!!!!!!WARNING!!!!!!

DO NOT READ OR USE THIS BOOK UNLESS YOU HAVE READ AND AGREE TO THE FOLLOWING STATEMENT:

   Rock Climbing is an inherently dangerous activity which may result in death, paralysis, or injury. Using this guidebook may increase that danger.

   This book is not an instructional manual. Do not use it as one. The information in this book is not designed to act as, or in place of, instruction in rock climbing. If you are in need of instruction pertaining to rock climbing, or using and understanding this guide, consult a professional climbing guide.

Assumption of Risk:

   This book is a compilation of opinions of the author and the people he consulted with. It is not verified information and should not be treated as factual. Information in this book pertaining to ratings of climbs, recommendations for protective gear, seriousness of attempting a climb, and more, are dependent on a climber's ability and are completely subjective. One person's opinions about difficulty and risk do not always match another's. Therefore, at all times, use your best judgement, and do not rely solely on the opinions expressed in this book to make risk based judgements. Information represented in this book may have changed due to factors beyond the publisher or author's control, such as man-made changes, changes due to weather, vegetation, wildlife, etc. Additionally, the information printed within this book has been through a long process of writing, editing, proofing, and printing, and has been through the hands of many different people. Inadvertent changes or mistakes may have taken place. Lastly, there are many other risks and hazards associated with rock climbing, and being outdoors in general, which are not described in this book. Therefore, do not assume that the information presented in this book is accurate, or that it accurately represents all the dangers associated with rock climbing.

   The publisher and author make no promises or representations about the accuracy of any of the information in this book, and are not liable for mistakes printed within. If you use the information printed in this book, either for its intended purpose, or not, you do so at your own risk.

Disclaimer of Warranties:
THE PUBLISHER AND AUTHOR MAKE NO REPRESENTATIONS OR WARRANTIES, EXPRESSED OR IMPLIED, ABOUT THE ACCURACY OF THE INFORMATION CONTAINED WITHIN THIS BOOK. THE PUBLISHER AND AUTHOR ALSO MAKE NO WARRANTIES REGARDING FITNESS FOR A PARTICULAR PURPOSE AND/OR MERCHANTABILITY OF THIS BOOK. THE PUBLISHER AND AUTHOR EXPRESSLY DISCLAIM THEMSELVES OF ALL LIABILITY ASSOCIATED WITH, AND NOT LIMITED TO, THE USE OF THIS BOOK.

THE READER AND USER OF THIS BOOK ASSUMES ALL RISKS ASSOCIATED WITH ANY USE OF THIS BOOK, INCLUDING, BUT NOT LIMITED TO, ROCK CLIMBING.

Rob Robinson on Afterburner, 5.13-, Jamestown, AL

```
   Climbing is a great game — great
 not in spite of the demands it makes
   but because of them. Great because
it will not let us give half of ourselves
— it demands all of us. It demands our best.

                            —Royal Robbins
```

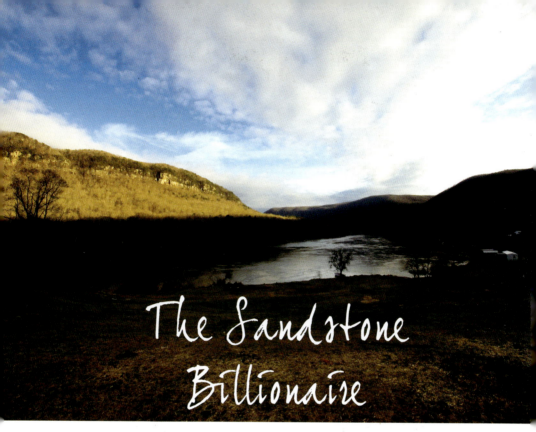

The Sandstone Billionaire

"I remember realizing as I moved deeper into climbing that I was living a truly extraordinary life. I was living the kind of life that people can only dream of, because I was living a dream. And I was living a dream that you can't buy...."

Rob Robinson

Scan these bar codes with a QR App. on your smartphone, or visit rockerypress.com to access the multimedia content available throughout ChattRad.

INTRODUCTION

CHATTRAD: A Comprehensive Guide to Chattanooga Trad Climbing

Copyright 2014 Rockery Press. All Rights Reserved. No part of this book may be reproduced in any way without the written consent of Rockery Press. Printed in Korea.

Author: Rob Robinson

Photography: Micah Gentry & Cody Averbeck unless otherwise credited

Front Cover Art: Rob Robinson on a 19th century ascent of The Prow at Sunset Rock with the old photography studio visible on the left. Photo courtesy of Tennessee State Library and Archives. Note: this image has been altered from its original format

Back Cover Art: A historic shot of downtown Chattanooga with its newest climbing addition, High Point Climbing Gym. Photo courtesy of Tennessee State Library and Archives. Note: this image has been altered from its original format

International Standard Book Number: 978-0-692-28835-1

The mission of Rockery Press is to produce the most unique, local-born content and multimedia designs that preserve the authentic Chattanooga rock climbing record for past, present, and future generations.

Rockery Press Publishing is continually expanding its guidebooks and loves to hear from locals about corrections to information. We also invite information concerning future additions to climbing in the Southeast. Please email us at rockerypress@gmail.com with updates and suggestions.

It's hard to look away.

INTRODUCTION

The publication of this guide — like the previous guides I've produced — has been an epic undertaking. It's a process which, to paraphrase Winston Churchill, has been "An adventure ... a toy and an amusement. Then a mistress, then a master, and finally a tyrant."

My escape from the tyranny of the word processor was aided by publishers Cody Averbeck and Micah Gentry of Rockery Press, to whom I give great thanks. Though I had written much of the content for this guide years ago, there was still a lot of heavy lifting yet to be done to get the book to press. Cody and Micah were the fulcrum that provided the leverage necessary to finish the task. Assisting them was Josh Livasy who was responsible for book design and review.

Additional leverage came in the form of photographers Corey Wentz, Mike Cork, Andrew Miller, Nathalie Dupre and Aaron Matheson who together put in untold hours behind the lens. Many climbers also came out to give it up for the camera; chief among them were Laban Swafford and Verena Draper.

Many of the (color) historical climbing images used in this book were selected from thousands of slides in my private collection, as well as from friend's collections including Todd Wells' library. These photos were taken by various climbing partners of mine going as far back as the mid 1970's. When I could remember who shot what I have provided attribution within the guide.

I've also republished in this guide (for the enjoyment of a wider reading audience) essays by Cody Averbeck, Rich Romano, John Bachar and John Gill which make for some entertaining and informative reading. Joining these authors in this publication is Matt Simms.

My final thanks are reserved for my wife, Susan Robinson, who has long understood, appreciated and supported my abiding passion for this magnificent sport of ours — and for my parents, Sam and Sally Robinson, who dispatched me on my first mountaineering trip back in the mid 1970's; in doing so, they opened the door to a life filled with unimagined riches.

www.rockerypress.com

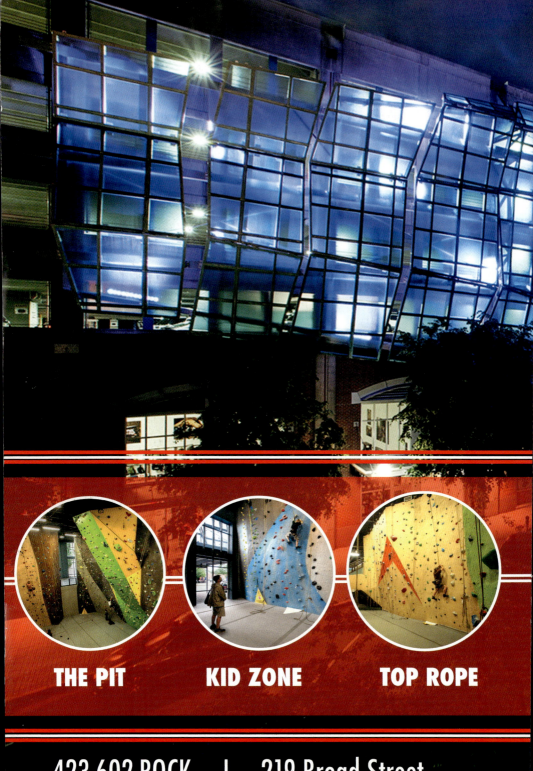

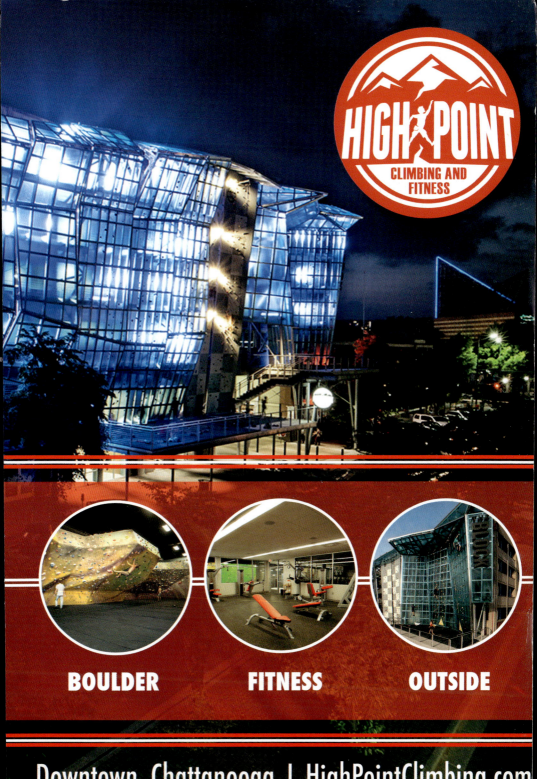

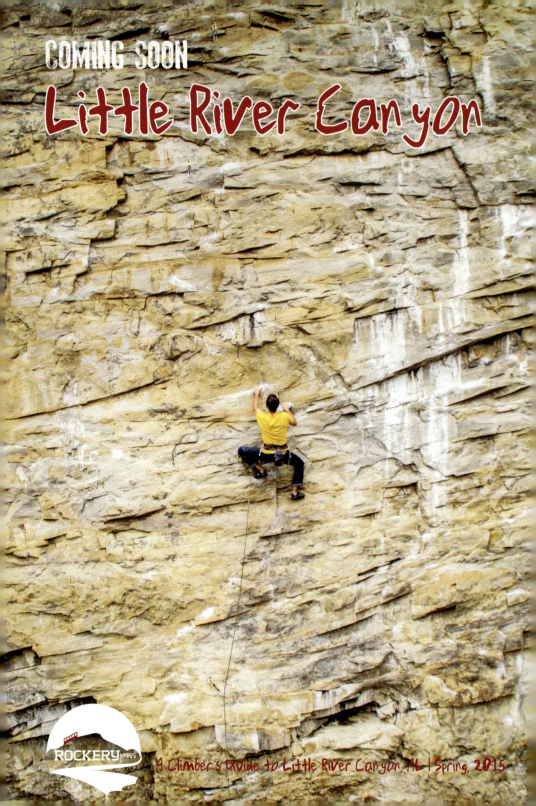

INTRODUCTION

CHATTRAD

A Comprehensive Guide to Chattanooga Trad Climbing

Forward 12

The F.A. of Vector Analysis 18

About Chattanooga 40

Using this Book 46

Sandstone Tips & Tricks 48

About the SCC 51

Sunset Rock 54

Suck Creek Canyon 184

The Tennessee Wall 296

The Promised Land 460

Big Soddy Gorge 488

About the Photographers 537

About the Author & Publishers 538

Route Index 540

LIVE WHERE YOU PLAY

featuring beautiful climb-in, climb-out homesites near Chattanooga

Miles of Cliffline

Acres of Boulders

Gateway to S. Cumberlands

WWW.TNLAND.COM | 1-888-777-5758 | DANEB@TNLAND.COM

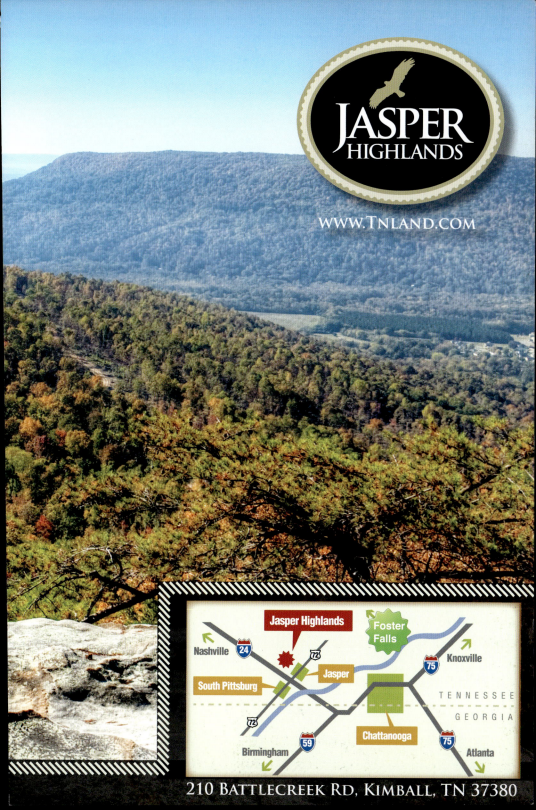

FORWARD

By Rob Robinson

Leading off into a life of climbing...

My first climbing experiences played out on one of the most scenic stages of American climbing: Wyoming's Grand Tetons. In the summer of 1975, when I was fourteen years old, my parents enrolled me in a month-long beginner's mountaineering expedition bound for this magnificent range of mountains. The trip was headed up by James "Pop" Hollandsworth — a man who, although in his mid 60's, could readily shoulder a 70 pound pack and hike for days on end through winding mountain passages.

With Pop at the wheel of a van, and a bunch of us kids in the back, we traveled from Tennessee to the Tetons. Our journey ended at a ranch overrun by tumbleweed and swirling dust, situated on the outskirts of a tiny tourist town called Jackson Hole. At the ranch, a couple of professional mountain guides joined us who, along with Pop, would lead me and my friends deep into that snow capped, rock-strewn cathedral of mountains.

Our guides had discovered the Tetons just as we were about to: by way of personal introduction. But they also depended on a trusty little guidebook published under the aegis of the American Alpine Club: *The Climber's Guide to the Tetons*. Packed into this small, brick-like book bound with a dark green cover were the details of a vast inventory of routes.

Back in town, I located a copy of the AAC's Teton guide on the bookshelves of a local mountaineering shop. Flipping through the book, it occurred to me that I might want to return to these spectacular mountains one day — on my own. So I bought a copy.

While I was at the shop, I tried on "real" climbing shoes (klettershoes made by "E.B.")for the first time. I scrunched my toes in a futile attempt to minimize the pain caused by stuffing my feet into shoes which were two sizes too small. One of our guides had advised me that pain was mandatory for a proper fit: "They don't fit if they don't hurt."

At night, I studied the AAC guide by the light of a candle lantern while I lay

FORWARD

cocooned in a snow covered tent. The guide made it easy to locate a route and envision the subsequent line of ascent. Of course, route descriptions were only latent blueprints for adventure, and fuel for the imagination. To experience the "rapture of the steep" you had to get out there and go for it.

Our guides made sure we got "fully raptured" — I'm certain my parents would have been terrified had they known the full extent of our activities. By the end of the trip, the mountains had cast a spell over me. I was hooked on climbing.

After my Teton epiphany, I returned to my home town of Chattanooga, Tennessee. It's beautiful, mid-sized American city, encircled by tree-covered mountains crowned with endless miles of sandstone cliff line. I was a long way from the big mountains out West, but it was easy to see there was plenty of rock climbing to explore. I bought a pair of climbing shoes and started bouldering at a crag on nearby Lookout Mountain called Sunset Rock.

The author bouldering at Sunset Rock.

At the time, there was no guidebook for the Chattanooga area. One was hardly needed. After all, Sunset had less than two dozen established routes. Of these, the hardest were a pair of 5.10's: Scream Wall Direct and Alpha Omega. (To give you an idea of where standards were at the time: I saw the former line top roped a handful of times, and the latter led only once by local "hard man" Bill Smith — with a few falls and considerable difficulty).

Guidebook absent, I started to explore the Sunset cliff line to look for new routes. I didn't have to look too hard! I had enough experience to begin to appreciate what passed for quality rock, though no idea that I was one lucky prospector who had stumbled into the middle of a southern sandstone goldmine!

In 1978, right about the time I was starting to get Sunset "dialed", I moved to North Carolina. At a local climbing shop I picked up a copy of Buddy Price's 1977 edition of the *Carolina Climber's Guide*. A black and white cover photo depicted a helmet-clad Gerald Laws starting the crux slab pitch of Stone Mountain's legendary Great White Way. His helmet struck me as … amusing. I also had a helmet, but found it hot and bothersome, so it lolled around in my gear box unused.

FORWARD

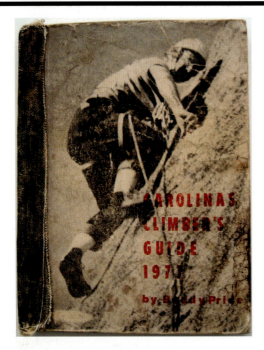

It wasn't too long after I picked up a copy of Buddy's guide, however, that I found myself poised on the exact same holds as him. As I contemplated the run-out above the crux — an unprotected 150' water-polished groove — I could only wish I had brought my helmet. Somehow, I managed to gather up enough courage to complete the run-out. Once I got started, however, there was really little choice. The fall was unthinkable, and down climbing would have been a nightmare.

Buddy's book also enticed me to explore that incredible North Carolina "granite ocean of eyebrow pockets" — Looking Glass Rock. Like all climbers, I marveled in awe at the monolith's massive, bulging north face, and romped up the classic corners and cracks that line its sunny south side. I also explored every quartzite nook and cranny of Moore's Wall, where I had the good fortune of crossing paths with Tim McMillan, a famous North Carolina climber.

Tim invited me to join him for an upcoming pilgrimage of sorts to a famous West Virginia climbing mecca called Seneca Rocks. Always on the lookout for a new adventure, I couldn't resist the invite. On the way up, Tim and I were joined by "Boone locals" Dan Perry and Lee Carter. We made the 12 hour trip at night, traveling in style in a classic, early 1960's car complete with rounded fins and a faded, light blue eggshell paint job.

Using the car's dome light, I pored over Bill Webster and Richard Pleiss's pocket-sized, powder blue book entitled Seneca Rocks, West Virginia — A Climber's Guide. I wondered what the colossal, white loaves of Seneca stone depicted in the guide's murky photos looked like up close and personal, and fretted about ratings wherein 5.10 denoted a level of difficulty "approaching human limitations", and 5.11 was "unbelievable!" (My reputation for rating Chattanooga area routes "stiff" can be traced to my formative Seneca experiences.)

We arrived at the crag just before dawn. The main Seneca cliff line, a high ridge crowned by a majestic swath of rock, lorded over the valley. A silver moon hung in a patch of sky above the Southern Pillar on the right, doing its best to wriggle free from a cocoon of drifting clouds. Capping the length of the central wall was an airy array of tiny summits. It was a skyline profile which, in my imagination, looked like the

FORWARD

Grim Reaper's lower jaw unhinged — with a gaping mouthful of jagged teeth ready for "climber chow." I was glad we had Bill and Richard's trusty little guide to back us up.

We spent the following two weeks doing some of the most enjoyable, exhilarating, and rewarding climbing I had ever experienced in my life. Seneca instantly became one of my all-time favorite areas, and I made several trips back to the area in subsequent years with Bill and Rich's guidebook (the 2nd edition red book) always close at hand. During my time at Seneca I managed to add a couple of new routes to the guide, as well.

In 1979, I returned to Chattanooga where I whiled away countless afternoons bouldering

The author and Forrest Gardner bouldering in Eldorado Canyon.

at Sunset. It was here, also, that I met another young local climber named Forrest Gardner. Like me, Forrest had a passion for doing new routes. Not surprisingly, we joined forces and went on a rampage throughout the Chattanooga area. In 1981, we took our skills on the road and spent the better part of the summer climbing around the Boulder, Colorado area where Jim Erickson's classic *Rocky Heights* climber's guide introduced us to a vast repository of world class climbs secreted away in the nearby Eldorado and Boulder canyons. In the evenings, after climbing, we sat around reading Jim's guidebook, drinking beer, eating pizza, listening to music (Neil Young, The Police, and Santana) and discussing the next day's agenda. Erickson's writing style — elegant and always entertaining — would greatly influence climbing guides I would later produce.

For years, I had been keeping notebooks detailing the climbs we had been doing around Chattanooga with an eye towards writing a guide for our area. By 1983, I had a half-inch thick stack of notebook paper packed with names, notes, and route descriptions. This stack was transformed into a small, spiral bound volume entitled *Southern Sandstone: A Climber's Guide to Chattanooga, Tennessee*; it was published in 1984 with the help of Paul Sloan, a Nashville-based climber and friend. Areas included were Sunset Rock, Suck Creek Canyon, Point Park and Bee Rocks. I also kept records of new routes at crags such as Foster Falls, Buzzard Point, Laurel Falls, Falling Water, Sand Rock, Chickamauga Gulf, Desoto Falls, Fullerton Bluff, Jamestown, Yellow Creek

FORWARD

The author on Flight of the Challenger, 5.12 at Steele, AL.

Falls, Sequatchie Valley — and many more.

Doing first ascents became a sort of monomaniacal vision quest that consumed me. There were just so many incredible new routes to do everywhere I traveled throughout the sandstone belt that the process just seemed to feed on itself — like an out of control wildfire. In my college dorm room, I covered an entire wall behind my bed with hundreds of images cut out of old climbing magazines. I installed a compact gym in the small living room that I shared with my roommates, and did thousands of pull ups in addition to marathon weight training sessions at the university gym. I also regularly swam, and jumped rope, for hours at a time. I was getting ready for something big, but had no idea what was coming. It was the Ultimate Sandstone Explosion™ of the mid 1980's.

On December 24th, 1984 — on the day before Christmas— we lucked out and stumbled across one of the best virgin sandstone crags in the world: The legendary Tennessee Wall. Over 200 new routes were established in 1985 alone; these were included in my second rock climbing guide called *The Illustrated, Underground Guide to the Tennessee Wall*.

In the early 1990's, I published a third guide, *The Deep South Climber's Companion*, which covered 20 sandstone climbing areas scattered throughout the region. 422 pages long, the guide would have been double in size had I included routes established at "access sensitive" areas.
Soon after the first edition sold out, I got burned out on writing guide books.

But then a few years ago, I picked up a copy of Ray Ellington's *Red River Gorge Rock Climbs*. I was so impressed with his work product that I got to thinking about publishing again. For years, I felt like the Tennessee Wall should have a new, stellar, stand alone guidebook. In 2009, inspired by Ray's work, I published a 184 page book dedicated to showcasing this world class crag. After most of the guides sold out, I decided to pull the plug on publishing once and for all. It takes a tremendous amount of time and energy to produce high quality books in this genre, and I had a lot of other things competing for my attention. But never say never!

In 2013, Cody Averbeck of Rockery Press looked me up to see if I would be interested in doing a guidebook dedicated to the Chattanooga area. His timing was perfect: I had actually written just such a guide, but not gotten around to publishing it. The copy had languished on the hard drive of my computer for years collecting cyber dust. All that was needed to put out the new guide was someone to shoot hundreds of photographs, lay the 500 page book out, edit it, proof read it, have it printed — and

FORWARD

then distribute it to shops. "All that was needed" was a huge amount of work. Rockery Press was up for the challenge, and I hope you are pleased with the results.

A couple of years ago I asked a few of my friends if they would share some of their experiences they've had while climbing in the Sandstone Belt of the South. The result is a delightful collection of anecdotes, vignettes, essays, and photos I have decided to republish in this guide. They are, if you will, "the party hats and balloons" for a book which is, at its essence, a celebration of the spirit of climbing.

Whether you're leafing through the pages of this book in 2014 (or a 100 years from now after I'm long gone) I hope it serves you well and, moreover, that it engenders an appreciation for the history of the sport as it was first established in the Chattanooga, Tennessee area.

I'll leave you with this. The great naturalist and outdoorsman John Muir once wrote: "The clearest way into the Universe is through a forest wilderness." If so, then outdoor guidebooks are informal books of common prayer for acolytes of the wilderness, of which I am one.

In Spirit,

Rob Robinson

The First Ascent of Vector Analysis

By Rob Robinson

The Atomic Buttress as viewed from the Bee Rock Falls Overlook. Vector Analysis climbs the face next to the arete on the right.

Vector: (physics): A quantity having direction as well as magnitude, esp. as determining the position of one point in space relative to another.

Analysis: A detailed examination of the elements or structure of something, typically as a basis for discussion or interpretation.

Vector Analysis: The quintessential southern sandstone "super desperate".

Men's resources in energy in the face of death are inexhaustible. When the end seems imminent, there still remain reserves, though it needs tremendous willpower to call them up.

— Maurice Herzog

```
*The following events took place at a pri-
vately owned and now-closed cliff and have
been included for historical reasons only.

     "I'm melting!" I screamed down to
"Jersey" Jeff Gruenberg who was belay-
ing me. "Ahhhh SHIIIEEAAAAAAAT!!!!!!!!!" I
couldn't hang on any longer. Up until that
moment, I had hung on — with everything I
had. It had been minutes at the most, but it
seemed like forever ... trapped in a sicken-
ing reality where time didn't exist anymore.
     Switching hands. Shaking out. Trying
to buy a few more seconds. Raised, gossamer
webs of dilated, pale blue veins inked my
forearms like writhing, 3D tattoos; the mus-
cles beneath them compressed into fibrous,
rock hard briquets lit on fire with pain.
     Trying to get something, anything, in
the pinched off, thin horizontal seam star-
ing me in the face. Torturing me with its
tantalizing possibilities. God, please ...
even a #1 stopper that I can at least body
weight, I thought in an almost feverish
delirium. Anything, to stop what was about
```

VECTOR ANALYSIS

to happen. I battled for control of my head space, trying to win the mind game, trying to squeeze out enough fractals of composure to keep hanging a little longer....

A sickening and overwhelming sensation began roiling through my imploding body in oscillating waves. It was the amplitude of impending death, and I knew it. I had felt this strange sensation before, but not this bad. It filled me up head to toe, ready to burst me from inside out, scattering the existential "me" into whatever it is that lies beyond this world.

It was going to be the longest lead fall of my life. And even if Jeff was able to rip the pair of 9 millimeter ropes back in through the belay plate — thereby shaving a few precious feet off my fall — it was likely I was still going to deck on our little belay ledge.

The final, few grains of sand left in the hourglass of my life had seemingly run out. The death grip I had fought to maintain in those precious minutes dissolved. The miserable, greased slopers slipped from my grasp as if they were half forgotten remnants of some fast-fading and surreal dream. Then they were gone — existing now in some other world — a world no longer reachable by me.

I plummeted towards the ledge below in a huge, loopy fall. It was raining all around me, but I was sheltered by the wall, which was severely overhung. I descended towards whatever my fate was going to be in a dry bubble of fear. My twin 9mm umbilical cords, — their tattered sheaths worn with white cores exposed in multiple places — whipped out through space, snaking back towards the wall to a small collection of pathetic #1 and #2 brass nuts laced behind an expanding flake. I put them in with the idea that they might at least slow me down if I blew it. Some distance below these worthless talismans was a lifesaving nest of bomber gear at a small roof which I knew would hold. If I didn't hit the ground first.

I was lost in a sea of blurs as I fell towards the ledge. Thooom! Thooom-thooom! ... the expanding flake bellowed out as the worthless brass nuts I had placed behind it were stripped loose by the impact of my accelerating fall.

Then, it was over. The gear below the roof that marked the start of the overhanging wall had done its job. I dangled in disbelief a short distance above Jeff and the ledge. The brass nuts which had ripped out spiraled down my ropes on carabiners, playfully thwacking me on my head.

I gazed up to where I had fallen from as Jeff dutifully fed the ropes out through the belay plate and lowered me

VECTOR ANALYSIS

the remaining distance to the ledge. He extended a hand to mine and pulled me over to a standing position alongside himself. He turned his head to one side and spit out a stream of spit laced with chewing tobacco. Jeff loved his dip.

"Damn" he said in his characteristically low key and understated tone.

"Yeah, I know" I said. "That was some shit."

I loosened the knots from my harness and sat down.

"What'da ya think?" he queried, testing my resolve.

"Well," I said, "it looks like the fall is pretty safe. Don't you think? I mean, we still got a couple of body lengths to go between us and the ground."

"You want to go back up and give it another shot after you take a break?" he offered.

I looked out across the valley through the pouring rain and thought about it. I turned back to him.

"You want to give it a shot?" I asked.

"Are you sure?" he replied differentially.

"Yeah, this is going to take both of us."

"Can we get any gear in that horizontal?" he asked.

"I don't know." I said. "Maybe, but it's going to take some work," I said flatly.

  It was apparent the horizontal seam I had fought so hard to place gear in was not going to give up any kind of placement without a ferocious battle, if at all.
  Jeff grabbed the business end of the ropes, tied in with a pair of figure 8 knots and started racking up ... all small wires on a couple of biners. I grabbed the ropes, stuffed the bights through the belay plate, locked the carabiners and clipped into the belay anchors.

VECTOR ANALYSIS

Jeff Gruenberg on an early ascent of "Nuclear Puppies" (5.11+) at Bee Rocks. Photo Credit: Rob Robinson

He stood before me girded for battle. Jeff was a tall and rangy climber with a powerful build, affectionately referred to by the locals at his home crag — the legendary Shawangunks of New York — as "Bones". He had done all the hardest, established trad lines at the Gunks and, in recent years, had completed a bonanza of new extreme trad routes which were a step beyond anything done previously ... routes like Nectar Vectors, Talus Food, Rings of Saturn and Skeletal Remains — just to name a few. He also regularly free soloed into the 5.10 and 5.11 range of difficulty, with ropeless ascents of routes such as Foops and The Yellow Wall. He was, straight up, one of the best trad climbers in the world. And for a route like the one we were now attempting, I couldn't have hoped for a stronger and more capable partner.

Jeff reached into his chalk bag, withdrew a hand caked in white and then clapped. Poof! An explosion of dust as fine as sifted flour lazily drifted off into space. He looked at me hard. I looked back just as hard. Our gazes locked and reflected our shared resolution.

"You ready!?" he barked.

"Go for it man," I replied.

He turned away, a hulking figure, and stepped onto the rock.

"Climbing!"

"Climb on," I replied.

* * *

VECTOR ANALYSIS

North of the overlook atop Bee Rock Falls, a giant outcrop of sandstone protrudes from the mountainside. Hailed by climbers as "the Atomic Buttress", the southwest corner of this 200' tall buttress is formed, in part, by a massive, overhanging wall. At the wall's right edge a spectacular, crescent-shaped arete bows outwards into space, fusing with the skyline in a perfect union of rock and air. The line Jeff and I were attempting tackled this overhanging wall, just left of the magnificent arete.

Looking up at the southern face of the Atomic Buttress. Photo Credit: Rob Robinson

The first route completed on the buttress was an awe inspiring line that penetrated the central southern face. "Trinity Site" (5.11) consisted of four short though memorable and unique pitches. Completed in October of 1982, the first ascent party consisted of myself, Forrest Gardner and Gene Smith. The first pitch featured a leisurely 5.7 jog up a nice buttress laced with good jam cracks to a pedestal. Pitch two climbed through a tiered 5.11 roof crack to a spectacular standing belay in a small pod on the wall above.

Rob Robinson leading pitch #2 of Trinity Site during the first ascent. Photo Credit: Gene Smith

Above the pod belay the wall dramatically changed in character: A beautiful, offset fist crack led for forty feet to a bank of massive and complex overhangs. It looked like we had our work cut out for us. But the crack turned out to be a scenic cruise, and we discovered an easy zig-zag through the overhangs. The climbing on this pitch never got any harder than about 5.9 or so.

Rob Robinson leading pitch #3 of Trinity Site during the first free ascent. Photo Credit: Gene Smith

At the end of the third pitch a narrow belay ledge, capped by another huge overhang, reclined towards the wall — like bucket seats in a car. Just off the ledge where the line obviously had to go was a razor sharp edge which we covered with athletic tape. Gardner led the final pitch, hand-traversing around an exposed, rock spike spiderwebbed with dangerous-looking hairline fractures. Fearing it might shear off if full body weight was applied, a single point of aid (a fixed pin left in situ) was used to surmount the final overhang above.

VECTOR ANALYSIS

Intro

Forrest Gardner on the final pitch of Trinity Site.
Photo Credit: Gene Smith

A few weeks later, I returned to the route with Gene who, in a coin toss, won the right to have first shot at eliminating the point of aid on the final pitch — which he pulled off with little effort — on his first try. Trinity Site instantly became one of the finest, multi-pitch sandstone routes in the Southeast.

Next to be climbed on the Atomic Buttress was an aid line soloed by Forrest Gardner in August of 1983, which he named "Beyond Berserk." His route took a line left of center up an overhanging wall, a short distance left of the new route Jeff and I were working on.

Not long afterwards, I attempted an on-sight free ascent of Gardner's route accompanied by Robyn Erbesfield. After turning a 5.11 roof down low, I placed a #2 Friend (with a Kevlar cord threaded through a small hole in the shaft) in a shallow horizontal slot on the overhanging wall above. Some distance above this piece, in the middle of some hard moves, I blew off a couple of sloping holds and took a huge, loopy fall. At the end of the fall, I swung into the underside of the 5.11 roof. I shot my legs upwards over my head in a desperate bid to protect my skull from impact. Though successful, the collision torqued my ankles and folded my toes back towards my shins. I was lucky I had hiked in wearing boots; lacing them up as tightly as possible, I managed to stumble and crawl back through the woods to our car that night.

I got lucky. At the hospital, X-rays revealed nothing had been broken. Prior to the fall I had, as part of my regular training routine, skipped rope (in bare feet) a few days a week for several hours at a time. The doctor who treated me in the emergency room surmised the resultant conditioning was likely the reason I hadn't torn any ligaments and tendons. I left the hospital sans casts, but with doctor's orders to lay off for awhile. Several months would pass before I recovered enough to begin climbing again.

VECTOR ANALYSIS

Rob Robinson sporting a custom "Beyond Berserk" T shirt made up just for the route.
Photo Credit: Robyn Erbesfield

In August of 1984, I returned to give "the Berserker" another go. This time, Jeff Gruenberg accompanied me. In the middle of the run-out, where I had taken the bad fall, I discovered a tiny vertical slot — perfect for a small, wired stopper. It was all I needed to keep pushing through the crux to reach a scoop on the vertical face above. Delicate moves following a vertical seam past a couple of manky fixed knifeblades left behind from Gardner's aid ascent ended at a ledge. At "middlin' 5.12" the route turned out not to be especially difficult. Though tricky to protect, it was nonetheless a fun and super classic trad line on perfect rock.

After completing Beyond Berserk, Jeff and I contemplated a potential line on the same overhanging wall out right. (The line that would become Vector Analysis.) It looked free climbable — provided we could get enough gear in to protect it. But even if we could, it seemed clear it would still be run out as hell, but with potentially clean air falls. In other words, it was exactly the kind of route we were looking for. Although we hadn't planned on attempting it, the forecast had called for rain for the next four days. So we decided what the heck, it's going to be dry, let's give it a shot. We hiked in the next day in light showers, climbed the first pitch of Trinity Site, spread out our gear on a small pedestal ledge and set up a belay. Looming overhead, the bulge of the overhanging wall shielded us from the rain.

And that's how we got to where we are now in this story ... with me chilling out at the belay ledge after taking what was my second huge fall on this same wall within 12 months. And with Gruenberg on his way up — to find out if he was going to "join the club."

* * *

VECTOR ANALYSIS

Jeff stepped off the ledge and onto the wall. A short distance higher, he eased over a strenuous 5.11 roof guarding the upper face which resembled the underside of a giant, tan colored blimp covered with undulating ripples. A few more moves, and he was at a stance that marked the point of no return. Directly overhead was another, smaller roof laced with bomber pro. On the overhanging wall above this feature the rounded flake I had placed a couple of miserable brass behind (that had ripped out during my fall) silently waited, licking its chops.

"Pay the rope out!" he called down.

"You got it!" I hollered back.

Even though the wall was severely overhung, a short fall starting up this section would be bad — you'd crater back into the vertical face. We had to fall past the 5.11 roof to be safe. I had not forgotten what happened to me the year prior while attempting Beyond Berserk. So without even stepping up into "the business," we were already on the hook for a solid 15 footer — plus rope stretch. It was unnerving.

Jeff powered out and up onto the rounded flake using open handed palming layaways, his feet smeared out left on the wall. From my observation point on the belay ledge, it was spectacular to watch. At the top of the flake, he shook out and prepped for a powerful undercling move to snag more rounded holds above. I paid out more slack through the belay plate as he made the move. Next up: "the crystal sequence" and the first really difficult move of the climb. A smooth, gumball-sized pebble protruded from the wall. Gripping this tiny knob with his left thumb, index and middle fingers, he shot his right hand up to some tweaks and then snagged a long horizontal weakness with a bank of rounded holds a bit higher.

"You got me man!?" he shouted.

"I got you covered! Go for it!" I fired back.

He was at my high point. The fall looked ... ghastly. The ropes bowed out into space in a sickening arc from his harness back down to the only protection we had at the roof below. He straight armed off the holds and switched out his hands, alternately dipping one and then the other into a chalk bag, sizing the insanity up, glancing up and then down, eyeing the monster fall, trying to recover long enough so he could commit to retrieving a biner full of small wires clipped to his harness. Got to get something in. Anything....

"Hang in there man!" I screamed.

"This is sick!" he screamed, quickly glancing down at me.

"Dude! There's got to be something in that seam! Hang on!"

He managed to get a biner full of tiny stoppers off his harness, none larger than a pinky fingernail. Desperate, he dragged one after another back and forth along the seam, hoping to get one to slip into a tiny, pinched off pocket.

"You got me man!" he screamed.

"I got you man!" My voice echoed across the amphitheater.

"Try to take in a little slack! I'm comin off!"

I watched in awe as he fell. I had never seen anything like it before. The impact at the end of the ropes snatched me off my feet and suspended me in space, taut against the belay anchors. His arms and legs and arms dangled, totally spent. I lowered him the rest of the way to the ledge.

We spent the rest of the day taking turns climbing to our mutual high point and melting off — never getting any gear in the horizontal.

The following day, I brought a pair of binoculars with me to scope out the wall, hoping I'd spot something we'd missed on the lead. Jeff played it hard core trad to the hilt and declined to use them, although I had no such misgivings. After all, climbers used spotting scopes for big walls and mountains all the time; I didn't

VECTOR ANALYSIS

Intro

feel like using them would diminish the integrity of the challenge. But they revealed nothing new. The wall above our high point was utterly devoid of cracks. Our only option was going to be to get something bomber in at our high point. If it was only a body weight piece we could conceivably clip into it, hang, then pull up a hand drill kit with the second rope and place a single bolt for pro. The only problem with that plan was neither of us a had a bolt kit. Bolt guns did not exist yet.

Above our high point were several small angular holds spaced apart about three feet from each other; they were all that stood between us and the top. We renewed our attack on the wall in a controlled frenzy, determined to get the gear needed to protect the moves above. But in spite of our valiant efforts, neither of us managed to finagle so much as a #1 stopper in. If the route was going to go we had to find a way to climb still higher and, apparently, without any more protection. Yet we could only risk a few more feet above our gear before things would go from merely being dangerous — to deadly. We were in a quandary.

I came up with an idea: I lowered Jeff after his last fall — until his shoes dangled a short distance above the ledge — and wrapped athletic tape around each rope where it fed through the belay plate. This way, whoever was manning "air traffic control" could call out to the person on lead and say where the tape was. When the tape passed through the belay plate the leader knew he was climbing into the death zone. We calculated that the rope paid out a couple of feet past the marking tape was the maximum acceptable risk. We made sure to take into account rope stretch. Our plan also called for whoever was on belay to take in a few feet of rope at the start of a fall.

Directly right of our high point, we had spotted a fingerlock behind a thick flake — on the nose of the arete which formed the right margin of the overhanging wall. If we could reach the flake, we might be able to place a medium-sized stopper behind it. If it was bomber, we could finish directly up the arete and, in doing so, achieve even more spectacular wall position.

The short traverse right to gain the arete looked reasonable, but it would require more forearm blasting, open handed palming maneuvers with foot smears on the wall below. The fingerlock we would be gunning for had to go "left hand, thumb up"; to get it would totally commit the leader to the arete — with the ropes paid out well past the tape markings. If Jeff or I failed to get some decent gear after completing the envisioned sequence, it was going to be very bad. We decided that the stopper, if we could get it, had to be placed before committing to the fingerlock.

***

It was our fourth day on the wall, and we were running out of time. Vacation was over for Jeff, and he had to head home the next day. It was now or never.

We had all the moves wired. Both of us had run laps on the route for days and taken a dozen or so huge falls in the process. Psychologically, we had come a long way from our initial push up the wall. We were, in fact, pretty comfortable with the climb ... except for the upcoming traverse of death — a transit which would take us to a new frontier of fear.

I started us out and climbed to our high point where I paused to grab a biner full of wires and clamp them between my teeth. I worked right along the rounded horizontal. Jeff hollered a warning as I passed the tape. I was close to the arete. I snatched the bundle of wires and then, pinching one by its looped end, stretched towards the flake. It was still two feet away, and I was pumped out of my mind. I clipped the wires back on a harness loop, clawed left a few feet, then melted off the wall. At the last nano second before impact, I tucked my knees up into my chest, hoping to save my legs if it was close. If I decked, it was going to be as an exploding ball of meat. But Jeff managed to reel in a precious few feet as I fell — and got the tape close to the plate.

Jeff "Bones" Gruenberg climbing at Little River Canyon late 80's or early 90's. Photo Credit: Robinson Collection

We traded out the lead ropes. Jeff cruised up the wall cleanly and smoothly, working hard not to waste an iota of unnecessary energy. In minutes, he arrived at our old high point, then eased right towards the arete. Hanging from one arm with his feet sprawled out in tech smears, he made the desperate reach for the arete, trying to sink a wire. But he couldn't get it either. In full burn mode, he wobbled back

VECTOR ANALYSIS

Intro

left then peeled off the wall. I ripped a few feet of rope back through the plate as he fell and stopped him a short distance above the ledge.

We took turns for the rest of the day going back up and trying to work out the the last moves to reach the arete to place a wire. But in the final analysis, the stakes were just too high. We packed up that evening and hiked out. It was still raining.

***

In December of that same year, on the day before Christmas no less, the Tennessee Wall was discovered. It was a first ascent goldmine. I burned through the inventory of untouched rock in a monomania frenzy. Within months, climbers from all over joined the party and descended on the crag. When summer came no one seemed to care, myself included, that the highs were in the 90's and sometimes the low 100's. We knew the Tennessee Wall was probably going to go down in history as one of the best sandstone crags in the world. And as history has borne out, we were right on the money.

Occasionally, I considered returning to Vector to try it again but didn't think I had it in me to commit to the last moves to the arete. I was also taking into account the possibility that the gear on the arete would turn out to be bogus. After all, it would be wedged behind a flake that could have a fatal hairline crack — a crack which might cause it to shear off the wall in a fall — or possibly even if a stopper placed behind it was body weighted.

In the summer of 1985, I met Japanese climber Hidetaka Suzuki at the Tennessee Wall. As I hiked up to the Amphitheater, I saw him trying a 5.12 stacked roof route called "Hands Across America", which I had completed back in May. His climbing style was mesmerizing ... he moved slowly and effortlessly and in a way that reminded me of a gecko. He fell at the big roof crux, and launched into an unintelligible tirade with his wife, Michiko, who was belaying him. She meekly lowered him to the ground and together they pulled the rope.

Eventually, Hidetaka was able to make a successful ascent after spending a little time on the route — just as I had. Turning the crux roof was highly sequential, and one side of the crack at the lip had a sharp edge to contend with. Never mind the rope drag issues....

I took Hidetaka under my wing and together we made the grand tour of our local crags — including Bee Rocks. Given his proficiency at crack climbing, I figured he might have a good chance of freeing another old Forrest Gardner aid route left of the Atomic Buttress called Seam Solibeam. Naturally, I also pointed out the unfinished Vector Analysis line. I was going to get around to trying it again soon I told him — after it cooled off a bit more. "It's not an open route please so don't get on it. And also it's very dangerous."

Not long after that, however, I hiked in to Bee Rocks to turn a couple of British climbers on to a stupendous set of stacked dihedrals called Cornered Rats.

Lo and behold, there was none other than Hidetaka! ... hanging at the end of his rope on Vector Analysis. He had made it up to the roof to the base of the overhanging wall — to the point where the last good gear was. I wasn't very happy.

Rob Robinson on pitch #1 of Cornered Rats (early 80's)
Photo Credit: Gene Smith

I hiked over to the base and shouted up at him, asking him what he doing. A classic case of "lost in translation" ensued. "Ohhh, ahhh, you not want me to climb on this one. I not understand" he said. However we both knew the score ... it was so good he simply "couldn't stop himself" from trying it.

I talked him down off the wall and decided that if he wanted to do a first ascent so bad I'd try and lose him for a few days. I dispatched him to the White Wall at Foster Falls. There was a spectacular finger crack ("Satisfaction") I hadn't gotten around to doing yet. Maybe, I figured, that would hold him off until I could try and finish Vector.

***

The next day, I drove up to Sunset Rock to try and rustle up a belayer. There was a single car at the parking lot. It was an out-of-state climber on his first trip to the area. And he had just pulled up.

"Are you a pretty good belayer?" I asked him. "You are? Great! Have you ever handled double ropes? No? Well don't worry

VECTOR ANALYSIS

Intro

about it. I'll show you how they work. Hop in your car and follow me. Sunset is great, but I'm going to show you a new area."

My new friend followed me to the parking area for Bee Rocks. I explained what my mission was, and the reward for him helping me out. After belaying me on Vector I would guide him on a couple of classic routes. He agreed it was a fair trade. Of course, he had no idea what he had signed up for....

We hiked down to the Bee Rock Falls overlook, and I pointed out the Vector line on Atomic Buttress. I gave him the rundown on the progress made to date and my plan to complete the route.

"So if I fall from that point right about there," I gestured, pointing at the wall, "what I want you to do is unclip from the anchors and jump off the belay ledge. We'll both end up hanging in the air."

"Dude," he exclaimed, "you're out of your freakin' mind! We'll both get killed!"

"No we won't," I said. "Trust me, it'll work. And besides, I'm not going to fall anyway."

These external regions, what do we fill them with except reflections, the escapades of death.

— Wallace Stevens

The rippling beige wall between Beyond Berserk and Vector Analysis is a no man's land of rounded holds with no obvious cracks for protection. But I had hiked to the base of the buttress several times over the summer, scoped it out with binoculars, and come up with a plan. From last year's high point I envisioned an alternate finish diagonalling left through this wasteland, then merging with the final headwall seam of Beyond Berserk. I knew if I could reach that seam I had Vector in the bag. This alternate way to the top looked substantially easier than a Vector direct finish. I was not prepared to rappel off Vector and place a bolt. This was a world class prize after all, and someone could pull it off. I hoped it would be me. Today....

Everything was likely going to depend on whether or not there was any pro on the alternate finish I envisioned. I would make sure I felt solid enough to reverse every move so I could jump off at a point where the ropes would still catch me. I also was banking on the hope that the horizontal seams that laced the

VECTOR ANALYSIS

wall might accept some small gear. I opted to carry a skeleton rack with a slew of small wires, a couple of Metolius cams, and a new kind of pro I had only used a few times before but loved when it worked — Sliders — which provided the perfect protection solution for straight in placements in thin, pinched off cracks. I also elected to carry a couple of long, knifeblade pitons. If I got a manky wire or cam in that I could hang from, maybe I could pull the hammer up from the belay to try and bang one in. Maybe.

Since my last attempt on Vector, I was in even better shape than before. For one thing, I had been climbing almost every day for months on end ... doing dozens of hard first ascents in the brutal heat at the Tennessee Wall.

But failing on Vector had revealed a heretofore unknown weakness in my strength: open handed palming. To remedy this, I set up a couple of wooden dowel bars of various diameters in my backyard to hang and swing from. To maximize the training effect during swings, I would shoot my hands back over the top of the bar — right at the moment I was melting off. That way I could "milk the melt" even after my forearms were flamed out. (I dubbed this "wave training".) I would occasionally strap on a scuba diver's weight belt loaded with ten or so pounds during some of my sessions to add heft to the routine. The goal was to build up my strength and endurance to the point where I could hang on to medium-to-large rounded holds (with a circumference ranging between that of a softball and a cantaloupe) anywhere on a route — for as long as necessary — without getting too pumped.

Rob Robinson on Grand Dragon, 5.12 (early 80's). Photo Credit: Rob Robinson Collection.

My preferred mode of climbing was to dominate a route — not merely get up it. There was safety in strength and power ... especially when doing routes with an "R" or "X" protection grade. On these type routes the safest climber was the one who didn't fall.

VECTOR ANALYSIS

Intro

We threaded along a precipitous cliff top trail to a tricky down climb gully which we descended to the base of Bee Rock Falls. We scrambled downstream between a few boulders, then commenced hiking towards the Atomic Buttress. As we approached, the immensity of the wall sprung into view. The horizon line where the rock met the sky at the right side of the wall seemed to shimmer faintly, as if it were the defining edge of a distant mirage. The oblique light of the morning sun splashed across the wall, infusing its tan hue with a slightly luminous and chalky incandescence. We arrived at the base and dropped our packs.

I assembled the rack, then tied into a pair of 9 millimeter ropes with a pair of figure eights, each backed up by half a grapevine knot. I soloed the first pitch of Trinity Site to reach the belay ledge and dropped a couple of anchors. I brought my belayer up. Above us, the wall bowed outwards — a silent sentinel lording over the valley below for untold millennia ... its rippled and planed surfaces melded together to form an inhospitable world of unmatched, overhanging chaos. I spent a little time to get my head space quiet for what was coming. My belayer was close to panicking.

"I don't think this is such a good idea," he whined. "This looks crazy. Why don't you come back another day with someone else? Can't we just go do that Astro Arete or something else like it you were telling me about?"

"Chill out," I said. "Everything is going to be cool. Trust me. All you have to do is pay the ropes out. Let me know when the tape reaches the belay plate. After that just tell me how much rope you pay out every three feet past the plate. So like 'three feet, six feet, nine feet.' If I start to downclimb then call that out to me in reverse. You got it?"

"What happens if you fall past that tape?" he asked.

"Well, if I'm too far out — I'll deck. So I'd want you to take in as much rope as possible if I come off the wall."

"What about that jumping off the belay ledge shit you were talking about?"

"Yeah. That too," I said. "If I pass the six foot mark you'll need to unclip from the belay. That's why I only got you tied in to the anchors with a locking biner. So you can unscrew it and unclip it fast. If I fall all you would do then is just jump off at the last second." He stared at me in a state of disbelief.

Before stepping up onto the wall, I laid the hammer out, and told him that — in the event I got something manky out in the middle of the face I could hang from — I might lower a bight of rope so I could pull it up to bang in a pin. If there was a place for one. On that note, I started to climb.

The Vector line starts out easy and serves as a bit of a warm up. I got to the first challenge ... a pumpy 5.11 roof. Not too hard, but I was careful not to blow any energy turning it. A few more moves above, and I was at the base of the overhanging face guarded by the small roof. I put in a couple of bomber pieces, doubled up on the slings and added a couple of extra biners to the mix. I lowered off the wall, and when I reached the farthest point that it was "safe" to fall, I had him wrap the belay ropes with athletic tape at the belay plate. I lowered the rest of the way to the ledge to take a short break before heading back up. By this point, I had my belayer's confidence.

The air between us was practically vibrating with energy, as I climbed back up to my highpoint.

"Pay me out about ten feet of slack and whatever you do don't pull me off the wall!" I hollered down.

Above the roof with the last good anchors, I launched up the rounded flake on the overhanging wall above with my feet smeared out left. At the top of the flake I palmed more rounded holds, got a good shake out, then powered past the undercling move. I set up for the crystal sequence with my left hand. Both feet rocked off the wall momentarily as I reached a half pad tweak above with my right hand. I quickly brought my left hand up and matched on another half pad hold. One more big move, and I was at the horizontal rail. I shook out again a couple of times and started traversing left. There was no gear anywhere, but a sequence over the bulge above materialized — more rounded holds. But I felt super solid.

"Where am I on the tape?!" I hollered down.

"You're right at it man!"

"OK watch me!"

VECTOR ANALYSIS

I bouldered out the bulge sequence, reversed it a few times, then committed to a delicate stand up move. Reversing this last move, though possible, would be difficult.

"Three feet of rope past the tape!" the call came from below.

The angle of the wall had eased off to near vertical. I cooly scanned the wall around me, looking for a spot to plug in a cam, or to slot a wire in one of the horizontal seams. Or poke in a Slider. But it was a sea of blankness. A few more feet though, and I could get off my hands a bit. But the next moves would put me six feet past the tape on the rope.

"Get ready to unclip from the belay!" I shouted. "I'm going to step up!"

Everything in my life as a climber had led up to this moment of truth. Was I prepared to risk pushing the envelope even further? Or should I downclimb as far as I could, drop off and hope for the best? Visions of rock climbing legends who had inspired me throughout my life flickered through my head. Memories of their achievements suffused me with a sudden burst of inspiration. I started inching higher on more insecure and sloping holds.

"Six feet!" the warning call rang out from below.

I stilled my mind. The exit seam of Beyond Berserk was a short distance away. I scanned the wall for gear. Out right, at about waist height, I spotted a small hole not much larger than the size of a #2 pencil. It looked as though it might take a Slider. Carefully, I reached down to my harness and retrieved a carabiner loaded down with several. *Blue. The blue one.*

It operated like a mechanical syringe. I grasped the device with my right hand, thumb through the cable loop, forefingers on the trigger. I squeezed gently; the brass wedges spread apart. The central cable bowed slightly with the force.

Palming the best rounded hold I could manage with my left hand, I dropped into a plié position and stretched towards the tiny black hole with my right hand. I probed the darkness with the tip of the Slider, jiggled it a bit, then watched excitedly as the wedges slid in. I eased off the trigger. The bottom wedge started to bite. I cranked on the cable loop and locked the

www.rockerypress.com

VECTOR ANALYSIS

wedges. It was only one piece, but it looked bomber.

    I called out for slack for my right rope which, with exquisite care, I slowly brought it up to clip into the biner dangling from the piece. I pressed the gate open and dropped the rope inside. The gate snapped shut. I added another biner for extra security.

"Is it good?" my belayer's voice boomed across the amphitheater.

"Yeah man. It's good."

    I diagonalled left on more sloping holds into the shallow bowl that comprised the upper section of Beyond Berserk. The Slider was well below and right of me. I sidled up to the seam and snatched a biner off my harness to clip one of Gardner's old fixed pins for my left 9mm rope. A few more moves and I clipped another pin. Then, I was at the top. Though it wasn't the perfect line I had originally envisioned, Vector Analysis was done. I set up anchors and lowered to the ledge. My belayer gave me a hand and pulled me in. He was still tied into the anchors.

"Dude!" I said, "you were supposed to untie from the anchors when I got six feet out from the tape. What happened?"

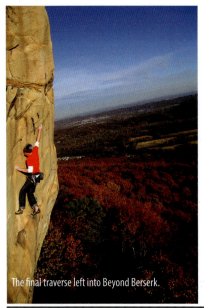

The final traverse left into Beyond Berserk.

"I thought you were kidding," he replied. So much for my plan.

    When I cleaned the route on top rope, I scoured the wall directly below the blue Slider for additional pro. There was nothing except for a horizontal sliver, which I managed to jimmy a long knifeblade pin into. I pulled the hammer up from the ledge and started banging away, hoping the pin wouldn't bottom out. It sunk to the eye with a rising pitch. It was good enough to protect the moves below the blue Slider, which I decided to leave fixed. Equipped thusly, Hidetaka could return to try it if he wanted to opt for an "R" version of the route vs. my "X" lead. Without the

VECTOR ANALYSIS

fixed gear, I surmised it would probably never get led again by anyone — a shame since it was such a world class route.

***

About ten years later a local, well known climber contacted me. He wanted to do a line on the same wall as Vector, and asked if I would agree to allow him to add bolts to the Vector line in furtherance of his desired objective. I could hardly comprehend his request. I said no, but he did it anyway. Beyond Berserk was also retro bolted (along with a host of other routes at the crag). As a result, two of the finest trad leads in the southeastern United States were summarily destroyed. But this was only the tip of the iceberg. Climbers wielding bolt guns have since gone on a retro bolting rampage throughout the region wreaking similar havoc. I'll leave it up to history to judge the probity of their collective actions.

Personally, I view such acts as short sighted, selfish and a pox on the history of our sport. Future generations of climbers are robbed of the opportunity to experience routes as they were originally done. As well, this kind of behavior is totally at odds with climbing ethics which have existed since the inception of the sport. Lastly, it is disrespectful of the efforts of one's fellow climbers.

Some "critics" will invariably point out that I added a fixed pin to Vector Analysis after I completed the route and, furthermore, that I left a piece of fixed gear in place. Vector, however, was my route. If anyone had a right to do this it was me — and me alone.

***

A few years ago I took my friend, John Bachar, out to see the wall. I had invited John to stay as a house guest with me for a couple of months while we travelled around the Southeast for him to do a slideshow. Bachar, for those of you who don't recognize the name, was arguably the best climber in the world "back in the day"; his free soloing exploits are the stuff of legends. Tragically, he died only a few months after departing Chattanooga in a free soloing mishap.

John and I stood there at the base of Vector Analysis, looking up. "Dude!" he exclaimed, "What the hell is up with all those bolts?" He turned and looked at me with an incredulous stare, eyes squinted, mouth slightly parted, arms crossed. I recounted the ignominious story. "Why haven't you taken them out?" he asked.

It's a great question. A great question, indeed.

Chattanooga

    Chattanooga is located in the southeast corner of Tennessee, just north of the Georgia state line. A large portion of the population of the United States is located within a day's drive of the city. It is the state's 4th largest city, with a population of approximately 170,000, although the metro regional population hovers around a half a million people.

    Sprawled across a wide valley situated approximately 680 feet above sea level, Chattanooga is ringed by low mountains, cloaked in dense hardwood forests, and capped by countless miles of sandstone cliffs. These cliffs comprise the biggest reserves of world class sandstone in the United States. From the downtown area, miles of cliff-line are visible. The vast majority of the region's sandstone treasures, however, are hidden within the convoluted folds of the surrounding mountains that form the rugged topography of the region.

Within an hour or so drive of Chattanooga is a seemingly endless supply of incredible crags to explore, with a route inventory that numbers in the thousands. (There is also unlimited world class bouldering.) Although the city's official nickname is the "Scenic City" some folks have taken to calling it the "Boulder, Colorado of the East." In 2008, Chattanooga was listed at the top of Rock & Ice Magazine's Top Ten Cities to live in if you're a climber. Alternate outdoor activities include whitewater kayaking, hiking, mountain biking, caving and hang gliding.

Housing in the Chattanooga area is surprisingly affordable when compared to many other metropolitan areas elsewhere in the country. That fact, coupled with a low cost of living and a strong economy, make Chattanooga a very appealing place to live-especially for climbers. If you are looking to buy or sell a home in the Chattanooga metropolitan area call Metro Real Estate, LLC at (423) 468-1111 and ask for Rob Robinson, or visit him online at: www.GoWithMetro.com.

CHATTANOOGA

Getting Here

Flying?
Visit http chattairport.com for detailed information.

Connecting flights into Chattanooga are available and affordable. It is recommended, however, that you consider renting a car once in town --- as many of the climbing areas are far enough away to necessitate frequent access to a vehicle.

Driving?
Car-less navigation and travel around the immediate downtown Chattanooga area has increased in popularity and ease within the recent past. Electric shuttles, city-run bike shares, and a general pedestrian-friendly design has helped to establish Chattanooga as a foot-friendly city.

However, if you are here to climb on our surrounding sandstone, having a vehicle or an extensive network of friends with vehicles is a must --- seeing that the climbing areas around Chattanooga are numerous, not in walking distance, and are very dispersed throughout a 50 mile radius from the city center.

Driving to Chattanooga

From Atlanta: Take I-75 North for 118 miles.

From Birmingham: Take I-59 North for 147 miles.

From Nashville: Take I-24 East for 133 miles.

From Knoxville: Take I-75 South for 112 miles.

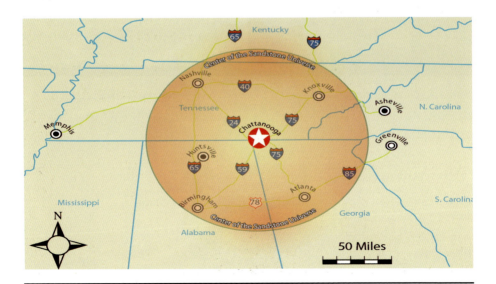

www.rockerypress.com

CHATTANOOGA

Where to Stay?
Hotel/Hostel
There are a multitude of hotels located in the Downtown Chattanooga area. Alternatively, you might also want to check out the local hostel, The Crashpad.

The Crashpad
29 Johnson Street
Southside Neighborhood
Chattanooga, TN 37408
call: 423-648-8393 or visit crashpadchattanooga.com for more information

Prentice Cooper State Forest (T-Wall)
The long-time preference of the traveling dirtbag is the FREE primitive camping (no utilities) in designated tent sites at the base of the Tennessee Wall in the Prentice Cooper state forest.

Directions:
❶ From Chattanooga, Take I-27 North (across Oligiati bridge) to the Signal Mountain Road exit. ❷ Continue 1.5 miles on US 127 North (Passing a Wal Mart Shopping Center) until you reach the base of Signal Mountain. ❸ At the base of the mountain, take a left onto Suck Creek Road (TN Highway 27 West) (If you start going up the mountain, you've missed the turn). ❹ Follow Suck Creek Road for approximately 4.0 miles to a bridge that crosses suck creek. ❺ Take a left at this bridge onto Mullins Cove Road (if you start going up Suck Creek Canyon, you've gone too far). Drive approximately 6 miles on Mullins Cove Road (be mindful of the blind curves!), and locate a large climber parking lot on your left.

Outfitters & Climbing Gyms
Visit Rock/Creek Outfitters for all of your camping and climbing needs. You can visit them online at www.rockcreek.com or stop by their retail storefront at 301 Manufacturer's Road (Phone: 423-265-5969).

For your indoor climbing needs, choose from this list of climbing gyms:

High Point Climbing Gym: 219 Broad Street, Downtown Chattanooga. (p)423-602-ROCK
Urban Rocks Climbing Gym: 1007 Appling Street (p)423-475-6578
Tennessee Bouldering Authority: 3804 St. Elmo Avenue, Suite #102 (p)423-828-6800

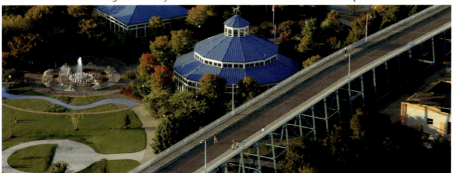

www.rockerypress.com

CHATTANOOGA

Season

The climbing season in Chattanooga (for those with a high-threshold for pain) is year-round. For those that like it a bit more comfy, take away 2 months of sweltering humidity & 2 months of sub-freezing temps, and you have 8 months of great climbing conditions (March-June ; September-December).

The best month to climb in Chattanooga is the month of November. The temps are perfect (low 60s), the leaves are beautiful (1st week of November), and each area despite being shady, sunny, or seasonally seepy are all in perfect equilibrium with the climbing world.

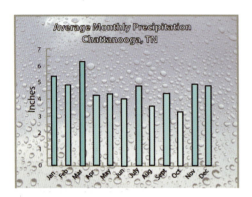
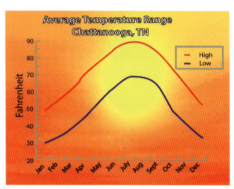

Where to Eat

While the quality of Chattanooga fine dining has improved over the past decade, the following list is not predicated on the traditional 5-star dining scale. Rather, this list is built on post-climbing grubbin' criteria: cost, portion, and beer.

Tremont Tavern: Best burgers in town, awesome prices, and FREE BEER once a week!!! 1203 Hixson Pike. Chattanooga (423) 266-1996

Amigos Mexican Restaurant: Great Americanized Mexican food with very large portions and excellent 32 ounce beer specials.
1906 Dayton Blvd, Red Bank (423) 499-5435

La Altena's Mexican Restaurant: Authentic Mexican food with mega burritos and good margarita & beer specials.
314 W Main St., Chattanooga (423) 266-7595

Sluggo's Vegetarian Cafe: Delicious vegetarian food (even for meat eaters) that is very well priced and comes with HUGE portions. They also have great beer on tap and frequently have live music downstairs.
501 Cherokee Blvd, Chattanooga, (423) 752-5224

CHATTANOOGA

Good Rest Day Activities

Chattanooga is full of great rest-day activities. Browse the Free & NOT Free list of awesome non-climbing opportunities available in our city.

FREE

Three Bridges Waterfront: You have to experience the Three-Bridges waterfront and art-district. We recommend you park on the North Shore, walk across the Walnut Street Bridge (walking bridge), and either walk left (to art district) or right to the waterfront where several public art displays will keep you entertained for an afternoon.

Stringer's Ridge: A recently acquired tract of public land located on the North Shore, Stringer's Ridge offers miles of hiking & biking trails --- as well as several art exhibits.

City Sponsored Festivals & Events: Your trip will most-likely coincide with any number of free festivals or concerts that are centered around the waterfront area. Whether it's the Night Fall/ River Front Nights Summer Series - or the Annual River Rocks Festival in October, make sure you check local media outlets (nooga.com) for show times and events.

NOT FREE

The Chattanooga Aquarium: The Aquarium is a long-time Chattanooga staple that offers a great day of educational fun! The Aquarium now has two components (Fresh Water & Salt Water). In particular, the TN River exhibit offers some great insight into the TN River Gorge environment and surrounding ecosystems that we, as climbers, often frequent on our trips out into the surrounding Chattanooga wilds.

Shopping: If that vacation cash is itching at your back pocket, check out the several boutique shopping districts that sell a wide selection of local crafts and goods. In particular, check out the Fraiser Street (North Shore) shopping district or the Warehouse Row shopping district.

Movie/ Concert/ Plays: Chattanooga provides several entertainment venues ranging from new release films to excellent live music. In particular, check out the new downtown venue, Track 29 (track29.com) for upcoming shows.

Boozin': For those creatures of the night that require some after-hours entertainment, Chattanooga has several local breweries and bars that serve local-brewed beers and whiskeys. In particular, check out The Terminal (terminalbrewhouse.com); Big River Grille (bigrivergrille.com); and the Chattanooga Brewing Company (chattabrew.com).

Chattrad Ranking Systems

Route Difficulty Ranking System
In keeping with the spirit that the simplest idea is often the most elegant: I wanted to skip the use of the popular Y.D.S. letter sub-grade system (a,b,c,d) in favor of a minus sign (-), plus sign (+) — or no sign at all — to signify approximate route difficulty. This is how I have graded traditional style climbs. However, sport climbers like letter grades and, as such, this guide utilizes letter grades for sport (all bolted) routes.

Route Quality Ranking System
The first half of the quality ranking system relies upon the traditional three star system. I have always appreciated rock climbing guides which incorporated the so-called "star system" of grading climbs for their aesthetic qualities. This classification is especially useful for vacationing climbers interested in sampling the very best climbs an area has to offer. The star system in this guide works as follows:

(N/A) A route without any stars does not mean you should automatically dismiss the climb as a candidate for fun and adventure. Rest assured, there are many climbs in this guide, sans stars, deserving of your time and energy. (There are very few climbs I have ever done that I didn't get something out of.)

One star - ★ - indicates a route of above average quality — perhaps flawed in some intrinsic way — but still good enough to encourage climbers to rope up and explore. If assigned a "report card grade," a one star climb would range between a B- and a C+. Frequently, one star routes will reward the curious with a pleasant surprise.

Two stars - ★★ - signify a climb that, for any number of reasons, seems to fall just short of the highly prized "mega classic" status. You'll find the overall rock quality is typically good, but not necessarily perfect. (There might be some choss, friable flakes or mossy holds to contend with.) The route will yield substantial, but discontinuous, stretches of quality climbing following aesthetically pleasing features. If assigned a "report card grade," a two star climb would range between a B+ and a B-.

Three stars - ★★★ - suggests a route which offers a combination of overall superior quality rock, beautiful moves and/or sequences, appealing features, nice wall position and/or exposure. If assigned a "report card grade," a three star climb would range between an A and A-.

Route Quality Symbol System
The second half of the quality ranking system relies upon three symbols to denote the highest quality this guide awards.

Take note that one symbol is not considered better or higher quality than another. They are all considered equal. Their purpose, however, is to represent distinguishing route characteristics and styles that would otherwise be omitted or ignored within traditional ranking techniques.

The three Chattrad symbols are as follows:

This route is **PURE FUN**. Some traits include: dynamic movement, JUGS, Sculpted features, all-around fun-style climbing. You want to do these routes every time you come to the crag.

USING THIS BOOK

This route has **got Soul!** These routes are distinguished by the best possible movement & route aesthetics.... Wall position, style, setting... etc.

This route is defined by **classic Southern Attributes**. Some of these include: steep, pumpy, powerful lines that define what it means to climb in the South.

Danger Ranking System
This guide incorporates a system of icons intended to serve as shorthand for additional route information that you might find helpful.

A **'leap of faith'** icon signifies a route that likely offers the experienced climber decent gear placements, but with a caveat: the potential for a long and "spicy" fall(s) will be present. In other words, plan on catching a bit of "big air" if you blow a run-out.

A **'Houdini'** icon indicates a "serious" lead. Of course, all leads are potentially serious, but tackling one of these routes will likely expose the experienced climber to an "enhanced" situation wherein a fall at the wrong spot could result in serious injury. This could mean striking a ledge during a fall, or perhaps the ground. A fall at the wrong spot will likely result in bodily injury, but most likely be survivable.

A **'meet your maker'** icon indicates a so-called "death route." Protection (if available) will usually be marginal at best, and is likely to fail in the event of a fall. Striking the ground from high up (decking) or clipping a nasty projection at a "high rate of speed" during a fall is a distinct possibility.

     Whatever the case, if a climb does not have a danger symbol — it does not mean it is a "safe" climb! There is no such thing. Safety is always a function of each climber's own independent judgment combined with his or her experience. This guide is not intended to replace, or serve as a substitute, for your own judgment. (Please refer again to the disclaimer in the front of this book.)

Insider's Tip: not into tackling one of these routes? Rig a toprope! Many of these lines offer excellent climbing well worth sampling.

INTRODUCTION

A Few Thoughts on Climbing & Safety

Climbing demands a tremendous amount of self-restraint and personal discipline. In general, the safer climber is one who:

❶ Knows, and does not exceed, his or her climbing ability.
❷ Possesses the requisite skills to arrange adequate protection ... and further has a keen appreciation for the limitations of that gear.
❸ Maintains a fanatical adherence to established safety practices.
❹ Can comprehend the "full spectrum of risk" presented by not only a particular climb, but the entire cliff line, and proceeds accordingly.

The subject of rock climbing safety is a complicated and extensive one. You can learn the basics from a qualified, professional rock climbing instructor supplemented by scores of books and videos commonly available at most outdoor shops these days.

Technical safety considerations aside, there are a few items I recommend you consider bringing with you to the crag:

❶ **A Cell Phone.** In the event you or someone else is involved in an accident; valuable time can be gained if you can call emergency personnel immediately. The alternative is tracking down someone else at the cliff with a cell phone, or hiking out to find the nearest land line. Insider's Note: The quality of reception at areas in this guide vary considerably from cell carrier to carrier, so bear in mind you may not always be able to get a phone connection just because you have a cell phone!

❷ **A Headlamp.** At minimum, I encourage you bring one, along with fresh battery back ups. No "light at night" is a pet peeve of mine, so I usually bring three lamps: a main light and a back up for myself, and a third light for anyone else I'm climbing with who might have forgotten theirs.

❸ **A Helmet designed for rock climbing.** Not only can a helmet provide some protection against head dings caused by dropped biners and pebbles ... it can also offer some protection in a bad fall. Remember, your skull is basically a heavy duty egg shell. It will crack surprisingly easy.

❹ **A Rescue Signal Laser.** Go to Greatland Laser company's web site at www.GreatlandLaser.com and check their product line. It might also help if you know how to use Morse code to signal "SOS."

❺ **A First Aid Kit.** To take care of the small stuff, and possibly give you an edge if you find yourself administering aid in the initial stages of a bad accident.

The consequences of an error in judgment can be tragic. Gravity is an equal opportunity "employer" ... and destroyer. Gravity doesn't care if you are a novice or an expert climber. Gravity doesn't care if you've been climbing one day — or thirty years. Gravity doesn't care how much, or how little, you know. When "gravity takes hold," and you hit the ground at a high rate of speed, the end result is the same for everyone: almost certain death. There is no margin for error.

Recommended Gear

Ropes
Many Chattanooga Trad climbs top out at about 100 feet. As such, I suggest you bring a 60 meter (or longer) rope to facilitate single line top-ropes and rappels. Note: If you are using a 60 meter rope, do not automatically assume that both ends will always reach the ground, as this is not the case!

Traditional Routes
For 90% of the "traditional style" free climbs a rack which includes the following will usually suffice:

A double set of steel or brass nuts
Triples in wired stoppers #3 through #6
A double set of Metolious cams #00 through #2
A double set of Camp Tricams #.25 and #.50
A double set of Camalots #1 through #3
A half dozen or more full length runners
Ten or or more quick draws (made from tripled full length runners)
Plenty of free carabiners
A nut tool for cleaning up seams

You also might want to lug a couple of the "jumbo" camming devices in your pack ... they occasionally come in handy.

On some of the more extreme free routes you might want to add a bit more gear to your arsenal, including:

A "fistful" of small brass and steel nuts
Extra sets of the smallest Metolious (or Alien) cams
A couple of Black Diamond Peckers
A couple of long knifeblade pins for hammer-less placements
A variety of skyhooks (and a roll of duct tape to secure them in place)
A couple of small Camp Ball Nuts
Double ropes!

And last but not least ... a patient belayer who won't take it personally if you lower off, screaming, totally freaked out and on the verge of a nervous breakdown as a result of the unrelenting mental anguish and tension occasionally experienced when tackling a "sandstone super desperate."

Sport Routes
In general, I recommend carrying at least 10 draws for all bolted routes, plus a couple of extras in case you drop one or two while trying to make a desperate clip. And don't forget clips for anchors.

Additionally, I recommend you bring a couple of extra carabiners and full length slings in case you need to "float the rope" through overhangs, work with zig-zags, or sling a tree at the summit.

INTRODUCTION

The Nature of Sandstone Climbing

Of all the rock types I've climbed on through the years, southern sandstone remains my all-time favorite. There are several reasons for this. One, I suppose, is this is the rock I "grew up on," and consequently that which I am most familiar and comfortable with. Southern sandstone is like an old friend to me. Beyond this, however, are many other factors which continue to hold my interest. One I would attribute to is simple aesthetics. Southern sandstone often presents an astonishingly wide palette of intermingled colors: oranges, greys, pale yellows, black varnishes, streaks of marshmallow white and dark chocolate are often melded into a gorgeous vertical tapestry that is as much fun to look at as it is to climb on.

Another draw is the overall challenge this rock type presents; it requires an "interdisciplinary approach." To wit: you cannot be the master of any one technique and expect a high rate of success. Time and again it seems southern sandstone conspires to throw a little bit of everything at you in an effort to stymie upward progress. So be ready to crimp thin face moves, rip through roofs, battle past baffling bulges, conquer cryptic cracks and hit the slopers — often times all in the same pitch!

In addition to the complexity of moves one often encounters there is the critical issue of figuring out how to rest. This demands great creativity and the ability to improvise under duress. At times, it seems one has to be an amateur contortionist to make the best use of holds in order to catch a break. It doesn't matter how good you are at everything else, if you don't know how to finagle rests while you're climbing … you're "goin' down." Good rest technique helps a climber shift the load from overtaxed hands, gain more time to get in extra protection, down climb into safety, or turbo through an eight cylinder crux with gas to spare.

As such, it will be of great benefit if you know (or are prepared to learn) how to cobble together rest stances that permit maximum conservation of strength and energy (thereby providing an opportunity to recover the same). Just a few examples of great rests include: A tiny heel stance in the middle of a "blank" face … a subtle thumb catch or a shallow knuckle undercling … an overhead heel hook … a hi-tech "knee bar" … a hip smeared into a corner. Climbers sometimes refer to these tricks of the trade as "skin catch" or "body English."

Regardless of whether you are a beginning climber or seasoned pro, this sandstone is going to challenge your creativity, test your courage and "willingness to engage," push you past the edges of your comfort zone, and ultimately — thrill you as only this incredible rock medium can.

Rob Robinson climbing Iron Maiden, 5.11.

Preserving Climbing Areas for Future Generations

///////// *The SCC Vision Lives On* /////////

The Southeastern Climbers Coalition (SCC) is a 501(c)(3) non-profit corporation dedicated to preserving climbing access in the Southeast. It started in 1993 when a group of climbers banded together to help out with ongoing access issues at Sunset Rock, atop Lookout Mountain in Chattanooga, Tennessee. The group had positive results from the start and went on to sponsor cleanups and trail days at climbing areas. Later, the SCC raised money to purchase land to keep climbing areas open for future generations. SCC volunteers are climbers from Tennessee, Alabama, Georgia, Florida, and elsewhere who have joined forces to resolve climbing access issues. The SCC aims to provide an ongoing means for climbers throughout the area to come together and respond effectively to access threats to crags, as well as the impacts of increasing use.

The SCC has effectively empowered climbers for 20 years now. In fact, many of the areas in this guidebook are open due to the hard work of SCC volunteers and activists. The SCC leases access to Castle Rock from private landowners. The SCC works with a private company to keep Leda open. The SCC has negotiated climbing management plans with state parks like at Foster Falls and Deep Creek to keep those areas open to climbers. The SCC hosts annual and biannual trail days on public and private lands to maintain positive relationships with land managers and to address the impacts of increasing use. If you have never been to a trail day, check the SCC calendar and join one at your favorite crag. The SCC has done more for climbing access and conservation in the southeast than can be listed here, but please visit our website www.seclimbers.org for more information.

From 1993-2013, the SCC has made significant accomplishments and contributions to climbing access in the southeast. The SCC owns six crags and leases two more, and the SCC has helped keep countless crags in the southeast open by maintaining positive relationships with landowners and land managers. BUT there is always more work to be done.

In fact, upwards of 50% of climbing in the southeast is on private property! Can you imagine if this guidebook had twice as many areas and a 1000 more routes in it? The SCC is the organization that is purchasing new crags and expanding access to existing climbing areas, be it sport climbing, trad climbing, or bouldering. The SCC's vision for climbing conservation in the southeast is clear, more access to more climbing areas.

Support from our members and volunteers is behind all the crucial work that the SCC does. The SCC is a grassroots organization to its core, and every new member and volunteer makes a difference. Join us now at www.seclimbers.org. Every climber makes our coalition stronger. And you, are no exception.

WHY JOIN THE  ?

THE SOUTHEASTERN CLIMBERS COALITION

is a 501(c)(3) non-profit corporation dedicated to preserving climbing access in the Southeast. The SCC was founded in 1993 when a group of climbers banded together to help with ongoing access issues at Sunset Rock, atop Lookout Mountain in Chattanooga, Tennessee. The SCC had positive results from the start and soon moved into sponsorship of cleanups and trail days at climbing areas. We've since expanded our scope to include fundraising and land preservation, purchasing many historic and threatened climbing areas around the southeast. The SCC's volunteers are climbers from Tennessee, Alabama, Georgia, North and South Carolina and the Ozarks who have joined forces to resolve local climbing access issues. The goal of the Southeastern Climbers Coalition is to provide ongoing means for climbers throughout the area to respond effectively to access threats at our crags and mitigate the impacts of their increased use. It's all about preserving climbing access,

SO THIS NEVER HAPPENS AGAIN

Boat Rock, Atlanta, GA - 2004

Photos by Wes Powell

www.seclimbers.org

2002

Raised $100,000 for the purchase and preservation of the severely threatened **BOAT ROCK** bouldering area, just 20 minutes from downtown Atlanta, GA. Over 260 boulder problems to date, and counting!

2003

Received a donation of the **KING'S BLUFF** cliffline, a limestone sport climbing area near Clarksville, TN. More than 160 routes from 5.3 to 5.13 on 9.78 acres along the Cumberland River.

2005

Purchased 1550 linear feet of classic sandstone cliffline on a 3.14 acre tract at **JAMESTOWN**, Alabama. Climbers had been visiting Jamestown since the 70's, but it had been closed since 1993.

2005

Negotiated a lease agreement for **CASTLE ROCK**, a sandstone cliff near Jasper, TN. Castle Rock is home to more than 50 established lines, including one of Tennessee's hardest, "Apes on Acid" - a 5.13d.

2009

Raised funds to purchase a portion of **YELLOW BLUFF**, near Huntsville, AL. Yellow Bluff is an historic sandstone cliff with both sport and traditional lines. The property had been closed for over 25 years.

2009

Purchased a 25 acre tract that includes a portion of cliffline at **STEELE**, AL. The property includes over 40 established climbing routes, both traditional and sport. Steele had been closed since 1987.

2011

Purchased a two acre parking area and approach trail for convenient access to Deep Creek and climbing areas along the Cumberland Trail near Chattanooga, TN. Relatively new, Deep Creek has Over 170 sport routes and counting.

2013

Southern bouldering is world-class and Hospital Boulders are no exception. Located 15 minutes from both HP40 and Steele in Alabama, the SCC purchased the Hospital Boulders.

FIND OUT HOW YOU CAN HELP ADD THE NEXT SUCCESS STORY HERE BY VISITING WWW.SECLIMBERS.ORG

A view of Lookout Valley as seen from Sunset Park.

If you were drawn to Sunset based on how promising the NPS owned and managed crag looked from the valley —you would likely be disappointed. Framed by trees, a lackluster, ash gray cliff line spans the northwest tip of Lookout Mountain. To be sure, there are a couple of eye-catching features including: Sunset Rock, the Space Ranger Buttress, The Towers, and a few taller outcrops towards the southern end of the crag—but by and large, Sunset appears like scores of other middlin' cliffs sprinkled throughout the region: a cobwebbed sandstone bank bereft of vertical treasure.

Sunset Park

Photo Credit: Micah Gentry

As luck would have it, however, Sunset holds significant reserves of world class rock. I envy you if this is your first trip to the area; get ready to ransack a rock vault replete with nearly three hundred climbs and a king's ransom in bouldering. If you're a long-time Sunset regular, I trust you'll pocket a couple of "newly minted coins of the realm" you might have missed previously.

SUNSET PARK

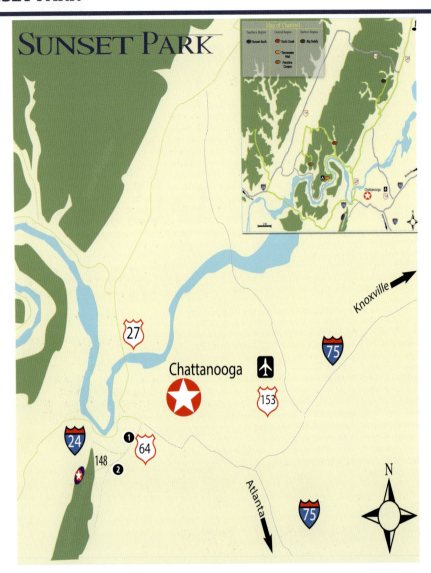

20 mins

Sunset Park sits atop the northwest shoulder of Lookout Mountain near its northernmost tip. ❶ Follow the Lookout Mountain/Ruby Falls signs from I-24. ❷ Follow 148 South past a tourist attraction, "Ruby Falls," to the crest of the mountain. ❸ Stay on 148 South for 4/10ths of a mile to a fork in the road formed by a stone traffic island. ❹ Bear right up the hill past the island, and continue along on West Brow Road for 1/2 mile. ❺ The truncated Sunset parking lot will appear on the left sandwiched in between a couple of houses. ❻ A gated entrance leads to a brief mountain stone trail which in turn leads down to the summit of Sunset Rock.

56   www.rockerypress.com

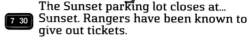
SUNSET PARK

Area Overview

Welcome to Sunset: the starcrossed crag that shines from the center of the southern sandstone solar system, the place where the first light of southern sandstone epoch kindled.

As late as the mid 70's this stellar area was largely unexplored—only a couple of dozen routes had been done. Most climbing activity revolved around main rock and adjacent cliff line. Developing Sunset was any starship trooper's game.

Throughout the 70's, 80's and 90's I spent more time climbing at Sunset than anywhere else. It was the first (local) area I climbed at, and obviously I came to love it. The locale has a unique sense of place and an astonishing array of great routes.

Sunset's 24 carat status can be attributed to its:

❶ Relative ease of access, civilized setting and proximity to a major urban center.

❷ Consistently superior rock quality: extremely solid, compact and fine grained.

❸ Plethora of two and three star routes.

❹ Huge inventory of high end boulder problems.

❺ Cognitively complex, sustained, asymetrical "in your face" (steep) climbing.

Work through the majority of Sunset's puzzles and you should be able to piece together hard sandstone routes just about anywhere in the world.

Rules & Regs

The Sunset parking lot closes at... Sunset. Rangers have been known to give out tickets.

1.) Observe all posted signs and regulations.
 2.) The parking lot is very small (~8-10 spaces) Arrive early or carpool. Do NOT park illegally.
If the parking lot is full, try parking at the Craven's House or at the Lookout Mtn. ball parks which you pass on your way in.
 3.) Camping and overnight use are prohibited in the parking lot.
 6.) Before the fixed anchor initiative of the early 2000s, Sunset had a major issue with unpadded anchor slings damaging trees. If you are in a position where you need to sling a tree, be sure to pad it first!
7.) Firearms, fireworks, or alcoholic beverages are prohibited.
 8.) All pets must be kept on a leash at all times.
 9.) The installation of new fixed hardware is prohibited without a permit.
10.) 'Sport' rappelling is prohibited.
11.) Large groups and guided tours are subject to NPS restrictions and guidelines

Area Logistics

Emergency
Dial 911

Season
Spring through Fall

Camping

There is a KOA in the valley, about a 20 minute drive from the Park. Check a city telephone book for details. If you want to "get plush" you can find a budget motel in Tiftonia at the foot of Lookout Mountain.

Park History

Sunset Rock played a minor part in the Civil War; it served as vantage point to observe rival troop movements in the valley below. Activity witnessed from here is said to have led to a skirmish known as the Battle of Wauhatchie.

After the war, the top of Lookout grew into an affluent residential area, and simultaneously became a destination for tourists. A nationally recognized luxury hotel, The Point Hotel (a.k.a. the Lookout Inn), was built at what is now Point Park.

Strangely enough, one mile south, a small frame house was built atop Sunset Rock. This location served as a photography studio (owned by J.B. Linn), and it was operated by two brothers, Charles and Harry Hardie. The studio was doubly unique in that it had a front porch which jutted out over the edge of the bluff—complete with rocking chairs! The iron poles still found atop Sunset Rock today secured the structure to its precarious perch.

During their stint at Sunset Rock, the Hardie brothers produced a classic, (and now very rare) small book of photographs detailing many of the mountain's scenic wonders, as well as their studio, the Hotel, and themselves. Even more bizarre than the studio was a narrow gauge steam railway, "The Little Dinky," that ran from the Point Hotel to Sunset Rock. This small train brought tourists to the Rock's base! If able bodied, visitors could clamber up the steep trail to the summit where (for a price) they could have their picture taken. Additionally, they might have purchased a tall, cool glass of lemonade from the concession stand, or bought a trinket or Civil War relic to take back home for a souvenir.

About 1910 the Point Hotel burned to the ground, the narrow gauge railway ceased operation, and the Sunset studio was abandoned and later razed. At the time, Sunset was privately owned by the Lookout Mountain Railway company, a subsidiary of the Tennessee Electric Power company. It was largely through the magnanimous efforts of the late publishing magnate, Adolph S. Ochs, that Sunset eventually ended up in public hands.

A 19th Century Scene from Sunset Rock.

Photo Courtesy of TSLA Archives.

Forrest Gardner, Time Travel Soloing.

Climbing History

Sunset was the first sandstone cliff in the mid South to be systematically developed. For this reason, it is of considerable historical interest to climbers. Though the following history is incomplete, it is nonetheless the most complete record assimilated to date. If you know of anything further regarding the development of climbing at Sunset prior to 1975 please contact the publisher via the address on the copyright page.

Presently, no solid documentation prior to the early 1960's has surfaced regarding climbing at Sunset. However, it is conceivable a husband and wife team, Harvey and Jewel Templeton, may have frequented the area—though at the time practice climbing on small cliffs in the United States was uncommon.

The Templetons, residents of Lookout Mountain, traveled and climbed throughout Europe in the late 40's and early 50's. They also served as mountain guides out West and made several first ascents in Wyoming's Grand Tetons with crack Colorado climber Dick Pownall. (**Insider's Appendix:** See Page 131 for a fascinating advertisement from 1944 that shows an unknown climber at Sunset Rock).

1960'S

In 1960, Tom Kimbro and Tom Martin met up and discovered they had a mutual interest in climbing. Armed with "an ancient hemp rope and some pointed pieces of steel" the pair headed to an obscure Lookout Mountain limestone cliff called "Eagle's Nest." Over several months, Kimbro and Martin managed to work out a half dozen climbs, ranging in difficulty up to 5.4. Soon thereafter, they contacted Recreational Equipment Inc. and mail ordered more climbing equipment, "the real stuff, just like that in the books." Tom wrote: "With our new gear in hand we were ready to move on to bigger projects. The Sunset area had the best access, and we soon found the rock much better than the shattered Eagle's Nest limestone."

First Ascent of Rusty's Crack

"The first route we did was Yellowbrick Road in spring of 1960. We also did The Womb accompanied by Noel McGlothin." Kimbro and Martin also managed the Bolt Pinnacle chimney, placing a bolt to escape from the crackless summit. The pair also climbed the Towers Chimney"and a few routes south of Sunset ,but I don' remember much about them." In fall of 1961, Kimbro was drafted into military service, and his climbing came to a temporary halt. Martin was still around, and likely went on to complete more first ascents. It is also known that Sir Edmund Hillary (of Mount Everest fame) visited Chattanooga on a lecture tour and managed to get away long enough to do some climbing with Martin whom he had met. Martin probably took him to Sunset.

SUNSET PARK

In 1964, Kimbro returned to Sunset, this time with none other than Steve Roper, author of the first Yosemite Valley guide and the book Fifty Classic Climbs of North America. The two had met while in the service; both were clerk typists at the same Army base. "Roper was an aid specialist, and he led several Sunset lines I can no longer identify. The hardest aid pitch we did was The Prow, or something close to it (Roper's Aid Route). He also did S'More, the free climbing testpiece of the area." From this last quote, we can deduce that in Kimbro's absence, first ascent activity had indeed continued.

S'More, rated 5.8, must have been done between 1961 and 1964. Although it is likely Martin or McGlothin made the first ascent, we can't rule out the possibility that Sir Edmund Hillary led it on his brief visit to the area! Inspired by Roper, the trio of Kimbro, Martin and McGlothin tackled Rusty's Crack, aiding out of the chimney on wooden blocks wedged in the imposing, 4" crack above. This was probably Kimbro's last climb at Sunset. Lured by tales of life on the big walls, he headed West for Yosemite Valley and never looked back.

The trail through the mid 1960's grows cold here. One report has it that a Park Service ranger climbed the Rattlesnake Route using bolts! (You can still see the quarter-inch studs today.) In the late 1960's, Tim McMillan, then a North Carolina climber, visited Sunset and made the first ascent of Walk In The Park. McMillan probably did the first ascent of Thin Pockets, too. Undoubtedly there were more climbers active throughout this period, but names and climbs have yet to surface.

1970'S

In the early 1970's, one name stands out clearly: Stan Wallace. It is reasonably certain Wallace made the first ascent of the classic dihedral Stan's Crack and the first free ascent of Alpha Omega. The latter, a technical and awkward crack climb, was unquestionably the free climbing testpiece of the area. Given this level of demonstrated expertise, Wallace may have made other difficult (though unknown) ascents. In 1974, Dennis Holland and Stephen Lepley worked out free leads of Scream Wall and Scream Wall Direct. These two climbs, along with Alpha Omega, represented the fringe of free climbing feasibility for local climbers at the time. Another significant ascent completed in the early 1970's was Steve Jenkins all-nut lead of Rattlesnake Route. Though technically easier than Alpha Omega and Scream Wall, Jenkins' efforts were laudable: The delicate face climb was very short on natural protection. In the mid 1970's, Bill Smith, noted for his red hair and calm demeanor, emerged as a central Sunset figure and first ascensionist. With a variety of partners, Smith branched out in the park, picking lines here and there like chocolates out of a large Whitman sampler. To his credit are classics such as Bill's Route, Friday the 13th, Afternoon Delight and Divinity Crack.

Rob Robinson on an Early Ascent of Bill's Route, 5.8

Climbing History

Rob Robinson's First Lead, S'more, 5.8

In 1975, fifteen-year-old Rob Robinson completed an "Outward Bound" style trip out West. Upon returning to his home town of Chattanooga he became an avid explorer of the region's cliffs. A few years later Robinson moved to North Carolina for a year where he "apprenticed" with one the state's then leading climbers, Tim McMillan.

Upon his return to Chattanooga in 1978, Robinson began to expand development of Sunset. Inspired by Godfrey and Chelton's book Climb and especially the biography of John Gill, Master Of Rock, Robinson intensified his efforts. That year, accompanied by Steve Goins, he completed two noteworthy ascents: Muscle Shoals and The Pearl. Though the former was a short toprope, it was nonetheless the first route in the region to earn a 5.12 rating. The latter climb was the first bona fide 5.11 lead in the mid South's sandstone belt.

A year later, Robinson met Forrest Gardner at a local university. It just so happened that at the time Robinson was looking for a climbing partner. One look at Gardner's cabled forearms, and he knew Gardner had to be a climber. The two forged a friendship and soon became a dynamic climbing team. In the ensuing years the frenetic pair systematically developed Sunset, and several other areas throughout the region.

Eric Janoscrat on an Early Ascent of the Pearl, 5.11

1980'S

1980 was something of a landmark in the history of Southern climbing. In an astounding effort, Gardner made the first free ascent of Jennifer's World. His ascent was doubly significant: not only was this the first solid 5.12 lead in the Sandstone Belt, but it was probably the first 5.12 lead in the southeastern United States as well. Gardner also excelled at high end free soloing. Just a few of his outstanding efforts include Euphoria, Flagstone and the Headwall. In the late 1980's Gardner shifted his focus to solo aid climbing; primarily in North Carolina. Today, quite a few of his routes are among the most difficult in the region.

Forrest Gardner Soloing the Headwall, 5.10+

SUNSET PARK

In late 1984 the Tennessee Wall was discovered, and Sunset experienced a brief lull in first ascent activity—but not for long. Enter the brothers Justin and Travis Eiseman. Throughout the mid 1980's, this energetic pair of high school kids strung together an amazing number of quality first ascents at Sunset and elsewhere. Classics such as A Carnival Of Sorts, and Tarantula are representative of their bolted efforts, though they managed first ascents of many traditional style routes as well. But Travis really excelled at bolted "sport" climbing. He was also capable of free soloing at a very high standard. His solo of the testpiece 5.12 roof Tantrum is among the hardest pitches done ropeless in the Southeast. About the same time Chris Chesnutt came onto the scene. Soon after zipping

Chris Chesnutt on the Prow, 5.11+

through the Sunset classics he, too, began adding new routes. Early on, this high school lad earned a reputation as a very bold leader. The Banshee and Dementia are but two examples of his considerable prowess. In later years Chesnutt acquired a taste for overhanging limestone, and recently he established several 5.12 and 5.13 all-bolted routes at a nearby Chattanooga limestone crag; his best efforts are among the most difficult free routes in the region.

1990s Fashion...

1990'S & Beyond

Today, Sunset's "first ascent bank" is notably depleted, though far from insolvent. Climbers continue to scour the park in search of hidden assets, and occasionally discover a gem of a pitch like Dennis The Menace or The Widow Maker.

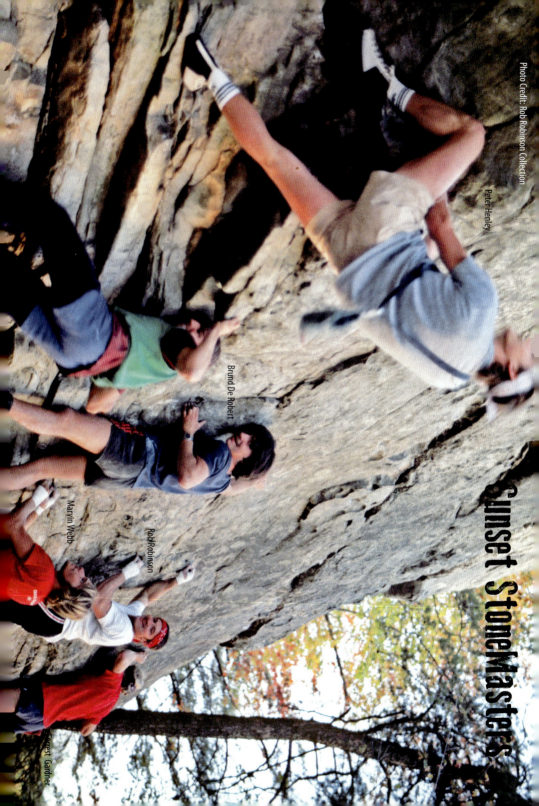

Photo Credit: Rob Robinson Colection
Peter Henley
Brund De Robert
Rob Robinson
Marvin Webb
Forrest Gardner

Sunset StoneMasters

Hedi Stanke on Another Fallen Angel, 5.10-

Sunset North

Access: From the parking lot, hike down the trail to the Sunset Rock overlook. From the overlook, hike left (South) along the rim to a stone staircase descent. At the bottom of this descent, you will encounter a junction in the trail. From this junction, hike right (North) back towards the Sunset Rock overlook, and you will encounter the Dick & Jane area within 100 feet. From here, navigation is easy seeing that the trail runs parallel to the base of all the climbing at Sunset North until terminating at the Craven's House just below Point Park.

Season: As is typical with many climbing areas throughout the Sandstone belt, spring and fall are the ideal times to climb at this locale. Not too hot ... not too cold. However, as Sunset in general is a northeast/northwest facing cliff, it is also an excellent summer crag. The sun first hits the crag at the far southern end, right around 2 p.m., then slowly arcs right about 45 degrees at around 5 pm when the entire crag is more or less bathed in full light. Sunset's circuitous cliff line provides plenty of cover from the late afternoon sun, as there are many niches, coves and recesses to take cover in.

Character: While North & South each have their own unique merits, the Northern end tends to be the more popular of the two. Sunset North is characterized by high densities of classic lines clustered together that tend to offer steeper routes on consistently clean and monolithic Sandstone. Oftentimes, routes are tucked away in overhanging alcoves which, by Sunset standards, are typically shorter and less exposed than the Southern end. But for what these climbs may lack, they make it up by packing in consistently steep and powerful testpieces - many of which are still revered as coveted Southern achievements.

Photo Credit: Micah Gentry

SUNSET PARK

NORTH

PM
10 mins

Sunset

DICK & JANE AREA

This is the first area you will come to if you take a right after descending down the access staircase. This box-like formation is popular for your first moderate toprope. This area also offers several rarely repeated 5.11 & 5.12 testpieces known for their high levels of commitment (Note: These higher end routes can easily be toproped).

Routes described starting from right to left of the gully descent.

❶ The Diamond 5.7
Start: 100' left of the switchbacks. Climb a crack with a diamond-shaped slot. 25'

Prisoner of Zenda, 5.11-

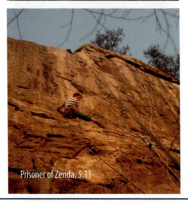
Prisoner of Zenda, 5.11-

❷ More Fun with Dick and Jane 5.9 ★
Start: 10' left of The Diamond. Climb a steep, right-facing flake. Keep left of an arete and wander up the wall. 70'
(First Lead) Forrest Gardner (summer of 86')

❸ Righthand Crack 5.8 ★
Start: Scramble up a gully to a ledge just left of Dick and Jane. Climb a right-facing corner with a jam crack. 40'
Unknown

SUNSET PARK

④ Lefthand Crack 5.9 ★★
Start: 10' left of Righthand Crack.
Climb a classic overhanging hand crack. 40'
Unknown

⑤ Tarantula 5.12- ★★
Start: Same as for Lefthand Crack. Boulder over a bulge with a sketchy bolt clip. Continue to the top past two more bolts on a blank-looking, overhanging face. 40' **Steve Goins (toprope, late 70's)**
First Lead: Travis Eiseman (3/88)

⑥ A Carnival of Sorts 5.12 ★★
Start: 5' left of Tarantula.
Climb an overhanging wall past a couple of fixed pins and a bolt. 50' **Travis Eiseman (3/88)**

⑦ Prisoner of Zenda 5.11- ★★★
Start: Atop a large boulder 5' left of A Carnival Of Sorts.
One of the greatest foes of any would-be Sunset king... Diagonal left and turn a bulge. Weave up the overhanging wall to a flake capped by a crack. Escape to the top. 60'
Toprope: Rob Robinson (7/79)
First Lead: Marvin Webb (7/82)

Photo Credit: Bob Robinson Collection

Forrest Gardner Free-Soloing the Headwall, 5.10

SUNSET PARK

❽ Cranial Reconstruction 5.11
Start: 10' left of Prisoner Of Zenda.
Climb a short jam crack. Continue right up the nose of a prominent arete to the top. 70' FA: Travis Eiseman (4/88)

❾ Rattlesnake Route 5.9 ★★★
See description on page 72.

Stop!: *The following 8 routes are closed to climbing and are included for historical purposes only.*

❿ The Fang 5.11 (closed) ★
Start: 15' left of Rattlesnake Route.
Scale a thin face protected by a single bolt; finish via Rattlesnake Route.
FA: Rob Robinson, Steve Goins (7/79)

Insider's Note: Presently closed to climbing. Bolt removed.

⓫ Typically French 5.11+ (closed) ★★
Start: Same as for The Fang.
Climb the face keeping left of the three bolts. As the angle lessens, diagonal right up a ramp to the top. 60'
First Lead: Bruno de Robert (9/81)

Insider's Note: Bolts removed.

⓬ The Headwall 5.10(closed) ★★★
Ultimately cool face climb, ultimate head trip.
Start: Same as for Typically French.
Climb a steep face with two thin sections to gain a "thank God" ledge. Zig zag through a few bulges (thin pro). Finish straight up the face (mega run-out) to the top. 60'
First Lead: Forrest Gardner (8/81)

⓭ Beginner's Gauntlet 5.6 (closed)
Start: 10' left of The Headwall.
Climb a short crack system to a ledge. Head left and up passing more ledges to the base of a vertical gully stacked with cracked blocks. Climb this to the top, favoring the gully's left side when difficulty is encountered. 60'
FA: Unknown

⓮ Yellowbrick Road 5.7 (closed) ★
Start: 15' left of Beginner's Gauntlet.
Layback a polished right-facing flake. Amble up a couple of ledges, then make a rising traverse left along smaller ledges to the top. 60'
FA: Tom Martin, Tom Kimbro (spring of 60')

Insider's Notes: Sunset's first recorded route.

⓯ Geek Motel 5.10+ (closed) ★
Start: 5' left of Yellowbrick Road.
Claw through a weakness in a small roof. Climb the wall above to a ledge. Finish up Yellowbrick Road. 50'
FA: Forrest Gardner, Jack Noonan (late 80's)

⓰ Screaming Turtles from Hell 5.10+ (closed) ★
Start: 5' left of Geek Motel.
Climb a short an easy right-facing corner; turn a small overhang. Knock over a low-angle bulge. Finish via Yellow Brick Road. 80'
First Lead: Travis Eiseman (8/87)

⓱ Complex Dexterities 5.11- (closed) ★
Start: 5' left of Screaming Turtles From Hell. Climb a short, left-arching flake. Creep onto slab above. Follow S'More to the top. 80'
First Lead: Travis Eiseman (9/87)

www.rockerypress.com 71

Rattlesnake Route 5.9 ★★★

Start: by a trailside slab 5' left of Cranial Reconstruction. Climb a nice ramp past a bolt (now chopped). Slither up the steep wall above, keeping right of two more bolts (chopped). Diagonal right up a tiny ramp; finish up an easy face to the top. 70'
FA: A "Park Ranger" (late 50s, early 60s)

Insider's Note: Bolts removed.

Photo Credit: Micah Gentry

SUNSET PARK

Sunset Rock
The next routes are located right below the main overlook and are loved by all for their high quality and convenience (topropers, please be courteous of parties below when dropping ropes).

⑱ S'more 5.8+ ★★★
Start: 10' left of Complex Dexterities. Climb a classic right-facing corner with a hand crack for about 15'. Step right beneath a roof to gain a smooth, right-facing corner. Tackle this (Super S'More) or move right and merge with Yellowbrick Road. 60' FA: Unknown.

⑲ Alpha Omega 5.10 ★★★
Start: Same as for S'More.
The beginning and end for all Sunset lifers! Climb a complex stack of short dihedrals guarded by small roofs and bulges. 60' FFA: Stan Wallace (early 70's) FA: Unknown.

⑳ Flagstone 5.11-
Start: 10' left of Alpha Omega.
Classic climbing in a picturesque setting! Boulder into a hanging right-facing corner and continue up the big overhanging flake and face above past two bolts. 70'
First Lead: Rob Robinson (4/81)

㉑ Total Eclipse 5.11+ ★★
Start: Same as Flagstone.
Climb a short, overhanging finger crack above a small, black roof. Finish up Flagstone or Carte Blanche. 70'
FFA: Ken Duncan (May/82)

㉒ Carte Blanche 5.12- ★★★
Here's one that'll ... wipe your slate clean? Powerful mix of roof work and overhanging terrain. Conquer Total Eclipse, cruise up the Flagstone flake ... iron cross right to a pocket; finish up a rounded groove. 60'
FA: Rob Robinson, Forrest Gardner (5/84)

㉓ Flute Loops 5.10- ★★
Start: 10' left of Carte Blanche.
Boulder up the wall for about 15'. Join a thin crack that leads up to and over a 3' roof. Finish up an easy prow. 90'
FA: Forrest Gardner, Rob Robinson (6/83)

www.rockerypress.com 73

SUNSET PARK

NORTH

Flagstone, 5.11-

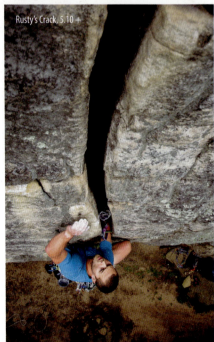

Rusty's Crack, 5.10 +

㉔ Another Fallen Angel 5.10- ★
Start: 5' left of Flute Loops.
Climb the steep wall; turn roof and continue to the top. 90'
First Lead: Travis Eiseman (10/87)

SUNSET PARK

25 Screamwall 5.10
Start: 5' left of Another Fallen Angel. Vertical filibuster? A trip to the podium no senator of sandstone should miss! Climb the face for 15' using a couple of small holds, then jam a short finger crack. Step right and continue screaming up a right-angling crack line to the top. 90'
FFA: Dennis Holland, Stephen Lepley (4/74)

26 Screamwall Direct Finish 5.10 ★★★
Step left at the top of the Scream Wall finger crack. Continue straight over bulges and blobby rock to the top. 90'

27 Euphoria 5.11
Start: 10' left of Scream Wall Direct. Boulder right past a small, but puzzling overhang. Face climb the blank-looking wall above, staying a few feet left of Scream Wall Direct. 90'
FA: Rob Robinson, Forrest Gardner, top rope (3/80) First Lead: Forrest Gardner (5/83)

Insider's Beta N' Notes: A.) A left leg cam (calf) at the opening overhang is helpful. B) Forrest Gardner free soloed this pitch shortly after leading it; he did a fully detached dyno at the crux. Think about that when you're doing it...

Photo Credit: Rob Robinson Collection

The Prow 5.12-
Classic sandstone air voyage. One of the Sandstone Belt's finest.
Start: 5' left of Pagan Rites.
Pitch #1: Boulder up a bulging overhang capped by a short arete and hidden ledge. (30') (5.12-)
Pitch #2: Dangle left through a reachy band of white overhangs. Hand-traverse right 15' to the final prow and the summit. (50') (5.11)
FA: Forrest Gardner, Rob Robinson (alt. leads, 6/80)

Climber: Rob Robinson

SUNSET PARK

NORTH

㉘ Dysphoria 5.11 ★★
Start: 5' left of Euphoria.
Pitch #1: Begin with a long reach to gain good holds. Trend left to a thin, vertical seam. Climb along this, eventually exiting left to the crack on pitch #1 of Rusty's Crack. 40' 5.11
Pitch #2: Climb one of several variations up the headwall above to the top. 50'
FA: Greg Smith, Rob Robinson (9/85)

㉙ Rusty's Crack 5.10+
Start: 10' left of Dysphoria.
Pitch #1: Climb a short chimney, "boulder" through a tricky roof capped by a classic 4" crack. (30') (5.10+)
Pitch #2: Pop through the slot overhang above. Finish up a spectacular headwall. (60') (5.9)
Variation (Flash or Crash) 5.10
Flash past a small overhang and finish up the exposed headwall.
FA: Tom Martin, Noel McGlothin, Tom Kimbro ('64) FFA: Unknown, FA Pitch two variation: Forrest Gardner, Rob Robinson ('83)

SUNSET PARK

㉚ Pagan Rites 5.12- ★★
Start: 5' left of Rusty's Crack. Boulder over low roof, turn the smaller roof above ,and then face climb a thin, water-polished face capped by a hidden ledge. 40' (Finish up any number of routes.)
FA: Forrest Gardner (late 80's)

㉛ The Prow 5.12-
See description on page 78.

㉜ Roper's Aid Route 5.12 ★
Start: 5' left of The Prow. Boulder past a very thin overhang; climb a short, rounded left-facing flake. Bucket right to a hidden ledge. 40' FA: Steve Roper, Tom Kimbro (64')
FFA: Rob Robinson (top rope, early 80's)

Cody Averbeck on the crux of Euphoria, 5.11　　　Photo Credit: Micah Gentry

SUNSET PARK

㉝ The Pearl 5.11 ★★★

A natural gem, but cracking this climbing oyster might prove to be a rare event. Start: 10' left of previous. Pitch #1: Climb a shallow left-facing corner to a couple of small ledges. (30') (5.9) Pitch #2: Stem up a severely overhung corner capped by a flared left-angling slot. (40')(5.11)

FA/FFA Pitch: Rob Robinson, Steve Goins (11/78)

㉞ The Edge of Might 5.12+

Or is it the edge of flight? Features a huge airborne dyno. Start: Same as for The Pearl. From ledge, move right above the lip of an overhang to gain spaced holds leading up an airy arete capped by a short, shallow, right-facing corner (crux). At big horizontal above, escape right. Finish over a small but tricky roof. (40') (5.12+)

FA: Rob Robinson (8/86)

㉟ Hyena 5.12+ ★

Start: 5' left of The Pearl. Toprope a burly face with a couple of (insanely) sloping holds; finish using the arete. 30'

FA: Travis Eiseman (6/88)

87 aint Sh*t

By: Matt Sims

In November 1989, I had my first real climbing experience. My high school buddy, Owen Megahee, introduced me to Sunset Rock on a rather cold day for a first timer. His experience didn't extend much beyond beginner either, but he had the necessary pieces of gear to get us sufficiently killed. We set up a top rope on Headwall 5.10 (now closed). I scraped and clawed my way to the top, wearing a pair of converse high tops (a.k.a "chucks"). I don't remember anything but the elation of rock climbing. Pure and Simple…I was hooked. I knew nothing about it, except that I wanted to do it. For Christmas that year, I received a locking D biner, 150' of static Bluewater gold line, a figure eight and a Misty Mountain Fudge harness. It was the best Christmas I ever had…

Afterwards I went into the Rock Creek Outfitters on Hixson Pike and bought my first pair of climbing shoes. 5.10 Verticals. They were pink and blue and I remember Jack Noonan, an employee

and later a great friend and mentor, made sure that they were almost 2 sizes smaller than my foot size. I still regret that purchase and actually wearing them for as long as I did. What's really funny now to think back about, was wearing tights. I had a drawer full of obnoxious tights and I wasn't alone. You didn't show up to climb without them. It almost became a contest to see who's were the ugliest. None of us wanted to admit that the only place you could fine them was in the women's section at TJ Maxx.

For almost an entire year, I went to Sunset Rock (the only climbing area that I knew existed) by myself and bummed rides on top-rope. I didn't care who you were, stranger or local. Experienced or novice, didn't matter. All I wanted to do was climb. I remember watching rock legends like Shane Reimer and Tommy Hayes climbing "Dance of the Demon".

I remember Chris Chestnutt top roping "Banshee" with a blindfold on. I belayed Jack Noonan up a very scary and runout Headwall 5.10+ on lead. To my recollection, it only took 2 pieces of good gear. Thinking back now, I can't believe he let me belay him. I guess it didn't really matter, since it was basically a solo. Speaking of solo's, I remember Derek Hersey making a visit one day and soloing a bunch of stuff on the main face of Sunset Rock. One of my fondest moments as a beginner climber was doing a bouldering circuit at Sunset Rock with Forest Gardner.

He was wearing white painter's pants and made me climb stuff I wouldn't normally do on my own. It wasn't too long before I got a good grasp on what I was doing and "who" was doing it better. I needed to find someone to teach me. I want to know how to lead!

In walked Lothar…long haired, scruffy and obscene. Lothar's birth name is Jonathan Clardy. Man, I got lucky. What a great teacher and friend he became. He was really rude, crude and socially unacceptable at the time, but for whatever reason we became the perfect "odd couple". I would sleep in my truck in his parent's driveway on Friday night in the summer time, so we could wake up early to go climb. 6:00am was the normal start time. I have great memories of him making me do "Back Street Revelation", the route I took my first lead fall on. He was never very sympathetic but he always pushed me in ways that only recently have proven to be a huge asset.

The cool thing back in the early 90's was that the climbers in Chattanooga could fill a small room. We all knew each other and socialized on a plane that can best be described as "equal". There was never any judgment on skill levels, or doing something technically wrong. I think I tied my top rope knot wrong for at least 6 months. I remember being very intimidated early on by such great climbers as Tim Williams, Jack Noonan, Forest Gardner and many others but they were always so very gracious to teach me and climb with me. Even the infamous Chris Chestnut, as wild and intimidating as he was, was nothing but gracious and understanding. We were all climbers of different abilities but the common goal was to climb and climb as much as possible. Sport climbing was basically non-existent in our world. I think Little River Canyon had a few sport routes and Foster Falls was just getting cranked up. Rob had bolted some really hard stuff at T-wall, but short of that, it was all about trad climbing. Now, having climbed in various places all over the globe, I still find my home here among the BEST climbing and honestly, the thing that makes it so great is the memories I have of all the guys that taught me what it meant to be a rock climber. It was and is still about style, not grade. See Bio on pg 539

Matt Sims on an early ascent of Scream Wall, 5.10

Shane Rhymer executing the rose crossover maneuver on Edge of Might, 5.12+   Photo Credit: Rob Robinson Collection

SUNSET PARK

THE ARENA
Rounding the corner from the main Sunset headwall, you will find this cluster of continuously shady routes on bullet grey and white rock. The classic first-lead for many, One-Ten, is also located here.

NO
15 mins

Sunset

36 The Womb 5.6
Start: 20' left of The Pearl.
Pitch #1: Wriggle up an awkward, body slot. Traverse right across gap to a ledge. (30')(5.4)
Pitch #2: Climb a vertical gully guarded by a roof. (40') (5.6)
FA: Tom Martin, Noel McGlothin, Tom Kimbro (60')

37 Muscle Shoals 5.12- ★
Start: On a ledge above the trail, perhaps 20' left of The Womb.
Boulder up a short left-facing corner capped by a bolt. Climb past a tiny roof; finish up the face with a pocket or two. 30'
Insider Beta: Barely enough pro. To wit: A few small wires after the bolt in a small horizontal. Tri Cams and/or TCUs in pockets at top.
FA: Rob Robinson (toprope, 5/78)
First Lead: Rob Robinson 8/86.

38 Zenobia 5.10- (PG) ★
Start: At trailside, 20' left of Muscle Shoals.
Diagonal right up a short ramp, traverse left and over a bulge to a small stance. Wander up a lichened slab to the top. 70'
FA: Forrest Gardner, Jack Noonan (4/85)

39 Hallucinating Insects 5.11- ★
Start: 10' left of Zenobia.
Climb a nice orange face with a bolt (now chopped). Ease through a series of small overlaps. Finish up the Zenobia slab. 70'
FA: Chris Chesnutt, Travis Eiseman (7/87)

> Insider's Notes: A) Getting past the bolt is definitely 5.12 for shorter climbers. B) The fixed pin in the overhang was added some time after the first ascent.

40 Scare Voyager 5.11 ★★
Start: 10' left of Hallucinating Insects.
Pitch #1: Cruise up the wall for 30'; turn a gnarly 5' roof and belay. (40') (5.11-)
Pitch #2: Climb into a right-facing corner, bobble left (crux) to the top in a shallow bowl. (30') (5.11)
FA: Forrest Gardner, Rob Robinson (alt. leads, 6/85)

> Insider's Note: Can be done in a single pitch.

41 Osmosis 5.11 ★★
Start: Same as for Scare Voyager.
Pitch #1: Cruise up the wall for 30', crab out a flared roof slot (crux) via a 10' hand crack.
Belay at a large horn just above the lip. (40') (5.11)
Pitch #2: Finish up short slabs. (30') (5.4)
FA: Rob Robinson, Forrest Gardner (9/79)

> Insider's Note: Combining both pitches into one is problematic due to rope drag at the lip of the roof.

SUNSET PARK

NORTH

42 In the Corner 5.7 ★
Start: 15' left of Osmosis.
Climb a steep crack system. Finish up a corner via a tricky (crux) finish. 70'
FA: Bill Smith, Steve Jones (late 70's)

43 Invisible Touch 5.12- ★★
But will the invisible be revealed?
Start: Same as for The Cobb.
Climb the Cobb for about 20'. Traverse right and follow a jam crack around a small roof. A bulging seam (crux) leads to the top. 60'
FA: Rob Robinson (4/86)

44 The Cobb 5.4 ★
Start: Just left of In The Corner.
Climb a short wide crack to a ledge. Head left up a gnarly chimney filled with horns and knobs. Traverse left a little, then on to the top. 60' FA: Unknown

> **Insider's Note:** The crux is near the top of the chimney.

45 Scandals in the Twilight 5.12 ★★
Start: 10' left of The Cobb.
Climb the face, up to a pocketed roof with a poor fixed pin (back it up!) and a committing back-handed iron cross maneuver to pull the lip. From the small ledge above, wander to the top. 60'
FA: Travis Eiseman (8/88)

46 Friday the Thirteenth 5.9 ★★
Today is your lucky day—a great lead with a circuitous crux.
Start: 5' left of Scandals In The Twilight.
Climb a face with a couple of nice flakes for about 10'. Step left and tiptoe up through a set of tiered, white roofs (crux) to a ledge. Easy rock leads to the top. 60'
FA: Bill Smith, Doug Grayden (late 70's)

Osmosis, 5.11

SUNSET PARK

㊼ Dire Straights 5.10+ ★★★
Full steam ahead? Classic, high end challenge for 5.10 leaders.
Start: 65' left of Friday The Thirteenth.
Climb a short vertical seam. Negotiate bulge, traverse left into a right-facing corner capped by a small roof. Wander up easier rock above to the top. 60'

FA: Rob Robinson, Forrest Gardner, Marvin Webb (8/81)

㊽ The Arena 5.11- ★★★
Dancing with the lion? A fierce piece of climbing for the sandstone gladiator.
Start: 10' left of Dire Straits. Climb through low overhangs capped by a short but classic finger crack ending at a bolt (now chopped). Battle past the former bolt (crux) to the base of a left-facing corner. Step right and wander to the top on progressively easier rock. 60'
First Lead: Rob Robinson (3/81)

> Insider's Notes: A) Grabbing the left edge of the arete lessens the difficulty by a half grade. B) You may find a good TCU to protect the crux in the place of the old bolt.

Forrest Gardner climbs One-Ten, 5.6

㊾ One-Ten 5.6 ★★
Surprisingly sustained—and devious all the way; a vertical labyrinth of sorts.
Start: 10' left of The Arena.
Climb a classic, left-facing corner. Zig-zag through bulges, worm through a notch in an obvious overhang. A short slot leads to the top. 60'
FA: Bob Mitchell (late 60's)

> Insider's Notes: Bring a 4" piece to protect the last wide section.

㊿ Crux Busters 5.12- ★
Start: Same as for One-Ten.
Face climb the left wall of the One-Ten corner following a shallow seam (crux). Finish up the headwall above. 60'

FA: Rob Robinson, Forrest Gardner (6/85)

SUNSET PARK

NORTH

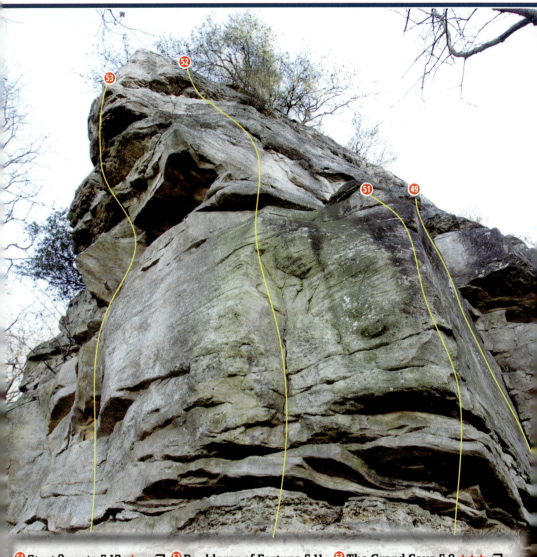

51 Stretcharete 5.12- ★
Start: 5' left of Crux Busters. Climb a short, blunt arete. Finish via Boulderer Of Fortune. 60'

FA: Tommy Hayes (toprope, 5/91)

52 Boulderer of Fortune 5.11 ★★
Perhaps the description provided by one climber sums this pitch up best: "it's like climbing up the side of a sandstone bowling ball." Start: 5' left of Stretcharete. Boulder up a shallow, right-facing corner capped by a bolt-protected bulge (crux). Wander up the headwall above to the top. 60'

FA: Rob Robinson (2/82)

53 The Grand Cave 5.9 ★★★
Start: 5' left of Stretcharete. Pitch #1: Climb one of two possible cracks formed by a semi-detached flake. Dive into the large overhang above, escape into a cave. (30' (5.9) Pitch #2: Zig left, zag right over bulges to the top. (30' (5.8)

FA: Tim McMillan? (late 1960's)
FFA: Rob Robinson, Steve Goins

Insider's Tip: Can be done in one pitch if you carry plenty of full length runners.

SUNSET PARK

GULLY WALLS

Snaking around the bend, the next section of walls are more broken than most and provide some quality, yet albeit forgotten routes on pebbly stone.

54 Green Hills of Africa 5.10- ★ ☐
Start: On the right wall of a recess just left of The Grand Cave.
Ease up the wall on sloping holds, sans gear, to a smooth, green face split by a thin crack.
Breech the face (crux) and continue to the top. 60'
FA: Rob Robinson, Forrest Gardner, Marvin Webb (8/81)

55 Congo Bongo 5.9 ★ ☐
Start: 15' left of Green Hills Of Africa. Bongo up little shelves to a small roof. Step right, then right up an arete peppered with
solution pockets to a ledge. 40'

FA: Bill Smith (late 70's)

56 Jungle Gym 5.8 ★ ☐
Start: 5' left of Congo Bongo.
Climb a left-facing dihedral with a jam crack to a ledge. 40'
FA: Unknown.

57 Apes Only 5.8 ★ ☐
Start: In a recess just left of Jungle Gym. Jam over a bulge using one of two cracks; continue to the top. 35'
FA: Unknown.

58 Point of No Return 5.12- ★ ☐
Bon voyage? A real head trip ... and possibly a trip to the graveyard.
Identify this route up and right, elevated off the trail on the right side of the gully.
Start: On the right side of a prow-like formation just left of Apes Only.
Power past the overhang (tech crux), move left to the prow; "solo" to the top. 45'
FA: Rob Robinson, Forrest Gardner (8/85)

www.rockerypress.com 91

SUNSET PARK — NORTH

59 Lost Digits 5.12- ★★
Start: At trailside, 50' left of Point Of No Return. Boulder up a right-facing flake for 15' with no gear. Escape left up crack. "Boulder" over a bulge capped by a shallow 3' hand crack. Engineer a few moves right to snag a small detached-looking roof. Paw over bulge (crux); easy rock leads to the top. 60'
FA: Rob Robinson (10/81)

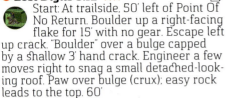

Insider's Tip & Trivia: A) Use double ropes. B) Named for the route's shallow hand crack that —when viewed from the top of Green Hill of Africa, et. al.—resembles the number "1."

60 The Birth Canal 5.10 ★
Start: 25' left of Lost Digits. Worm up an imposing chimney-crack. Finish to the top with easier chimneying. 60'
FA: Bill Smith (mid 1970's)
FFA: Rob Robinson, Clint Henley (2/81)

Insider's Note: Bring some big big cams.

61 The Erroneous Zone 5.10+ ★★
Nothing wrong with this pitch ... unless sustained and hard climbing qualifies as such. Start: On a ledge 35' left of The Birth Canal. Follow a thin crack splitting a steep headwall. The crack dead ends just before the top; detour right and continue to the summit. 40'
FA: Rob Robinson, Gene Smith (4/83)

62 Fault Line 5.9 ★★
Start: 15' left of The Erroneous Zone. Scramble up ledges. Follow a finger crack up a shallow right-facing corner to the top. 40' FA: David Broemel, Ted Evans (70's)

Grand Cave, 5.9

SUNSET PARK

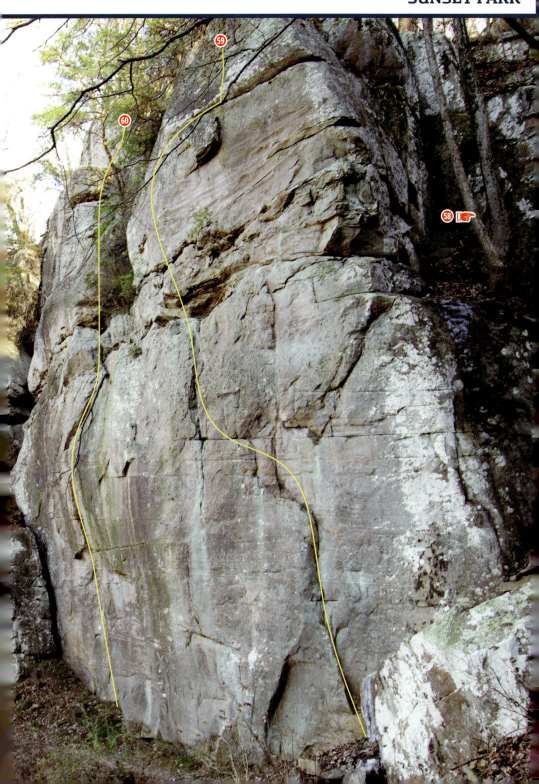

SUNSET PARK

NORTH

15 mins

LICHEN WALL

Though short, this wall's bullet rock and elevated position above the canopy give the routes here a taller and somewhat adventurous feel. Short & sweet - Check em' out!

63 Lichen to Lose It 5.10- ★★
Start: On a ledge 45' left of Fault Line. Turn a smooth bulge to garner a small stance. Step right and ease up the wall with sloping holds to the top. 40'
FA: Rob Robinson, Forrest Gardner (early 80's)

64 Crazy Eights 5.8+ ★★
Start: 15' left of Lichen To Lose It. Blast? straight up the wall past a spot of overhanging rock (scant pro) to the top. 40' FA: Bill Smith, Steve Jenkins (late 70's)

65 Copperhead 5.7 ★
Start: 10' left of Crazy Eights. Climb a shallow crack. Angle right and back left up a ramp, passing a horn to the top. 40'
FA: Bill Smith, Doug Grayden (mid 70's)

66 Whiz Bang 5.7 ★
A worthy route that is rarely repeated!
Start: At trailside, 30' left of Copperhead.
Pitch #1: Follow a "V"-shaped corner guarded by a roof; belay on a hidden ledge. 20' 5.6
Pitch #2: Traverse left across loose? rock to a hand crack hiding behind a block. Follow it to the top. 40' 5.7

FA Unknown.

Wills Young showing some 'grit' on Crazy Eights, 5.8+

Photo Credit: Cody Averbeck

Great White Fright, 5.11+

AM

20 mins

Sunset

Jennifer's World

Rounding the corner, the cliff takes on a dramatic transformation into a tall & intimidating section of hard routes on classic white and salmon colored Sandstone. For those seeking the 5.12 grade - don't miss the requisite Southern experience: Jennifer's World!

(67) Kaleidoscope Eyes 5.11+ ★ ❐

Start: 10' left of Whiz Bang. Climb the face following a thin crack. Turn the large roof above on the right; finish up a headwall to the top. 70'
FA: Travis Eiseman (2/88)

(68) Caught Red-Handed 5.10-, A2 ★ ❐

Start: On the right wall of a large, rectangular cave 35' left of Whiz Bang. Free climb to, then aid past two bolts to a small, triangular roof. Continue right under the roof above ... a finger crack leads to a small recess. Revert to aid; clip bolt above and dangle left through white overhangs past a few fixed pins. Escape right to the top. 75'
FA: Forrest Gardner, Marty Gibson (12/81)

(69) The Drainpipe 5.11- ★★ ❐

Start: In the back of the large cave, 15' left of Caught Red-Handed. Undercling a 4" roof crack past three bolts to a small cave. Follow Lost Arrow Chimney to the top. 100'
FA: Bob Mitchell (late 60's)
FFA: Rob Robinson, Steve Goins (5/78)

(70) Lost Arrow Chimney 5.11- ★★ ❐

Start: In the back of a large cave, 15' left of Caught Red-Handed. Conquer an overhanging crack capped by a small cave. Traverse left in through a meatgrinder slot. Waltz up a giant, left-facing corner with a wide crack to the top. 65' **First Lead: Rob Robinson, Steve Goins (5/79)**

Insider's Notes: There are a couple of short (but hard) toprope problems and variations on the wall just left of the opening crack.

(71) The Great White Fright 5.11+ ❐

Here comes the boogeyman ... airy, hairy and a little bit scary. Start: Same as for Lost Arrow Chimney. Pitch #1: Conquer the overhanging crack (attentive belay here!), traverse right beneath a steepled roof and up a short finger crack to a hanging belay. (40') (5.11-) Pitch #2: Blast straight up past a bolt in the white roofs. Traverse right along a break in the wall to the top. (40') (5.11+)
FA: Rob Robinson, Gene Smith (6/84)

Direct Finish 5.12- ★★ ❐

Climb straight up the wall above the bulge, staying left of a small, left-facing corner.
FFA: Rob Robinson, Robyn Erbesfield 11/84

(72) Jennifer's World 5.12- ❐

How about a piece of free climbing that is out of this world? This route is tied with Space Ranger for the best 5.12 pitch at Sunset (Both are among the best the Sandstone Belt has to offer.) Start: 25' left of Lost Arrow Chimney. Climb a beautiful overhanging flake with a fingertip crux, traverse right to a stance by a pedestal. Handrail left, turn a bulge split by a thin cobbled crack. Traverse right and finish via an overhanging, pocketed crack that merges with the final moves of Lost Arrow Chimney. 70'
FFA: Forrest Gardner, Rob Robinson 11/80

Rob Robinson, Prep School Climbing Attire.

SUNSET PARK

73 Perfect Sinner 5.12 ★★★
Prepare to be burned?
Start: Same as for Jennifer's World.
Climb the J World flake for 12'. Juggernaut left to a horizontal crack and turn several bulges. 70'
FA: Rob Robinson (10/86)

74 Deaf, Dumb, and Blind 5.14- ★
Start: 10' left of Perfect Sinner. Toprope a trailside roof, tweak up an overhanging seam to a horn by a small ledge. 40'
FA: Forrest Gardner, Rob Robinson (mid 80's)
FFA: Travis Eiseman (89')

Insider Trivia: A) Bolted and then lead free after a doctored fingertip fissure was opened up. In protest, Rob Robinson removed the bolts amidst considerable controversy.

Andrew Miller executing the technical layback crux on Jennifer's World, 5.12- Photo Credit: Micah Gentry

SUNSET PARK

75 Turkey and Coke A3 ★
Start: 15' left of The Cross. Climb a shallow, seamed corner. Traverse right beneath the Tantrum roof along a disappearing footwall onto the wall above. Finish right to a small ledge with horn, or continue to the top. 50'

FA: Forrest Gardner, solo (mid 80's)

76 Tantrum 5.12
Furor brevis. Short but spectacular piece of southern roof work.
Start: Same as for Turkey And Coke. Clamber up to and out a 20' roof via flakes and a few jams...50'
FA: Bill Smith (late 70's); FFA: Ken Duncan (5/82)

> Insider's Note: Incredibly, Travis Eiseman free soloed this route back in the late 80's or early 90's. Think about that if you find yourself flailing at the crux lip.

Laban Swafford demonstrating some spoiler beta on Tantrum, 5.12

Photo Credit: Micah Gentry

Sunset Boulevard

The Boulevard is a great place to come to mow down a bunch of Sunset classics all in a row. The routes have smooth monolithic features with great moves and rock. Don't miss the classic corner of Broken Arrow!

The following 5 routes are located on a short cliff line right above the trail a few hundred yards past Tantrum.

(77) Crispy Creme 5.12- ❐
Start: 350' left of Tantrum.
Toprope an overhanging, grey face using a combination of small edges and sloping holds. 30' **FA: Unknown.**

(78) The Banshee 5.13- ★ ❐

Start: 10' left of Crispy Creme.
Boulder about 15' to a tiny mantel shelf; mount this, make a few more moves to escape. 30'
FA: Chris Chesnutt (late 80's)

Insider's Trivia: This has reportedly been toproped blindfolded by Chris Chestnutt!

(79) Test Tube 5.7 ★ ❐
Start: 40' left of The Banshee.
Jam (and face climb a bit) a low-angle 6" crack. Exit through a jug-filled notch; finish up a curving hand crack. 60'
FA: Unknown

(80) Roach Crack 5.10 ★ ❐
First Lead: Unknown.
Start: 150' left of Test Tube.
An overhanging crack splits the center of an outcrop. 25'
FA: Tim McMillan (toprope, late 60's)

(81) Dynamic Salvage 5.11+ ★ ❐
Start: At the left side of the outcrop, 15' left of Roach Crack.
Climb an outside corner. 25'
FA: Rob Robinson, free solo (early 80's)

(82) Diamond in the Rough 5.10 ★ ❐
Start: 200' left of Dynamic Salvage.
Step left onto face above a flared, left-facing slot. Follow an obvious, thin crack to a roof, sparkle left to ledges.
50' **FA: Rob Robinson, Peter Henley (11/81)**

(83) A Sense of Adventure 5.9+ ❐
Short but sweet vertical safari for the 'adventurous traveler.'
Start: 10' left of Diamond In The Rough.
Scamper up a smooth chimney capped by a left-facing corner with roof. Turn the roof and a slight bulge above (crux) to gain a narrow ledge with several trees. 50'
FA: Rob Robinson, Peter Henley (11/81)

(84) Puppy Rodeo 5.10 ★ ❐
Start: Same as for A Sense Of Adventure. Paw left through the tiered white roofs straddling A Sense Of Adventure and Broken Arrow. Finish on the upper corner of the latter. 50'
FA: Forrest Gardner, Rob Robinson (7/84)

(85) The Whitewall 5.12- ★ ❐
Start: 5' left of Puppy Rodeo/A Sense of Adventure. Toprope to a tiny stance atop a short, shallow "V" corner. Climb the crispy face; turn overhangs above capped by ledges. 50'
FA: Unknown

SUNSET PARK

NORTH

86 Broken Arrow 5.10- ☐
Start: 10' left of The White Wall. Climb a perfect, left-facing dihedral to an overhang. Work right to gain a steep ramp, follow this up and right to a good ledge. 50' **FA:** First ascent unknown.

87 Alternate Start 5.9 ★★ ☐
Start: Same as for Broken Arrow. Climb a thin crack on the left wall of the dihedral.

88 Alternate Finish #1 (The Shaft) 5.10 ★★ ☐
Start: From the belay ledge at the end of pitch #1, climb a roof crack up and left from the ledge. 30'

89 Hit the Slopers 5.11- ★ ☐
Start: Same as for Broken Arrow. Climb a face with shallow pockets on the left wall of the dihedral. Traverse left beneath roof; finish on Bare Elegance. 70'
FA: Rob Robinson (toprope, early 80's)
First Lead: Mark Douglas 8/87)

90 Bare Elegance 5.10- ★ ☐
Start: 15' left of Broken Arrow. Begin by climbing the left wall of a rounded arete with small knobs. Diagonal right at the roof to a bulge split by thin cracks. Over this and on to the top. 70'
FA: Rob Robinson, Forrest Gardner, Curt Merchant (6/84)

91 Up In Smoke 5.10- ☐
Start: 10' left of Bare Elegance. Turn bulge above a short finger crack to gain a stack of cracked blocks. Wander up the wall to the top. 70'
FA: Rob Robinson, Brian Holdam (8/77)

92 Sunset Boulevard 5.10+ ★★★ ☐
Pedal to the metal. Hang on to your gear shift. Cruise it or lose it? Hard-to-protect climbing that will require plenty of horsepower to hang on! Start: 15' left of Up In Smoke. Climb a short but classic flake to a small ledge. Cruise? through a band of white roofs capped by a tricky slab and overhang. 60' **FA:** Rob Robinson, Forrest Gardner, Jim Vanburen (toprope, 5/80)
First Lead: Forrest Gardner (8/80)

Memory Fog

Longtime Shawangunks climber Gene Smith (pictured here) introduced double rope technique to climbers in the South when he moved to the region in the early 1980's. The benefits of this protection system were immediately recognized and put into full use. The result was a revolution of sorts, with a surge in both the difficulty and quantity of new "R" and "X" rated trad routes.

Gene Smith utilizing the double rope technique; A Sense of Adventure, 5.9, Circa 1980   Photo Credit: Rob Robinson Collection

SUNSET PARK

NORTH

Broken Arrow, 5.10-

Sunset Boulevard, 5.10+

93 Thin Pockets 5.8 ★★★
Superb face climbing, with a nice jam crack to top it off.
Start: 40' left of Sunset Boulevard. Weave up the wall to a bolt. Pass on the left (harder) or right. Jam the crack to the top. 60' FA: Tim McMillan? (late 60's)

> Insider's Note: The bolt might have been placed by Paul Landram, so one assumes he may have done the first ascent.

94 Ghost Dancers 5.8 ★★
Start: 10' left of Thin Pockets. Boulder up tricky face moves (crux) ; merge with a crack; turn lip of small cave above. 60'
FA: Paul Landram, unknown partners (mid 70's) FA Alternate Start: Ted Evans? (mid 70's)

95 Alternate Start 5.10+ ★★
Start: 5' left of the regular start. Climb the shallow-pocketed face. Finish via Ghost Dancers.

96 Spring Break 5.8 ★
Start: 20' left of Ghost Dancers. Climb a short, flared crack. Turn a small roof, wander up a lichened arete to the top. 70' FA: Rob Robinson, Forrest Gardner, Peter Henley (2/81)

97 Water in Motion 5.12- ★★
Look ma—no hands! Sunset's slopiest route. Start: 10' left of Spring Break. Climb a water-polished slab past three bolts. Ripple left near the top of the wall to the woods. 70' FA: Rob Robinson, toprope (5/81) First lead: Chris Chestnutt, late 80's

> Insider's Trivia n' Notes: A) Originally done in a pair of "E.B.'s." B) In the late 80's, Chris Chesnutt led this pitch after placing two bolts. Even so, this was an extremely serious lead—the run-out past the second bolt included 5.11 moves, with the likelihood of a ground fall (a bolt now protects these). C) It has also been rope soloed by Steve Goins.

97 Variation (On Ballet) ★
Start: A few feet right of the regular start. Crank onto the face with a nice crimp and rejoin the regular route. 70'
FA: Rob Robinson, Mid 80's

SUNSET PARK

SUNSET PARK   NORTH

98 Beginner's Route 5.4
Start: 15' left of Water In Motion.
Climb a "V"-shaped chimney barred by a small overhang. Finish up a slab. 70'
FA: Unknown

99 Special Delivery 5.9+ ★
Start: 10' left of Beginner's Route. Clamber over a rock-scarred bulge capped by a delicate crux. Proceed to better holds and continue to the top. 70' FA: Rob Robinson, Bruce Rogers, Fred Moore (3/80)

100 Spud Boys 5.10 ★
Start: 15' left of Special Delivery. Spudder up a left-facing corner capped by a roof. Finish up a slab split by a crack. 60'
FA: Marvin Webb, Al Whaley (2/81)

101 Fat Crack 5.8
Start: 10' left of Spud Boys.
Climb a right-facing corner with a wide crack. Continue past a roof to a ledge. 40' FA: Bill Smith and partners (late 70's)

102 Heavy Hands 5.8
Start: 15' left of Fat Crack.
Dispatch overhang, climb a short crack above to the top. 40'
FA: Unknown

103 Rushin' Roulette 5.11- ★
Start: 10' left of Heavy Hands, near an arete.
Roar over roof, creep up cross-hatched cracks to a bulge. Step left, finish up arete. 40'
FA: Rob Robinson, Tod Anderson (7/84)

104 Terrier in Trouble 5.8 ★★
Start: 15' left of Rushin' Roulette starting up and off the trail.
Climb a shallow corner with a splitter finger crack. 40'
FA: Unknown

105 Inside Moves 5.4
Start: 30' left of Terrier In Trouble.
Climb a chimney splitting the wall. 70'
FA: Unknown

Edward Yates blasting off on the final aerial mantle of Space Ranger, 5.12-   Photo Credit: Micah Gentry

SUNSET PARK   NORTH

AM
25 mins

Space Ranger Buttress
This proud protrusion of Sandstone offers some of the park's highest quality routes distinguished by difficult, airy, and oftentimes scary movement in an out-of-this-world vertical position.

106 Golden Ledges 5.11- ★★★
Or is it "bloody ledges?" Spectacular and airy but somewhat run-out. Start: By a trailside guardrail 20' left of Inside Moves. Pitch #1: Turn roof split by a hand crack. Motor up a left-facing corner to a ledge. (50') (5.9) Pitch #2: Bongo up tiny "ledges," sans pro, to a small bulge. Unlock this (crux) and finish up an airy, run-out slab on washed-out solution pockets. (50') (5.11-)
FA Pitch #1: Bill Smith and partner (mid 70's) FA Pitch#2: Forrest Gardner, Mike Lewis (5/82)

107 Dementia 5.11+ ★★★
A psycho "path" of sorts. The run-out on pitch two is … slightly demented. Start: 10' left of Golden Ledges. Pitch #1: Traipse up face through a few dabs of questionable rock. Tackle the triangular roof above at its widest point. Belay on ledges above. (5.11) (50') Pitch #2: Climb the steep headwall above past a single bolt. (50') (5.11+)
FA: Chris Chesnutt, Randy Lane (7/87)

108 Final Frontier 5.11 ★★★
Its space of course … and you'll find plenty of it here.
Start: 10' left of Dementia.
Pitch #1: Rocket over bulge capping a band of loose rock. Shoot left up a short, right-facing corner. Grooved cracks lead to a flat ledge. (70') (5.10-)
Pitch #2: Jockey left a bit, then up a bit on a steep, lichened wall. Drift left about 10' to a beautifully exposed position. Launch straight up on fingertip holds (crux), merge with a thin crack. Escape to the top. (50') (5.11)**FA: Rob Robinson, Forrest Gardner, alternate leads (5/84)**

109 A Stitch in Time 5.10+ ★★★
A belay plate in time? Pitch two is tailor made for the crafty trad technician: its a spectacularly steep and exposed line with plenty of pro—but will you be able to hang on long enough to place it? Want some added excitement? Tack on the Rocketman alternate finish.
Start: 10' left of Final Frontier.
Pitch #1: Climb a left-facing corner, turn roof at notch, belay on ledge above. (70') (5.9)
Pitch #2: Step left and zip up a steep lichened wall split by a thin crack. At small roof, escape left to the top. (40') (5.10+)
FA Pitch #2: Forrest Gardner, Rob Robinson (9/81) FFA Alternate Finish: Chris Chesnutt (late 80's)

110 Alternate Finish (Rocket Man) 5.11- ★★★
As the crack ends on pitch two … persevere straight up then slightly right to the top.

Space Ranger, 5.12-

111 Space Ranger 5.12-

Houston we have lift off. One of the Sandstone Belt's finest trad-style air voyages and arguably Sunset's ne plus ultra for the grade. Start: 15' left of A Stitch In Time. Rocket over roof, blast up overhanging cracks to a small overhang and bolt. Turn overhang (crux) on the left that leads to a ledge. Crouch right and turn a flat 4' roof and climb a short overhanging crack... at chockstone, iron cross right to the top.100' **FA: Rob Robinson, Forrest Gardner, alternate leads (9/81) FFA: Chris Chesnutt (6/88)**

> Insider's Note: In spite of this routes very intimidating appearance, there are quite a few no-hands rests to be found. Bring a #4 Camalot to protect the final iron cross sequence.

112 Power Ranger Project 5.14?

Start: 10' left of Space Ranger. Follow a white face to a ledge and then overcome an overhanging pin-protected seam providing double-digit boulder moves along the way. The face has been top-roped into the Space Ranger finish at 12+ by **Cody Averbeck and Laban Swafford.**

> Insider's note: This route has the potential to be one of the hardest and most committing trad climbs in the South.

Climber: Ben Hornesby Photo Credit: Micah Gentry

Jefferson Airplane 5.10-
A popular flight plan for sandstone test pilots. A nice, long well-protected runway. Start: Atop a large boulder 5' left of Mineral Fright. Climb a steep, left-facing flake capped by a small overhang and left-facing arch. Lower angle rock leads to the landing strip above. 100'
FA: Bill Smith, Tom Popp, Steve Jones (fall/78)
FFA: Rob Robinson, Bruce Rogers (3/79)

SUNSET PARK

NORTH

Bolt Pinnacle

This beautiful wall is home to arguably Sunset's greatest collection of classics all of which surround the area's iconic natural attraction: the Bolt Pinnacle.

113 Malfunction Junction 5.9
Start: Above the trail, 15' left of Space Ranger. Stem up a smooth corner to a ledge. 15'
FA: Unknown

114 Dennis the Menace 5.10 ★★
Start: 40' left of Malfunction Junction. Claw onto wall at a square jug (about 6' right of Ambidextrous.) Climb face past a useless fixed pin ...gravitate right to a gently overhanging white face; jugs lead to the top. 90' FA: Tim Williams, Philip Hyman (4/92)

Insider's Trivia: Named after a popular Sunset ranger.

115 Ambidextrous 5.10 ★★
A pair of good hands—supported by two well-connected and functioning brain lobes supplying ample nerve—is prerequisite. Start: 5' left of Dennis The Menace. Boulder into a small, right-facing corner above an overhang. Tiptoe up a shallow, right curving arch. Head for hole, then pass bulge at weakness; more run-out (but much easier) face climbing leads to the top. 100'
FA: Rob Robinson (toprope, 8/80) First Lead: Forrest Gardner (9/81)

SUNSET PARK

116 Bolt Pinnacle 5.11- ★★
The summit of this beautiful, free-standing blade of rock has been a popular destination for decades. Pitch two provides the icing on the cake. Start: 30' left of Ambidextrous. Pitch #1: Climb a classic but unprotected chimney to the top of the pinnacle. (40') (5.5) Pitch #2: Span gap to gain main cliff wall, climb to a bolt above a small ledge. Solve this (crux) and zither to the top on a short but potentially serious run-out. (50') (5.11-) FA Pitch #1: Tom Martin, Tom Kimbro (61') FFA Pitch #2: Eric Janoscrat (10/81)

117 R.J. Gold 5.9+
Yields a complex and subtle blend of premium grade sandstone ... not surprisingly, one of Sunset's most popular face climbs. Start: 10' left of Bolt Pinnacle. Tiptoe up the face with a short thin crack. Merge with wider crack above, turn a small roof (go left, right or straight up). Claim summit after dealing with a minor run-out past a bolt using small but good holds. 100' FA: Rob Robinson, Peter Henley (10/80)

Insider's Trivia: "R.J. Gold" is sweet-tasting chewing tobacco sold in a gold foil pouch.

118 Mineral Fright 5.11- ★★
"Lunatic fringe" face climbing. Start: Same as for R. J. Gold. Follow an overhanging seam to a bulge. Brave on to the steep face above, steering clear of crispy edges. Escape over R. J. Gold bulge and continue to the top. 100' FA: Rob Robinson, Gene Smith, Curt Merchant (5/84)

119 Jefferson Airplane 5.10-
See description on page 112.

Memory Fog

Eric Janoscrat (pictured below) met Rob Robinson in the late 1970's during one of Robinson's many trips to Seneca Rocks in West Virginia. At the time, Janoscrat was part of a talented and driven team pushing Seneca's already extreme trad climbing to the next level. For many years after they first met, Janoscrat would journey southward to visit Robinson to check out the "latest and greatest" sandstone super classics. Usually all it took was an enthusiastic phone call from Robinson for him to make the 600 mile drive down from his home in Pennsylvania to see what was up.

Eric Janoscrat on RJ Gold, 5.9

Photo Credit: Rob Robinson Collection

CONTACT 9.8

If only all your cragging partners were this reliable.

Petzl's durable new 9.8 mm single rope

The CONTACT 9.8 was designed from the ground up to be tough yet smooth-handling, thanks to Petzl's EverFlex heat treatment. This versatile cord will hang with you, pitch after pitch.

Learn more about our full line of ropes at www.petzl.com/ropes

SUNSET PARK — NORTH

120 Bill's Route 5.8 ★★★
Superbly rendered sandstone composition; hits all the high notes—and then some. Start: 5' left of Jefferson Airplane. Climb a beautiful right-facing Yosemite style flake capped by a roof. Work left a few moves, now up through a slot into a left-facing dihedral. Turn overhang above, continue to the top. 100'
FA: Bill Smith, Steve Jones (77')

121 Horribilus Maximus 5.10+ ★★
Start: At trailside, 15' left of Bill's Route. Hop atop a short, right-facing corner. Jockey left up the steep face following an inverted flake ... to a tenuous stance on the lower-angle face above. Merge with Bill's Route. 100'
FA: Rob Robinson, Forrest Gardner (4/82)

> **Insider's Note:** The crux is a unique inverted flake that makes for several blind gear placements. Might be a strain and a stretch for the 5.10'er.

The Cornerstone, 5.11-

122 Broemel's Route 5.8 ★★★
The compressed view from trailside really doesn't do this pitch justice. Offers a truckload of good climbing following classic wall features. Start: 20' left of Horribilus Maximus. Ease up loose-looking rock for about 15'. Finagle right to gain a long, vertical crack system topped by a small cave; turn lip and continue to the top. A wonderful vertical adventure recommended to those seeking this grade...100'
FA: David Broemel, Steve Jones, Bill Smith (mid 70's)

SUNSET PARK

123 Twilight of the Idols 5.12- ★★
Start: 10' left of Broemel's Route. Toprope through a gap in a small overhang to the base of a tiny left-facing corner. Shoot right a few moves on shallow "bullet holes." Gun for easier rock above. 80' **FA:** Rob Robinson (5/89)

> Insider's Note: This used to be a two-bolt protected lead; the bolts have disappeared....

124 The Cornerstone 5.11-
Sunset's reputation for perfect rock is built on a foundation that includes scores of incredible routes like this one: the archetypal arete. Start: Same as for Twilight Of The Idols. Hustle up wall to the base of a small, left-facing corner. Teeter left a few moves, tackle a superb, sharp-edged arete. Zip over the lip of the recess above. A casual slab leads to the woods and bolted anchor. 80'
FA: Rob Robinson, Steve Poupore (5/79)

Shane Rhymer on the now stripped masterpiece, Dance with the Demon, 5.13   Photo Credit: Rob Robinson Collection

SUNSET PARK

125 Dance of the Demon 5.13 (Currently Stripped) ★★★

For all you sport climbing fiends out there, this devilishly difficult piece de resistance should keep you hoppin' for an afternoon or two. Bring your pitchfork, and an attitude to match.
Start: On the right wall of a gully, uphill and 20' left of The Cornerstone.
Follow a serpentine crack up a bulging wall. Rip over 5' roof, continue churning up the overhanging wall above to the top. 60'
FA Pitch #1: Rob Robinson, aid solo (5/79)
FFA: Shane Rymer (6/91)

126 No Hand's Land 5.12- ★★

Occasionally found lurking in Sunset's dark coves are little free climbing chimeras like this "R.P." masterpiece. The name? A play on words, and a subtle clue that could help you at the crux.
Start: On the wall opposite Dance Of The Demon. Climb a short left-facing corner with a seam to a tiny roof. Break right over a baffling bulge (crux). Continue right over another bulge, finish up a slab. 70'

FA: Rob Robinson, Robyn Erbesfield (7/84)

THE TOWERS

The following 13 climbs are located on 'the towers,' a striking bastille-like formation split by a 90' chimney. Make sure not to miss Stan's Crack and the Toothpick, two of Sunset's best!

127 Twilight Zone A2 ★

Start: 100' left of No Hand's Land, on a cliff band behind The Towers.
Climb an overhanging seam. (Use nuts, etc. and hand placed pins.) 30'
FA: Bill Smith and partner (late 70's)

128 Submission 5.12

Ready for a little "power play?"
Start: On the back wall of The Towers, directly across from Twilight Zone. Toprope a steep face past old bolt holes. 40' Insider's Note: Used to be a lead protected by four bolts.
FA: Chris Chesnutt (7/88)

129 Trickle Down Effect 5.10 ★

Start: 5' left of Submission.
Climb a crack formed by a flake; continue up a blunt arete to the top. 50'
FA: Unknown

PM
25 mins

SUNSET PARK — NORTH

Stan's Crack, 5.8

130 Peace and Tranquility 5.8+ ★
Start: At trailside, 35' left of Trickle Down Effect. Pitch #1: Climb a right-facing corner for a couple of feet. Traverse left a bit, then gingerly up a series of small shelves and shallow corners to a scenic ledge. (50') (5.8+) Pitch #2: Finish up the right wall of a short arete. (20') (5.8+)

FA: Rob Robinson, Bruce Rogers (8/79)

131 Infidel Zombies 5.9+ ★
Start: 15' left of Peace And Tranquility. Climb a wide, left-facing corner to ledge. Shoot straight up a steep headwall to the top. 90'

FA: Chris Chesnutt, Randy Lane (6/87)

132 The Toothpick 5.11

Technician's finger crack ... a popular entree at the "Sunset North Cafe."
Start: Same as for Stan's Crack. Climb Stan's for 15'. Traverse right a few moves and climb a thin, overhanging crack. 60'
FA: Rob Robinson (7/79)

> **Insider's Tip:** Use double ropes. (Run the left rope up Stan's high enough to protect the traverse out to the crack.)

The Toothpick, 5.11

SUNSET PARK

133 Stan's Crack 5.9
See description on page 124.

134 Direct Finish #1 5.9+ ★★
From the ledge continue up the corner via an overhanging flake. 30'
FA Direct Finish #1: Steve Goins, Doug Merriam (10/78)

135 Direct Finish #2 (Pleasant Diversions) 5.9+ ★★
From the end of pitch one—float left through a band of tiered overhangs. 30'
FA Direct Finish #2: Forrest Gardner, Peter Henley (3/82)

136 Towers Chimney 5.4 ★
Start: 5' left of Stan's Crack. Climb a wide chimney. 90'
FA: Tom Martin, Tom Kimbro (61')

137 Deceive Me 5.9+ ★
Start: Same as for the Towers Chimney. Climb an arete formed by the left side of the Towers Chimney. Finish up thin cracks. 40' FA: Chris Chesnutt (6/87)

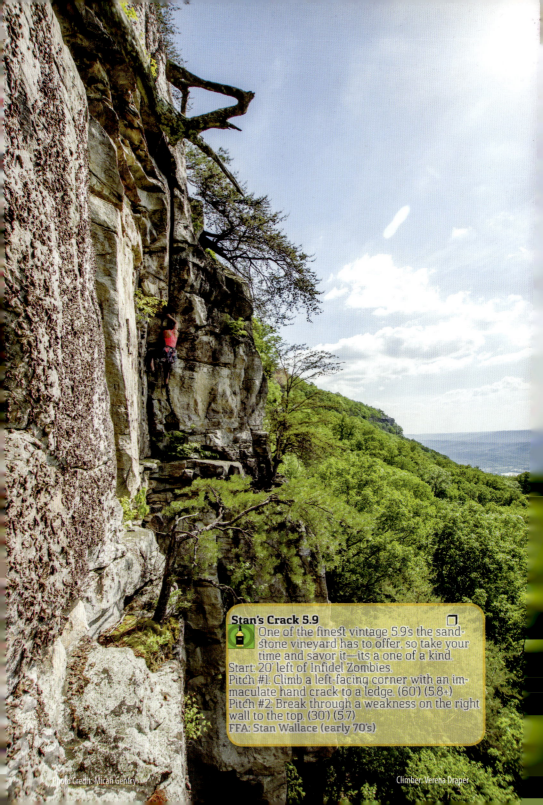

Stan's Crack 5.9

One of the finest vintage 5.9's the sandstone vineyard has to offer, so take your time and savor it—its a one of a kind.
Start: 20' left of Infidel Zombies.
Pitch #1: Climb a left-facing corner with an immaculate hand crack to a ledge. (60') (5.8+)
Pitch #2: Break through a weakness on the right wall to the top. (30') (5.7)
FFA: Stan Wallace (early 70's)

SUNSET PARK

NORTH

🔴138 Moccasin Bend 5.10+, A2 ★
Start: 15' left of Deceive Me.
Climb a short jam crack to a long ledge; continue up a left-arching thin crack. Aid over a bulge and continue to the top. 60'
FA: Forrest Gardner, Rob Robinson (2/80)

Insider's Note: If you're over six feet tall and can dyno four or so feet you might be able to eliminate the final point of aid.

🔴139 Thin Slivers A2 ★
Start: 10' left of Moccasin Bend.
Follow a thin seam (using all natural gear) to a good ledge. 15'
FA: Forrest Gardner, solo (2/80)

🔴140 Bubble Bath 5.9 ★★★
Good clean fun, decent exposure. Terry-cloth robe optional.
Start: 50' left of Towers Chimney.
Bubble up a thin crack and face to a narrow, horizontal roof. Slip over this (crux) and slide up a short, right-facing corner. Time to pull the plug: exit left to a ledge. 60'
FA: Forrest Gardner, Rob Robinson, Peter Henley (4/81)

🔴141 Slip Stream 5.7 ★★
Good chunks of classic climbing packed between ledges.
Start: 10' left of Bubble Bath.
Stream up a right-facing corner with a jam crack. Knock off a short, left-facing corner. Aim right to easier rock and continue to the top. 60'
FA: Unknown

Slip Stream, 5.7

Edward Yates in much need of a Bubble Bath, 5.9

Photo Credit: Micah Gentry

Becca Greene on Broemel's Route, 5.8
Photo Credit: Micah Gentry

SUNSET PARK

🔴 **143** **Dobermanns 5.11-** ★★★ ☐
At my command: unleash hell. The perfect climb for all you teeth-gnashing trad dogs on the prowl for a little "fight n' bite." Crank past flake to a small rounded bench. Stand up, "dobe" right via fingery moves (crux), gnash up broken face merging with an incipient crack that fizzles out at a very smooth bulge. Finish with a surprise escape to the top. 60'
FA: Rob Robinson (6/01)

> Insider's Tips: A) The first 20' are a bit "gear cruxy," but there is excellent pro to be had; you're just going to have to work to get all of it. B) Double ropes will also be helpful.

Doberman's Direct 5.11 ★★★ ☐
Just in case the regular route wasn't feral enough for ya'--jump this! One of Sunset's best face climbs for the grade.
Start: Same as for Dobermanns. Crank past a flake to the small rounded bench. Now attack the face straight on - cranking through a couple of stacked cruxes ---directly to the top. 60'

> Insider's Tips: A) The first 20' are a bit 'gear cruxy,' the rest of the route is pretty much 'plug and play.' B) Single rope lead is O.K.

🔴 **142** **Jams and Shams 5.10** ★ ☐
Start: 15' left of Slip Stream.
Climb a short, overhanging hand crack. Traverse left, climb a right-facing corner. Turn a small roof and continue to the top. 70'
FA: Marvin Webb, Ronnie Shehee (81')

SUNSET PARK

NORTH

Sunset

144 Devil Dog 5.9 ★★
All you'll need to "walk" this beast is a "nylon leash," a standard rack and a little time to burn. Muzzle, prong collar optional. Start 10' left of Dobermanns. Climb a left-facing flake for 10', turn bulge (crux), merge with short vertical flared slot (funky). Continue up and slightly right on face above to the top. 60'
FA: Unknown.

145 Unleashed 5.11- ★★
Start: on a gently overhung wall, 10' left of Devil Dog. Climb a very steep left-facing flake, boulder through face moves, passing a single brown bolt (crux). Continue past horizontal breaks to the top. 50'
FA: Rob Robinson (6/01)

146 Nuclear Blue 5.10 ★★★
Understarred, underrated and underappreciated for years ... one of Sunset's best bomber cracks.
Start: 5' left of Unleashed.
Nuke a gently overhanging finger and shallow hand crack. 50'
FA: Rob Robinson, Forrest Gardner (6/80)

147 Alan Gold's 5.9 ★★
Silver ingot discovered in the dusty back room of Sunset's precious metals department. Start: several hundred feet left of Nuclear Blue.
Suss out a slightly off kilter sequence to snag a big pasted flake (crux). Continue up the wall following zig-zag staircase stances. Sketch right at top across sloping summit on rounded holds (a little tricky). 50' FA: Unknown

> **Insider's Freak:** "Alan Gold's" is Chattanooga's "alternative" night club. Regardless of your, umm, orientation—this is a great dance club and place to watch some really off-the-wall people strut their stuff.

148 Jungle Boobies 5.9
Start: left of Alan Gold's.
Boulder up left-facing corner (crux). Climb short vertical crack (crux), ease left around small roof, now back right and straight up to a hand-holdless finish on a sloping ledge beneath a short headwall. 50'
FA: Rob Robinson, Jared Chastain (6/01)

> **Insider's Beta:** Although there is some other gear available, a blue Camalot might also fit in a horizontal slot somewhere before you commit to the finish. Bring a nut tool as well to dig around for better gear.

Broemel's Route, 5.8

www.rockerypress.com

The first ascent of Flagstone, 5.11- (lower right): an advertisement from the 1940s showing a rock climber at Sunset Rock.

Sunset South

Access: From the parking lot, hike down the trail to the Sunset Rock overlook. From the overlook, hike left (South) along the rim to a stone staircase descent. At the bottom of this descent, you will encounter a junction in the trail. From this junction, hike left (South) away from the Sunset Rock overlook. From here, navigation is easy seeing that the trail runs parallel to the base of all the climbing at Sunset South until terminating at Covenant College.

Season: As is typical with many climbing areas throughout the Sandstone Belt, spring and fall are the ideal times to climb at this locale. Not too hot ... not too cold. However, as Sunset in general is a northeast/northwest facing cliff, it is also an excellent summer crag. The sun first hits the crag at the far southern end, right around 2 p.m., then slowly arcs right about 45 degrees at around 5 pm when the entire crag is more or less bathed in full light. Sunset's circuitous cliff line provides plenty of cover from the late afternoon sun, as there are many niches, coves and recesses to take cover in.

Character: While the Northern end is characterized by shorter, steeper, and generally harder routes, the Southern end of Sunset has a very special characteristic: exposure. The cliffline on the Southern end has fewer bends and lays consistently parallel to the valley. Coupled with the height of the cliff (80-100'), the Southern end has an extremely airy personality where it is not unusual to be staring down 5.11 face cruxes 100 feet off of the deck with all of the Tennessee Valley acting as your audience.

256 Blonde Ambition
244 Silent Runner
227 Train Time
215 Wind Walker
211 Deck Party
200 Optical Delusion
184 Black Magic
158 Raiders...

Rob Robinson staring down the belly of Raiders of the Lost Arch, 5.12-

SUNSET PARK

SOUTH

149 Lizards in Action 5.9
Start: 100' right of the base of the switchbacks. Climb short corners to a ledge. Climb the face on the left side of a prominent arete. 50'
FA: Forrest Gardner, Marvin Webb (6/82)

150 Off to See the Lizard 5.10- ★★
Start: 5' right of Lizards In Action. Climb the prominent arete. 50'
FA: Steve Goins, rope solo (4/94)

151 New Age 5.11- ★
Start: 100' right of Lizards In Action. Climb small ledges beneath a white face. Adle right to an arete; continue to the top. 60' FA: Chris Chesnutt, Randy Lane, Travis Eiseman (late 80's)

152 Colors Like a Tropical Fish 5.9, A3 ★
Start: 40' right of New Age.
Climb casual cracks splitting a cracked bowl capped by a small roof; continue with a few fingerlocks up a shallow corner. From an old fixed bashie (?) aid past a smooth bulge; switch back to free climbing mode and swim to the top. 60'
FA: Forrest Gardner, rope solo (7/83)

153 Stretchum' Armstrong 5.12 ★★
Even if "your reach exceeds your grasp"—you'll still do fine on this one.
Start: 20' right of Colors Like Tropical Fish. Scramble up and left on small ledges to a large ledge with a pine tree.
Face climb past two bolts; join an arch and rally to the top. 40'
FA: Jay Bell (7/88)

154 The Widow Maker 5.11 ★
Start: Same as for Stretchum' Armstrong. Scramble up and right to the start.
Tiptoe up the face following a black water streak, sans pro, past a fixed wire (?) to the top. 45'
FA: Tim Williams, Jack Noonan (4/91)

155 Rude Awakening 5.11- ★
Start: At trailside, 100' right of The Widow Maker. Meander up the center of a deceptive, severely overhung tan wall. 50'
FA: Forrest Gardner, Jay Bell (9/86)

156 Flarewell to Arms 5.9+ ★
Start: At a small outcrop 400' right of Rude Awakening, by the trailside guard rail. Climb the face, turn a small roof split by a a flared, four-inch crack. 30'
FA: Rich Gottlieb, Shannon Stegg (4/81)

Memory Fog

Just south of Sunset Rock, a massive sandstone arch towers above the trail. For decades, climbers had turned a blind eye to the possibilities this spectacular block of rock posed. Of course, it was understandable. But in the early 80's with standards in the region rapidly evolving, this king line was bagged on aid using a rack fortified by a couple of pitons and a pair of etriers. A few years later the inevitable free climbing assault went down in a no falls, stemming frenzy — even the crux was unlocked using a contorted, side split backstep. A handjam or two near the lip followed and it was over. "Raiders free" became the mind-blowing route it had always had the potential to be, and set to become the stuff of legends.

Rob Robinson on the First Free Ascent of Raiders of the Lost Arch, 5.12-

Photo Credit: Rob Robinson Collection

SUNSET PARK

SOUTH

PM
20 mins

Sunset

HARRISON FORD WALL
Look out, Dr. Jones! 150 feet right of Rude Awakening is a spectacular sandstone arch split by a 15 foot roof crack known as *Raiders of the Lost Arch*!

157 Replicons 5.10
Start: At the arch's left side.
Pitch #1: Climb a right-facing corner to the highest ledge. (30') (5.7)
Pitch #2: Traverse left under the arch above. Finish up a lichened headwall. (30') (5.10)
FA: Forrest Gardner, Rob Robinson (9/84)

158 Raiders of the Lost Arch 5.12-
Drop your fedora, grab your bullwhip and get ready for some serious "crackin." One of the Sandstone Belt's "big ten" roofs. Start: Same as for Replicons.
Pitch #1: Climb the corner to a ledge and belay. (50') (5.8)
Pitch #2: Traverse left along a crack with a hanging foot wall; span gap, join the roof crack splitting the span. (30') (5.12-)
FA: Peter Henley, Rob Robinson (8/81)
FFA: Rob Robinson, Robyn Erbesfield (7/84)

159 Blade Runner 5.11- ★
Start: At the arch's right side.
Pitch #1: Climb a left-facing corner to a suitable belay. (30') (5.7)
Pitch #2: Do a (highly improbable and very exposed) right rising traverse beneath a huge swoop of a roof. (30') (5.11-)
FA: Peter Henley (aid solo, 11/83)
FFA: Peter Henley, Rob Robinson, Forrest Gardner (11/83)

Insider's note: The fixed pins have been removed.

160 Murfreesboro Blues 5.11 ★★
Start: 15' right of Blade Runner. Weave through a gauntlet of roofs on an overhanging face. Finish up a jam crack. 60'
FA: Randy Lane, Travis Eiseman (7/88)

About 400' right of Murfreesboro Blues is a trailside guard rail.

SUNSET PARK

SUNSET PARK

SOUTH

25 mins

LOWER TIER

The following routes are located below the main trail on a lower band. This largely undeveloped tier runs below most of the proper cliff at Sunset and holds several worthy routes. In particular, don't miss the overhanging pump of *Illusions*. Either rappel or snake down a descent gully to the base of these routes.

161 Illusions 5.10 ★★
Start: On an outcrop below the trail, 50' right of Flarewell To Arms. (Rappel to the base of the climb.) Blitz up a short hand crack. Work left and up a shallow, left-facing corner capped by a bulge. 40'
FA: Rob Robinson, (toprope, 1/80)
First Lead: Marvin Webb (3/81)

162 Hell in a Bucket 5.9 ★
Start: 10' right of Illusions. Climb directly up an arete to the top. 70' FA: Shane Rymer, Randy Lane (8/87)

163 Saint Pauli Girl 5.10 ★
Start: 20' right of Hell In A Bucket. Turn a 5' roof; continue up a lichen covered headwall to the top. 70'
FA: Randy Lane, Chris Chesnutt (7/87)

At this point, routes regain the upper band and are located above the standard hiking trail.

164 Pete's Back 5.10-
Start: At a trailside outcrop 200' right of Illusions. Climb a gruesomely overhung wall rippling with cracks. Hump right at juggy bulge, savor a short slab, exit to the top. 40'
FA: Peter Henley, Forrest Gardner (11/83)

165 Generation Gap 5.9 ★
Start: 100' right of Pete's Back. Scramble up the hill to the right side of a shallow alcove. Tunnel through overhang capping an obvious cave. Continue up a short crack to a small ledge. A left-leaning, overhanging offwidth crack leads to the top. 60' FA: Rob Robinson, Bill Smith (mid 70's)

> **Insider's Tip:** Carry a couple of large cams.

SUNSET PARK

BLACK MAGIC COVE

Located approximately 200' right of Generation Gap is a tall buttress joined by a shallow cove. Route layout begins up and left of the central buttress. Scramble up a steep hill and walk left approximately 125' to locate the first climbs noted below.

166 Yin 5.11- ★
Start: 200' right of Generation Gap, and 125' left of Black Magic Buttress. Climb a surprisingly steep face with a short, vertical seam. Tiptoe into a shallow bowl capped by a tiny, triangular roof. Yang past this and continue to the top. 40'
FA: Chris Chesnutt and partner (late 80's)

167 Yang 5.11- ★
Start: 10' right of Yin.
Climb the face with a thin crack. Yin right to the top. 60'
FA: Chris Chesnutt and partner (late 80's)
Insider's Note: Protection difficult.

PM
20 mins

SUNSET PARK — SOUTH

168 Dyno Land 5.12-
Start: 50' right of Yang.
Dyno over roof to reachy-but-good holds; churn through a juggy roof and on to the top. 40'
FA: Rob Robinson (free solo, mid 80's)

170 Gut Strings 5.12- ★
Start: 10' right of Overhead Smash. Climb a 10' angled roof with thin "spaghetti" cracks. 40'
FA: Forrest Gardner, Rob Robinson (11/83)

171 Little Pearl 5.7 ★
Start: 100' right of Gut Strings. Putter up a left-facing corner, layback a flake on the right wall. Finish over pocketed bulges. 40'
FA: Rob Robinson, Walter Forbes (5/81)

Confederate Arete, 5.10+

Dodge City 5.9 ★★★
Minor but immensely enjoyable showdown at the Sunset corral.
Start: 5' right of Sinsophrenia.
Climb a small left-facing corner offering a bit of good jamming and stemming. 50'
FA: Rich Gottlieb, Shannon Stegg (4/81)

Climber: Beckett Honnicker   Photo Credit: Cody Averbeck

SUNSET PARK — SOUTH

THE TREASURE CHEST
There's gold in them hills! Ten quality climbs are located in this small shoe-box like alcove, all of which feature superb, yet albeit pebbly stone.

172 Beyond the Obvious 5.10- ★★
Believe me—it's not obvious—but this one is better than it looks.
Start: 15' right of The Little Pearl. Yard past an overhang to gain a large flake ... cap this and continue up the face to the top. 50'
FA: Jack Noonan, Tim Williams (8/90)

173 Confederate Arete 5.10+ ★★
Good for a rebel yell, or two.
Start: 20' right of Beyond The Obvious. Work past an overhang and climb an outside corner (crux) with a former fixed pin to the top. 50'
FA: Shannon Stegg (89')

Insider's Tip: A very dangerous outing without the pin in place.

174 Sinsophrenia 5.10- ★★★
A very steep hand-eating crack slices this unusual wall of tight grained conglomerate.... Start: 10' right of Confederate Arete. An orangutan overhang guards the crack; swing past this and start stylin'. 50'
FA: Rob Robinson, Walter Forbes (5/81)

175 Dodge City 5.9 ★★★
See description on page 141.

SUNSET PARK

Portal to 2nd pitches on Black Magic Buttress

176 The Cobbler 5.9 ★★
Start: 5' right of Dodge City. Climb a pebble-studded "piranha" crack. Cruise through finger pockets over bulges. 60' **FA:** Bill Smith and partner (mid 70's)

Insider's Tip: TAPE!

177 Catatonia 5.10-
Start: 5' right of The Cobbler. Toprope the center of the pebbly face. 50'
FA: Travis Eiseman, Mark Douglas (toprope, 6/87)

178 Remain in Light 5.8+
Start: 5' right of Catonia. Climb a wide crack in a left-facing corner. 50' **FA:** Unknown

179 Golden Years 5.11- ★★★
Fast lane free climbing right off the bat; move it grandpa! Start: 5' right of Remain In Light. Climb a fierce—but oddly elegant—overhanging crack system. 50'
FA: Rob Robinson, Marty Gibson (10/81)

180 Tequila Sunrise 5.11+ ★
Start: Same as for Golden Years. Toprope the opening moves of Golden Years; traverse right and up an arete. 60'
FA: Travis Eiseman, Justin Eiseman (toprope, 6/87)

181 Hueco Twelve 5.10- ★
Start: 15' right of Golden Years/Tequila Sunrise. Climb the face capped by a poorly-protected arete. 50'
FA: Jack Noonan, Tim Williams, Marvin Webb

Laban Swafford & Beckett Honicker retiring Golden Years, 5.11-   Photo Credit: Cody Averbeck

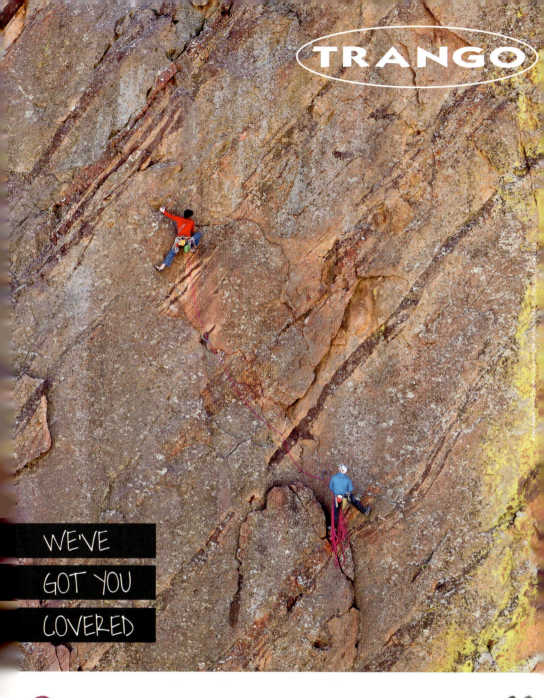

SUNSET PARK — SOUTH

20 mins

Black Magic Buttress

Ummm, here's the rack - you first!... To start these climbs on the spooky Black Magic Buttress, climb the 1st pitch of Black Magic, or crawl through the 'portal' in the right side of the Treasure Chest. Belay from a set of bolts. Supernatural Sandstone at its best!

182 Trailside Trials 5.10+ ★
Start: At trailside, at the extreme left edge of Black Magic Buttress. Toprope a steep lichened face with a tiny roof. 40'
FA: Rob Robinson, Bruce Rogers (toprope, 9/81)

183 Battle Above the Clouds 5.9 ★★
Start: Just left of the second pitch of Black Magic. Climb a short corner. Float right, then up an exposed left-facing corner. Finish right around a roof. 55'
FA: Rob Robinson, Marty Gibson (10/81)

SUNSET PARK

184 Black Magic 5.10
"Air voyage of the aristocrats." One of Chattanooga's finest for the grade.
Start: 30' right of Trailside Trials. Pitch #1: Boulder up the wall for 10', turn a roof split by a hand crack. An easy dihedral leads to a hidden belay ledge. (60') (5.9) Pitch #2: Flounder(?) over a small flat roof (crux) capped by a thin crack sporting a fixed pin (?). A glove-like hand crack leads over a 4' black roof (crux); continue up an overhanging spacey headwall to the top. (50') (5.10) FA: Rob Robinson, Clint Henley, Peter Henley (10/81)

Insider's Note: Climbed on Halloween, hence the name.

185 Wigged Lycra Warrior 5.10 ★★
Diaper deluxe lead: airy, scary and committing. Start: Same as for pitch two of Black Magic. Climb a severely overhung face 10' right of pitch two of Black Magic. 55' FA: Chris Chesnutt, Travis Eiseman, Kent Ballew (7/87)

186 Chaos Out of Control 5.10 ★
Start: 10' right of Wigged Lycra Warrior. Climb a corner to a roof, chaos left and up to the top. 55' FA: Travis Eiseman, Mark Douglas (6/87)

Photo Credit: Rob Robinson Collection

Memory Fog

A giant, white capstone buttress, framed by a cerulean blue sky bereft of clouds, juts into space. Will it go?! We carry a few pins — just in case. Above the first pitch, a small overhang split by a thin seam slows me down. The moves are spooky-looking, and the crack won't take a wire. I hammer in a pin above the lip, then ease past it using a couple of crimps to reach a spectacularly exposed roof. Black as midnight — and split by a perfect handcrack — it's the prize we had coveted from far below. I follow the crack out into infinite space. An overhanging headwall guards the summit, but the holds are good. I'm 21 years old. This must be a dream. But it's not. I'm awake, and this is as real as it gets. I am living the dream....

SUNSET PARK

The following two climbs—Adaptive Radiation and Slip Slot—are situated located below the trail and just left of the main face of Black Magic Buttress.

187 Adaptive Radiation 5.11 ★★
A socio-anthropological phrase which describes the behavior of a species "expanding and adapting to an environment"—a vertical one in this instance. Start: On the cliff below the trail. The upper half of the climb is visible from the trail. A short rappel is necessary. Launch up the face following a pair of classic thin cracks to a small ledge. Feral finger cracks breech an overhanging, orange wall. Tame it. 60'
FA: Rob Robinson, Forrest Gardner (9/82)

188 Slip Slot 5.10- ★
Start: The second crack on the wall left of Adaptive Radiation.
Slip through a roof slot, jam a hand crack, finish over a final bulge. 60'
FA: Rob Robinson, Eric Janoscrat (5/81)

We rejoin climbs on the upper tier at this point.

189 Marty's Misconceptions 5.10
Start: By a trailside guardrail 60' right of Black Magic. Boulder past an overhang. Continue up a steep lichened wall to the top. 40'
FA: Marty Gibson, Rob Robinson (10/81)

Black Magic, 5.10+

SUNSET PARK — SOUTH

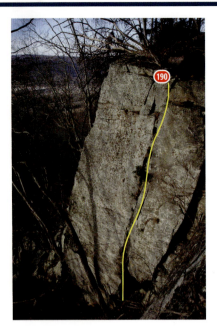

The following climbs are found on the cliff line below the trail in a shallow "shoe box" about 150' wide, formed by two opposing dihedrals. Walk past Marty's Misconceptions for approximately 200'—to a point where the trail makes an abrupt, short left. A few paces past this point, locate a (somewhat inobvious) 3rd class gully which can be used to descend to the lower cliff band's base, or simply rappel.

190 Safari With Friends 5.10- ★
Start: At the far left side of "the box." Safari through a flared slot capped by a vertical crack system which leads to the top. 60'
FA: Marvin Webb, Walter Forbes, Ronnie Shehee (4/81)

191 Diagonal 5.9+ ★
Start: 130' right of Safari With Friends. Follow a striking thin crack that slices left across a steep face and turns a small roof. 60'

FA: Rob Robinson, Walter Forbes (10/80)

192 Rip Cord 5.12- ★★
Great line to log a little "flight time" on. Parachute (not rope!) is optional.
Start: 40' right of Diagonal.
Toprope a severely overhung wall. 60'
FA: Randy Lane (89')

Insider's Note: The bolts have been stripped.

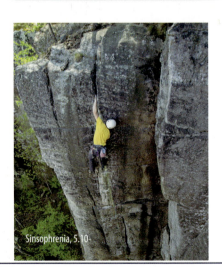

Sinsophrenia, 5.10-

SUNSET PARK

Once again, we rejoin climbs on the upper tier at this point.

🔴193 Ode to the South 5.10- ★
Start: 30' left of Anteater, (and five right of a small cave.) Subdue a small roof to gain ledge. Subtle moves and long reaches lead to easier ground; finish over a small roof that caps the top of the cliff. 60'
FA: Rolf Fraunfelder, Matt Sims (8/97)

🔴194 Anteater 5.6 ★★
Poke your snout in this Sunset cubbyhole—you'll discover a tasty sandstone snack packed with jugs, jams and good pro. Start: 30' right of previous. Scramble up the hill to a small buttress of bullet white rock. Climb a left-facing corner to a ledge. Step left; a crack continues up the wall to the top. 60'
FA: Steve Jones and partner (mid 70's)

Direct Afraid, 5.13- Photo Credit: Cody Averbeck

SUNSET PARK — SOUTH

PM — 25 mins

The Beauty & The Beast
What fantasies are made of! Grab your rack (pitchfork optional) and go storm this castle made up of tall & sustained routes on perfect white rock - the summit of which is guarded by a beast(s) that lurks above!

195 Greenpeace 5.10 ★
Start: 175' right of Anteater, a few steps left of a pair of obvious thin, white cracks crowned by a small roof.
Froth left following a thin diagonal crack to stacked roofs. Ship over these and dock at a ledge with a pine tree. 40'
FA: Rob Robinson, Forrest Gardner (4/83)

196 The Beauty 5.12-
Features a gorgeous piece of sustained hard climbing through a stellar band of white rock. Start: 5' right of Greenpeace. Climb a thin seam up to and over a small roof (crux). Boil left out of a kettle scoop; finish up a moderate crack. 60' FA: Rob Robinson, Peter Henley (10/80)

197 The Beast 5.12
Anyone out there willing to spend some quality time with this ... poor little neglected trad monster? A classic Sunset claw fest. Start: Same as for The Beauty. Climb The Beauty for 10'. Burn right ... snag a fingertip seam, churn to and through small roofs above; finish up and right. 60'
FA: Rob Robinson, Forrest Gardner (8/85)

SUNSET PARK

200 Optical Delusion 5.10 ★★★
Sandstone kaleidoscope offering an eyeful of beautifully varied climbing. Visine optional. Start: 10' right of Grounds For A Peel. Balance up a steep wall, float past a thin crack and blank section to gain an easier crack. Join face moves above. Break left at horizontal, jam a crack to the top. 60'
FA: Rob Robinson, Peter Henley (9/81)

201 No Pro Glow 5.11- ★
Start: 4' right of Optical Delusion. Climb face via thin face moves, sans pro, for about 20'. Continue up face past another crux (with pro) to the top. 60'
FA: Matt Sims (97')

202 Crack-a-Smile 5.8+ ★★
Start: 4' right of No Pro Glow.. Follow a hand crack past two small trees to the top. 60'
FA: Matt Richardson, Matt Sims, Natalie Zahn (4/97)

198 Divinity Crack 5.9 ★★
Start: 20' right of The Beast. Follow a crack through two overhangs to the top. 60' FA: Bill Smith and partner (mid 70's)

Insider's Tip: The crack at the first roof is a little on the wide side, you might want to throw a couple of bigger cams on the rack if leading 5.9 is your limit.

199 Grounds for a Peel 5.11 ★★
Start: 10' right of Divinity Crack. Climb a very shallow corner and steep face with bottoming seams. 60' FA: Rob Robinson (8/86)

The Beauty, 5.12-

www.rockerypress.com

SUNSET PARK   SOUTH

203 Shy Line 5.10+ ★
Start: 35' right of Crack-A-Smile.
Climb the face to an arete; continue to the top. 60'
FA: Steve Goins, Tim Presley (10/96)

204 Overbearing Elders 5.8+ ★
Start: 10' right of Shy Line.
Climb the face past a weakness to gain a crack; continue to the top. 60'
FA: Tim Presley, Steve Goins (10/96)

205 Grim Reaper 5.9+ ★
Start: 10' right of Overbearing Elders.
Begin beneath a small roof ... climb to a thin crack, move left under bulge. Cruise up a slab to the steep face and continue to the top. 40'
FA: Matt Sims, Matt Richardson, Natalie Zahn (4/97)

206 Sudden Journey 5.8 ★
Start: 10' right of Grim Reeper.
Blast up a finger and hand crack to the top. 40'
FA: Rob Robinson, Peter Henley (10/80)

207 Lesbians in Politics 5.10 ★
Start: 10' right of Sudden Journey.
Boulder over a low roof onto a steep face. Follow a thin seam to the top. 60'
FA: Steve Goins, Tim Presley (10/96)

Afternoon Walk, 5.11-

Memory Fog

Marvin Webb was one of the early pioneers of the Chattanooga climbing scene. Aways smiling, he seemed to exist in a state of perpetual mirth — as if simply being alive was, in and of itself, a highly amusing affair. But his laid back attitude took a back seat when he was on the sharp end. Sporting only a swami belt, he was all business on the lead — and always ready to run it out on gnarly moves above thin gear. Today, Marvin is co-owner of the successful Rock Creek Outfitters, which keeps him smiling.

Marvin Webb making an early ascent of Deck Party, 5.11-

Photo Credit: Rob Robinson Collection

SUNSET PARK — SOUTH

DECK PARTY
Welcome, brother! Setup your lawn chair, soak up some rays, and dive into some steep, splitter Sandstone. Just don't 'crash' the party!

208 Dreamway 5.8 ★
Start: 10' right of Lesbians In Politics. Follow a shallow chimney and right-facing corner to a small cave. Exit left to the top. 40'
FA: Rob Robinson, Peter Henley (12/80)

209 Escape from Ventura! 5.12- ★★
Start: 10' right of Dream Way. Turn a small roof and "boulder" up a steep face past two bolts to a small cave; continue over the lip to the top. 50'
FA: Rob Robinson (5/89)

210 Agrippa 5.10+ ★★★
Features bomber "buried to the 3rd knuckle" finger locks.
Start: 5' right of Escape From Ventura! Conquer a small roof (crux), join a sinker finger crack that ends at a cave. Exit right to the top. 50'
FA: Rob Robinson, Bruce Rogers (12/80)

PM
25 mins

SUNSET PARK

211 Deck Party 5.11- ★★★
Party on, Garth! Set up a light rack, break out a fresh block of chalk, cinch those laces down and get ready to strut your stuff. Start: 20' right of Agrippa. Scamper 10', unlock sequence guarding a flat, crackless roof (crux). Join pumpy steep cracks capped by a delicate bulge; drift to the top. 50'
FA: Rob Robinson, Peter Henley (12/80)

212 Sunset Sonata 5.8+ ★
Start: 10' right of Deck Party. Zing through slot, salsa up a right-facing corner capped by a crack with horizontal holds. 40'
FA: Rob Robinson, Bruce Rogers (12/80)

213 Defender 5.11 ★★
To win the summit of this sandstone fortress you'll have to breach a wall protected by a regiment of fingertip holds. Start: 35' right of Sunset Sonata. Toprope the center of a smooth-looking wall capped by a thin crack and small roof. 40'
FA: Rob Robinson (toprope, 4/82)

Rob's Sunset Select

- Blonde Ambition, 5.7
- Walk in the Park, 5.8
- R.J. Gold, 5.9
- Alpah Omega, 5.10
- Traintime Direct, 5.11+

☐ ☐ ☐ ☐ ☐

Photo Credit: Rob Robinson Collection

Pigs in Space, 5.10, with Marvin Webb

A Retrospective Look at the South
By: John Gill

By the late 1950's I had rejected the mainstream perception — unspoken, but nevertheless exerting a strong existential effect — that rock climbing was an extension of walking or hiking. I knew that my engagement with the rock was clearly an extension of gymnastics. By that time, several climbers had followed my example of chalking up, just as a gymnast does when preparing for a routine. Although by no means a versatile gymnast, I loved the still rings and 20', inch-and-a-half (diameter) speed climbing rope. Looking for analogies in nature requiring strength and dynamic motion, I found that firm sandstone was an excellent natural apparatus that evoked an exotic artistry. I first encountered that sandstone in the Deep South.

In graduate school at the University of Alabama in the early 1960s, I would drive a few miles north to Shades Mountain in Birmingham, and, out of the trash and debris at the base of the short cliffs, pull up onto the wonderful acrobatic solidity of sandstone overhangs. I recall bouldering at DeSoto Canyon on a couple of occasions, listening to the infant-like bleatings of semi-wild goats in the woods. I knew of no other climbers working the southern rocks. Rock climbing, for those Southerners who were aware of its existence, was considered esoteric and somewhat deviant. Bouldering was not recognized among climbers as a worthwhile activity in isolation from a larger context, and sport climbing (its logical extension) didn't even exist as a concept. Little had changed since I had begun climbing in 1953; serious rock climbing — like civil rights — was only beginning to emerge.

In the mid 1960's I lived in Murray, Kentucky, a brief drive from Dixon Springs and other sandstone outcrops to the north of the Ohio River. At Dixon Springs I found an unexpected playground of large boulders and short cliffs: quantum rocks — existing in a nebulous state only as part of a scenic environment, waiting to be brought to life in the mind of a climber. I was happy to provide that focus of consciousness. This is always the best part of bouldering, establishing a rapport with virgin rock and melding your spirit with the Spirit that dwells in the stone.

One Christmas I enticed Rich Goldstone, Ray Schrag, and Bob Williams to drive down from Chicago and go bouldering in southern Illinois. The day we climbed at Dixon Springs, the temperature was 5 degrees, but sunny. Rich kept saying as he crept around patches of snow, flexing his cold fingers in lined gloves, "I can't believe we drove all the way down here for this!" My VW bus was uncompromisingly frigid. We crossed the Ohio River on a ferry boat that skirmished with floating chunks of ice. Bundled in down, and with the curious silent fixation of arctic explorers, we sipped hot coffee from a thermos and steamed up the interior glass of my vehicle.

I put up many routes at Dixon Springs and surrounding areas in a period of two years, sometimes using a rope, either for leading or top roping, but more frequently, bouldering free and free soloing. I recall first coming upon a bulging overhang amid the trees while accompanied by a fellow math instructor from Murray State who was fascinated by my weird athletics. I christened it "Jumbo" and told him I thought it might not be too hard to climb. He guffawed and immediately wagered that evening's meal on my putting my body where my mouth was. Poor fellow, a non-athletic product of a more gentile and provincial Deep South, he held the top rope for me as he lost his bet. At Murray State, I made an agreement with a physics student named Mohammed Shams to teach him climbing if he taught me some of the skills of soccer. He and I climbed on a short cliff near "Jumbo" that became known as the Persian Wall.

I left the South permanently in 1967, and moved to Fort Collins. There I found a marvelous Dakota sandstone playground, virtually untouched. What a wonderful thing, a stroke of good fortune again, to explore and develop that primal connection between man and stone.

See Bio on pg 539

SUNSET PARK

SOUTH

SUNSET PARK

Bell Buttress

The bell tolls for you! Heed the call and come journey up these serpentine, tall, and exposed routes on great rock. Recommended for those breaking into the grades found here! Watch the ends of your rope!

Train Time, 5.10-

214 Freedom Chimney 5.7 ★
Start: 5' right of Defender. Chimney a casket-width crack to the top. 40' Insider's Note: Classic chimney! Unfortunately, there's not one iota of pro.
FA: Rich Gottlieb, free solo (4/80)

215 Windwalker 5.9
Ready to catch some big air? Start: At trailside, 50' right of Freedom Chimney. Climb through a weakness and small tiered roofs. Climb straight to an overhang, work right, then climb a thin fissure. Friction left across an airy slab, finish up a fine crack. 120'
FA: Bruno de Robert and partner (6/81)

> **Insider's Tip:** Carry about a dozen runners, and watch out for rope drag at the lower roof.

216 Windmill 5.10- ★★
Liberty Bell's big cousin.
Start: Same as for Liberty Bell. Crack the Liberty Bell roof slot. Breeze left a few moves ... mill up shallow cracks splitting the increasingly airy steep wall. 120'
FA: Forrest Gardner, Jack Noonan (9/86)

217 Liberty Bell 5.9
You'd have to be —cracked—not to want to hang a rope on this classic Sunset pitch.
Start: 15' right of Wind Walker. Begin with a couple of boulder problem pull-ups ... squiggle through a tricky roof slot. Merge with a long and lovely crack system that disappears to the top 120'
FA: Rob Robinson, Peter Henley (9/80)

> **Insider's Tip:** Aid the first 20' (crux), and the rest of the climb is a three star 5.7.

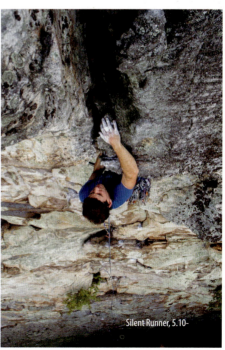
Silent Runner, 5.10-

SUNSET PARK SOUTH

218 King's Roof 5.10 ★
Start: 150' right of Windmill, on the right wall of a left-facing cove above the trail.
Ease through a spot of "suspect" rock; continue up a wide dihedral to a large, flat roof. Dethrone this (crux) and exit to the top. 60'
FA: Rob Robinson, Forrest Gardner (early 80's)

219 Grip Stone 5.10- ★
Start: 10' right of King's Roof.
Face climb a bit, then ease up a narrow and very steep left-facing corner. 60'
FA: Rob Robinson, Forrest Gardner (9/80)

Sunset 'Big Air' Routes
Stan's Crack (direct finish), 5.9+
Black Magic, 5.10
A Stitch in Time, 5.10+
The Prow, 5.11+
Space Ranger, 5.12-

Photo Credit: Rob Robinson Collection
Rob Robinson rides airy arete, 5.10-

SUNSET PARK

CELEBRITY FLAKE
Strike a pose! This is one of Sunset's hottest scenes for seeing and being seen. The Celebrity Flake is a large semi-detached flake that holds 9 high quality lines.

220 Temple of Doom 5.10 ★★
Where's the stained glass? More like a sandstone cathedral. Features a beautifully backlit tunnel around sunset.
Start: In an obvious tunnel right of Grip Stone. Climb an overhanging crack, span gap ... chimney right a bit to join an off-width crack in a right-facing corner. 60'
FA: Rob Robinson, Gene Smith (6/84)

> Insider's Note: Bring a couple of big cams (#5) and a headlamp.

221 Back Street Revelations 5.11- ★★★
Eureka! What do we have here?! Lurking in dark coves.... Start: 20' right of Temple Of Doom. Attack the overhanging wall: charge over a bulge staying just right of a thin crack. "Turn on auto-pilot" and cruise to the top of the pinnacle following a classic finger and hand crack highway. 60'
FA: Rob Robinson, Marvin Webb (3/81)

> Insider's Upgrade: Stick with the crack at the opening bulge for a "full value" 5.11.

222 Facts of Strife 5.10 ★★
Start: 5' right of Back Street Revelations. Chow down on a chocolate-colored wall packed with tasty jugs. Turn a calorie-burning roof (crux). Finish following an enjoyable jam crack. 60'
FA: Rob Robinson, Tim Cumbo (5/84)

223 Jug Mania 5.7 ★
Start: Right around the corner from Facts Of Strife. (On the front face of Celebrity Flake.) Weave up the arete following a trail of big and incut holds to the top of the pinnacle. 60'
FA: Unknown

PM — 30 mins — Sunset

www.rockerypress.com

SUNSET PARK

SOUTH

224 Afternoon Delight 5.7 ★★
Start: Same as for Jug Mania.
Ease up the wall using sloping holds; turn a minor bulge (using one of two cracks.) Step right and follow a delightful, straight-in jam crack to the top of the pinnacle. 60'
FA: Bill Smith, Steve Jones (77')

225 Afternoon Walk 5.11- ★★
Start: Atop a ledge just right of Afternoon Delight. Climb a steep green lichened face past a bolt (crux). Turn a 2' roof; face climb an exposed headwall to the top of the pinnacle. 70' FA: Forrest Gardner and partner (mid 80's)

226 Walk in the Park 5.8
Classic Sunset stroll.
Start: Same as for Afternoon Walk. Face climb to a small ledge, continue up a short, left-facing corner. A perfect, straight-in 3" to 4" crack leads to the top of the pinnacle. 70' FA: Tim McMillan? (late 60's)

> Insider's Tip: Bring at least one #4 cam for the headwall crack.

The First Ascent of Train Time Direct, 5.11

227 Train Time 5.10-
Wildly varied, engaging climb up very steep and absolutely perfect rock.
Start: 10' right of Walk In The Park. Rally up the wall to the base of a tiny, right-facing corner. Step left, shadow a right-facing arch that leads to a small notch. The top of the pinnacle is just ahead. 70'
FA: Rich Gottlieb, Forrest Gardner (4/80)

228 Train Time Direct 5.11

You might let out a whistle when you come round the bend and see this one. World class quality—one of the finest pitches of 5.11 in the guide.
Start: Same as for Train Time.
Tiptoe up the face and "boulder" into a tiny right-facing corner ... battle through bulge split by a thin crack. Escape through a small notch, continue to the top of the pinnacle. 70'
First Lead: Forrest Gardner, Rob Robinson, combined effort (9/80)

229 Pancake Flake 5.9 ★★

Mouth watering stack of "Yosemite style" jams. Pass the syrup.
Start: 10' right of Train Time Direct. Layback, jam and face climb along a classic right-curving arch with a fist-sized crack to the top of the pinnacle. 70' Insider's Tip: Bring several bigger sized cams.
FA: Bill Smith? (mid 70's)

Marvin Webb making an early slung hexcentric ascent of Pancake Flake, 5.9 Photo Credit: Rob Robinson Collection

SUNSET PARK

Pigs Buttress

Bring home the bacon! The following climbs are located on a formation known as the Pigs Buttress - a soaring 100' wall identified by a prominent arete on its left margin.

230 Airy Arete 5.10 ★★★
See description on page 171.

231 Direct Finish (Barnyard Zen) 5.10+ ★
Finish directly over the small roof capping the arete.
FA Rob Robinson, Gene Smith(4/84)

232 Baby Cats 5.11 ★★★
Feed me ... now! Recommended to Sunset tigers on the prowl for "the perfect trad meal."
But look before you leap—you'll earn your stripes on this one.
Start: 10' right of Airy Arete.
Follow an obvious flake to a small ledge. Continue up a narrow dihedral to a bulge... swing right, then up and left to a fixed rurp. Claw up the thin overhanging face (crux) to a jam crack—escape to the top. 100'
FA: Forrest Gardner, aid solo (11/83)
FFA: Forrest Gardner, Rob Robinson (11/83)

PM

30 mins

Based out of the incredible new climbing gym, High Point Climbing & Fitness, in downtown Chattanooga, the High Point Climbing School was founded by world renowned climbers Lisa Rands and Wills Young.

Guiding: We offer guided climbing at local venues! Learn to lead, to belay, to set up anchors, to trad climb, or even sport climb. Get out climbing with us and take in some expert advice.

Classes: Come to the gym and join one of our regular classes to improve your technique, or hone your rope handling skills.

Private Coaching: Fast results from undivided attention.

Club, Team & Training: We have youth clubs, a youth team and training camps.

For more information, call Wills Young at 760-920-5348 or find us online (see below).

www.highpointclimbing.com/climbing-school

SUNSET PARK — SOUTH

233 Pigs in Space 5.10
Award winning sandstone Bar-B-Q flavored with a dash of spicy exposure. Guaranteed to put some "extra curl" in your tail.
Start: Same as for Baby Cats. Pitch #1: Trot up the wall to a ledge. Gobble up a wide dihedral, squeal right across the face to a ledge and belay. (75') (5.8+) Pitch #2: Traverse left and—sink your hooves—into a tasty finger crack (crux) that leads to the top. (25') (5.10)
FA: Clint Henley, Clay Henley, Peter Henley (spring of '80)

234 Pigs in Space (direct) 5.10 ★★★
Even better than the "original recipe." Don't let the little run-out spoil your picnic!
Start: 5' right of Pigs In Space. Climb a left-facing corner to a ledge. Turn bulge split by a thin crack (crux). Step right at the small roof. Thread through notch and tackle a long 5.6 run-out which ends at a ledge. Finish via the airy finger crack (crux). 100'

FA: Rob Robinson, Forrest Gardner (10/80)

Airy Arete 5.10 ★★★

On the prowl for ... a little exposure? Gorgeous flow of face climbing grace this beautiful arete which offers more "big air" than a clothesline caught in a summer rainstorm. Start: At trailside, 40' right of Pancake Flake. Float up the right side of the arete to a short left-facing corner. Top this, boulder up the left wall for a ways, swing back onto the exposed right wall. At the base of a short left facing corner (capped by a 1' roof), diagonal right a few feet and finish up a short jam crack splitting the overhanging wall. 100'
FA: Rob Robinson, Bruce Rogers (4/84)

Photo Credit: Rob Robinson Collection

SUNSET PARK

SOUTH

NORTHWEST BUTTRESS

PM
30 mins

May the wind always be at your back, the walls steep, and the cracks splitter! Set your course for the N.W. Buttress - as it won't steer you wrong!

235 Experimental Animals 5.10+ ★★
Welcome to the Sunset lab? Trad surgeons take care wielding this scalpel of an arete. Doctor's smock, stethoscope optional.
Start: 90' right of Pigs In Space Direct.
Pitch #1: Climb past weakness. Trend left to a belay at the base of the arete. (50') (5.6) Pitch #2: Turn overhang to gain ledge. Scratch up the left wall of the arete following a thin crack (crux). When reasonable, claw right onto the arete's nose and proceed directly to the top. (70') (5.10+)
FA: Rob Robinson, Forrest Gardner (8/83)

236 Lichen or Not 5.10- ★★
Lots of lichen (climbing through a bowl of sugar frosted flakes) but pitch two is greaaat! Start: Same as for Experimental Animals.
Pitch #1: Hustle through weakness. Trend left to a belay at the base of an arete. (50') (5.6) Pitch #2: Turn the overhang on the right. Link up with a thin crack which tracks straight up the licheny head wall to the top (70') (5.10-)
FA: Chris Chesnutt, Randy Lane (6/87)

237 Northwest Conversion 5.9 ★★★
See description on page 173.

238 Direct Finish (Good Fortune) 5.10 ★
Finish straight over the summit bulge capping pitch two.
FA Direct Finish: Rob Robinson, Tim Cumbo (mid 80's)

239 Disintegration 5.8
Start: Same as for Northwest Conversion.
Pitch #1: Do the pitch one of N.W. Conversion. (50') (5.7)
Pitch #2: Continue up pitch two of N.W. Conversion for about 20'. Head out right and meander up the lichened wall, climbing through bulges to the top. (80') (5.8)
FA: Rob Robinson, Pam Thompson (11/83)

240 Prior Consent 5.10
Start: 10' right of Northwest Conversion.
Climb through lichened rock to a ledge; continue to a small cave. "Boulder" over the cave's lip (crux), cruise past a fixed pin, finish up a steep headwall. 100'
FA: Forrest Gardner, Rob Robinson (6/85)

Northwest Conversion 5.9 ★★★

In spite of the route's initial mediocrity, I've upgraded this route to three stars to honor pitch two, which is deserving of the grade. A Sunset South classic!

Start: Same as for Experimental Animals/Lichen Or Not.

Pitch #1: Climb straight up the wall to a ledge. Continue up a right-facing corner, then left to a belay. (50') (5.7)

Pitch #2: Follow a long, steep, exposed and beautiful crack that splits the lichened wall. Avoid the summit bulge; step left and climb a short (crux) crack. (60') (5.9)

FA: Marvin Webb, Rob Robinson (8/81)

Climber: Emily Hon
Photo Credit: Micah Gentry

SUNSET PARK

SOUTH

241 The Day After 5.9+
Start: 20' right of Prior Consent.
Blast up the wall past a small corner that forms part of a roof. Turn another roof and dock at a long ledge beneath large, white overhangs. Find or set anchors and rappel. 80'
FA: Forest Gardner, Clint Henley (11/83)

242 B-52 5.8
Start: By a pine tree 5' right of The Day After.
Climb the face following a thin crack to a band of loose overhangs. Work around left and up to a long ledge. Find or set anchors and rappel. 80'
FA: Rob Robinson, Forrest Gardner, Bruce Rogers (6/80)

243 Idiot Savant 5.12 ★★
An aerial asylum of sorts; features a short bit of psychotic roof work.
Start: From the long ledge where B-52 ends. Face climb a few moves ... ease into huge, tiered white overhangs via a short, right-facing corner. Traverse left a few feet, turn the lip, passing two s#$# fixed pins and a few rotten wires. Escape to the top. 60'
FA: Forrest Gardner, Jack Noonan (11/86)

244 Silent Runner 5.10-
Eclectic mix of continuously challenging climbing with three unique cruxes; the latter is very exposed. Always a top finisher in the Sunset 5.10 popularity contest.
Start: 15' right of B-52. Pitch #1: Take aim and shoot up the face (crux) and climb a pair of thin, parallel cracks (crux) to a long ledge. (70') (5.10-)
Pitch #2: Swing through the white overhang above at its right side (crux). Much easier climbing leads up and left to the top. (60') (5.10-)
FA: Rob Robinson, Bruce Rogers (7/79)

> Insider Notes: A) Originally done as one mega pitch. B) Pitch one is a spankin' three star route in and of itself. C) Pitch two is superb through the overhang, but then fizzles out into a nondescript jug haul. As such, it is worth noting that—after doing pitch one—you can escape left along the ledge to a pine tree and rappel. Flaws assayed, I still recommend doing the entire route at least once.

Idiot Savant, 5.12 — Edward Yates　　　Photo Credit: Micah Gentry

SUNSET PARK

SOUTH

SUNSET PARK

245 Draft Dodger 5.10- ★
Start: 10' right of Silent Runner. Climb past a thin flake and up a steep, bouldery wall past a bulge. Now jam a crack to a ledge. Finish through fragmented rock to the top. 130'
FA: Rob Robinson, Forrest Gardner, Bruce Rogers (6/80)

246 House of Cards 5.9+
Start: 20' right of Draft Dodger. Shuffle up unstable rock to a roof. Turn this at a pair of thin cracks. A direct line of jugs leads to a pine tree. 60'
FA: Forrest Gardner, Clint Henley (11/83)

247 Mercenary Territory 5.8 ★
Start: 15' right of House Of Cards. Gun up questionable quality rock ... turn roof, subdue another roof with a single hand jam. Finish with a runout up a steep slab. 120'
FA: Kyle Leftkoff, Buddy Thompson (6/80)

248 Space Flaps 5.8
Start: 25' right of Mercenary Territory. Wander up a lichened covered wall, avoiding roofs and turning bulges for the better part of a rope length. Finish up a crack near the top of the wall. 130'
FA: Forrest Gardner, Pam Thompson (6/83)

249 Decoy Buckets 5.9 ★★
Start: 20' right of Space Flaps. Climb about 20' and pass a short, right-facing corner. Follow a line of buckets for a bit. Motor past a few bulges, trend right up a headwall (crux) to the top. 120'
FA: Forrest Gardner, Rob Robinson (6/83)

250 Flash Dance 5.10 ★★
A bit of a lichen safari—but its a small price to pay for such an enjoyable and highly improbable vertical adventure. What a feeling!
Start: Same as for Decoy Buckets.
Pitch #1: Climb Decoy Buckets for 20'. Dance right 15', flash a left-slanting finger crack. Continue to a small ledge and belay. (60') (5.10)
Pitch #2: Balance right through a blank section capping a small roof. Climb up, then diagonal left ... finish on the final moves of Decoy Buckets. (60') (5.10)
FA: Forrest Gardner, Rob Robinson, alt. leads (6/83)

Beckett Honicker on the rarely repeated, Direct Afraid, 5.13-   Photo Credit: Cody Averbeck

SUNSET PARK

THE GIANT'S NICHE
FE...FI...FO...FUM
Big roof. Hard climbs. Sunset's steepest wall. BUT...don't miss some of Sunset's best moderates located right around the corner.

251 Direct Afraid 5.13-
Nothing to fear here—only Sunset's hardest (and one of its coolest) roof problems.
Start: In a shallow cave known as "The Giant's Niche," immediately right of Flash Dance. Turn a small roof (5.10) and climb to a spectacular 15' roof crack. Crank to lip (crux), claw up the thin crack above. Continue straight up the lichened headwall to the top. 100'
FA: Forrest Gardner, Rob Robinson (4/80)
FFA: Hidetaka Suzuki (11/86)

252 Dementol Bridge 13a ★★
Start: Same as for Direct Afraid.
Climb to the base of the roof. Climb right following a horizontal crack splitting the roof which ends—engineer moves out to the lip. Lower from fixed gear above, or continue up face to the top. 120'
FA: Steve Goins, Truly Bracken (4/92)

PM

35 mins

www.rockerypress.com

SUNSET PARK — SOUTH

SUNSET PARK

253 La Pishnibulle 5.10+ ★
Start: At the right side of the Giant's Niche, and 20' right of Dementol Bridge. Climb a left-facing corner at the right side of the Giant's Niche. Traverse right beneath the roof (crux), continue up a right-facing corner and on to the top. 130' **FA:** Bruno de Robert, Marty Gibson (9/81) **FFA:** Chris Chesnutt, Forrest Gardner (8/87)

> **Insider's Note:** Done in two pitches by some parties.

254 Jugular Vein 5.7 ★★
Start: 30' right of La Pishnibulle. Track left across the wall, join a juggy vertical crack. Move right past a pine tree(?), turn a small overhang. More face climbing leads to the top. 80'
FA: Rob Robinson, Peter Henley (10/80)

255 Second Sun 5.9+
Light this! High wattage pitch of 5.9; guaranteed to provide a bright spot in your day.
Start: 5' right of Jugular Vein. Beam up the wall to a bulge split by a thin crack. Cruise over this (crux) and continue up a long, right-facing corner. Cipher a small roof (crux); finish up a left-facing dihedral. 90'
FA: Rob Robinson, Peter Henley (10/80)

256 Blonde Ambition 5.7
A dream of a pitch: one of the most classic climbs for the grade in the Sandstone Belt.
Start: 10' right of Second Sun. Climb to a small scoop. Unlock face moves above (crux) to gain access to a long, vertical crack brimming with bomber jams and jugs. 90' **FA:** Rob Robinson, Peter Henley (10/80)

> **Insider's Note:** Named after a beautiful blonde-haired girl that jogged past the base of the route at the time of the first ascent.

257 Whistler's Mother 5.10 ★★
Start: 10' right of Blond Ambition. Zoom up the wall, keeping left of a vertical gully. Transition through a notch, move right, then left along a thin, arching crack (crux). Whistle to the top. 90' **FA:** Forrest Gardner, Rob Robinson (6/83)

The First Ascent of Blonde Ambition, 5.8

Second Sun, 5.9+

SUNSET PARK

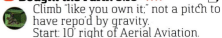 SOUTH

258 Trivial Pursuits 5.9
Start: 15' right of Whistler's Mother. Climb the face to a shallow crack in a white headwall. Migrate left and up a bit ... then back right and up a short slab and thin crack to the top. 90'
FA: Rob Robinson, Forrest Gardner (6/83)

259 Ghostly Grabber 5.10-
Start: 80' right of Trivial Pursuits. Climb 30', turn an 8' roof with a thin crack. Continue up a grungy crack and corner. 80'
FA: Marvin Webb, Rob Robinson (9/80)

260 Apogee 5.12- ★
Start: 15' right of Ghostly Grabber. Climb 30', turn 8' roof (crux) split by a thin crack. Continue to the top. 80'
FA: Forrest Gardner (8/86)

> Insider's Tip: Bail above the roof.

261 Aerial Aviation 5.9 ★
Start: 60' right of Ghostly Grabber. Climb a thin crack and a steep, left-facing dihedral. 70'
FA: Rob Robinson, Forrest Gardner (9/80)

262 Bought the Farm 5.10+ ★★
Climb "like you own it;" not a pitch to have repo'd by gravity.
Start: 10' right of Aerial Aviation. Climb the face, diagonal left and weave up the arete to the top. 80'
FA: Rob Robinson, Steven Farmer (mid 90's)

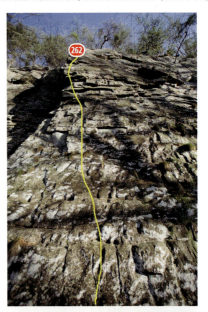

SUNSET PARK

263 Terminal Impatience 5.8+
Start: 15' right of Bought The Farm.
Climb 25', pass a roof on the left. Wander to a smaller roof a bit higher, pass this and trend left to the top. 80'
FA: Forrest Gardner, Rob Robinson (9/80)

264 Airbrush 5.6 ★
Start: 15' right of Terminal Impatience.
Scramble up small shelves, climb a hand and finger crack. Angle left to the top. 80'
FA: Rob Robinson, Peter Henley (9/80)

265 Squeeze Box 5.8 ★
Start: 40' right of Airbrush.
Follow a wide crack through large tiered overhangs. Continue up slab cracks to the top. 80'
FA: Rob Robinson, Peter Henley (8/80)

267 The View From Above 5.9+ ★★
Sunset loyalists should check this crack line out at some point in their climbing career ...its a sight worth seeing.
Start: Walk a short distance past Squeeze Box to an aluminum bridge. Continue for approximately 1/4 mile until you come to a large boulder on the right side of the trail. Rappel to the cliff's base down and left of the boulder. Climb a long and classic hand crack capped by a small roof. 90'
FA: Rob Robinson, Bruce Rogers (4/85)

Insider's Note: was discovered while doing photo fly bys for a guide.

268 Evening Flight Out 5.7 ★
Start: 10' left of The View From Above.
Climb a right-facing corner with good hand jams and stems. 50'
History: Rob Robinson, free solo (4/85)

Suck Creek

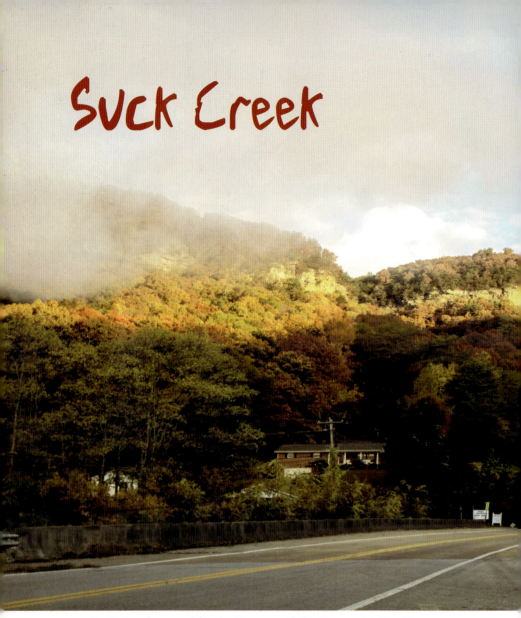

Suck Creek crags like the Arena and the Concentration Camp are owned and managed by Prentice Cooper WMA and are closed during managed hunts and subject to the additional regulations. Unfortunately, forest service personnel do not (as yet) post any signs indicating these particular areas are closed during managed hunts (either at the mouth of the canyon or at the trailhead for the Concentration Camp.) However, managed hunts are regularly conducted during the spring and fall months. I recommend you save yourself a chalk bag full of grief and call the Tennessee Wildlife Resources Agency at 1-800-262-6704 or 615-484-9571, to get the year's hunt dates before making plans.

If Prentice Cooper is closed for a hunt, don't even think about slipping in! Forest service personnel will not be amused, and the $130 fine they levy for trespassing could pay for 1) a handful of brass nuts, 2) a tank of gas, and 3) a couple of pitchers of Big River's Vienna Ale (my favorite beer of all time.) I'm speaking from personal experience.

All of the rock on the right side of the Canyon is not part of the Prentice Cooper, so you have carte blanche. This serendipitous fact can come in handy if you've headed out for a day of cragging at the Tennessee Wall, the Promised Land, Crystal Buttress or the left side of the Suck Creek Canyon ... and have the misfortune to discover these cliffs are closed to climbing for another managed hunt. Instead of heading to the climbing gym to pump some plastic you can simply switch to back up Plan B: visit any one of the five areas on the right side of Suck Creek.

SUCK CREEK

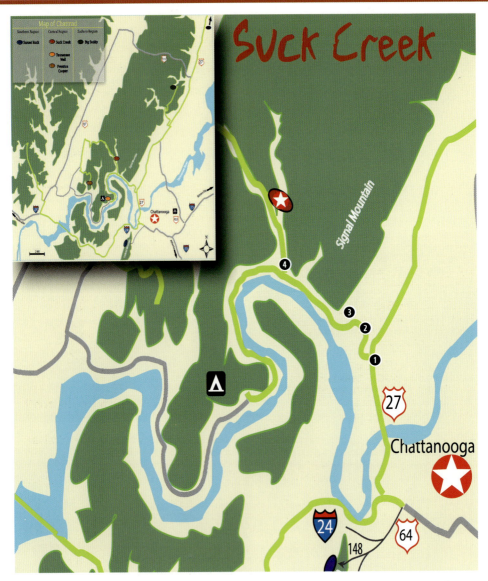

20 mins

❶ From Chattanooga. Take 1-27 North (across Oligiati bridge) to the Signal Mountain Road exit. ❷ Continue 1.5 miles on US 127 North (Passing a Wal Mart Shopping Center) until you reach the base of Signal Mountain. ❸ At the base of the mountain, take a left onto Suck Creek Road (TN Highway 27 West) (If you start going up the mountain, you've missed the turn). ❹ Follow Suck Creek Road for approximately 4.0 miles to a bridge that crosses suck creek. See directions to crags from here.

SUCK CREEK

Area Logistics

Emergency
Dial 911

Season
Spring through Fall

Amenities

Budweiser and Slim Jims are yours for the asking at a little ole' country store situated right at the mouth of the canyon (now closed unfortunately). At the intersection of Highway 27 and 127 (Signal Mountain Road and Suck Creek Road) you'll find:

Shuford's Bar-B-Que: Never eaten there, but it smells good, and probably tastes even better (if you're into pork.)

Subway sandwiches: for the lunch you forgot to bring, or "dinner" after snacking on sandstone all day.

Camping

Are you crazy!? Broken beer bottles and shell casings at most of the roadside pull-offs and … you get the picture. Flip to the Tennessee Wall intro for suitable, nearby venues where you can commune with the wilderness, not wild Bubbas.

Rules & Regs

1.) Have you checked to make sure that it's not a Prentice Cooper scheduled hunt date? In which case climbing will be temporarily prohibited within the park until the end of the hunt.

You can check scheduled hunt dates by following this link:

http://www.tn.gov/agriculture/forestry/stateforest07.shtml

3.) Firearms are prohibited in park if not under a Wild Hunt permit.

4.) Possession of drugs or alcohol is prohibited.

Climbing Specific Regulations

1.) All new routes requiring fixed hardware must be approved through Prentice Cooper Management. Consult the SCC website for more information.

Layout of the Canyon

The essence of Suck Creek is found in seven concentrations of routes: on the left side of the Canyon is: The Arena and the Concentration Camp. On the right side: The Upper Passes, Malevolence Wall, Hidden Wall, The Roadside Wall and White Cove. (see following pages for details)

Crags on Left Side of Canyon

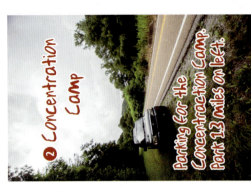

② Concentration Camp. Parking for the Concentration Camp. Park 1.3 miles on left.

① The Arena. Parking for the Arena at Lusk Point Overlook. See pg 194 for driving directions.

Mouth of Canyon. Set Odometer Here.

Crags on Right Side of Canyon — SUCK CREEK

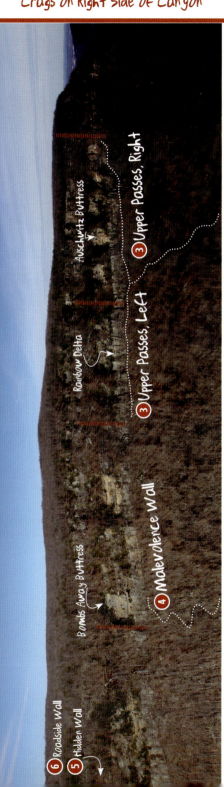

- Auschwitz Buttress
- ③ Upper Passes, Right
- Rainbow Delta
- ③ Upper Passes, Left
- ④ Malevolence Wall
- Bombs Away Buttress
- ⑥ Roadside Wall
- ⑤ Hidden Wall

⑥ Roadside Wall

Parking for the Roadside Wall. Park 1.8 miles on right.

⑤ Hidden Wall

Parking for the Hidden Wall. Park 1.6 miles on right.

④ Malevolence Wall

Parking for the Malevolence Wall. Park 1.1 miles on right.

③ The Upper Passes

Parking for the Upper Passes. Park .7 miles on right.

SUCK CREEK

Todd Wells

Rob Robinson

Climbing History

Travis Eiseman

WELCOME ... TO SUCK CREEK CANYON!

You are undoubtedly familiar with an old adage which claims what you see is what you get. Frequently this is true, and hence the saying. If it were always true, then few climbers would venture to explore a complex of cliffs that— at first glance—looks to be "long on sand and short on cement."

At the mouth of this "creek" (more a small river) climbers are greeted by a spectacular but crumbling 200' high swath of stratified choss; an undulating buttress of rotten rock affixed to a wide point on the left side of the canyon. If this were any indicator of what the rest of the area is like—who could blame you just blowing the area off? After all, the solid gold, sun drenched Tennessee Wall is situated just a few miles distant.

SUCK CREEK

What the heck ... you're already here. Looks like there's a lot of rock; you continue up the canyon in hopes you'll catch a break and see something better. Soon after crossing a bridge (at the canyon's entrance) the point on the left disappears behind a curtain of trees. Replacing it is another dreadful colossus of rotten rock; this time on the right side of the canyon. That's it. No doubt about it: This place is a pile! Time to turn around at the next pull-out. Who suggested we come here?!

There is another popular saying: Don't judge a book by its cover. This is the adage that best applies to the cliffs of Suck Creek. Tucked just out of sight beneath those interlaced rotten walls is a rock solid foundation of more high quality sandstone than you can "shake a stick at." The fact is Suck Creek is home to some of the finest cragging in the region. There are many routes comparable in quality to the best of the Tennessee Wall. So take a moment and look closer now—do you see the promise of things to come rising from the tree tops? Ah ha!

An early ascent of the Rose - 5.10-

The cliffs of Suck Creek can be roughly divided into two geologically distinct bands: A monolithic, complex, rotten upper crust perched atop a compact band of predominately high quality stone. You might be surprised to know Suck Creek shares a similar geology with the Tennessee Wall.

Occasionally, Suck Creek's upper crust is capped by a tippy-top band: A complex and scattered constellation of "summit crags." Routes "up top" are difficult to access, and without a future revised edition of this guide, you'll be wasting your time trying to locate any climbs of substance.

Forrest Gardner in his element

Suffice to say: Ole' Rob has plenty more in store for you.

Suck Creek also offers many serious aid climbs that worm through the crumbling upper crust proper. Conquer a couple of these chimeras, and you'll have enough experience under your harness to tackle hard aid climbs elsewhere in the country. (Aid savant Forrest Gardner "made his bones" here.)

Not surprisingly, Suck Creek is also home to some loose and potentially scary free routes. Because these routes offer a venue for learning how to deal with the terrors and triumphs of climbing on unstable rock, I've chosen to include them!

Todd Wells doing his Summit Dance

Climbing History

How It All Got Started

Who actually placed the first klettershoe on Suck Creek rock is unknown. However, the first routes recorded were done way back in the 1980's when Forrest Gardner, Peter Henley and Rob Robinson teamed up with each other (and with various partners) and blew through many of the creme de la creme classics.

The latter part of the 80's saw a spike of activity led primarily by Todd Wells, Rick Mix (and Gardner) and various partners — mostly complex aid stuff, with a couple of classic free lines thrown in for good measure.

In the early 90's, the area was closed by the Klu Klux Klan for several years to allow the endangered plastic pink flamingos native to the area an opportunity to rebreed and re-infest the trailer park

Rick Mix enjoying a 'mini-bigwall' Belay

located at the mouth of the canyon. The re-population program was a huge success; in the late 90's the Klan removed all burning crosses and, thankfully, new route activity was allowed to resume. Subsequently, Darrow Kirkpatrick and Rob Robinson added a small but superb string of classic free climbs to the kitty.

In the opening years of the 21st century, the west walls of the Upper Passes were rediscovered.

Laban Swafford after a 'near deck' experience in Suck Creek

Elements Of Style

Suck Creek has long been the "domain of the trads" (and just down the road from another traditionalist strong hold — the Tennessee Wall.) However, like its richer cousin, a handful of sport routes have successfully been integrated into the area's inventory of climbs.

Nonetheless, if you're afflicted with bolt gun fever, or consider yourself a natural born driller, I suggest finding another locale (southern Hilti? the suburbs of Bosch?) to drain batteries, sink sleeves and don hangers ... the Canyon has seen its fair share of bolt chopping.

It can get expensive....

A normal day with the Suck Creek "Wild Life"

Today 4:39 PM

> We found a body.

> Waiting on ambulance.

Text Message

> She's ok. Passed out drunk.

iMessage

> It was scary.

AM
20 mins

The Arena

The Arena: a beautiful, overhanging alcove of Sandstone sporting a spectacular waterfall. Beautiful and isolated, intimidating and serious - this unique area is recommended only to the expert Trad climber.

Bottom Access: Same driving and hiking instructions as for the Concentration Camp (see 205), but when you reach the base of the cliff head left and... continue hiking for a burly mile. Eventually you'll be smitten by a spectacular waterfall cove. Total hiking time from car to the cove: approximately 45 minutes.

Top Access (Recommended): Instead of approaching the Arena from the Concentration Camp, the preferred method (especially when the trail to the arena is non-existent (IE Summer Time) is to approach the area from Lusk Point Road in the Prentice Cooper Forest above. From the mouth of Suck Creek, drive 4.0 miles up the canyon and take a left turn at a sign for Prentice Cooper WMA. Continue .3 miles following signs for WMA until the road turns to gravel and you enter into the forest. From here, drive 2.3 miles on gravel road to a LEFT turn at a sign that reads 'Lusk Point Road.' Head to the end of this road making sure to stay straight avoiding any left or right turns. This road will dead end at a nice graveled cul-de-sac with a great view of the TN River Gorge.

From the overlook, walk left and down a steep hillside for a hundred or so yards to a point where you will intersect the Cumberland Trail. From here, the outline of the Arena Amphitheater will become visible. Now cross the CT and head steeply down the lower slope to the top of the cliff. Look for an obvious 6 foot long jutting overlook. Peek over the edge of this overlook on the falls side, and you will find a bomber SS bolted rap station below on a small ledge (the anchors of Going Off the Deep End). Squirm down to the station and rig a rappel down.

Insider's Tip: Though the upper approach is logistically more involved than most other Suck Creek areas, you can be from your car to the arena in 10-15 minutes. And actually, this approach makes for a good half-day or after work summertime activity, especially if you rap in over the Deep End and chalk it up for your buddy and then top this route out. Just make sure to be out before dark, as the PC gate closes at sundown!

N ▷

CHATTRAD

Going Off the Deep End, 5.12

Climber: Laban Swafford   Photo Credit: Cody Averbeck

SUCK CREEK

the Arena

AM
20 mins

The Arena
For those about to fly, we salute you! Now prepare for some blood sport! Your options are limited, so let's get down to it -- don't miss Sudden Death Playoff, Going Off the Deep End, and Suck Crack -- recommended in this order.

❶ **Temporary Like Immortality 5.9** ★
Start: Approximately 250' right of Sudden Death Playoff.
Pitch #1: Climb a steep, smooth slab with a "candelabra" of thin cracks. Turn a small roof, continue up a right-facing flake and corner to a second roof. Belay a bit higher beneath a band of tiered overhangs. (70') (5.9) Pitch #2: Traverse right across easy ledges to a shallow left-facing corner. Work onto face right of the corner (freaky). Turbo to the top. (70') (5.8)
FA: Rob Robinson, Gene Smith (1/84)

❷ **Panzer Leader 5.10-** ★★
Start: ' left of Temporary Like Immortality. Description.
FA: Rick Mix, Jeff Burton (96' or 97')

❸ **Sudden Death Playoff 5.10+** ★★
Pitch one involves "an intricate and tricky dance across the vertical ball room floor," with the Grim Reaper leading. The crux pitch is a two star tango featuring solid rock, superb natural features and superior wall position.
Start: left of Panzer Leader, (on the right wall of the Arena amphitheater). Pitch #1: Boulder over a bulge and through a "sandtrap" to a massive roof. Traverse left 20' beneath roof on granular holds to a collection of small ledges. A secure belay is difficult to arrange. (45') (5.10) Pitch #2: Continue up a left-facing corner, work left n' up via sloping holds to gain a spectacular, left-facing slot. Chimney to slot's top. Finish straight up a steep headwall. (80') (5.10 +)
FA: Rob Robinson, Peter Henley (4/83)

> **Insider's Beta:** You might find it worth your time (and possibly your life) to avoid pitch #1 by climbing another route, traversing to the top of S.D.P., then rapping off to a belay at the base of pitch #2. After completing the route: return the base via a two rope rappel, or traipse right about 75 yards to a point where it is fairly obvious you can make two single rope rappels.

❹ **The Jesus Chainsaw Massacre 5.11+** ★★
You will become a believer....or else! Start: Same as Sudden Death Playoff. P1. From SDPO, traverse hard left to the base of the vertical crack and corner system. P2. Follow the left facing system up the wall to a large roof. Turn the roof and journey to the woods and a rap station above.
FA: Tyler Stracker and Todd Wells, 2007

SUCK CREEK

⑤ The Ho Chi-Min Trail 5.11+ A1
An incredibly long free route: pending a couple bolts and some eager strongmen. Start: at a tree 20 feet left of Sudden Death. Climb the tree and traverse across jug laced ledge trending left to a good stance. P.1 5.7 60 feet. P.2 crank straight up the vertical crack system and surmount a roof (bolt needed here) keep cranking the left margin of the arete past some tiny gear to an alcove w/ a single SS bolt, 80 feet 5.11d. P.3 leave the belay low and left, tricky poorly protected moves gain questionable rock. Head up to the huge left facing corner, a tips seam gains better gear and easy climbing to the top, A1 (5.12ish likely) 60 feet. Rap off the Jesus anchors at the tree, one 70 gets you to the pool. FA: Tyler Stracker, Kirk Brode

SUCK CREEK — the Arena

6 Going Off the Dead End 5.12-
Head games, anyone? If the hike in doesn't make a nut case out of you—the climb will for sure! An airy, very overhanging pitch incorporating all the best that Southern sandstone has to offer. Straight jacket optional.
Start: several hundred feet left of Sudden Death Playoff, on the left side of the Arena amphitheater and just left of the waterfall. Climb a short right-facing corner, exit right. Continue directly up the overhanging wall on jug holds to a small roof. Rip through this (5.11+), roar into a smooth-looking, left-facing dihedral. Turn another small roof with a bolt (5.12-). Worm right a move or two. Conquer a band of small tiered summit roofs (5.11-). Belay on scenic ledge at a pair of bolts.

Direct Start 5.12- ★★★
Start: A few feet right of the regular route. Power up the wall on jugs, jams and pockets for about 15 or so feet, merge with the regular route.
FA: Rob Robinson, Darrow Kirkpatrick (4/99) FA Direct Start: Rob Robinson (5/99)

> **Insider's Tips:** To obtain the full flavor of the route I recommend tackling this route when the adjacent waterfall is running full force. A spring or fall (or a warm winter) day are your best bets. Maximize your chances of "a flash": use double ropes, bring plenty of runners and carry a lightweight (but full spectrum) rack. The crux seeps for a few days after steady rains.

Laban Swafford about to Go Off the Deed End, 5.12- Photo Credit: Cody Averbeck

Are You Ready to Rumble?

By: Jeff Achey

Bob was from Atlanta, and a big, big boy. Where I come from, Bob could avert a fight just by standing up — or, should it come to that, settle the matter with a bear hug. So when he told me the story of stepping through the splattered remains of the turtle he was trying to save near his parking spot at Yellow Creek, dodging a flying beer bottle, and then putting six 9mm slugs through the tailgate of a rag-tag pickup, I knew the South was a little different.

If I wanted to climb in the South, I needed guidance and protection. At first I considered packing a pistol under the seat of my Honda, until Will recounted an incident that escalated from small-arms fire to assault rifles to plastic explosives. I realized that carrying any kind of firearm I could purchase legally would only guarantee that I'd be outgunned and shown no mercy.

When I actually started touring the Sandstone Belt, I learned that, in fact, the South is a pretty friendly place. Plaster some NRA decals over your Save the Whales bumper stickers, don't drive a vehicle with New Jersey plates, change out of your tights before entering a bar, and you're good to go. You stay out of trouble by paying attention and having a sense of the terrain — true for coping with local rednecks, but truer still for dealing with the trad climbing.

I was from Eldorado Canyon, land of fancy footwork and brass nuts, so in the South, I learned to stick to open ground, where I could keep my escape routes open. Runout face? Plenty of that here, but you can see it coming. You get through with a show of feet instead of arms, and flee if necessary. Splitter cracks? These, too, fight fair, in a style easily learned out West.

One serious bully just comes with the territory, however. Run from this one and you haven't fully appreciated the Sandstone Belt. Sometime on your visit you're going to back yourself up underneath one of the big Southern roof cracks. When you step up, no bumper sticker or pussyfooting is going to save you. You'd better be ready to rumble.

See Bio on pg 539

SUCK CREEK

❼ Dying on the Vine 5.9 ★
Start: 300' left of the waterfall, at a distinctive black and orange dihedral approximately 30' above the ground. Pitch #1: Climb to a bulge and hand traverse left into the black and orange dihedral; continue to a ledge. Move left and seek sheltered belay. (85') (5.8+) Pitch #2: Step left and climb steep orange face to gain another ledge. Continue up a distinct trough; bypass detached block on its left side and proceed to the top. (90') (5.9) FA: Todd Wells, Mark Cartwright (12/01)

Insider's Tip: Use double ropes. The first ascent party trundled a dump truck's worth of loose rock and suggests wearing ... "helmets and shoulder pads."

❽ Suck Crack 5.12-
This is the new-age crack classic of the Canyon, which is thought to be one of the best finger cracks in Suck Creek. This line is similar to Special O, but this time features ORANGE rock in a beautiful, remote setting. Follow a finger-tip-to-hand sized fissure up the beautiful monolithic swath of orange streaked sandstone to a fixed anchor. Make sure to bring plenty o' small gear.
FA: Todd Wells, Ed Marshall
FFA: Tyler Stracker, Kirk Brode, 2009

❾ Angst 5.10- ★
Start: Approximately 200' left of Dying On The Vine. (A few feet left of the 5.12 seam, Suck Crack) Pitch #1: Scramble to ledge and climb a right-facing orange corner for about 40'. At band of crud, traverse right to a spacious belay ledge. (75') (5.10-) Pitch #2: Climb right and over a bulge, pulling onto an arete (with interesting face climbing for 20'). Scruffier rock leads to the top. (75') (5.8)
FA: Mark Cartwright, Todd Wells (12/01)

❿ Lusk Point Horror 5.10- ★★
"In terms of training for climbing loose rock ... Lusk Point Horror (a.k.a The Horror) remains one of the test pieces of Suck Creek Canyon. Its been around a long time, and it's still no gimme. — *Todd Wells* Start: At a gigantic open book complex 500' left of Angst. Pitch #1: Climb the huge, central open book corner to a scenic belay ledge. (90') (5.8) Pitch #2: Continue up the corner a few feet, work right around a small roof (crux). Continue into the bowels of prominent, hanging roof slot. Exit left and up to a large ledge. (70') (5.10-) Pitch #3: Continue up the corner to the top. (40') (5.9)

Variation 5.10-
Below the hanging roof slot on pitch #2 ... traverse right a few feet, now up on friable rock (crux), sans pro. Ease back left into the corner above the roof and continue to a ledge. Finish up pitch #3 of the regular route. 80'

Original Route 5.10-
Below the hanging roof slot on pitch #2 ... face climb right (crux) on crumbling rock for 30' to an arete with a junky fixed pin. Escape to the top via moderately difficult climbing on better rock.(70') FA: (Original Route): Forrest Gardner, Peter Henley (8/84) FA: L.P.H. Direct (Variation): Mark Cartwright, Todd Wells (6/99) FA: L.P.H. Direct: Todd Wells, Rick Mix (5/00)

Insider's Notes: A "must do" for all long time locals. The route has just enough loose rock to inhibit "a mad rush to the summit." You can probably get by carrying a standard trad rack which includes lots of runners (mainly for the second pitch); however, I recommend using double ropes and carrying as many as six larger sized cams (#4 and up).

AM
25 mins

The Concentration Camp

The Concentration Camp, as the name suggests, offers a high concentration of climbs only ten minutes uphill from the parking pull-off. However, this area (like the Arena) is recommended to experienced climbers looking for more ... "complex" adventures.

One of the first things you'll probably discover sooner than later is a patina of very fine lichen common to many Camp routes. It varies in texture from a talc-like powdery consistency to almost like bread mold. To remedy this problem a quick "finger brushing" usually suffices, at least for the easier routes. **Insider's Tip:** Carry a small toothbrush or wire bristle brush. Cleaning holds on difficult, lichened climbs (5.11 or harder) is a different matter. Done on-sight the task can be Herculean, not to mentioned scary. If greasing off holds 20' above your last piece (with a cleaning brush clamped between your teeth like a cheap dentist's mandible restraint) is not your cup of tea I suggest the civilized alternative: Rap and clean. Insider's Tip: To "save" a route for an on-sight ascent, ask your partner to rap off and brush the holds for you.

Lichen problem solved, there is another "growth" to contend with. Late spring through early fall the cliff line from "the Camp" to the Arena is awash in waist high poison oak and "Cambodian jungle" undergrowth. **Insider's Tip:** Visit this area late fall through early spring when the worst of it has died off.

The Camp gets morning to early afternoon sun, providing a venue for winter morning cragging (or afternoon summer cragging if you're willing to brave the vegetation.) **Insider's Tip:** If it has been raining steadily for several days the Camp walls typically require the same to dry out.

The Camp may also be home to the longest roof bouldering traverse in the region. This enduro problem encompasses about 100' of low roofs found between the climbs Fascist Leader and The Burn Ward/Aryan Way. Why hasn't it been done? Well, for one thing it needs some T.L.C. (Tenacious, Laborious Cleaning.) If you're up for the job e-mail me and let me know when its done. Don't forget to do the entire crux sequences are the far left side!

Access: As you cross the bridge at the mouth of the Canyon ... drive for 1.3 miles uphill and pull off the road into a large parking loop. Just as you pull in to the loop look for a small square white blaze on the pavement. On the other side of the main road is a dirt jeep trail (blocked by boulders) leading up a steep hill into the woods. Hike up this till flat; bear right up the hill and follow a brief trail that fizzles out. Continue to the cliff's base via a scramble up a streambed terracing the hillside. Total time hiking from car to base: approximately 10 minutes.

SUCK CREEK

Concentration Camp

AM

25 mins

While never reaching the popularity of it's next door neighbor, the Roadside Wall, the Concentration Camp has some really outstanding walls offering a high density of good to great routes - all without the nuisance of a river crossing...

*The following two routes begin **right** of the creek bed that is encountered when first intersecting the cliff line.*

❶ Buff Rubes 5.8, A2+ ★★★
Classic "rottwand thuggery"... pack an attitude. Start: Approximately 200' right of the streambed, at a prominent buttress. Pitch #1: Climb an obvious, right-facing corner to a ledge, then straight up a loose, low-angle face to a hanging belay. (60') 5.8, A1) Pitch #2: Move right and up on steep rock following an obvious weakness bristling with semi-detached blocks. Continue to a break leading left to more "reasonable" rock and on to the top. (80') (A3) Descend by bushwhacking right and rap off some trees.
FA: Todd Wells, Rick Mix (1/96)

> **Insider Notes:** Frozen choss and a huge hanging icicle facilitated the first ascent.

❷ Redneck Direct 5.8, A3 ★★
Yeehaw! Break out yer' overalls and Cat diesel cap, an' don't fergit to brang yer hammer. Start: Same as for Buff Rubes. Pitch #1: Climb an obvious, right-facing corner to a ledge, then straight up a loose, low-angle face to a hanging belay. (60') (5.8, A1) Pitch #2: Climb directly over a bulge past blocks and more bulges; finish through a final roof. (85') (A3)
FA: Jeff Burton, Todd Wells

❸ Blue Collar 5.8, A2
Start: Same as for Buff Rubes/Redneck Direct. Pitch #1: Same as for Buff Rubes. (60') (5.8, A1) Pitch #2: Move left at the ledge and up a steep buttress via aid. Free climb past a huge perched block (bolt for pro) and continue to the top. (85') FA: Forrest Garner (10/96)

> **Insider's Note:** This route can be done in one long pitch using strategically placed long slings and judicious back cleaning.

*All routes from this point begin **left** of the creek bed that is encountered when first intersecting the cliff line.*

❹ The Faucet 5.10- ★
Start: On an obvious vine-strewn (poison oak) ledge; left of the streambed approach. Boulder steeply up to a "well-pasted" left-facing flake. Pass this and continue up the face (a bit loose) to the ledge below the Mace And Chain (see route description) buttress. 50'
FA: Todd Wells, Forrest Gardner (6/88)

> **Insider's Trivia:** During rainy spells, a spring spouts from a crack low on the climb, giving the route its name.

❺ The Entrance Crack 5.10- ★
Start: 15' left of The Faucet. Climb a hanging right-facing dihedral until it's possible to swing left onto good face holds. Continue up an intermittent crack to the trees above. 60'
FA: Todd Wells, Forrest Gardner (6/88)

206

SCC

SOUTHEASTERN CLIMBERS COALITION

www.seclimbers.org

Preserving Climbing Areas for Future Generations

Photo Credit: Micah Gentry

Forrest Gardner on the First Ascent of Maice & Chain, 5.9 A3+

Photo Credit: Tod Wells Collection

SUCK CREEK

6 Mace And Chain 5.9, A3+ ★★★

Perhaps the classic rottwand route in the canyon. Bring all of your beaks, RURPs and blades ... the final pitch used 49 of the latter! Start: 15' left of Entrance Crack (where the approach trail intersects the wall.) Pitch #1: Climb a big right-facing corner sporting a huge wedged block (called "the pony"—ride it?!) Exit right around roof to a large vegetated ledge. (80') (5.8) Pitch #2: Set up on the left side of the soaring orange buttress above. Climb loose, low-angle rock to a roof. Aid over this, move right and up an arete to a ledge. (50') (5.7, A2) Pitch #3: Work left from the belay, now weave up flakes and seams in the overhanging headwall. Aim for an obvious break in the left side of the summit visor. (80') (A3+)
FA: Todd Wells, Forrest Gardner (7/96)

Insider Notes: Pitch one is regarded as a climb in and of itself (called "Ride The Pony). Two rappels via trees to the ground.

7 Plate Lunch 5.8+, A2+

Start: Same as for Mace And Chain. Pitch #1: Climb pitch one of Mace And Chain; continue up to the vegetated ledge at the base of the upper headwall. (90') (5.8+) Pitch #2: Climb into huge cleft the splits the left side of the Mace And Chain buttress. Balance up loose blocks and surmount a bulge to arrive at a stance with a two bolt anchor. (40') (5.8) Pitch #3: Continue up the cleft, through soft rock, over and around wedged blocks and up to a final overhang. Surmount this with difficulty, move left on solid pins to a good ledge and belay. (50') (A2+) Pitch #4: Continue up a short offwidth crack to the top of the buttress (20') (5.6)
F.A.: Todd Wells, rope solo (5/01)

Insider's Notes: An incredibly aesthetic line when viewed from a distance, but seen up close it is obvious this soaring vertical slot bristles with detached blocks—it is one of the most objectively dangerous routes in Suck Creek. The line saw serious attempts by several "canyon locals" before finally succumbed in the spring of 01'. It might be safer to climb this route (rope) solo rather than expose a belayer to the catastrophic rock fall potential on pitch #3.

www.rockerypress.com

209

SUCK CREEK

Concentration Camp

❽ Free, White And Twenty One 5.10+ ★★
So you're all grown up now and ready to take on the world. Give this one a little spin.... Start: 10' left of Mace And Chain/Plate Lunch, where the approach trail intersects the cliff band. Face climb just left of a blunt arete past a bolt to a ledge with a perched block. Continue up a right-leaning dihedral to a second bolt. Exciting moves directly left of the bolt lead to good face holds. Now climb straight up, merge with a hand-crack splitting a small roof; continue to the top. 70' **FA:** Forrest Gardner, Jay Bell (5/88)

❾ Inches Despair 5.12- ★★
Inspiring climbing, where inches (coupled with the ability to stretch your mind and body) will make the difference between success and failure. Start: 10' left of Free, White And Twenty One. Climb a steep and bulging face past two gray bolts (crux). Weave through gauntlet of small roofs, trend right, then into a short left-facing corner capped by a small roof. Turn this and finish with a couple of delicate face moves. 80' **FA:** Rob Robinson, Darrow Kirkpatrick (9/97)

Insider's Note: Shorter climbers will probably find the climbing past the initial bolts to be more difficult than 12-.

❿ Free James Brown 5.11+ ★★
Flash this and you're sure to say "I feel good!" Start: 15' left of Inches Despair. Boulder past (crux) a fixed pin ... break dance up the bulging face above. Continue on (withering?) arms to a thank God stance beneath a final bulge. Turn this and finish up a shallow dihedral. 80' **FA:** Todd Wells, Lee Munson (5/89)

⓫ The Obvious Crack 5.8+
Start: In a recess about 60' left of Free James Brown. Climb a finger-crack to the left edge of a prominent roof (about 15' above the ground.) Now step left and jam a widening crack until it becomes a slot. Grunt past this, then savor? the scruffy climbing which continues to the top. 50' **FA:** Todd Wells, Rick Mix (4/98)

⓬ Forearm Magazine 5.11 ★★
Start: 13' left of The Obvious Crack. Toprope through a series of diminishing stances to a pumpy headwall, staying left of an obvious thin flake and right of "Rapture Of The Steep" (see next route description); gradually trend right and finish to the top. 80' **FA:** Forrest Gardner, Todd Wells, top rope

SUCK CREEK

⑬ Rapture Of The Steep 5.11 ★★★
Pack your wings, wires and three-cam units ... its time to tour a vertical version of Valhalla. Start: 10' left of Forearm Magazine. Climb a short, small corner. "Boulder" up the right side of a very steep arete to a single bolt clip. Pull directly over apex of small roof above. Continue straight up the nose of the arete, finishing with a fine sequence of tricky climbing favoring the right wall. 80' **FA:** Rob Robinson, Darrow Kirkpatrick (9/97)

> **Insider Notes:** Bring several blue Metolious to place en route to the bolt. The bolt was added by Robinson after the first ascent.

⑭ Soapstone 5.11- ★★
This route's slippery crux occasionally "hoses" the inept or brash. Otherwise, good clean fun. Start: 5' left of Rapture Of The Steep. Boulder up the face past a pair of finger pockets. Continue past a fixed pin and bolt (crux). Step left over a small overhang and on to the top. 80' **FA:** Forrest Gardner, Todd Wells (5/88)

> **Insider's Lament:** Thanks to global warming, Soapstone is more often dry then in times past.

Just past "Rapture Of The Steep" is an obvious drainage peppered with Class 2 and 3 ledges. Continue past this feature a short distance via the narrow trail to the next block of good rock.

⑮ Fascist Leader 5.11- ★★★
Proceed on bended knee? Surprisingly difficult ... features a sporty, authoritative crux. Start: Approximately 300' left of Soapstone, at several huge, flat slabs sprawled across the trail—you can't miss them. Climb a short, right-facing corner (capped by a large flat roof) for a few feet. Make a short, easy traverse left. Now follow an obvious weakness up through a shallow bowl past a fixed pin (crux) to the top. 80' **FA:** Jay Bell, Forrest Gardner (date unknown)

⑯ Truancy A2+
Start: 20' left of Fascist Leader. Aid over low roof and up seams (fixed bashie) leading past the right side of the Nazi Party Animal roof (see next route description.) Thin moves angling left "over the void." (staying just right of a huge roof) lead to a crack just below trees above. (80')
FA: Rick Mix, Todd Wells (1/99)

SUCK CREEK   Concentration Camp

17 Nazi Party Animal 5.9, A3 ★★★

An inspired solo ascent by "the master" — not for the squeamish. Heil Forrest! Start: 12' left of Truancy. Free climb a hand-sized crack (just past a large flat roof) for 30' to a huge roof. Nail right two moves, then back left. Dangle into space, nailing a horizontal seam on increasingly insecure wafers to a single rivet. Continue straight up the bulging headwall to the top. 130'
FA: Forrest Gardner, solo (10/88)

> Insider Tip: Don't forget your chest harness!

18 Caesar's Palace A4 ★★

Named for the site of one of motorcycle daredevil Evil Knievel's famous smash ups; don't let this climb be one of yours…. Start: 15' left of Nazi Party Animal, and just right of an obvious wide dihedral. Pitch #1: Turn a pair of low roofs and aid up seams via fixed heads to a hanging belay beneath the roof. (50') (A2+) Pitch #2: Move right on good gear, then launch directly out the ceiling on "esoteric" RURPs to a pair of rivets. Angle left up the headwall to the top. (95') (A4) FA: Rick Mix, Jeff Burton (date unknown)

> Insider Tip: A large hook (I'm laughing too) works well at the belay at the end of pitch #1.

19 Steggish Boy 5.10+ ★

Start: 5' left of Caesar's Palace. Climb through low roofs and up an obvious wide dihedral to slot (at left margin of giant roof). Climb left past slot and up wall above. Finish right of obvious flat (summit) roof. 100' FA: Shannon Stegg, Curtis Glass (date unknown)

> Insider's Note: I personally have not done this route, nor have I spoken to anyone who has. Nonetheless, I have given it "one star" (because it looks pretty good) but it may deserve more. Email me if you happen to do it and let me know what you think.

20 Crankin' Juicy 5.13a (sport) (chopped)

A controversial route that climbs up the center of a orange-dripped wall passing unique oppositional grips. This route's estimated difficulty was around 5.13a before the lead bolts were removed amid considerable controversy.
FA: Edward Yates & Johnathan Swader (Fall 2013)

21 Pleasure Burn 5.11

So decadent! Indulge yourself in the steamy, hot-blooded pleasures of southern sandstone … all rolled up into one fever-inducing encounter. Begin with a bit of engaging bouldering past a bolt (crux) in a corner capped by a tiny roof. Step left and climb a narrow corner capped by a stretch of moderate face climbing (run-out). Merge into short, right-facing corner capped by roof tiers; finish through these (crux) staying to the left. 100'
FA: Forrest Gardner, Jay Bell (date unknown)

SUCK CREEK

SUCK CREEK — Concentration Camp

㉒ Fire In The Belly 5.12 ★★
Fairly hot piece of free climbing, in spite of the upper face being a bit on the dusty side. Start: 30' left of Pleasure Burn. Smoke past three bolts (multiple cruxes) through small overhangs to a stem stance. Break left and burn up a funky steep face with sloping holds to a small roof capping the wall. Exit right beneath this, via off kilter moves, to the top. 100'
FA: Rob Robinson, Darrow Kirkpatrick (10/99)

㉓ The Burn Ward 5.11+ ★★
Forearm cooker and ego debrider — with a classic flamer finish. Start: 40' left of Fire In The Belly. Boulder a few moves off block to gain fingertip horizontal crack. Move right a few moves, now follow a crack up the wall to a small overhang. Conquer this and churn dead center up a very steep headwall (crux). 100' FA: Rob Robinson, Darrow Kirkpatrick, Justin Eiseman (10/97)

> **Insider's Tips:** Although the FA was done "on sight," I recommend you rap and clean it — the upper headwall seems to stay perpetually dirty. The crux is the very last move.

㉔ Aryan Way 5.10
Start: Same as for The Burn Ward. Boulder up the face, turn a small bulge via a thin crack. At roof above, step right. Continue straight to the top via an obvious weakness in the wall. 100' Alternate Start 5.9 Start: 10' left of the regular route. Climb an obvious right-facing corner with a hand crack.
FA: Shannon Stegg, Curtis Glass (80's)

㉕ A Matter Of Degrees 5.10+ ★★
A fairly hot free climb "designed" with the budding sandstone scholar in mind … minimum requirements for graduating to the summit include a bachelor's degree in gear placement and a high school education in route finding. Start: Around the corner, 20' left of Aryan Way/The Burn Ward. Face climb for 15', traverse right across wall (crux) just above the lip of a roof to gain a stance in a short corner. Climb this, turn a small roof, continue up a steep headwall (crux) with several "boulder problem style" moves to the top. 100' FA: Rob Robinson 10/97

> **Insider's Tips:** You may find the traverse hard to protect, but look hard high and low— there's bomber gear. Double ropes useful.

Rick Mix, 'Mini Big-Wall Belay' Photo Credit: Todd Wells Collection

SUCK CREEK

Concentration Camp

Just past A Matter Of Degrees is a break in the cliff line. Continue a short distance to the next block of rock: a large buttress peppered with lots of small, exfoliating roofs about 100' above the ground.

㉖ Mountaineer's Route 5.8+ ★ ☐
Start: Perhaps 100' left of A Matter Of Degrees. Pitch #1: Climb past loose blocks (just right of an obvious dihedral) to gain a series of solid shelves; gradually diagonal right (for a long ways) to a large grassy ledge with a large tree. (85') (5.7) Pitch #2: Climb directly up a broken buttress left of the tree (knifeblades protect this section well). At the top of the buttress angle right and mantle a large ledge. (75') (5.8) Pitch #3: Climb wall, turn orange roof above using a crack and horizontals. (35') (5.8+)
FA: Todd Wells, Forrest Gardner (11/93)

Insider's Tip: Rap back to the ledge at the top of pitch #1 (two ropes needed), then rap from a large tree to the base.

㉗ Steve McQueen Memorial 5.7, A4★ ☐
Start: 12' left of the Mountaineer's Route. Pitch #1: Climb a "pinched off" dihedral using a variety of hooks, heads and "tied off trinkets." Belay on a ledge. (80') (A4) Pitch #2: Climb left and out the roof via an obvious weakness to the top. (80') (5.8, A2)
FA: Forrest Gardner, Rick Mix (90's)

Insider's Tip: An additional belay above the second pitch roof may help reduce rope drag.

㉘ Zyklon B 5.7, A4 ☐
Start: Same as for Steve McQueen Memorial. Pitch #1: Same as for Steve McQueen Memorial. (80') (A4) Pitch #2: Aid up to and right beneath the roof, then out a blocky weakness to the top. (60') (5.8, A2+) **FA:** Forrest Gardner, Rick Mix (90's)

Insider's Trivia: Pitch two has been the scene of at least one headlong screamer.

www.rockerypress.com

SUCK CREEK

㉙ This Ewe's For Bud 5.11- ★★
Not for the "sheepish," one presumes. Start: 60' left of Zyklon B. Begin with a couple of interesting boulder moves, trend slightly left to stance at the base of a thin crack. Clip a fixed pin, power up (crux) to bulge with better holds. A fist crack leads to a ledge with a single bolt. Easier climbing leads to the tree ledge above. 100'
FA: Forrest Gardner, Todd Wells (mid 80's)

㉚ Corner Bar 5.8 ★★
It's happy hour in Suck Creek Canyon! Time to belly up to the wall for some classic jamming and stemming. Start: 5' left of This Ewe's For Bud. Climb a long, right-facing corner with lots of hand and finger jamming. As the corner ends, trend left to the top. 100' FA: Forrest and Donna Gardner (mid 80's)

Insider's Note: Swizzle stick optional.

㉛ Honeycomb Hideout 5.10+ ★★★
To bee or not to bee? By some accounts a real forearm stinger.
Start: Approximately 30' left of Corner Bar. Power up the wall on good but reachy holds above a ground level roof; pump into a wide open corner with ratchet lock jams. Crank past shakey flakes protected by a single bolt (left wall) to gain stance beneath a sweet 5' "honeycombed" roof. Turn this (crux) and buzz up the steep wall above to a cedar tree. 100'
FA: Tyler Stracker, Kirk Brode (5/08)

Suck Creek Super Classics
Rockwork Orange, 5.10- ☐
Five Roofs in Reverse, 5.10+ ☐
Special Olympics, 5.11 ☐
Rainbow Delta, 5.11 ☐
Anyway You Slice It, 5.12- ☐

Photo Credit: Micah Gentry

Cody Averbeck on the crux face of Anyway You Slice It, 5.12-

SUCK CREEK

Concentration Camp

Mein Kampf, 5.10

㉜ Ballew Balls 5.9 ★★★
Start: Walk about 50' left of Honeycomb Hideout where the trail passes beneath an over-hang. Start just past this at a large boulder in the trail. Undercling right past initial roof, pull into shallow corner with a hand crack. Climb the corner till it ends, continue up the face above, then traverse hard left for 40' to bolt anchors. 100' **FA: Kent Ballew, Forrest Gardner (date unknown)**

Insider's Afterthought: Don't forget to throw in a couple of pieces on the long traverse to cover your partner.

㉝ Commandant's Choice 5.10- ★★★
Ten hut! A favorite warm up route of the Camp regulars. Start: 15' left of Ballew Balls. Face climb past a fixed pin and up a shallow left-facing corner. Continue with a spate of crack climbing, finish with face moves, trending left to a good ledge with a pair of bolt anchors. 100'
FA: Forrest Gardner, Jay Bell (mid 80's)

㉞ Mein Commandant 5.10 ★★★
A popular route combining some of the best features of two superb routes. Start: Same as for Commandant's Choice. Climb Commandant's Choice for about 30'. Traverse left a few moves and join the thin crack and headwall of Mein Kampf (see next route description). 100'
FA: Todd Wells, Stuart Chapin (late 80's)

㉟ Mein Kampf 5.10
See description on page 222.

SUCK CREEK

㊱ Extreme Prejudice 5.11+ ★★★
Prepare to be terminated? Famous for its pissy boulder problem start (which has torched many an ego). The final headwall regularly sets the stage for "a cruel exercise in forearm annihilation"— and belayer entertainment! Start: 10' left of Mein Kampf. Boulder a few moves up the face (tech crux). Now face climb (also hard!) past three huge bolts to small ledge stance. Follow squiggly crack line peppered with face holds up a sustained and steep headwall to a ledge with bolt anchors. 100' **FA: Forrest Gardner, Jay Bell (mid 80's)**

㊲ March Into The Sea 5.11 ★★★
Start: 10' left of Extreme Prejudice. Climb a deceptively difficult crack to a ledge. Step right a few feet and begin weaving up the steep headwall, slowly trending right past several beefy cruxes to the anchors atop Extreme Prejudice. 100' **FA: Tyler Stracker, Kirk Brode 9/08**

Mein Kampf 5.10

Although the route itself presents a bit of ... a struggle, you may discover the real battle lies on the ground—with your partner—over who's gets the lead! Start: 5' left of Commandant's Choice. Climb a shallow slot-crack capped by a small overhang. Exit right, follow a squiggly crack line peppered with face holds up a (very) steep wall to a ledge with a pair of bolt anchors. 100' **FA: Forrest Gardner, Kent Ballew (mid 80's)**

Climber: Laban Swafford Photo Credit: Micah Gentry

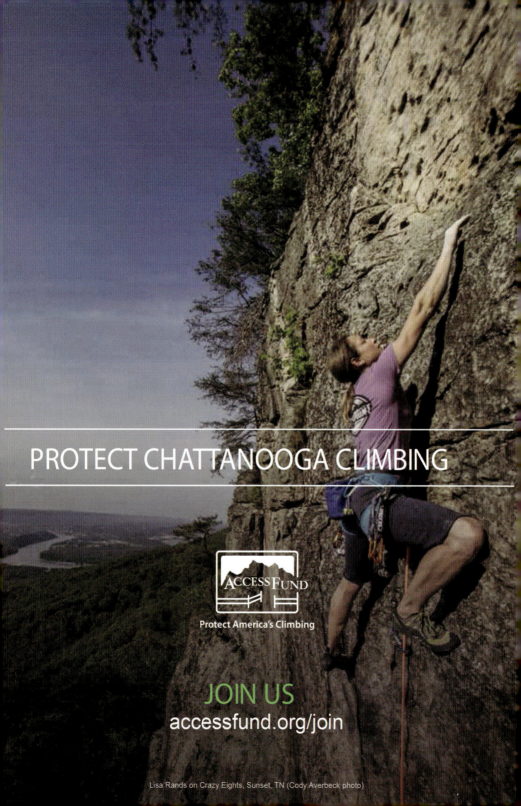

SUCK CREEK

Concentration Camp

38 Burstin' At The Seams 5.12 ★★★

Top out on this one, and your forearms will probably look like they've just fallen off the back of a watermelon truck. A real "down n' dirty" trad style hangfest. Start: Same as for March into the Sea. Climb a deceptively difficult crack to a ledge. Burst straight up a beautiful, seamy orange headwall. At the top, traverse right to the bolt station above Extreme Prejudice. 80'
FA: Rob Robinson (late 90's)

> Insider's Notes: The headwall is heinously sustained, with one very difficult crux near the top. I strongly suggest using double ropes. Not up for the lead? Toprope it! This a great piece of climbing!

39 Mountain Madness 5.12-

Sip (or is it slip) on this! Pooowerful good climbing ... packs a punch similar to a mason jar full o' copper-kettled moonshine. Start: 10' left of Burstin' At The Seams. Pitch #1: Climb an obvious, straight-in crack to a comfortable ledge. (35') (5.11-) Pitch #2: Continue up a splitter crack past a few fixed pins (in gorgeous orange rock) past a short, left-facing corner capped by a small roof. Over this (crux): diagonal right to the bolt station atop Extreme Prejudice. (45') (5.12-) FA Todd Wells, Scott Fisher, Forrest Gardner

> Insider's Tip: I recommend leading the second pitch with double ropes.

40 Rolling Rock 5.5, A3-

Start: 5' left of Mountain Madness. Climb a cracked stack of blocks resembling a small pyramid. Aid up a wide dihedral to a bolt at the base of a roof. 80'
FA: Todd Wells, Rick Mix (date unknown)

41 Mr. Big Stuff 5.10- ★★★

This "top hat" line will have you snappin' biners and twirling your nut tool. Start: 10' left of Rolling Rock. Strut right up an obvious, left-facing dihedral, sporting a 3" to 5" crack, to small ledges. Traverse left to the bolt station atop Any Way You Slice It. 80'
FA: Forrest Gardner, Todd Wells

42 Any Way You Slice It 5.12-

 See description on page 226.

SUCK CREEK

🔴 43 The Knockout Artist 5.12 ★★★

A respectable prize fight for up-and-coming heavyweight sandstone contenders. Better be light on your feet though, or you may find yourself foundering "on the ropes" in the standing-eight-count corner. Start: Same as previous. Face climb following the initial "Slice" crack to good stances. Diagonal left over a small roof past a couple of questionable (former aid?) clips, then up a very steep and technical corner (crux). Traverse right to the pair of bolts atop Any Way You Slice It. 80'
FA: Rob Robinson, John Barr (3/97)

> **Insider's Tips:** As luck would have it! ... an old, worn down #3 or #4 brass provides just enough "transition pro" beneath the tiny roof in the crux corner. In any event, use double ropes.

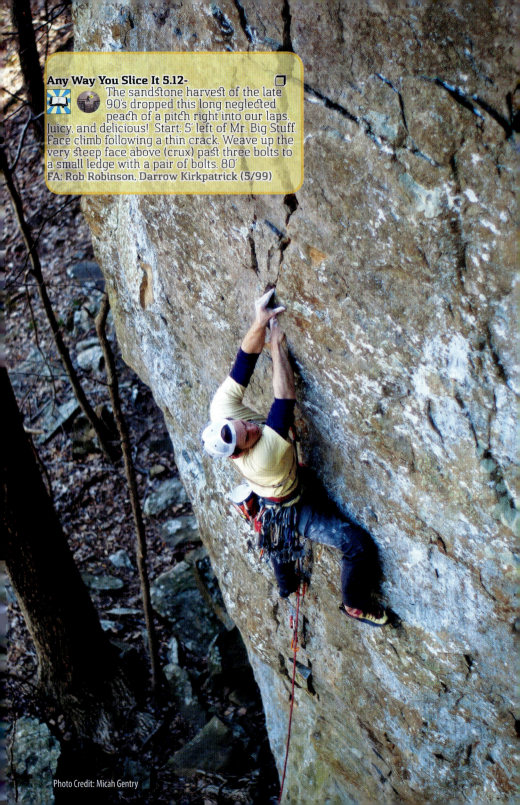

Any Way You Slice It 5.12-
The sandstone harvest of the late 90's dropped this long neglected peach of a pitch right into our laps. Juicy, and delicious! Start: 5' left of Mr. Big Stuff. Face climb following a thin crack. Weave up the very steep face above (crux) past three bolts to a small ledge with a pair of bolts. 80'
FA: Rob Robinson, Darrow Kirkpatrick (5/99)

Photo Credit: Micah Gentry

SUCK CREEK

㊹ Pilgrim's Progress 5.8+
Start: 20' left of The Knockout Artist. Climb an obvious, wide corner. At broken rock traverse left to a ledge with a tree. 50'
FA: Ed Marshall, Rick Mix (date unknown)

㊺ Shoot To Thrill 5.11+ ★
Start: 10' left of Pilgrim's Progress. Climb a corner for 15'. Follow a crack through a pair of stacked triangular roofs (crux). Continue to a ledge above. 60'
FA: Arno Ilgner, Jack Noonan (date unknown)

Ballew Balls, 5.9

SUCK CREEK　　　　　　　　　Concentration Camp

Layaway Plan, 5.10+

㊻ Fuhrer's Fury 5.12- ★
Start: 15' left of Shoot To Thrill. Boulder up the left side of a crackless arete for 15' to a bolt clip. Continue a few moves to a small roof. Smolder right along roof line for 12' (crux) to gain blotch of broken rock (directly above a large flat roof.) Continue to a ledge above. 60' **FA: Rick Mix, Ed Marshall, Todd Wells (date unknown)**

㊼ Layaway Plan 5.10+
A wildly popular but equally challenging climb. Might require a "lactic acid down payment" (or two!) before you're able to check out at the summit register. Start: 5' left of Fuhrer's Fury. Climb a long and superb crack line (crux) with small overhangs; "boulder" into a tricky scoop above. A bit more "crackin" leads out of the scoop ... now dodge right, now left, now up a short headwall to a narrow ledge and anchors. 100'
FA: Jack Noonan, Arno Ilgner (date unknown)

㊽ Diesel And Dust 5.11+ ★★★
In-your-face "Mack truck" power climbing, with two cruxes that'll do their best to ... knock your forearms out of alignment. Start: 5' left of Layaway Plan. Follow seams over bulge (crux) and up wall, conquer a roof (crux) guarding a very short, left-facing corner. Turn final hang and motor to a ledge above. 100'
FA: Rob Robinson, John Barr (10/97)

SUCK CREEK

49 Violent Twisting 5.10 ★
Start: 12' left of Diesel And Dust, and just right a wide corner with crack. Climb face with a short and shallow, left-facing corner. Continue up face above to right margin of a large square roof. Turn this on the right, now step into a nice dihedral capped by a small triangular roof. Hand traverse left, turn bulge and continue up the face to a ledge. 100'
FA: Todd Wells, Forrest Gardner (date unknown)

50 Elective Dentistry 5.10-
Start: 8' left of Violent Twisting, on the left wall of an obvious corner. Climb a short face following a seam past small ledges to gain big ledge above. Continue up the wall above via obvious weakness to another ledge. 100'
FA: Rick Mix, Ed Marshall (date unknown)

Andrew Miller exploding on all cylinders, Diesel & Dust, 5.11+ — Photo Credit: Micah Gentry

SUCK CREEK

51 Rainy Day 5.7 ★
Start: Around the corner and 30' left of Elective Dentistry. Follow an obvious left-facing dihedral up and right past several ledges to a narrow ledge with a couple of cedar trees. 90'
FA: Todd Wells, Perry Key (early 90's)

52 Heavy Hor's D'oeures 5.10, A3 ★★★
Here's one sandstone "dinner party" you won't soon forget. Bon apetit? Start: 5' left of Rainy Day, by a large rock pile in the trail.
Pitch #1: Free climb following obvious line of cracks in a cascading streak of eye-catching orange rock for about 70'. At this point, the rock quality begins to deteriorate—break out the aid gear. Continue up flakes, then gingerly alongside "the garage doors" (huge multi-layered, semi-detached "doomsday" flakes) past a rivet to a hanging belay. (90') (5.10, A3)
Pitch #2: Angle right and climb choss through an overhang to a large ledge with fixed pins. (60') (A3) Pitch #3: Move right from the ledge and up a strenuous slot to the top. (65') (5.9, A2)
FA: Todd Wells, Forrest Gardner (3/99)

Little Tree, 5.9+

> **Insider Tips**: Don't be sucked in by the appealing vertical features on pitch #2 ... the route goes straight over the roof via horizontal placements. Descent: Rap from trees back to ledge, fix gear (your own "throwaway pieces") and rap on to the ground. Note the pile of rocks in the trail at the climb's base ... these are the "heavy" hor's d'oeuvres!

(53) Squeezing Out Sparks 5.9+ ★ ❒
Start: 60′ left of Heavy Hor's D'oeures. Climb a short crack with small ledges for 10′ to a larger ledge. Place gear in thin corner above, climb face just right of this feature to gain an obvious horizontal weakness in wall. Continue up the face above via vertical cracks to a wide ledge. 80′
FA: Todd Wells, Jay Bell (date unknown)

(54) Fantastic Voyage 5.10, A2 ★★ ❒
Vertical journey to the overhangs at the end of your mind, or possibly the end of your rope. A beautifully exposed line on generally solid rock with outstanding wall position. Start: Same as for Squeezing Out Sparks. (See previous route description). Pitch #1: Climb Squeezing Out Sparks and belay on the big ledge at bolt station. (80′) (5.9+) Pitch #2: Climb right towards a huge alcove capped by a roof; belay on the right side of the alcove beneath a striking roof crack. (50′) (5.6) Pitch #3: Aid the crack out the roof to a stance with rivets on a steep headwall. (40′) (A1) Pitch #4: Climb directly up a steep orange headwall and through a weakness on the right side of the summit bulge. (pitch length unknown) (5.9) (A2) Alternate Starts: Kaboom!(5.10+), Club Fighter (5.10) or Little Tree (5.9+). If you do one of these routes, simply traverse across the big ledge (at the end of the pitch of your choice) to the bolt belay at the base of pitch two of Fantastic Voyage. **FA: Rick Mix, Ed Marshall (9/95)**

Insider's Tip: **Once on the summit: bushwhack left a bit; descend via two rappels.**

(55) Kaboom! 5.10+, A2 ★★ ❒
As the name implies: a trundler's delight. Expect some close (and exciting) "encounters" with loose rock on pitch two. Start: 10′ left of Squeezing Out Sparks/Fantastic Voyage. Pitch #1: Scramble 8′ to a ledge. Follow an elegant thin crack system up the wall, turn a small bulge, trend left to a thin crack in orange rock. Up this, then back right on to the bolt station on the large ledge above. (80′) (5.10+) Pitch #2: Climb directly up flakes to a huge orange protuberance split by a crack; aid out this and belay above. (50′) (A1)
Pitch #3: Continue up a steep headwall to the top. (50′) (A2) **FA: Forrest Gardner, Chris Chesnutt (7/89) FFA Pitch #1: Forrest Gardner, Jay Bell (90's)**

Insider's Notes: **Pitch #1 is a stellar free climb in and of itself. Descent from the summit: Same as for Fantastic Voyage (see route description.)**

(56) Club Fighter 5.10 ★★ ❒
Start: 20′ left of Kaboom!, at the right margin of a large, shallow recess that resembles a giant shoebox. Climb the right side of "the box." When feasible, traverse right to a short, left-facing flake on the face; continue straight up the wall above following a thin crack. Pass through a band of orange rock, work through bulge (crux) to gain a big ledge. 80′
FA: Forrest Gardner, Todd Wells (date unknown)

Suck

Memory Fog

I first ran into Forrest Gardner at the University of Tennessee at Chattanooga as a freshman student. Forrest had a pair of thick, wiry forearms which I imagined he could use to rip the crimped cap off a Coke bottle if the mood struck him. We teamed up at Sunset Rock first and began checking off established routes, then putting up dozens of new ones. On lead, after sizing up the gear, Gardner would frequently run it out — like he was shot from a bazooka — in a go-for-broke effort. Not surprisingly perhaps, he was also a bold free soloist. Many local climbers are familiar with the story of him climbing Euphoria (5.11) without a rope and doing the crux using a huge, airborne dyno. Later on in his climbing life Forrest channeled his energy into extreme aid routes. Many of his first ascents in the Southeast stand as lasting testaments to his ingenuity and boldness.

Forrest Gardner in his element.

Photo Credit: Todd Wells Collection

SUCK CREEK

Concentration Camp

SUCK CREEK

⑤⑧ Green Dreams 5.11- ★★
Begin in a left facing corner, to a pair of thin seams that merge with into the final moves of Club Fighter.

⑤⑨ Little Tree 5.9+ ★★★
Start: 8' left of Club Fighter, at the left side of a large, shallow recess that resembles a giant shoebox. Follow a prominent handcrack through a small roof (crux) and up the wall past a small tree growing in the crack till it ends. Merge into short orange corner (crux) capped by a large bulge. Bypass this on the right via face climbing (crux) and continue to the big ledge above. Belay here, or stroll right approximately 30' to a bolt belay station (at the top of Squeezing Out Sparks (see route description.)
FA: Todd Wells, Shannon Stegg (date unknown)

⑥⓪ Steggosaur 5.9+ ★★★
Start: 20' left of Little Tree. Follow a right-leaning, right-facing corner featuring a bit of "slot work" and plenty of burly hand and fist jamming. At the top of the corner, "tunnel" through a collection of cobbled overhangs. A crack above leads to a big flat ledge. 90'
FA: Shannon Stegg, Todd Wells (date unknown)

> **Insider's Tip:** Bring plenty of long slings and/or use double ropes.

⑥① Stracker/Eiseman 5.11+ ★★
Start: 5' left of Steggosaur. Follow a left facing corner to a squiggling crack that leads to a blunt, overhanging arete. Power through steep slots finishing at a single bolt anchor.
FA: Tyler Stracker, Justin Eiseman, 2013

⑥② Snag the Ear! 5.11- ★★
Start: same as Stracker/Eiseman. Follow a left facing corner to a stance below a series of horizontal 'pillowed' rails. Climb the steep rail features to a dynamic snag to a unique 'ear' feature. Climb the lower angle finish to a single bolt anchor.
FA: Tyler Stracker, Kirk Brode 2008

www.rockerypress.com 235

Johnathan Swader clawing up the final bulge of Steggosaur, 5.9+

Photo Credit: Micah Gentry

SUCK CREEK

63 Goin's Route 5.12 ★
Start: 10' left of Snag the Ear! Climb a narrow, overhanging corner with a thin crack for 15' to a 3' roof. Follow seam over this obstacle to a small stance. Face climb the steep wall above following a thin vertical seam to a sloping ledge. 40'
FA: Steve Goins

64 Chesnutt's Roof 5.11+
Start: 25' left of Goins' Route. Climb face with crack for 10'. Handrail out a small horizontal crack in large flat roof for 12'. Turn lip and continue up a featured face to a tree ledge. 40'
FA: Chris Chesnutt (date unknown)

65 Karate Chop 5.10 ★
Start: 75' left of Chesnutt's Roof. Boulder a few moves up a face with three short vertical seams. Continue through bulge above via a short handcrack (crux) to gain stance above. Wander up the left side of a featured arete to a ledge. 75'
FA: Todd Wells, Ed Marshall (date unknown)

Variation (Total Recall) 5.10 ★
Start: A few feet left of the regular start. Climb the face (crux) for 15'. Climb through a body-length corner, step right and join the regular route.
FA: Jeff Burton, Rick Mix (date unknown)

66 Couch Banana 5.9+ ★★
Start: 15' left of Karate Chop, and just left of a tree butted up against the cliff line. Sketch up face a few moves to gain good jams and gear in a short horizontal hand slot. Turn smooth bulge above (crux), work left into a short, shallow right-facing corner. Continue more or less straight up, or (better!) angle left through tan rock and finish following Dos Padres (see next route description.) 75'
FA: Ed Marshall, Paul Sloan (date unknown)

67 Dos Padres 5.8+ ★★★
Start: 15' left of Couch Banana, at a roof line just a few feet above the ground. Pull onto the face above a low roof using a couple of large solution pockets. Follow a thin crack above to a good ledge. Step right, climb a short right-facing corner. Turn bulge above defined by a distinct crack; continue up face to a small flat roof. Turn this, angle left up face to ledge. 90'
FA: Forrest Gardner, Todd Wells (90')

68 Crankus Maximus 5.10+ ★★
Start: 10' left of Dos Padres. Begin with a boulder problem move to turn a low roof, now turn a bulge and face climb past a fixed pin. Turn small roofs, step left and climb face for 10' to gain a good horizontal. Traverse right 10', turn another bulge to gain a vertical crack splitting a headwall; follow this to the top. 90'
FA: Todd Wells, Perry Key (1990)

69 Crowbar 5.10
Start: 10' left of Crankus Maximus. Boulder over low roofs (crux) and climb crack-filled face above for 15'. Turn 5' roof peppered with lots of flakes. Continue up an obvious weakness in wall to the top. 60'
FA: Todd Wells, Ed Marshall (date unknown)

70 Reach For The Sun 5.12- ★
Start: 15' left of Crowbar. Climb face for 15', claw through 15' of tiered flat roofs (fixed pin) via horizontal holds and some crack work. 50'
FA: Robyn Erbesfield (mid 80's)

PM
25 mins

The Upper Passes

The Upper Passes are home to the Canyon's greatest concentration of high quality free climbs. Darrow Kirkpatrick describes the area as "the little Tennessee Wall." Indeed, the climbing and rock quality are as good as the best that the Chattanooga area has to offer. Here you'll find a hard, compact band of grey sandstone (dappled with beautiful orange hues) that provides several killer crack lines, beautiful corners, the occasional roof puzzle and several gorgeous faces.

The walls are shady in the morning but baking in the sun by noon—making this a perfect destination for late fall through winter and on into spring. And thanks to the sun and cliff aspect, the walls tend to dry off very quickly after rain. If the T Wall is closed for managed hunts, the Upper Passes are the next best alternative.

Access: Scramble, skid, slide, tumble, roll or cartwheel down a short but very steep embankment following a few blazes to the creek below. Cross the creek via boulder hopping, wading, or a combination of the two. On the other side of the creek, just left of a pair of stacked boulders emblazoned with an "A" (for "airplane," which the stack resembles), is a large, angular blaze. Enter the woods just left of the "airplane" boulder pile, at a small and obvious gully. More blazes lead up a shallow stream bed; a storm drain which ends at a small and nondescript, crumbling "cliff." Here, a trail defined by more blazes zigs right up a short but steep hillside, then zags left into a narrow and well defined gully. Its a straight shot up this gully (no more blazes) to the base of the cliff.

Note: If you are are headed for the west (right) walls of the Upper Passes: look for a short climber's trail veering right through the woods just before the gully ends. This cuts out a final bit of steep scrambling.

Insider's Tips: Shorts and sandals come in handy if faced with a high water crossing. Determined to keep your boots on? Ah, you love a challenge! O.K., but bring an extra pair of socks; you'll appreciate a dry pair if you end up taking a bath. If it has rained recently for any length of time there's a good chance the creek will be impassable, so have a back up climbing plan. In general, allow one dry day to pass for every day of rain before assuming the creek can be crossed.

Photo Credit: Micah Gentry

SUCK CREEK

Upper Passes, Right

PM

35 mins

The Upper Passes – RIGHT

Welcome to Adventure! The following routes are located climber's right of the approach gully and see little to no traffic. There are some classic routes here, but don't expect them to be in the same clean, user-friendly condition that you might expect of 'normal' classics. Bring your wire brush and a 'sense of adventure!'

The Smith Wall is located a short distance right of the gully. The climbing is reminiscent of Jamestown, Alabama.

❶ Weird Load 5.9 ★

Start: On a ledge above the trail and approximatively 100' right of the gully. Climb short parallel cracks. Step left and continue upwards through a maze of blobby tan rock to a small roof. Turn this on the left and continue up the face above to the top. 90'

❷ Asleep at the Wheel 5.10- ★★★

Wake up for this one!
Start: 10' right of Weird Load. Landmark alert: Just left of the route is an 8' tall, rectangular boulder resting close to the cliff's base.
Boulder a few moves up a slabby face (crux). A faint left-angling ramp leads to a recess. Climb the short, shallow left-facing corner above (crux). Follow the line of least resistance through a tan band. Trend right to the top in a shallow, rounded left-facing corner (crux). 90'

❸ The Last Detail 5.9+ ★

Start: Same as for Asleep At The Wheel. Boulder a few moves up the slabby face. At the base of a faint, left-angling ramp step right and climb a steep face cross-hatched with shallow cracks. Meander through band of broken rock, continue up headwall above to the top. (90')
FA: Rob Robinson, Gene Smith (5/83)

❹ Roadkill Bill 5.10- ★

Start: right of previous. Scramble up a couple of ledges to the base of the climb. Climb face for 10' to a roof. Step right, tiptoe up a short orange corner (crux) split by a seam. Feint left a few moves and climb blobby rock on right side of small arete to the top. 50'
FA: Rob Robinson, rope solo (12/02)

Past the Smith Wall are several un-recorded or never-climbed routes, including a striking right-facing corner crack which has been climbed but never named.

Amplitude 5.8

Suck Creek super classic: The best 5.8 in the canyon ... equal in quality to any dihedral for the grade found at the Tennessee Wall. Start: 10' right of Tora Bora.
Face climb following a short thin crack for a few feet. Diagonal right across a couple of small ledges. Continue to the top in a long, wide-angle dihedral tattooed with a patch of orange. 75'
FA: Rob Robinson, Eric Janoscrat (10/81)

Insider's Errata: Needs a bit of brushing ... please help clean it up a bit if you happen to have a wire brush in your pack. The crux is just below the patch of orange.

SUCK CREEK

Rob Robinson on the First Ascent of Amplitude, 5.9+. Photo Credit: Rob Robinson Collection

SUCK CREEK — Upper Passes, Right

❺ Kandahar Falls 5.9 ★
Start: One ledge down, and right of Roadkill Bill.
Turn a tricky overhang (crux) to gain slabby face. Trend right to the base of a prominent arete. Finish up a left-facing corner with crack. 50'
FA: Rob Robinson, rope solo (12/02)

❻ Tora Bora 5.9 ★
Start: At trailside, 10' right of Kandahar Falls.
Scramble up the wall and climb a short wedge-shaped corner, exit right around roof and continue to the base of the prominent arete. Step left and finish up the final corner of Kandahar Falls. 60'
FA: Rob Robinson, rope solo (12/01)

❼ Amplitude 5.8
See description on page 240.

❽ Alternate Start 5.9+ ★★
Start: 10' right of the regular start.
Climb a short and broken left-facing dihedral for 20' (with a small roof on its left wall). Join the corner and continue to the to top.

❾ Wash Board Blues 5.10- ★★
Slip sliding away....
Start: Same as for the Amplitude Alternate Start.
Climb the Amplitude alternate start for 20' to a stance. Work right one or two moves, then over a small boulder problem overhang (crux). Tiptoe up the water-polished "washboard" arete (past another crux or two) to the top. 75'
FA: Rob Robinson, top rope (spring, 2002)

SUCK CREEK

🔟 Golden Delicious 5.10 ★★★
One of the juiciest sandstone apples plucked from Suck Creek's "produce section."
Start: Same as for Wash Board Blues. Climb Wash Board Blues for 20' to a stance. Worm right and up short, shallow corners to gain an imposing open face. Peel right up the face ... turn bulge (crux) using a couple of sweet crimps. 75'
FA: Rob Robinson, Alex Kirkpatrick, Darrow Kirkpatrick (12/02)

⓫ Without Worms 5.10 ★
Start: right of Golden Delicious. Scramble up small ledges and climb face with thin cracks on right side of arete. Exit left onto the Golden Delicious face and continue to the top. 75'
Variation: Once on the Golden Delicious Face: Climb right and up a juggy arete to the top.

SUCK CREEK

Upper Passes, Right

PM

35 mins

The Auschwitz Buttress

Just right of a seasonal waterfall is a 200' high stack affectionately known among local 'storm troopers' as the 'Auschwitz Buttress.' The rock quality that comprises the stack's base is nice and solid; classic, clean lines compete for the slither of rope and tinkling of a rack. But lording over this benign band is a heaving hellscape of huge crumbling overhangs. Giant, tiered layers of rock ripple towards a surreal skyline in metastatic, angular waves that crash into one another along the way. Gaze up into this beast, and you'll swear it can't be real! But it is! Moreover, the routes are actually fun to climb -- in, uh, a demented sort of way. So it's 'on belay and on to the top' if you dare; do so, and you'll be rewarded by some of the most exciting 'asymmetrical' rock-a-neering Suck Creek has to offer!

⑫ **Battle Wagon 5.10-** ★★
Mount your choss chariot and ride for the sky! The rock Gods favor the brave! Start: on the left side of the formation in an obvious right facing corner.
Pitch #1: Climb a classic open book corner to a ledge system and change corners into another right-facing dihedral that leads to a ledge and tree (80') (5.8)
Pitch #2: Leave the ledge and meander up and left to the base of an undulating stacked arete. (5.9)
Pitch #3: From the belay, climb up and right of the arete for several body lengths, then move left around the point to a ledge and pin (possible to belay here). Next, continue up on the left side passing some thin crack features. When the wall steepens, cautiously move right to more 'crack' features to where it becomes possible to access a summit chimney and ledges. Scamper to the top (510-).
FA: Clint Henley, Peter Henley, Forrest Gardner, 1981

⑬ **Hate Crime 5.10** ★
Start: same as Battle Wagon.
Pitch #1: Climb a classic open book corner to a ledge system and change corners into another right-facing dihedral that leads to a ledge and tree (80') (5.8)
Pitch #2: From the belay ledge, clamber up and right to a ledge. When the wall steepens, find a crack on the left and climb through bulging rock and mantel onto another ledge.
Tread lightly towards another ledge and a fixed pin & belay (45') (5.10-)
Pitch #3: Trampse left on the ledge to a series of pins leading out a loose, blocky face. Find a handcrack and meander out left and right to a mantel maneuver and belay. (55') (5.10)
Pitch #4: Easy climbing on ledges leads to the summit. (40') (5.7)
FA: Forrest Gardner, Jay Bell, 1987
FFA: Todd Wells, Mark Cartwright (12/02)

> **Insider's Tidbit:** Formerly an A4 route

⑭ **The Auschwitz Crack 5.11-** ★★★
A classic pitch in its own right and the preferred start to the 'upper stack' routes. Start: 10' right of the starting corner for Battle Wagon / Hate Crime.
Climb a long, straight-in jam crack to a ledge. (80')
FA: Forrest Garder, Todd Wells

> **Insider's Trivia:** This was the original start to Hate Crime.

⑮ **Blood Assurance 5.9, C1**
Start: same as Battle Wagon / Hate Crime.
Pitch #1: Climb the corner of Battle Wagon.
Pitch #2: Climb part of the 2nd pitch of Hate Crime, breaking right to a thin crack in a bulge (C1).
Pitch #3: Finish on the final pitch of Whack and Dangle.
FA: Todd Wells & Rick Mix, 1999

SUCK CREEK

SUCK CREEK

Upper Passes, Right

⑯ Clay Fighter 5.10 ★
Start: same as Auschwitz Crack.
Pitch #1: Climb the first 20' of the straight in Auschwitz Crack to a ledge where it is possible to traverse out right to a loose ledge and belay. (60') (5.8)
Pitch #2: From the belay ledge, climb between loose ledges (optional belay) aiming for a giant bombay right facing flake system. Stay just right of this flake, climbing from here to the top. (100') (5.9)

⑰ Whack and Dangle 5.8, A2+ ★
Start: 20' right of Clay Fighter.
Pitch #1: Climb easy, ledgy terrain to a ledge and belay (80') (5.7)
Pitch #2: From the belay ledge, the route crosses over Clay Fighter, hacking towards the steep cornice above with a rotten chimney feature 40' (A2+)
Pitch #3: Aid through the cornice of choss via the shale slot which leads to a ledge above 30' (A2+)
Pitch #4: Climb a long, featured face to the top 100' (5.6)

Scholarly in appearance and perpetually sporting a pair of round, gold rimmed glasses, Todd Wells is a teacher by profession and as well a "rock scholar with a Ph.D.". Its a degree he earned by dent of a lifelong dedication to the art of climbing — an art which he has pursued with a largely private, but relentless, passion. A strong advocate for traditional routes, Todd's impact on the local climbing scene resonates to this day. The wild and untamed aid routes found on the soaring walls of Suck Creek Canyon have always had a special place in his heart.

Memory Fog

Todd Wells doing his summit dance.

Photo Credit: Todd Wells Collection

SUCK CREEK

Upper Passes, Right

⑱ Star Tide Rising 5.12- ★★★
Start: at the left margin of the orange outcrop.
Diagonal right up the wall, following a striking thin crack system. Boulder through roof complex (crux) protected by a future pair of bolts. Continue straight up the overhanging headwall to the top. 60'

Insider's Unfinished Business: This pitch has not yet had the bolts added and has not been led. INCREDIBLE PITCH.

FA: Kirk Brode & Rob Robinson (top rope) (1/02)

⑲ Variation 5.11- ★
At the top of the thin crack system ... traverse left a few moves, then climb straight up through a band of orange rock to the top.

FA Variation: Kirk Brode (top rope) (1/02)

Just right of the previously mentioned routes the trail drops down a short but steep hill. Scramble right across jumbled boulders, beneath a buttress capped by several impressive overhangs. Right of the overhangs is a steep wall with a couple of smaller roofs and lots of mixed features. Towards the right side of this wall, locate a couple thin parallel finger cracks running up the face, just left of a left-facing corner.

⑳ Art-a-Majig 5.10 ★★
A sustained jug haul with lots o' variety. Hard-to-forge rests.
Turn a small roof and climb short, parallel finger cracks to gain a line of good holds leading up and left into a short, left-facing corner (bypassing small roofs.) Solve a tricky face move a bit higher, now trend left to the top. 60'

FA: Rob Robinson, Darrow Kirkpatrick (late 1990's)

This corner has been climbed, but the details are unrecorded.

Verena Draper on the final roof traverse of Shelob, 5.8

Photo Credit: Micah Gentry

SUCK CREEK

Upper Passes, Left

PM

25 mins

The Upper Passes – LEFT

If the hike has left you 'unconvinced,' do yourself a favor and head to this area to sample the highest concentration of classic climbs that Upper Passes has to offer. Pick a line, any line - at, near, or around Rainbow Delta, and you may reconsider your initial impression! The following routes are described from right to left of the approach gully.

❶ Tombstone 5.10+ ★★★

A bit of a roof brawl, but not to worry; offers good gear despite its allusive appellation (which refers to the huge flake chinked in the roof.)
Start: 15' left of the intersection formed by the landslide gully and base of the cliff.
A classic 15' finger crack leads to a ledge. A thinner crack continues to large tiered roofs split by an obvious weakness. Conquer these (crux); continue to the top via a jam crack. 70'
FA: Rob Robinson, Eric Janoscrat (12/81)

❷ Sandstone Cemetery 5.9 ★

Start: 150' left of Tombstone.
Scramble to ledge, turn roof at crack. Pass a second roof, then follow an obvious, left-curving hand crack (crux). Finish up and right across slabs. 75'
FA: Rob Robinson, Marty Gibson (10/81)

Rockwork Orange, 5.10-

Rob Robinson on the First Ascent of Tombstone, 5.10+   Photo Credit: Rob Robinson Collection

SUCK CREEK

Upper Passes, Left

❸ Shelob 5.8 ★★
Classy stem job; if you're on the 5.8 circuit you'll want to "brave the hike up" and do it.
Start: 70' left of Sandstone Cemetery. Climb an acute angle corner capped by a large roof. Traverse right to a ledge. 75'
FFA: Peter Henley, Forrest Gardner (10/81)

> **Insider's History Note:** Large spiders web the corner when climbing traffic falls off. The name references the huge arachnid in Lord of the Rings.

❹ Rockwork Orange 5.10-
One of the Chattanooga area's finest, most esthetically pleasing 5.10's ... need I say more?
Start: 5' left of Shelob.
A short, moderately difficult crack leads to a small recess. Climb cracks above (lesser crux) to good stances. Above lies a classic, left-facing corner. Improvise (crux) to the top. 75'
*Alternate Start: Climb a thin crack just left of the regular start.
FA: Rob Robinson, Gene Smith (5/83)

❺ The Cauldron 5.11+ ★★★
A complex witch's brew ... bubbling over with a hodgepodge of heavenly rock and calamitous cruxes. Wear ruby slippers, bring magic rope.
Start: 30' left of Rockwork Orange.
Pitch #1: Climb wall for 15', turn roof via hand crack; continue to tiered roofs. Step right, pull up, labor left (crux) to a small standing belay. (50') (5.11+)
Pitch #2: A thin crack seams the white wall above the belay. Follow it (crux) to a small band of orange overhangs (lesser crux). Easier rock lies above. (50') (5.11+)
FA: Forrest Gardner, Clint Henley (fall/82)
FFA: Rob Robinson, Philip Fisher (9/84)

Verena Draper on the immaculate orange stone of Rockwork Orange, 5.10- Photo Credit: Micah Gentry

SUCK CREEK

Upper Passes, Left

PM
25 mins

Rainbow Delta Wall

Did I hike up here for a big grey and brown slab!? No, no, no - don't let the muddled, neutral tones of this wall deceive you --- this is one of the tallest, most vertical and hyperly sustained walls of splitter cracks found in the Chattanooga area -- unparalleled quality & movement!

First Ascent of Confetti Fingers, 5.11+

❻ Panty Raid 5.11- ★
Start: 50' to 75' left of The Cauldron. Climb a steep, pocketed face. 80' **FA:** Forrest Gardner, Peter Henley (8/86)

❼ Native Tongue 5.11+ ★★★
A seraphic "sermon in stone." Listen close enough, and you may hear the sandstone Muse whispering in your ear. Start: 5' left of The Powers Of Will. Scramble up crack to ledge. Churn past overhang (lesser crux) at cracked block with thin crack. Turn small roof above capped by an overhanging face. A seam leads to a bulge, sans holds. Assemble moves (crux), escape to easy rock and the top. 100'
FA: Rob Robinson, Steve Goins (4/93)

> **Insider's Tip:** Use double ropes. The top piece of pro at the crux is a #1 or #2 steel which you can high clip with a second rope. May be as hard as 5.12-.

❽ Rainbow Delta 5.11
The archetypal crack of gold at the end of the sandstone rainbow. Start: Same as for Native Tongue. Climb a long, left-arching, finger-to-shallow-hands crack. From a small ledge above: Finish up a short face. 100'
FA: Rob Robinson, Peter Henley (10/81)

> **Insider's Notes:** This incredible line is one of my all-time favorite 5.11 sandstone cracks. Unusually sustained, though I don't feel any single move is harder than "middlin' 5.10." I recommend taping up if 5.11 is your limit—tape will allow you to "sag" onto the jams for better rests. Superb for toproping laps as well.

SUCK CREEK

9 Confetti Fingers 5.11+
Delta's distinguished companion, and the "other crack" at the end of the sandstone rainbow. Start: 20' left of Rainbow Delta. Flutter over small roof with power sequence. Climb a long, fingers-to-hands crack capped by a hold-less bulge. Float over this (crux); finish straight past small ledge to the top. 100' **FA: Rob Robinson, Robyn Erbesfield (7/84)**

Insider's Note: The crux is comparable to Native Tongue. Bring tiny steel nuts if you want "gear at your nose" for the hardest moves. Double ropes recommended for high clip to manky steel at crux.

10 Sea of Slopers 5.12- ★★★
One of the best trad face pitches for the grade in the Chattanooga area. Start: 10' left of Rainbow Delta. Layback over low overhang using large, cracked block. A short jam crack leads to a ledge. Turn the small overhang above, then climb a spectacular, steep face laced with shallow thin cracks capped by a blank-looking bulge. Finish to fixed anchors. 100'
FA: Rob Robinson, Cody Averbeck (2008)

Insider Tips: Double ropes recommended. Small to medium wires, lots of small Aliens and TCU's.

Cody Averbeck on the technical upper jams of Rainbow Delta, 5.11 Photo Credit: Micah Gentry

SUCK CREEK

⑪ Big Leg 5.9 ★
Start: In a giant, right-facing corner 10' left of Sea of Slopers.
Climb a narrow chimney — with a bit of sporty offwidth — to the top. Traverse left to anchors. 80'
FA: Marty Gibson, Rob Robinson (12/81)

> Insider's Tip: Bring some big cams, including "Big Bro's" if you've got'em.

⑫ Sundown Syndrome 5.11- ★★★
Start: 10' left of Big Leg.
Climb a short face to ledge. Continue up the bulging wall above past two bolts to a ledge with anchors. 90'
FA: Tyler Stracker, Steve Curtis, Cody Averbeck (10/08)

⑬ Agony to Ecstasy 5.10+
Start: 15' left of Sundown Syndrome.
Pitch #1: Jam and layback a crack through a minefield of disintegrating roofs. Belay at a small ledge. (40') (5.10+)
Pitch #2: Step left around arete where feasible; continue to the top.(60') (5.6)
FA: Robyn Erbesfield, Rob Robinson (alt. leads) (7/84)

⑭ On Any Sunday A2 ★★
Most good Suck Creek aid climbs are notoriously loose, but not this one. A surprisingly solid, clean-looking natural line.
Start: 25' left of Agony To Ecstasy.
Nail, hook and nut through an imposing block of tiered roofs capped by a headwall. 100'
FA: Forrest Gardner and partner (late 80's)

> Insider's "bird dog": Long overdue for a free ascent.

⑮ Star Search 5.9 ★★
Nifty space shot for the up-and-coming sandstone astronaut. "Starship troopers" can tack on the more difficult direct finish for added fun.
Start: 200' left of Agony To Ecstasy. Face climb alongside a pair of thin cracks that fade out. Traverse right across a low-angle slab to the top. 80'
FA: Rob Robinson, Mike Lewis (1/83)

> Insider's Tip: Combine with the direct finish for an overall three star climb.

⑯ Direct Finish (Reach for the Sky) 5.11+ ★★
Start: On a ledge at the top of Star Search. A classic jam crack splits a black, 10' roof. 45'
FA: Marvin Webb, Forrest Gardner (8/86)

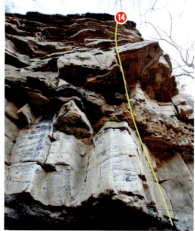

Malevolence Wall

25 mins

The Malevolence Wall area offers a hodge podge of decidedly mediocre to abysmally poor quality lines with loads of loose rock, but if its adventure climbing you're looking for then welcome, my demented, self-loathing friend!

All this said, the classic Malevolence Wall route, 'Bombs Away' 5.8 which clocks in at an astonishing 250' in height has become a 'popular' introduction to suck creek upper stack routes.

Area Access: As you cross the bridge at the mouth of the Canyon, drive for 1.1 miles and park on the right by a white blaze on the guardrail. Descend to the creek, cross it, hike uphill paralleling a small streambed. As the hillside steepens, begin diagonaling right to the cliff's base. Total time from car to cliff's base: approximately 20 minutes.

Insider's Tips: Even in the summertime, you can view this buttress from the parking pull off. You now know where you need to get to; now go get there.

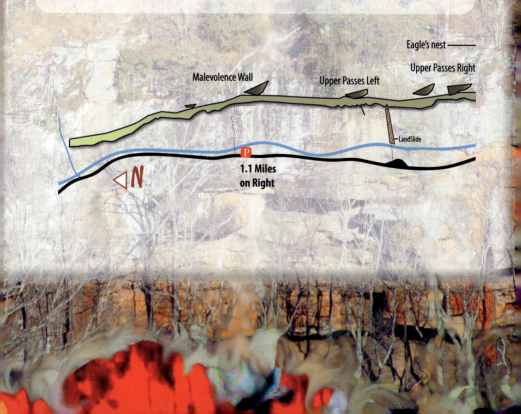

SUCK CREEK — Malevolence Wall

❶ Shock Collar 5.9
Pitch #1: Climb the first pitch of Flying Fortress (See below) and move hard left to belay. 80' (5.8)
Pitch #2: Climb a crack left of the overhead arete and then move back right at a break and belay. 60' (5.9)
Pitch #3: Climb up and right passing broken, loose terrain and a slot that leads to lower angle terrain up high. 60' (5.9)

FA: Todd Wells, Ed Marshall (2000)

❷ Flying Fortress 5.10- ★
Soaring to approximately 250', this is one of the tallest walls in the Chattanooga area. Although the first one third of the wall is comprised of mostly solid rock, the upper two thirds was described by the FA party as "free climbing on the loosest rock imaginable." Plan on carrying a full trad rack — and also bring ten pitons (with an emphasis on knife blades). A "must do" for hard core canyon aficionados.
Start: At the left side of the wall and about 50' left of Bombs Away.
Pitch #1: Climb a combination slab and corner. Belay up and right. 80' (5.8)
Pitch #2: Traverse right a few moves and climb a rotten band of rock for about 25' then turn a small roof. Belay on a ledge above. 75' (5.10-)
Pitch #3: Work directly up the overhanging wall above following disconnected cracks. Head left to a ledge above and belay. 75' (5.10-)
Pitch #4: Wander through a couple of bulges to the top. 50' (5.6)

FA: Peter Henley, Clint Henley, Forest Gardner (5/84)

❸ Bombs Away 5.8+ ★★
A great introduction to Suck Creek 'Upper Stack' routes. The moderate grade and relatively solid rock gives this route a 'popular' reputation.
Start: 50' right of Flying Fortress.
Pitch #1: Clamber up to a ledge and climb a right-facing flake, whereupon a step right will deposit you at a base of a bulging wall. Climb through a slot here and climb up and right to a big grassy ledge. Look 30' to your left for a cedar tree with slings. 140' (5.8)
Pitch #2: Leave the belay on the left side (loose) and aim for a big right-facing corner with good rock and gear in horizontals that lead to a ledge and tree belay. 100' (5.8+)
Pitch #3: From here, head generally up and left passing very loose blocks to the summit 75' 5.8 (70')

FA: Forrest Gardner, Peter Henley (1985),
FFA: Mark Cartwright, Todd Wells (1999)

❹ Sand Jive 5.10+
Start: A couple of hundred feet right of Flying Fortress and, more notably, some 20' right of an easily identifiable, bloodred streak staining the wall.
Climb a long, left-facing corner peppered with boulder problem moves to a large roof. Finish left with a moderate but unprotected hand traverse along a sandy horizontal crack to a ledge. 85'

FA: Forrest Garner, Rob Robinson (5/84)

❺ Finders Keepers 5.9+ ★★
Climb an excellent dihedral with an arching finger crack splitting the right side of the upper wall. 70'

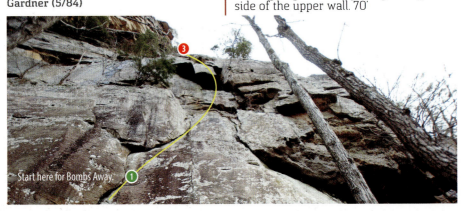

SUCK CREEK

Hidden Wall

Hidden Wall offers fast access and several nice chunks of high quality rock. The Ramp is one of the Canyon's few decent 5.8's. Five Roofs In Reverse (5.10+) features an enticing crack line slicing through a virtual tidal wave of overhangs, while next door is The Puzzle Palace — you'll want to be a solid 5.11 climber to do either of the latter. Odyssey, checking in at 5.12, is one of the few sport routes in the canyon. Around the corner and beyond the whine of canyon traffic are several superb, must-do routes ... 5.10 climbers should take the time to find Needle In The Haystack, and 5.11 climbers should try their hand at sewing up The Thread That Runs So True or Let's Dance. 5.12 climbers should add the sustained and elegant Strictly Ballroom to their tick list of face climbs.

Access: As you cross the bridge at the mouth of the Canyon ... wind up into the canyon for 1.6 miles. Park at a small pull-out in front of a guard rail marked by a yellow and black safety reflector. (Also look for a large white blaze on a tree.) Look right, and you'll see a prominent block of rock peeking through the trees. Descend a steep slope, cross a creek, wind up the adjoining hillside littered with boulders to the base of the cliff. Total hiking time from car to cliff: about 15 minutes.

Insider's Tip: You can almost always manage a creek crossing even it its been raining, since it is a smaller stream that feeds into the main Suck Creek tributary. If its been raining a lot, however, you may have to hike upstream a bit to find a suitable spot to cross.

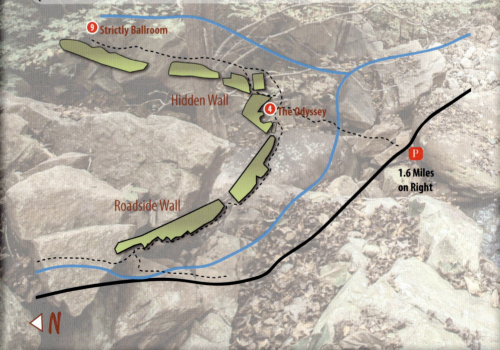

SUCK CREEK
Hidden Wall

15 mins

Five Roofs in Reverse

This box-like alcove offers several chunks of high quality rock. The centerpiece of this area is a tall, orange and tan buttress offering several very tall and very high-quality routes. Make sure you don't miss the classics, Five Roofs in Reverse and the Odyssey

❶ The Ramp 5.8 ★★
Start: Hike up from the creek bed (as described previously, see page) and you'll come to a jutting block of rock. Locate a very obvious ramp running left up the wall. 80'
FA: Peter Henley, Rob Robinson (2/81)

❷ The Puzzle Palace 5.11+ ★★★
Sandstone jigsaw artists on the prowl for unusual rock puzzles should check this brainteaser out.... Start: Same as for The Ramp. Climb a right-facing corner for 10'. Turn a tiny overhang on the right wall of the corner ... crawl into a cave strewn with blocks. Step off big block and turn roof of cave (classic!) and continue in a short, right-facing corner (watch for loose block at end?).

Traverse left a few feet and climb another short corner. Continue up a steep, small, left-facing corner. Turn devious, small bulge above split by a thin crack (crux); finish left past a small roof. 80'
FA: Rob Robinson, Darrow Kirkpatrick (5/97)

> Insider's Tips: Double ropes will help minimize rope drag. Regardless, bring plenty of runners. Cryptic clue for the crux: You don't have to be a wizard of cracks to succeed.

❸ Five Roofs In Reverse 5.10+
Boot camp for the 5.10 sandstone warrior ready to graduate to the 5.11 trad battlefield. Be prepared to kick ass ... or have yours kicked. Semper fi. Start: 10' right of The Ramp/The Puzzle Palace. Follow an obvious crack line (mostly hands) linking shallow corners and as many as five roofs. Multiple cruxes. 100'
FA: Rob Robinson, Peter Henley (2/81)

> Insider's Tips: In addition to a hefty rack of cams, I recommend using double ropes and carrying at least a dozen runners.

Laban Swafford blooming on Five Roofs in Reverse, 5.10+ Photo Credit: Micah Gentry

❹ **The Odyssey 5.12b (sport)**
Nice clip n' trip through the vertical world. Start: 10' right of Five Roofs In Reverse. Follow a line of bolts up a very steep wall and out through overhangs. 80'
FA: Travis Eiseman (9/99)

Photo Credit: Micah Gentry

SUCK CREEK
Hidden Wall

❺ Equal Rights 5.10+ ★
Start: 200 yards right of The Odyssey, on the left wall of an obvious large alcove capped by roofs. Climb an overhanging left-facing corner barred by small roofs; polish off a short but blank-looking wall. 40'
FA: Greg Collins, John McKigney (12/82)

❻ Needle In The Haystack 5.10+ ★★
Never know what you'll find if you keep digging around in the "Suck Creek haystack".... Start: 230' right of Equal Rights. Climb an obvious, straight-in crack system with fun finger and hand jams. Finish in a steep, bowl-shaped dihedral. 60'
FA: Rob Robinson, Darrow Kirkpatrick (4/97)

❼ The Thread That Runs So True 5.11 ★★★
A well-tailored line, though a bit hard to hang on and sew up — a stickler of sorts. Start: 10' right of Needle In The Haystack. Follow a thin crack up a steep and sustained blank-looking wall. 60'
FA: Rob Robinson, Peter Henley (8/81)

F.A. of Equal Rights, 5.10+

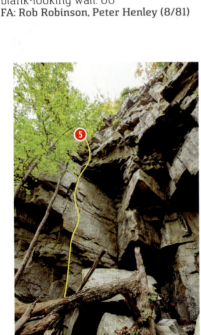

SUCK CREEK

⑧ Last Feast Of The Crocodiles 5.11- ★★
Hungry for a little pump? Sink you teeth into this savory sandstone snack. Start: several hundred feet right of The Thread That Runs So True. Chow down on a shallow right-facing corner with fingerlocks to a 2' roof split by a crack. Turn this, thrash right (crux) and finish via a bulging crack to a tree and the top. 50'
FA: Rob Robinson, Darrow Kirkpatrick (5/97)

Insider's Challenge: Can you find the no-hands "on-the-heels" rest stem in the corner?

⑨ Strictly Ballroom 5.12 ★★★
Features a brilliant, opening sequence worthy of a Baryshnikov. Belongs on the tick list of all "lords of the dance." Extremely sustained. Start: 15' right of Last Feast Of The Crocodiles. Power over a 2' roof and tango up a dead vertical face split by "R.P." seams. Continue straight up the wall above (avoiding a crack on the left near the finish.) 50' **FA:** Rob Robinson, Darrow Kirkpatrick (5/97)

Insider's Tip: If you want to do this amazing route (but not lead it) I suggest you do Last Feast, step right to trees and rig a toprope.

The Roadside Wall

PM — 10 mins

The Roadside Wall was the first crag in the Canyon to be developed. Hardly surprising, since you could practically hit the wall with a block of chalk from the parking pull-off. The cliff line is jam-packed (like a "Whitman's Sampler candy box") with a wide variety of tasty climbs. Bon appetit!

Access: As you cross the bridge at the mouth of the Canyon ... drive for 1.8 miles. When you see an obvious cliff line paralleling the road, immediately pull off at a wide parking spot on the right (after a sharp, right hand curve.) Look for a white blaze on the guardrail. Don't cross the creek here. Instead, walk uphill paralleling the guard rail for 175 yards and cross where the creek is practically right next to the road. You'll also find a white blaze on the guardrail at this point. (Insider's Note: You can also park here, but by parking downhill you can generally keep an eye on your vehicle.) Diagonal right up a short, steep embankment and follow a trail hugging the cliff's base to the right. Hiking time from car to crag: 10 minutes.

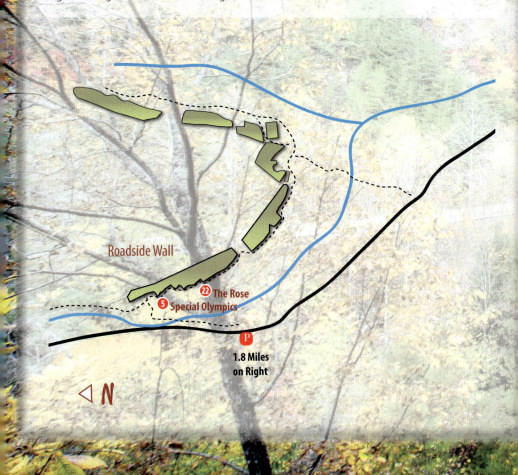

Roadside Wall
5 Special Olympics
22 The Rose
P 1.8 Miles on Right
◁ N

Emily Hon on GPS Crack, 5.9
Photo Credit: Micah Gentry

SUCK CREEK — Roadside Wall

Special-O Wall

NO
10 mins

Ok, well if you're THAT climber that is only here because T-WAll is closed, then let's face it, just come to this wall! Canyon locals will roll their eyes and call you cliche, but it's only because they know it's true ---- this is one of the best, most easily accessible clusters of routes in the canyon.

❶ A Good Root 5.10
Start: By a giant hemlock, about 300' right from where the trail begins at the cliff's base.
Root over rough roof and jam a short crack. Step left, climb a similar crack to the top. 25'
FA: Marvin Webb, Peter Henley (12/81)

❷ Jawbone 5.8
Start: 100' right of A Good Root. Climb a right-facing flake. 40'
FA: Rob Robinson, et. al. (2/81)

❸ Nifty Nine 5.9 ★★
Continuous, "cool" corner designed for the 5.9 climber. Start: 100' right of Jawbone. Climb a left-facing dihedral. 50'
FA: Rob Robinson, Forrest Gardner, Water Forbes 5/80

❹ Battle of the Bulge 5.12 (sport) ★★
Start: Same as for Nifty Nine.
"Special O's" denigrated cousin—a survivor of the Suck Creek bolt wars.
Climb a thin, overhanging crack with a slight bulge (crux) and several petzl long-life bolts. 50' FFA: Travis Eiseman (9/99)

> Insider's Note: Some time ago a flake popped off at the crux and revealed a key face hold.

❺ Special Olympics 5.11
Just as well could have been named "Welcome To Yosemite." Rare, straight-in overhanging crack—one of "the Belt's" top ten. Start: Same as for Battle Of The Bulge. A gently overhanging, tight-hands-to-fingers crack splits a wall of gorgeous white sandstone. 50' FA: Rob Robinson, Chick Holtkamp, Eric Zschiesche (8/80)

❻ Uncle Pervy's Playhouse 5.12a (sport)
Provides a short but powerful piece of "twisted" arete climbing. Start: Same as for Special Olympics. Hump the wide arete with half-pad edges bisecting the blank white and grey wall past four bolts. Though short, this is one of the finest pieces of arete climbing found in the immediate area! 50'
FA: Chris Chesnutt, Jay Bell (6/88)

Rob Robinson on an early ascent of Special Olympics, 5.11

SUCK CREEK

Verena Draper chuggin' away on Cruise Control, 5.8

Suck Creek Sleeper Classics
Amplitude, 5.8
Layaway Plan, 5.10
The Thread that Runs so True, 5.11
The Puzzle Palace, 5.11+
Going off the Deep End, 5.12-

Photo Credit: Micah Gentry

Cody Averbeck on the classic arete of Uncle Pervy's Playhouse, 5.12a. Photo Credit: Micah Gentry

SUCK CREEK

❼ Jerry's Kids 5.10+
Start: 10' right of Uncle Pervy's Playhouse. Climb the Cruise Control corner (see below) for a few feet. Crank left a few moves onto steep face and follow a thin crack to the top. 50'
FA: Paul Piana and partner (mid 80's)

❽ Cruise Control 5.8 ★
Start: Same as for Jerry's Kids. Motor up a right-facing dihedral with a jam crack. 60'
FA: Rob Robinson, Peter Henley (10/80)

❾ Welcome to the Machine 5.11+ ★★
Eat my (drill) dust? Gear grinding, dual exhaust, turbo-charged face climbing. Start: 20' right of Cruise Control. Climb the face past two bolts to a ledge. 30' FA: Travis Eiseman (7/88)

> Insider's Note: The bolt clips are "a bit necky." Double rope technique recommended.

❿ Psycho Fingers 5.10-
Start: 20' right of Welcome To The Machine. A steep hand and thin finger crack leads to a ledge. Finish up "vegetable" corner. 70' FA: Rob Robinson, Mike Lewis (9/83)

⓫ Sterling Mosh 5.10-
Start: 25' right of Psycho Fingers. Climb a mossy, left-facing dihedral guarded by a small roof. 30'
FA: Rob Robinson, Peter Henley (10/80)

www.rockerypress.com 277

SUCK CREEK Roadside Wall

⓬ Pete and Rob's 5.10+ ★★
Sketchy, but hugely popular, face route throughout the 1980's and beyond. Excellent, sustained, varied and eclectic. Start: 5' right of Sterling Mosh.
Climb a steep slab laced with vertical seams (subordinate crux) for about 30'. "Boulder" past a short crackless section (crux). Gallop up easier rock a ways; turn a small overhang. Finish straight over a rounded bulge (crux) at the top. 90' FA: Rob Robinson, Peter Henley (10/80)

Insider's Note: As is the Southern tradition ... topping out by grabbing a hanging rhodedendron branch is considered de riguer.

⓭ American Sportsman 5.11+
Start: 15' right of Pete And Rob's. Climb the arete past a single bolt (crux.) Merge with Bad Apple (see below). 90' FA: Rick Mix, Jeff Burton (96' or 97')

⓮ Poultry Boy 5.9 A2+ ★
Start: 20' right of American Sportsman. Pitch #1: Climb an obvious crack to an imposing 10' (or so) roof and belay. (60') (5.9) Pitch #2: Turn the roof and wander via aid through an immense band of overhangs to the top. (50') (A2+) FA Pitch #1: Rob Robinson, Marty Gibson (81') FA Pitch #2: Todd Wells, Chris Hyson (96')

⓯ Bad Apple 5.9 ★
Start: 20' right of Poultry Boy.
Pitch #1: Climb an obvious offwidth crack in a giant left-facing corner to roof and belay. (50') (5.9) Pitch #2: Traverse left beneath the roof along an obvious horizontal break (past an ugly semi-detached block.) Continue around arete and belay. (45') (5.9)
Pitch #3: Trend up and left to a giant hemlock at the top of the cliff. (45') (5.8+)
FA: Todd Wells, Tim Williams (95')

⓰ Happy Holidays 5.12- ★★
Successfully wend your way through this aid eliminate, and you and your partner will, indeed, have cause for much celebration. Party hats optional. Start: 10' right of Bad Apple.
Pitch #1: Climb a short, left-facing corner capped by a smooth roof split by a thin crack. Work right, up, then left across the lip. Jug haul to a semi-hanging belay. (40') (5.12-) Pitch #2: Inch up a shallow, left-facing corner, face climb past a worthless bolt, skate over a thin bulge (crux) sporting a token fixed Rurp. At the band of large roofs ... traverse right for 20' to a small cave and comfortable belay. (50') (5.11) Pitch #3: Roll past the bulge capping the cave. (15') (5.8)
FFA: Rob Robinson, Greg Smith (alt. leads) (9/85)

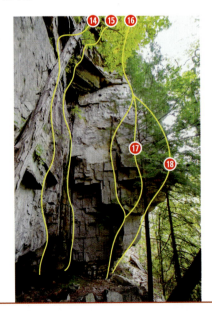

Memory Fog

Right off the side of the road in the canyon is an absolutely amazing crack climb with the bizarre name of Special Olympics. My discovery of this spectacular line was like raw jet fuel dumped into the afterburner engines of my young sandstone climber's imagination. In my mind, there had to more cracks like it out there — all I had to do was go find them. I scoured the Sandstone Belt for decades afterwards but never did find the mythical twin of Special O. I did, however, discover plenty of other "crack relatives" holed up throughout the region. Hope, anticipation and optimism fueled my outings. And of course there was the fact that I didn't want to miss out on finding something equally incredible — like "the mother of Special Olympics" which I stumbled across years later in nearby Sequatchie Valley (subsequently named "The Trumpet Unblown.")

Rob Robinson free-soloing "Special O," 5.11. Photo Credit: Rob Robinson Collection

Climber: Laban Swafford

Milky Way 5.12+

Star studded trip through a small galaxy of roofs. Rarely repeated area testpiece. Start: Same as Happy Holidays.

Pitch #1: Scamper up the left-facing corner, tiptoe right to stance. An imposing crack system splits a 12' tiered white roof—conquer it. Belay on the wall above. (40') (5.12+) Pitch #2: Climb a thin crack/corner, turn a small roof. Trend right to and up an arete capped by a cave and belay. (40') (5.10)

Pitch #3: Roll past the bulge capping the cave. (15') (5.8)

FA: Forrest Gardner, Rob Robinson (alt. leads) (4/81) FFA: Rob Robinson, Robyn Erbesfield (7/84)

Photo Credit: Micah Gentry

SUCK CREEK

Roadside Wall

⑰ Milky Way 5.12+
See description on page 282.

⑱ Cornhole 5.10, A4 ★
Start: A few feet right of Milky Way.
Pitch #1: Aid a short bulging wall, then dangle out a giant white roof with a discontinuous crack/seam. (40') (A4) Pitch #2: Step left and follow Milky Way. (40') (5.10) Pitch #3: Finish over the final bulge of Milky Way. (15') (5.8)
FA: Jeff Burton, Rick Mix (97')

> **Insider's Tip:** The real appeal of this predominately aid climb is the first pitch; you may want fix pieces and simply rap off above the lip. Also, a possible 5.14 if ever freed.

⑲ The Obsessed 5.11
Start: 20' right of Milky Way. High quality crack line you'll probably want to do more than just once—whether afflicted with climber O.C.D. (Obsessive Climbing Disorder) or not. Climb a jam crack bisecting small roofs (crux) capped by "an eight footer." The crack continues but thins above the lip ... face climb along this, finally finishing up a small summit corner. 100'
FA: Rob Robinson, Forrest Gardner (11/80)

> **Insider's Note:** Named after Shannon Stegg's valiant attempts to garner the first ascent.

⑳ G.P.S. Crack 5.9 ★★
Start: 30' right of The Obsessed. Named after the local Girl's Preparatory School. As you might surmise: One of Roadside's easier climbs, but it's still no giveaway.
Worm into a hanging chimney (crux). Gain the main wall of the cliff above ... climb a hand crack through a small roof, angle left and up a right-facing corner to the top. 100'
FA: Rob Robinson, Peter Henley (5/80)

Memory Fog

I worked hard and without respite, both on the rock and in the gym, for years on end, striving to get stronger and stronger. My goal was to become so strong that I could dominate any climb I set my sights on. I loved roofs and overhangs. Merely getting up a route wasn't good enough; it was this god-like feeling of total mastery that I lived for and which drove me. I was obsessed. I dreamed of becoming a "master of rock" — like the legendary boulderer John Gill about whom a book was written by that same title.

SUCK CREEK

Roadside Wall

The Rose, 5.10-

The Obsessed, 5.11

㉑ Pink Flamingos 5.11- ★★★
Trailer park classic! "Local color" climb loaded with burly roofs—you might have a hard time finding a good leg to stand on in the middle of pitch two. Start: 35' right of G.P.S. Crack. Pitch #1: Climb a short, left-facing corner with small roof. Continue up a thin face/crack to a small perch belay. (50') (5.10) Pitch #2: Flap right and up to cubby hole. Flap left through roof band laced with cracks (crux) to an alcove. Finish right over a tricky sloping bulge. (40') (5.11-)
FA: Rob Robinson, Peter Henley (1/81)

㉒ The Rose 5.10- ★★★
An "American Beauty" plucked from the sandstone flower garden. Full stems ahead. Start: 15' right of Pink Flamingos. Pitch #1: Climb a classic, left-facing dihedral with a perfect hand-to-fingers crack. Belay at a nice long ledge. (40') (5.10-) Pitch #2: "Stroll" right, snag a white flake, follow it past a large spike onto the main wall. Wander to the top, passing a pine tree. 70' 5.8 FFA: Rob Robinson, Peter Henley (10/80)

> **Insider's Notes:** Pitch two is interesting and probably worth doing if its your first time on the route. However, most climbers just do the first pitch and bail at fixed anchors on the ledge. The three star rating is for pitch #1 only.

SUCK CREEK

23 Ethiopia 5.10+ ★★
Emaciated face climb: Big, fat jugs are few and far between. Start: Same as for The Rose. A discontinuous network of thin cracks spans the right wall of The Rose dihedral. 40'
FA: Greg Collins, Alex Karr, John Bremmer (3/83)

24 The Entity 5.11+ ★★
Start: Same as for Ethiopia. Handrail right across the lip of a large overhang; "umphh" onto wall above. Follow crack, then trend right to an arete and on to the ledge above. 40'
FA: Mark Cole, Chris Chesnutt (7/88)

SUCK CREEK

Roadside Wall

㉕ Bitch in Heat 5.11- ★★★
Start: 65' right of The Entity. Climb the opening corner of The Way With Girls (see next route). Labor left beneath roof and up a left-facing corner (crux). Traverse right to a belay ledge (at the end of pitch one of The Way With Girls.). 50'
FA: Rob Robinson, Pat Perrin (7/86)

㉖ The Way with Girls 5.10 ★
Start: Same as for Bitch In Heat. Pitch #1: Climb a left-facing corner, ease through a band of roofs (crux); continue up and right to a belay ledge. (50') (5.10) Pitch #2: A long, left-facing corner leads to the top. (70') (5.8)
FA: Marvin Webb and partner (5/81)

㉗ The Suck 5.9+
Start: Same as for The Way With Girls. Pitch #1: Climb the left-facing corner to the roof band. Traverse right, rounding an overhanging arete. Continue to a ledge. (50') (5.9+) Pitch #2: Meander to the top. (50') (5.7)
FA: Rob Robinson, Rich Gottlieb (early 80's)

㉘ Happy Birthday 5.11- (sport) ★
Start: Same as for The Suck, et. al. Climb an overhanging arete past a small roof. 50'
FA: Justin Eiseman, Travis Eiseman (summer/89')

㉙ It's Bad A4 or 5.13a ★
Start: 10' right of Happy Birthday. Climb into a wide, right-facing corner. Turn a small flat roof, proceed to ledge via a short, left- facing corner. 50'
FA: Forrest Gardner (solo) (late 80's)

Insider's Note: Freed by Anthony Meeks.

㉚ Tight Cat 5.10+ ★
FA: Peter Henley, Clint Henley (late 70's)
Start: 25' right of It's Bad. Claw into a flared chimney (crux) and follow it to the top. 100'
FFA: Rob Robinson, Marvin Webb (1/81)

SUCK CREEK

SUCK CREEK — Roadside Wall

㉛ Primitive Man 5.12 ★★★
A modern Cro-Magnon classic of sorts: Yields about a half a rope length of brutally sustained face climbing. Start: 15' right of Tight Cat.
Climb an old aid line up the face past bolts, sans hangers, and a fixed pin or two through small roofs. 100'
FA: Forrest Gardner (aid solo) (late 80's)
FFA: Travis Eiseman, Justin Eiseman (to-prope) (12/97)

㉜ Sandtrap 5.10 ★★
A grand course of sorts for the experienced and ambitious 5.10 aspirant. Always interesting, intermittently sustained, tricky to protect in spots with an occasional bit of questionable rock. Start: 10' right of Primitive Man.
Follow a thin crack via face moves (crux) to a small roof; turn this (crux) at an obvious jam crack. Turn larger roof. Coast up, zig left a bit, now right past a tiny, left-facing corner. Putter up ledges to the top. 100'
FA: Rob Robinson, Forrest Gardner (9/80)

㉝ End of the Road 5.8
FA: Forrest Gardner & partner (80')

Laban Swafford rides American Sportsman, 5.11+   Photo Credit: Micah Gentry

White Wall

NO
5 mins

Last but not least is White Cove. This neat little roadside cove makes for a nice, one-time visit. Out To Launch and Strategic Arms Control (both stout 5.11's) are well worth doing.

Access: Park at the same pull-off as for the Roadside Wall (see above). Walk uphill about paralleling the guard rail for 350 yards, hop across the creek and you're there. Total time from crag to cliff: Faster than you can tie a bowline on a bight (with your eyes closed).

So there you have it: Suck Creek made simple! Now, let's get climbing!

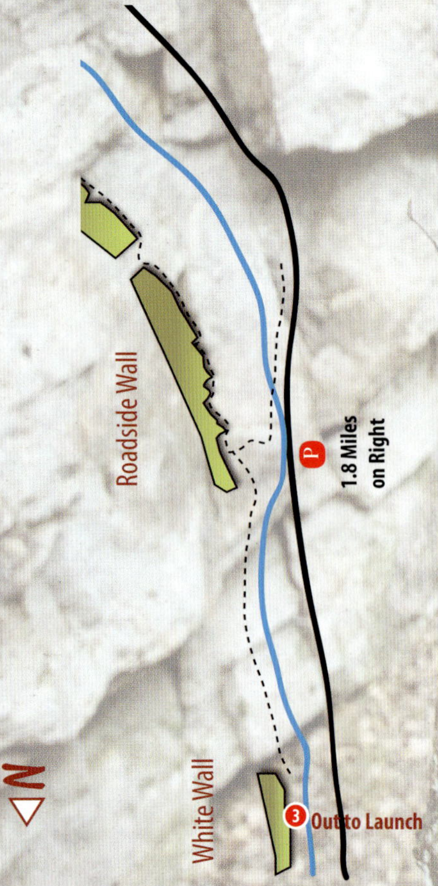

Roadside Wall

P 1.8 Miles on Right

N

White Wall

❸ Out to Launch

SUCK CREEK

White Cove

❶ Tweak Analysis 5.11-
Start: Near the right margin of the wall. A thin crack leads past a bulge to a small roof. Step right and on to the top through moss-covered rock. 65'
FA: Philip Fisher, Rob Robinson (9/84.)

❷ Fist Pocket 5.8 ★
Start: 10' left of Tweak Analysis. Scamper up a shallow, left-facing corner past a steepled roof. Finish via an enjoyable jam crack. 65'
FA: Peter Henley, Rob Robinson (5/81)

❸ Out to Launch 5.11 ★★
Houston, we have lift-off. Sandstone test pilot's "challenge of the day." Jet fuel, afterburners optional.
Start: 10' left of Fist Pocket. Giant stems lead up a wide dihedral (crux) to a large roof. Blast right a few feet, pass the roof where opportune. Rocket up a headwall to the top. 65'
FA: Rob Robinson, Philip Fisher (9/84)

Insider's Tip: Double rope technique highly recommended.

❹ Strategic Arms Control 5.11 ★★
Good luck brokering a "non-aggression pact" with gravity. An "arms race" will (in all likelihood) erupt en route to the summit if 5.11 is your limit.
Start: 10' left of Out To Launch.
Climb a thin crack through a small overhang (crux) past a fixed pin. Turn tiered roof (crux) and continue to the top in left-facing corners. 65'
FA: Forrest Gardner, Peter Henley (81')
FFA: Rob Robinson, Philip Fisher (9/84)

Insider's Warning: Beware "unexploded bombs" (a.k.a. "u.x.b.'s) poised above the tiered roof.

❺ Another Roadside Attraction 5.11★
Start: 100' left of Strategic Arms Control. A giant flake leads out along the lip of a large overhang to a rest. Reverse it. 30'
FA: Rob Robinson (early 80's)

Insider's Note: More a ropless boulder problem than actual climb.

Christmas Time in Suck Creek with Rick Mix

Photo Credit: Todd Wells Collection

Andrew Miller on the final roof splitter of Tamper Proof, 5.13-

The Tennessee Wall is named for the Tennessee River that meanders through the Tennessee River Gorge just at the wall's base. The Prentice Cooper State forest owns and manages the cliff and is home to miles of hiking trails, 4x4 roads, and T-Wall Sandstone! Luckily for climbers, Prentice Cooper manages their lands with a very pro-recreation stance that has helped to establish Prentice Cooper State Forest as one of the most popular and well-used recreational resources in the region.

TENNESSEE WALL

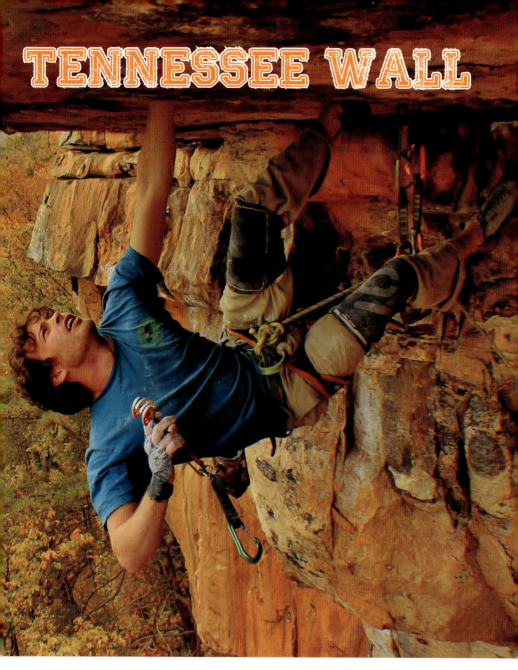

T-Wall itself is a South facing crag sitting high atop the TN river gorge whose 80' to 120' walls tower above tree-lines and soak in sun and exposure. For this reason, the season at T-Wall is from Fall to Spring.

TENNESSEE WALL

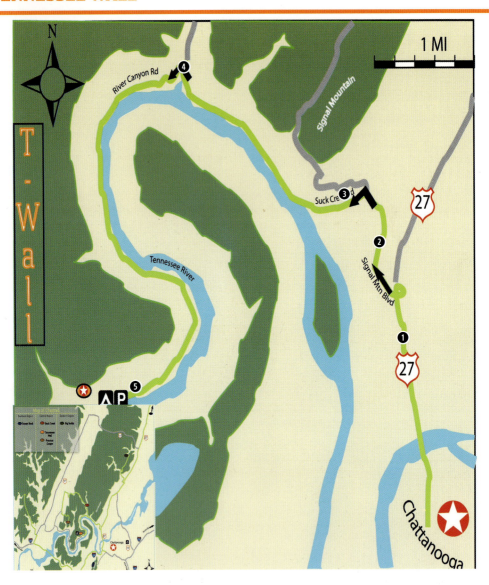

35 mins

❶ From Chattanooga, Take 1-27 North (across Oligiati bridge) to the Signal Mountain Road exit. ❷ Continue 1.5 miles on US 127 North (Passing a Wal Mart Shopping Center) until you reach the base of Signal Mountain. ❸ At the base of the mountain, take a left onto Suck Creek Road (TN Highway 27 West) (If you start going up the mountain, you've missed the turn). Follow Suck Creek Road for approximately 4.0 miles to a bridge that crosses suck creek. ❹ Take a left at this bridge onto Mullins Cove Road (if you start going up Suck Creek Canyon, you've gone too far). Drive approximately 6 miles on Mullins Cove Road (be mindful of the blind curves!), and locate a large climber parking lot on your left ❺.

TENNESSEE WALL

Parking

At your 6 mile mark from the last turn at the bridge, slow down and begin looking for an obvious trail head on the right. A stone's throw past this point and on the left is a big oak tree towering alongside a gravel parking lot that can handle about a dozen or so cars. Please make sure you only take up one parking space (vs. "a space and a half"). If you roll past your seven mile mark ... you've gone too far. This is where you will park if accessing climbs located at Paradise Walls, the Wasteland, the Amphitheater or the Orange Blossom Walls.

If the parking lot is full there is usually ample space to park alongside the road. Watch out for ditches though ... of especial note is a dastardly car-eating culvert right adjacent the trail head. If you get stuck try Cain Wrecker Services at (423) 875-9900.

Camping

There is an unofficial camping area adjacent to the main parking lot. Prentice Cooper officials have kindly allowed the climbing community to make use of this location, but only when managed hunts are not in progress. Moreover, camping is only allowed on the same side of the road as the parking area. Please use fire rings, and extinguish all fires before leaving your site. As well, please make a special effort to keep close tabs on your trash, and pick up any which others may have left behind.

Rules & Regs

 1.) Have you checked to make sure that it's not a Prentice Cooper scheduled hunt date? In which case climbing will be temporarily prohibited within the park until the end of the hunt.

You can check scheduled hunt dates by following this link:

http://www.tn.gov/agriculture/forestry/stateforest07.shtml

3.) Firearms are prohibited in park if not under a Wild Hunt permit.

4.) Possession of drugs or alcohol is prohibited.

Climbing Specific Regulations

1.) All new routes requiring fixed hardware must be approved through Prentice Cooper Management. Consult the SCC website for more information.

www.rockerypress.com 299

TENNESSEE WALL

Area Logistics

Emergency

Dial 911 (Cell Service is Limited)

Season

It is unlikely you'll desire to savor, firsthand, the grim conditions that dominate the Tennessee Wall during the months of June through August, when the area is superheated by a raging, demonic sun. However, if cragging in the "blast wave of a thermonuclear explosion" (which, come to think of it, the sun is) appeals to you ... then this south-facing wall is the place to do it! Add to the Stygian heat a blanket of 70+ percent humidity, and you have the worst of all possible worlds — a scorching desert overlaid by a steamy jungle. If you've never climbed in conditions like these, get ready to add a whole new meaning to your definition of "tough."

        Paradoxically, the juxtaposition of the cliff aspect to the sun is also one of its greatest assets. Come autumn, as the daytime highs begin dropping towards the magical mark of 50 degrees, the area metamorphoses into a snake-less "Garden of Eden"— no bugs, briers, debilitating heat, or humidity. Not surprisingly, late fall, winter, and early spring are my favorite times to frequent the area, and I expect this will be the case for you as well.

Food

For groceries and dining opportunities, your best bet is to return to Chattanooga and visit the Bi-lo or Walmart at the base of Signal Mountain. There are also several options for dining out in this area as well. In particular, check out Shuford's BBQ at the base of Signal Mountain.

Approaches

Cibola, Valhalla, and Serenity Walls

If you plan on climbing at Cibola, the Valhalla Wall or Serenity Walls: continue 0.6 miles past this parking lot to a shoulder pull-off on the left that can accommodate about a half dozen cars. (see page 308 for details)

For Paradise Walls & The Wasteland

❶ From the parking lot, cross the street and locate the marked trailhead leading up to T-Wall. ❷ Follow the main trail for approx. 10-15 minutes to a spur trail located on your left (marked by cairns) (if you pass a large house-sized boulder next to the trail --- you just missed this side trail, and you need to back track a few minutes). ❸ Take this (Paradise Falls Trail) to the base of Paradise Falls where you will intersect the route Stonhinge (pg 348) on the right side of Paradise Falls.

For the Wasteland, Amphitheater, and Orange Blossom Walls:

Take ❶-❸ to the split off of the main T-Wall approach trail. Do not split left. Instead, follow the main trail to its terminus where you will meet up with the impressive Amphitheater & waterfall as soon as you finish the uphill approach. ❹ Hike left for the Wasteland, or ❺ hike right for the Orange Blossom Walls.

TENNESSEE WALL

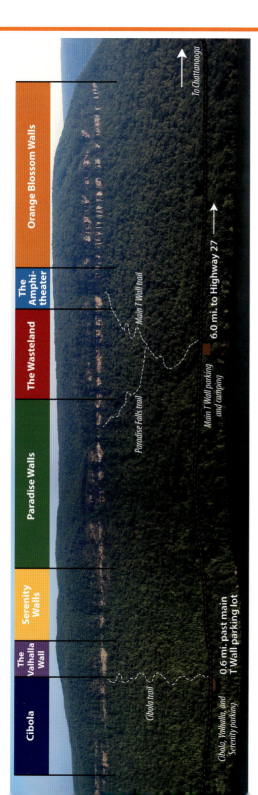

LAYOUT OF THE CLIFF

The Tennessee Wall is a complex and highly varied cliff line approximately two miles long. I seem to recall someone writing somewhere that the wall had a north end and a south end. This, however, is not the case. It faces southwest by southeast.

Soon after discovering the Tennessee Wall in 1984, I began subdividing it into areas. Though somewhat arbitrary and completely imaginary, this divvying up process was intended to help facilitate locating and identifying routes. (Plus, it was just fun to dream the whole thing up.)

The lower tier of the Tennessee Wall consists of seven primary divisions, some with several "subdivisions." From left to right (west to east) they are as follows: Cibola, the Valhalla Wall, Serenity Walls, Paradise Walls (consisting of Paradise Lost, West Paradise and East Paradise), the Wasteland, the Amphitheater, and the Orange Blossom Walls (consisting of West Blossom, Middle Blossom, East Blossom and Lost Blossom.)

There is also an upper tier of rock, dubbed Highlands which, in my estimation, is about 95% "choss." (Watch future climbers prove me wrong!) All lower tier routes end at a tree-covered ledge that runs along the base of this upper tier, in case you want to check it out for yourself.

www.rockerypress.com 301

WELCOME HOME...

THE TENNESSEE WALL

A stone's throw from my home, the main highway of Signal Mountain carves an asphalt ribbon through a narrow wilderness valley which local residents call "green gorge." On both sides of the gorge, sandstone outcrops framed by broad-leaf trees dot the slopes. At its mouth, the road unfurls in a series of precipitous curves which snake across an exposed shoulder of the mountain where a massive sandstone cliff towers over the passing traffic. A sheer drop below the roadbed provides drivers a brief but spectacular view of the Tennessee River Gorge. In the distance one can see the city of Chattanooga encircled by mountains — all capped by never ending mile after mile of sandstone cliffs.

At the foot of Signal Mountain, a turn onto Highway 27 will guide you alongside the Tennessee River and into the sacred heart of the Tennessee River Gorge. Just past a canyon bridge, a final turn leads even deeper into this ancient fold of water riven land. Cherokee Indians who, not so long ago, lived in the region lovingly called it O-tulla-ton-ton-kumma-ee, or "Mountains Looking at Each Other."

The final seven mile stretch of River Canyon Road leading to the Tennessee Wall navigates a twisted landscape comprised of small hills linked by death defying curves; it's an asphalt roller coaster as dangerous and unpredictable as an Eastern Diamondback Rattler trying to scramble sidewards towards safety across a pile of jumbled rocks. Dotting the roadside is a collection of modest homes (some on stilts in case the river floods), a couple of small country churches, and the occasional junked out single-wide trailer. Together, they make up what passes for "the neighborhood."

After a couple of miles, what remains of (what passes for) civilization in these parts thins out, and the road begins to get ... a little rougher. Then, right as you might start to wonder "Have I gone too far?" and perhaps more importantly, "Is it safe to go any farther?" — the parking lot for the Tennessee Wall suddenly appears.

T-Wall as seen from Raccoon Mountain

TO THE T-WALL...

★★★

    I began climbing at the Tennessee Wall in late 1984. Since that time I have made the short hike up to the cliff more times than I can remember. It's a hike I never tire of (how could I?) since, after all, some of the finest sandstone in the world is waiting at the top of the trail.

    The rock here is amazingly compact, fine grained and usually "bullet hard." It's also easy on the fingertips, and the soles of climbing shoes will adhere to small edges and smears with a tenacity that might even make the local mascot of the crag — the lizard — take notice. Most of the routes are in the 5.7 to 5.11 range of difficulty and, more often than not, offer excellent protection. The summits of many routes have been equipped with anchors ... a boon for setting up top-ropes and expediting rappels.

    The Tennessee Wall has a complex and multi-faceted personality. It'll take a fair amount of climbing here in order to fully appreciate all that this diverse cliff has to offer: straight-in splitter cracks, thin face climbs, knife-edged aretes, immaculate dihedrals — and lots of overhanging walls and roofs. The latter are a common feature of crags throughout the region, and this sun drenched, south-facing wall has been blessed with more than its fair share. Indeed, the Tennessee Wall is jam packed from one end to the other with — not hundreds — but thousands, of overhangs. These obstacles vary from in size from "manageable" on up to 30' monsters (with a reputation for chewing climbers up and spitting them out like discarded pieces of bubblegum).

    Across the breadth of the wall you will encounter swathes and patches of beautifully colored orange rock. Sometimes the color saturation is so intense you'll swear the color is hemorrhaging out of tiny pores in the rock. It was this aspect of the cliff which played a hand in the naming of the wall; the state of Tennessee's "official" color is, you guessed it, orange.

    Whether you are new to the sport or a seasoned "rock rat": the Tennessee Wall is going to amaze, inspire, and delight you for as much time as you have here — be it days, weeks, or years. The Tennessee Wall is an extraordinary resource we need to preserve — not only for our own enjoyment — but also for the generations of climbers yet to come. And there will be many. Please, take care of it.

Hangin' down by the River.   Photo Credit: Ben Ditto

TENNESSEE WALL

DISCOVERING THE T-WALL

Quickly, Now! Fall is Coming...

Although rock climbing in the Chattanooga area can be traced back as far as the 1940's, it wasn't until 1984, on the day before Christmas, that Tennessee Wall made its debut.

The relative late date of its discovery is likely attributable to several factors. One is that — until the mid 1980's — only a small fraternity of climbers lived in the Chattanooga area. Most locals were content to frequent Lookout Mountain's popular and easily accessible Sunset Rock (a superb crag in its own right).

Secondly, the wall lies hidden in the serpentine folds of the Tennessee River Gorge; a wilderness paradise located on the outskirts of the city.

Had a climber driven along River Canyon Road (at the cliff's base) on the prowl for new crags, it's unlikely he or she would have followed up on what they might have seen. To wit: although the upper tier is partially visible from the road, it looks, well, less than inspiring. The lower tier, where virtually all of the best rock is found, is obscured by a dense forest canopy.

The only way a climber might have stumbled across the wall would have been to have visited the hydroelectric power station situated atop Raccoon Mountain. Here, perched on the mountain's shoulder, is an imposing concrete pillbox with an overlook which provides a gorgeous panoramic view of the Tennessee River Gorge. On the far side of the gorge, beneath the crown of Walden's Ridge, lies the crag — a long ribbon of rock split into two tiers separated by a tree ledge. From this vantage point you couldn't miss it if you tried.

Though bursting with potential roof climbs, the discerning eye of the veteran climber will quickly size up the pastel-colored upper tier for what it is: a band of rubble and ruin. A cursory inspection through a pair of binoculars only confirms the unfortunate diagnosis.

In stark contrast stands the lower tier. Even a novice climber would be capable of discerning the profusion of obvious, high quality routes. When climbers talk about the Tennessee Wall, this lower tier is the cliff they are referring to. Best described as a smoldering tapestry of molten orange rock accentuated by intertwining shades of ash grey, the Tennessee Wall yields one of the sandstone belt's most beautiful and colorful mosaics.

Ironically, the discovery of the wall would have been made by Sunset Rock climbers decades prior but for the local topography. Sunset and the Tennessee Wall are situated laterally opposite one another, with the bulk of Raccoon Mountain in between. If you could grind Raccoon down to the size of a big hill you'd have a perfect view from one to the other.

The day of discovery was a momentous occasion. Arno Ilgner and I had been on the hunt for new crags for many months. Visiting the same areas (whether locally or requiring a bit of a road trip) time and again was getting old for both of us. Not that there wasn't plenty of new stuff left to do — far from it.

CLIMBING HISTORY

I just needed the infusion of energy a virgin area with lots of classic routes would provide. We hoped to get lucky and find a suitable candidate relatively close to Chattanooga.

As history now knows we hit the sandstone jackpot, but it took awhile for the winning number to come up.

Arno and I began meeting in Chattanooga to recon unexplored areas gleaned from a stack of topographic maps. An earlier recon into the periphery of the Tennessee River Gorge had revealed the existence of a long, tall, and solid-looking cliff line; its walls dripped with shades of lava orange infused with hues of grey. Unfortunately, it was located on private property. Though hardly keen on being blasted with rock salt (or worse) by a "Billy Bob" or his brethren kin for "trespassin'," we decided to risk a romp up to and along the base of the wall for one good look. Later, we'd decide if greater risks were warranted based on what we found.

We met up early one Sunday morning in downtown Chattanooga. Arno arrived en route from Nashville riding shotgun with Roger Sherman, whose four-wheel-drive truck was to serve as our "tank without tracks."

To access the wall we exited the interstate and, a few turns later, found ourselves on a scenic rural road which ran along the base of Elder Mountain, parallel to the Tennessee River. Soon we arced around the mountain's base, approaching the inner sanctum of the Gorge. To our considerable dismay, we were met by a padlocked gate. On the right side of the road and just beyond the gate was a chicken coop of a house encircled by a small army of barking dogs. Disappointed, but with no alternative, we retreated to look for another point of ingress.

On the way out, we spotted an "Elder Mountain Road" sign and decided to follow it to the top. According to our detailed map, the road continued down the mountain's backside and into the heart of the Gorge. We hoped to find a side road, sans gate, permitting a go at the Elder Wall from the opposite direction. We were about to get lucky, but still had no idea of what was waiting for us.

TENNESSEE WALL

At a place on the topo map marked "Pan Gap," we crossed the mountain's back and began a winding descent. Through the trees and on the far side of the Gorge, we began to make out bits and pieces of what appeared to be a cliff line — but not the one we were looking for!

Our odometer crept forward a click or two when, suddenly, a pastiche of tantalizing rock fused into a solid whole. Beneath a cobalt blue sky, basking in the heat of the quintessential winter morning sun, was one of the finest sandstone cliffs any of us had ever seen. Roger skipped pulling over to the side of the road. Instead, he cut the engine and set the parking brake. We tumbled out into the middle of the road ... and just stared. Seared into the flank of the south face of the mountain opposite us was a furious blaze of scintillating orange rock covered by a mottled patina of ash grey.

We passed around a pair of binoculars, and took turns panning the cliff line. It was obvious that, though viewed from afar, the wall possessed an un-godly concentration of natural lines. Raked by the sun from east to west, the contrast of light and shadow highlighted a multitude of spectacular aretes, and revealed a handful of deep, cave-like recesses. The latter were capped by massive, hulking roofs. Across the entire complex of the cliff line sprouted countless smaller roofs and overhangs, with a notable concentration towards the wall's center. We lost count of the number of clean, sheer faces. Rounding things out was a fat inventory of superb-looking dihedrals. At first glance, it didn't seem like one could design a more appealing crag, if such a thing were possible.

Our "question of the day" was at hand: what were we going to do with the rest of ours? Continue with our original itinerary? Or drive back around into the canyon from the other side, try to locate the wall from below and hike up to it? Winter days were short, so we decided on the former.

We found the side road we had hoped for; it dropped like a roller coaster through the woods, past several small, modest homes domiciled in a most enviable setting. A bit further, the road degenerated into an obstacle course of potholes, ruts, and downed trees. Roger expertly wheeled his rig through the minefields without mishap.

Limits of Sanity, 5.11

Eventually we reached the end of the "road" which, in a final bit of luck, dead-ended beneath the most impressive portion of the Elder Wall. After disembarking, we shouldered our packs and clawed up an ever-steepening slope. The last 100 yards was a devil of a sliding board littered with loose rocks obscured by leaves.

The Elder cliff line was amazingly monolithic; cracks necessary for on-sight trad leads seemed in short supply. So we hurried along the base, hoping to stumble upon a three-star stash of easy-to-protect classics. We came to a prominent, square cut cave capped by a giant roof.

On the overhanging left wall of the cave an "inch and a quarter" crack zig-zagged for 60'. It looked to be about 5.12 in difficulty. No question now what we were going to climb! We broke out the rope and rack and went for it. The day had been chock full of surprises, and we were in for yet another. A few feet up, the friendly-looking crack revealed its nasty secret. Ragged edges — almost as sharp as dull razors at some points — threatened to flay my fingers. I might as well have been sticking my hands into the jaws of a great white shark.

TENNESSEE WALL

I came close to conquering the Chimera, but in the end pain triumphed over will. Sans tape, the crack had taken its toll. I lowered off and relinquished the lead to Arno, who — in one clean shot — churned through the meat grinder cruxes and finished off what remained. At a small stance he stuffed in a couple of cams and lowered off. Wisely, Roger decided to skip the bloodbath. This left me to clean the pitch on top-rope, which I did, though endeavoring to not lose any more flesh. At the anchors I traded out a couple of "throwaway" pieces and lowered to the ground. It was getting late, so we packed up and headed down the mountain towards the river below; a trip to the new wall foremost on all our minds.

On the drive out, we struggled to come up with an appropriate name for this incredible "crack from hell" (which today still ranks among Chattanooga's top ten of the genre.) A crazy idea floated into my head: "limits of sanity." A nonsensical name for sure, but it sure seemed to fit!

Arno was not able to make it back to Chattanooga as soon as hoped, so another friend of mine, Peter Henley, joined me for the first "up close and personal look" at the new crag downstream and across the river.

It was the day before Christmas. After a short drive from Chattanooga, we puttered along River Canyon Road for a half dozen miles or so before spotting the upper tier of the T Wall peeking through the tree tops. We slowed to a crawl, looking for a suitable point of ingress. Without much searching we found one: an old, overgrown logging trail. Just past it was the perfect pull-out. Serendipity!

We followed the trail until it fizzled out, then continued up the slope to a gully which, in turn, led directly to the wall's base. Intersecting the cliff at this juncture was a major letdown. The rock wasn't junk by any means, but it didn't appear to be the 24 carat sandstone gold we had first glimpsed from across the gorge. Where was that rock?!

We decided to hike in opposite directions for a short distance, rendezvous back at our starting point, discuss what we'd found and go from there. Peter hiked to the left into what is now called Paradise East, and I ventured right into an area now called The Wasteland.

A short time later we regrouped, only to lapse in a quandary. Both of us had seen plenty of good routes, but had a tough time "outselling" the other on the merits of our respective finds. The sleepy sun began its slow motion fall towards the horizon; shadows crept through trees. We risked losing what little time we had left ... it was time to seize the day. Hastily, we threw a rack together, roped up, and tackled a long, left-facing corner near the top of the gully. This turned out to be an enjoyable, two star 5.8.

From the top of the corner we could see across the river to the Raccoon Mountain hydroelectric power station. The phrase "in sight of power" floated into my mind and it seemed like a fitting name.

★★★

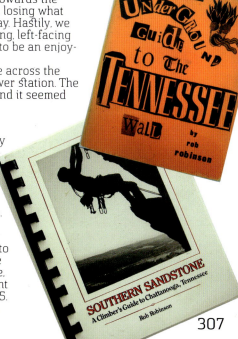

A few days later Arno arrived. Joined by a rotating cast of climbers, we began to explore the rest of the cliff. It didn't take long to figure out the wall was indeed as good as it had first appeared. Moreover, we had found the crag at the perfect time, since the Tennessee Wall is the archetypal south-facing winter wall paradise. Here, "sunny with a high of 45" means optimum climbing conditions.

1984 came to a close. Bruce Rogers and I added to the logging trail, extending it to the bottom of the cliff and then along its base. Trail system in place, the way was paved for a huge spike of first ascent activity that continued unabated throughout 1985. By the end of that year the area had a collection of 200+ routes.

307

CIBOLA & VALHALLA WALLS

25 mins

Cibola and the Valhalla Wall are long overlooked sections of the cliff line which comprise the left-most portion of the Tennessee Wall.

Parking: Park at a pull-off located 0.6 miles past the main Tennessee Wall parking lot (see Parking, pg. 299). The left shoulder of the road can accommodate four or so vehicles. (Insider's Tip: make sure your tires are completely off the pavement when you park or risk having your vehicle towed by the Marion County sheriff's department.) A hydroelectric power station will be directly across the river from the pull-off.

Approach: Opposite the pull-off, look for a paint blaze on a tree. The trail begins here. Follow paint blazes uphill. The trail will slowly become steeper and less defined. As the cliff line comes into view, the trail will disappear and you'll have to resort to scrambling. Make a bee line for an obvious wide outcrop at the wall's base. Head left(west) below this feature to access Cibola at its rightmost side. Head right (east) to access Valhalla at its leftmost side. Look for a 120' tall, exposed face peppered with discontinuous vertical cracks; "waves" of rippling, rounded-looking horizontals; several shallow corners — and a smattering of overhangs.

Routes are numbered left to right. However, you will encounter them walking right to left.

Boulder marking the Cibola, Valhalla Wall, and Serenity Wall Trailhead. The trail becomes more defined about 100' into the woods.

The small cave where the trail meets the cliff. Head left to Cibola or take a right to access the Valhalla Wall.

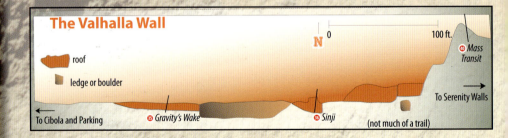

Kentucky Fried Fingers, 5.11-

Photo Credit: Luke Laeser

TENNESSEE WALL

CIBOLA

25 mins

CIBOLA

This long overlooked section of cliff line makes up the left-most portion of the T-Wall and is recommended to climbers looking for a bit of adventure climbing off the beaten path. Of especial interest is the deep, orange color the rock frequently exhibits and which, at times, is so intense that it appears as if the color is bleeding out of the rock...

❶ Then Everything Begins 5.10 ★★
Start: Atop a ledge in a recessed wall several hundred yards left of where the trail meets the base of the cliff. Face climb following a thin crack system angling left up the wall to bolt anchors. 60'
FA: Cody Averbeck, Nathaniel Walker ('07)

❷ Transient Chronology 5.6
Start: Same as for Then Everything Begins. Climb a chimney/offwidth. Ends at a single bolt on the left side of the wall. 40'
FA: Nathaniel Walker, Cody Averbeck ('07)

❸ Where The Sidewalk Ends 5.11- ★★★
Start: 20' right and downhill of Transient Chronology. Climb an orange, right-facing dihedral to a large ledge with a bolted belay. 70'
FA: Cody Averbeck, Nathaniel Walker ('07)

❹ The Gambler 5.11 ★
Start: 10' right of Where The Sidewalk Ends, just left of an arete. Follow a thin, left-arching crack over a bulge to a pillar, straight up via jugs to a ledge. Committing moves to more gear and the anchor on B.U.A.B.S. (see below) 80'
FA: Tyler Stracker and partner ('07)

❺ Born Under A Bad Sign 5.11+ ★★
Start: On a ledge 5' right of The Gambler. Get established in the corner and take on a series of committing moves to a good stance. Continue up corner, out roofs, and up a spectacular finger crack up high. Finish at bolted belay. 90'
FA: Cody Averbeck, Nathaniel Walker ('07)

> **Insider's Note:** It is possible to move left at crux corner — yielding an easier, but more circuitous and less classic, variation.

TENNESSEE WALL

6 Prepare To Dye 5.11+ ★★
Start: 10' right of Born Under A Bad Sign. Balance up the steep face with horizontals. Move straight up a vertical system to finish on Dreaming Of Beauty. 80'
FA: Nathaniel Walker, Cody Averbeck ('07)

7 Dreaming Of Beauty 5.11+ ★★
Start: 5' right of Prepare To Dye. Begin on Taming The Flaming (see below) but break left up a left-leaning finger and hand crack. Climb weakness to its end; finish on a series of side-pulls. End at bolted belay in roof. 70'
FA: Nathaniel Walker, Tyler Stracker ('07)

8 Taming The Flaming 5.11 ★★
Start: Same as for Dreaming Of Beauty. Climb orange flake/ corner to base of roof. Traverse roof to anchors. 80'
FA: Nathaniel Walker, Tyler Stracker ('07)

9 Send Lawyers, Guns, And Money 5.10 ★
Start: 15' right of Taming The Flaming. The obvious splitter hand crack ending below the roof. Climb up to and out a strenuous three foot roof. Cruise up orange face, to a ledge, and end up in a final white corner. End at a bolted anchor up high. 60' FA: Cody Averbeck, Nathaniel Walker ('07)

TENNESSEE WALL

CIBOLA

⑩ Hookers And Blow 5.10+ ★★★
So much fun it should be illegal, as the name implies.
Start: 10' right of Send Lawyers, Guns, And Money. Cruise up the ill defined right-facing corner to a ledge, protect here and jug haul up to the corner. Jam out the roof crack and mantle to another corner, pull another roof to a fixed anchor. 100'
FA: Tyler Stracker, Rod Thomas ('07)

⑪ Ghost Dance Of The Rednecks 5.10 ★★
Start: 30' right of Hookers And Blow. Climb a long and disjointed dihedral system barred by the occasional roof to the top. 100'
FA: Kirk Brode and Samantha Christen (4/07)

⑫ Disturbing Immortality 5.8 ★
Start: 10' right of Ghost Dance Of The Rednecks.
Climb the obvious "black hole" chimney. End at a bolted belay.
FA: Nathaniel Walker

> Insider's Tip: Consider bringing at least one #5 Camalot.

⑬ Resident Alien 5.11 ★
Start: 5' right of Disturbing Immortality. Climb a short, left-facing corner capped by a small roof. Exit right onto the bulging face, then slightly left and up (crux). Continue to the top. 100'
FA: Harrison Shull, Rob Robinson (4/09)

⑭ Electric Ambiance 5.9+ ★★
Start: On a ledge above the trail 15' right of Resident Alien.
Climb the obvious left-leaning hand crack, out a roof, and up a fun face to a bolted belay. 100'
FA: Nathaniel Walker, Cody Averbeck ('07)

F.A. of Electric Ambiance, 5.9+

TENNESSEE WALL

⑮ Safer By Design 5.10- ★
Start: At trailside, 10' right of Electric Ambiance. Ease through a couple of low hangs to gain a short corner capped by a roof. Work onto the right wall at a thin crack... ease around an outside corner to gain the face above (crux). Diagonal right up the wall over a bulge with great incuts to a small ledge. Head left, then right, up the headwall to the top. 100'
Variation: 5.10. From the small ledge above: climb a short corner on the right past a roof. Continue to the top.
FA: Tyler Stracker, Harrison Shull ('07)

> Insider's Note: Both the crux of the regular route, as well as the variation, are challenging to protect.

⑯ Rumble Fish 5.11-
Start: 10' right of Safer By Design. Wander up the wall to the base of a flared offwidth formation. Squeeze past this and into a tight hand crack. Ends at a single bolt belay below a choss band. 80'
FA: Tyler Stracker, Nathaniel Walker ('07)

⑰ Fiddlehead 5.8
Start: 200' right of Rumble Fish. Climb a splitter finger and hand crack. 40'
FA: Samantha Christen, Theresa Averbeck ('07)

⑱ Raptor Rapture 5.7
Start: 40' right of Fiddlehead. Climb obvious splitter hand crack to a bolted belay. 50'
FA: Samantha Christen, Nathaniel Walker ('07)

TENNESSEE WALL

CIBOLA

F.A. of Sewanee Gun Club, 5.11+

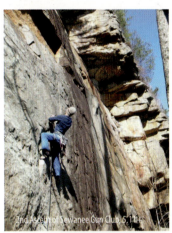
2nd Ascent of Sewanee Gun Club, 5.11+

19 Sewanee Gun Club 5.11+ ★★

Start: 200' right of Raptor Rapture. Turn a small overhang and traverse left in pockets to the base of the rightward-arching seam. Follow this (crux) to a small ledge. Clip bolt above, turn a small roof and continue up face to a bolted belay below roofs. 70'
FA: Cody Averbeck, Nathaniel Walker ('07)

Insider's Note: Reminiscent of, but much easier than, *Fear On Ice* (see pg. 416).

TENNESSEE WALL

20 All The Colors Of Love 5.10+ ★★

Start: 25' right of Sewanee Gun Club. Climb the obvious right-leaning hand and finger crack. Balance it out and run to the anchor of the previous climb. 70'
FA: Nathaniel Walker, Samantha Christen ('07)

21 The Blue Wall Of Silence 5.12 ★

Start: 20' right of All The Colors Of Love and at the left margin of a large and shallow cave.
Stick clip a bolt and conquer a fierce, boulder problem crux. Climb the left-facing corner system above to a bolted belay. 70'
FA: Nathaniel Walker, Cody Averbeck ('07)

The Sandstone Flux

-By Cody Averbeck

If you were to ask Rob Robinson, he might tell you it's the cosmic alignment of the quartz crystals on the rippled face of Super Slide, or the sharp but fleeting glint of blood orange reflection from the steeps of Tamper Proof and Wrectum Wrecker, or maybe even the Sandstone Flux - the force that percolates through the greys and the tans - through the slabs and the hangs - and from greasy rock edges to shaking tissue. He might tell you it's the force that oozes from the green ceiling of Celestial Mechanics - the same stuff that drips and buries itself deep in the earth only to be released and made airborne by the relentless uphill march of pumped calves. He might tell you it's the stuff that, once freed, infects our muscles and minds - causing us to storm headlong into cruxes with chipped and scratching fingernails and failing arms. It's the force that tells us to ignore the sound of our grinding vertebrae as we strain upwards. It's what pushes us to dream-to-life the vertical. It's the power that pulses through all of us. And it is the beacon that brings us all back to the Tennessee Wall.

I believe that Nathaniel Walker was probably somewhere in the Sierra when he heard the call of the Sandstone Flux. Bobbing and throwing his head forward with every ebb and painful rotation of his "rig" as it chugged up the steep ways of Tioga Pass, I imagine that between the explosions, he heard the organic whisper. Bouncing off the distant walls, it would have registered faint and fleeting. But as the hours and summer months passed by, the whisper would have grown more crisp and clear. Banging and scratching at his head, the voice would have become stronger as state lines and welcome centers blurred in the periphery. Soon, west would become east, and Nathaniel would step out one morning to a replacement landscape of hardwoods and flat top mountains. And as it travels on the fall winds, the Flux would smack into his face. And as if waking from a spell, the morning fog would lift to reveal golden visions through the uphill trees.

I met him there. I thought I was the first to the crag. Breathing deep and long, I stood at the trail's top. It was still cold. The haze hung low. And as I gazed up, greeting the wall as we all do, I suddenly saw a figure there at the base of the shale pedestals below Hands Across America. "Hey!" I yelled up at the figure. He stood eerily motionless as the fog wrapped around his small frame. Curious, I climbed up to meet the man. "Hey!" I called again. Still, he remained unmoving. So I brought my face around to meet his. And what I saw suddenly caused me to slip a little on the moss covered stones. Head cocked back and eyes closed, the man breathed infrequent deep breaths as he slept standing there with a drop of water from the falls kissing his forehead every so often. "Hey," I whispered - poking him slightly. "Wa!" he said in a startled tone. I nearly fell. "Sorry," he said as he lowered his head and looked

Nathaniel Walker

at me for a moment. His small and slightly stubbled visage hid below an old wool cap that was pulled down flush with the tops of his egg-shaped glasses. He wore baby blue scrubs that were scuffed around the knees and an ancient down jacket that oozed a veritable snow storm with every movement. I told him it was fine. And with nothing else said, he again turned his focus to the tiers above.

So we did not find each other immediately. But something kept drawing us together. From a distance, I'd see his giant pack bobbing with his three pairs of shoes jangling as he silently passed others on the trail. And on days when my hunger for new stone sent me to the far ends, we'd nearly collide as our vertical mindsets caused us to ignore all on the temporal plane. And when night had fallen - when the pack train of lights had faded from the parking lot, I'd see his solitary beacon there as it snaked down from above. And soon, we met there again. Below that wall, our paths stopped, and we tied them together as we strove to sate the powerful upwelling in us that entered our bodies and twisted and contorted them and set them on fire and watched them as they stormed off to rip down and topple great rocks.

And it was the Flux that we sought. We searched in splitters that arched to the horizon - in hangs that creaked and laughed at us - and in mud-choked corners that left us pawing. To distill and bottle the feeling of the finger locks on Fly With The Falcon - or the dirt-laced fear of a new route - or the warm glow of the fading western sun - it was all part of what we were searching for.

And no one can ever quite capture it. When you think you got it, you latch on and squeeze with all you have. But changing and always shifting, the flux falls away. Leaking through clenched fists, it drips back into the earth to await those down the line. And so Nathaniel and I closed our fists around what we had. And opening our eyes and hands slowly, we saw nothing there but some old sweat and chalk. But the essence of it floated there for a moment. Swept up and carried on the breeze, we breathed it deep and watched it swirl and spin away. And then, we left.

I often find myself trying to recreate some of the best times of my life. I'll place my hand there. Put my foot here. And position those people like it was. And then, I'll try. I'll try and push and squeeze it into that past mold. But inevitably, the mold will creak and break. My fingers will fail. My foot will pop. And those people will be looking away or be gone forever. And so I'll sit there mourning the loss of youth and passion. But I and you mustn't forget that the Sandstone Flux is eternal. And while it can never be captured or recreated, it will never fail to return. And while some of us believe it to have all passed, if you just listen and follow that whisper, you will find more than you thought possible.

Cody Averbeck & Edward Yates

TENNESSEE WALL — CIBOLA

㉒ Arsonists For Christ 5.10+ ★★
Start: Atop a ledge about 15' above the trail, and 200' right of The Blue Wall Of Silence.
Climb a wide, right-facing corner capped by a roof. Finish on Kentucky Fried Fingers (see below). 110'
FA: Cody Averbeck, Tyler Stracker ('07)

㉓ Kentucky Fried Fingers 5.11- ★★★
Start: Atop a ledge and 10' right of Arsonists For Christ.
Savor deep fried finger locks for 20', turn a small roof and continue to the top following an outside corner. 110'
FA: Cody Averbeck, Nathaniel Walker ('07)

㉔ Cast Iron Image 5.10 ★★
Start: 10' right of Kentucky Fried Fingers. Climb a short finger and hand crack capped by a small roof. Continue up the open face above to the top. 110'
FA: Cody Averbeck, Nathaniel Walker ('07)

㉕ Two Sides To Wisdom 5.12+ ★★
Start: 10' right of Cast Iron Image. Stick clip a bolt and climb the orange face above following double seams. Turn a small roof and continue up the casual face above. 110'
FA: Nathaniel Walker, Cody Averbeck ('07)

TENNESSEE WALL

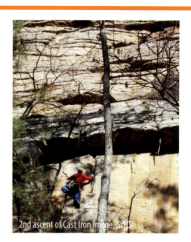

2nd ascent of Cast Iron Image, 5.10

T-Wall

㉘ Looking For Gold 5.11- ★★★
Sandstone prospectors willing to make the hike up to Cibola will be rewarded with this 24K climb.
Start: 15' right of Bomb Proof Roof. Climb the center face of the shallow amphitheater following a collection of tan-colored, cracked "dinner plate" flakes to a very small and improbable-looking roof. Conquer this (crux) and escape to the top. 80'
FA: Rob Robinson, Steve Goins (early 90's)

Insider's Notes: Double ropes recommended. Good gear, but strenuous to place at crux.

㉙ Trample Proof 5.9
Start: 10' right of Looking For Gold. Climb the obvious hand crack with a tree in the middle. Climb a section through a small roof, to a tree, to a hand crack. Traverse right to sling anchor on small pine. 50'
FA: Luke Laeser, Cody Averbeck ('07)

㉚ Golden Child 5.8 ★
Start: 15' right of Trample Proof. Climb an obvious "golden" finger and hand crack. More fun climbing above leads to a webbing anchor. 50'
FA: Cody Averbeck, Sam Miles ('07)

㉛ Talisman 5.8
Start: 20' right of Golden Child. Follow finger and hand crack up the face to a tree anchor. 50'
FA: Samantha Christen, Nathaniel Walker ('07)

㉖ No Name Number One 5.11 ★★
Start: Same as for Two Sides To Wisdom. Climb past a bolt and continue up a right-facing, right-arching corner that ends at a stance beneath an arete. Continue up the arete to the top. 110'
FA: Tyler Stracker, Cody Averbeck ('07)

㉗ Bomb Proof Roof 5.11+ ★★
Start: 10' right of No Name Number One, in the back of an obvious cave. Climb a strenuous roof crack to the "bomb shelter." Follow a hand crack to a series of corners. Break left out roof to a fixed anchor. 100'
FA: Nathaniel Walker, Cody Averbeck ('07)

Cody Averbeck on the 2nd ascent of All the Colors of Love, 5.10+

Photo Credit: Luke Laeser

TENNESSEE WALL

VALHALLA WALL

This area encompasses about 100 yards of cliff line. The main face has a 'mini big wall' feel to it, with routes suitable for only very experienced climbers. Much the same can be said of routes situated on the right side of the buttress. Here you will find a 'bullet hard,' overhanging white wall outfitted with a few sport lines... and what is likely the boldest trad line to date at the Tennessee Wall - Breaking the Waves.

③② Chalkdust Memories 5.10- ★
Start: Near the left side of the face. Face climb (crux) past a shallow and rounded right-facing flake. Continue up the short crack above, over a bulge and on to a ledge. 90'
FA: Rob Robinson, Emily Hon (3/08)

③③ Virginia Reels 5.10- ★★
Long, airy and surprisingly sustained. Start: 20' right of Chalkdust Memories, just left of small recesses and overhangs. Climb a black-varnished face. About 20' up, merge with a thin, rounded crack. Follow this up to and over a small crackless bulge, then up another thin, rounded crack. Finish past a small, right-facing corner. 120'
FA: Rob Robinson, Darrow Kirpatrick (10/97)

Insider's Note: From the book by writer Bill Hoffman of the same name.

③④ Time's Witness 5.11- ★
Start: 20' right of Virginia Reels. Scramble up the wall and turn a small roof. Continue out larger roof above (crux) capped by a shallow, rounded out crack. Continue up a second crack above with clean jams, turn a bulge and continue to a ledge. 90'
FA: Harrison Shull, Rob Robinson (3/08)

Insider's Note: Difficult to protect to the roof crux, with little margin for error.

③⑤ Gravity's Wake 5.9 ★
Start: 30' right of Time's Witness. **Pitch 1:** 5.9. Scramble up a short left-facing corner, step left onto ledge. Work through a spot of poor rock, then through a shallow gap in tiered overhangs with better stone. Belay on the wall above. (60') **Pitch 2:** 5.7. Climb straight up the exposed face above, finish through a small overhang, bearing left above the lip to the top. (60')
FA: Rob Robinson, Jared Chastain (3/01)

Insider's Note: This route is NOT suitable for a 5.9 leader. Beware loose rock on pitch one.

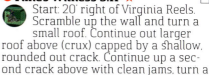
AM
25 mins

"3rd Class" up narrow, grassy ledges at the right side of the wall to access the following climbs.

T-Wall

www.rockerypress.com 321

TENNESSEE WALL

VALHALLA WALL

㊱ Sinji 5.10 ★★
Ready for a "mini big wall" adventure?
Start: 40' right of Gravity's Wake.
Climb a heavily-pebbled face to a crack
which leads through a small roof. Continue up the wall into a right-facing corner with large, hanging roofs. Traverse
out the left wall of the corner ... above
the lip of the biggest roof. Continue up
the face above to the top. 100'
FA: John Jolin, Ray Dobkin (3/86)

㊲ Breaking The Waves 5.12+
This "on-sight" trad test piece — one of the Tennessee Wall's most difficult and dangerous — surfs dead center up through a perfect wave of gorgeous white sandstone.
Start: 50' right around the corner and uphill of Sinji. Climb a left-facing corner capped by a roof. Trend right up the center of the wall. "Boulder" over a ball-breaker bulge (crux) to gain a tiny roof in a band of tan rock. Fire through a flared slot in the big roof above; finish through small tiers to the top. 85'   FA: Rob Robinson ('98)

> Notes: Use double ropes. Gear for the crux is small, hard to place and highly questionable. There is no fixed pro. A few bolts were inadvertently added about ten years after the first ascent. They have subsequently been removed. An alternate start can be done by beginning uphill a bit.

TENNESSEE WALL

㊳ Homemade Sin 5.12c
Super sustained, steep crimping on perfect rock.
Start: 15' right of Breaking The Waves. Pull a small roof and plow straight up through wild moves to chain anchors. 60'
FA: Cody Averbeck, Luke Laeser (spring '07)

㊴ Hot Off The Griddle 5.11+ ★★
Start: 5' right of Homemade Sin. Top-rope the steep tan and orange face to chain anchors.
FA: Cody Averbeck, Luke Laeser (spring '07)

㊵ Mass Transit 5.7 ★
Start: 5' right of Hot Off The Griddle. Climb a big, right-facing corner to trees above. 60'
FA: Judd Layman, Rob Robinson (10/97)

> Insider's Note: This might gain an extra star if it was cleaned up a bit. Needs traffic!

㊶ Soylent Green 5.9 ★
Start: 10' right of Mass Transit. Wander up the lichened face to the top. 60'
FA: Steve Goins, Rob Robinson (mid 90's)

㊷ The Schrodinger Equation 5.9+ ★
Start: 240' right of Mass Transit, the right-most route at Valhalla Wall. Climb an obvious corner loaded with lots of orange stone. 80'
FA: Judd Layman, Andrew Martin, Steve Goins (12/97)

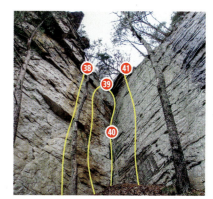

SERENITY WALLS

35 mins

This stretch of the cliff line is situated between the Valhalla Wall and Paradise Lost. It is the least developed and least frequented section of the Tennessee Wall. That said, there appears to be ample room for future development of many moderate and classic routes (which the Tennessee Wall is generally lacking). The area encompasses several hundred yards of cliff line. Much of the trail along the base of this section of the wall is ill-defined and sees little foot traffic, so be prepared for a bit of a tromp (especially if you visit the area during the warmer months, when there may be a lot of undergrowth).

Parking: Park at a pull-off located 0.6 miles past the main Tennessee Wall parking lot (see Parking, pg. 299) The left shoulder of the road can accommodate four or so vehicles. **Insider's Tip:** make sure your tires are completely off the pavement when you park or risk having your vehicle towed by the Marion County sheriff's department.) A hydroelectric power station will be directly across the river from the pull-off.

Approach: Opposite the pull-off look for a paint blaze on a tree. The trail begins here. This is the same trail as for Cibola and the Valhalla Wall. Follow paint blazes uphill. The trail will slowly become steeper and less defined. As the cliff line comes into view, the trail will disappear and you'll have to resort to scrambling. Make a bee line for an obvious wide outcrop at the wall's base. Head right (east) and skirt an impressive 120' face, the Valhalla Wall, pg. 322. Ascend a couple of narrow and grassy "3rd Class" ledges and a steep hillside at the wall's right margin. Hike right (east) beneath a long, low roof with a jumble of boulders beneath it to enter the area.

Routes are numbered left to right, and you will encounter them walking left to right (west to east).

Boulder marking the Cibola, Valhalla Wall, and Serenity Wall Trailhead. The trail becomes more defined about 100' into the woods.

The small cave where the trail meets the cliff. Head right and pass the Valhalla wall to access the Serenity Walls.

Serenity Walls

- ㊷ The Schrodinger Equation
- ㊸ Step Right Up
- ㊹ Big Orange Country
- ㊺ Little Steps
- ㊻ Falling Out

To Valhalla Wall and Parking ← | → To Paradise Lost

Serenity Falls

trail · seasonal stream · roof · ledge or boulder

(trail is vague or non-existent)

TENNESSEE WALL

㊸ Step Right Up 5.7 ★
Start: 80' right of The Schrodinger Equation.
Climb a 10' corner, ease right around a minor overhang with a detached-looking block. Follow a short crack to a short bulge with a rounded crack ... ease up a short, steep face with sloping holds. Continue to the top. 60'
FA: Rob Robinson, Susan Robinson (10/97)

㊹ Big Orange Country 5.8 ★
Start: 130' right of Step Right Up.
Climb the wall following an eye-catching crack line arcing right to the top. 80'
FA: Rob Robinson, Darrow Kirkpatrick (10/97)

Insider's Note: With a little bit of strategic cleaning this route might become popular.

㊺ Sundance 5.6 ★★
Quality stone, with good gear all the way.
Start: 70' right of Big Orange Country.
Dance up the face using the right-hand crack. Do a short section of steep face with horizontal holds and a thin vertical crack. Wander up the wall above and finish in a nice corner. 80'
FA: Rob Robinson, Darrow Kirkpatrick (10/97)

Insider's Note: The first 20' is not as hard as it looks.

㊻ Little Steps 5.7 ★★★
Great stone, good gear, cool moves — and it climbs alongside a leafy tree (which makes the route especially nice to do during the spring or fall season.)
Start: 10' right of Sundance.
Climb an obvious dihedral with lots of good holds. 80'
FA: Rob Robinson, Darrow Kirkpatrick (10/97)

Insider's Note: Using the tree at the start is considered part of the route since it's kind of hard to avoid it.

㊼ Starting Point 5.6 ★★
Start: 10' right of Little Steps.
Make a couple of awkward moves up a short, wide crack to gain a small ledge on the left. Continue directly up the arete to the top. 80'
FA: Darrow Kirkpatrick, Rob Robinson (10/97)

Insider's Note: There is no pro for a move or two above the small ledge, however, if you can lead 5.7 or 5.8 you should be fine.

gearX.com

GearX Web Manager Ivan Tighe keeping his composure on Fear and Loathing in Keene Valley (11b) in the Adirondacks, NY

The Best Selection of New & Discounted Gear Everyday Online.

Find our brick and mortar store in Burlington, VT

TENNESSEE WALL

48 Harvest Time 5.10- ★★

Pretty face climbing on sun baked stone. Watch out for da' Grim Reaper though.
Start: 5' right of Starting Point.
Step onto the face at a football-sized scoop. Turn a 1' roof a bit higher. Finesse the wall above; finish following thin cracks. 80'
FA: Darrow Kirkpatrick, Rob Robinson (10/97)

Insider's Note: Well worth top-roping in case you don't want to risk taking the run-out.

49 Falling Out 5.10- ★
Start: 160' right of Harvest Time, and 80' left of Maxwell House. Face climb to a shallow bowl, continue up a finger crack and over roofs to the top. 80'
FA: Tim Presley, Steve Goins (2/97)

T-Wall

www.rockerypress.com 327

PARADISE WALLS

Paradise Walls are home to a highly diversified collection of world class climbs. As is the case with much of the Tennessee Wall, there is an abundance of overhangs in all shapes and sizes. There are also several steep and sustained face climbs, along with a couple of splitter crack lines.

To facilitate locating routes, I divided the area (back in 1985) into three "subdivisions." They are as follows (from left to right): Paradise Lost, Paradise West and Paradise East.

Parking: Park at the main Tennessee Wall parking lot.

Approach: Hike up the main Tennessee Wall trail for about a quarter mile to an obvious fork where there is an obvious cairn as a marker. Make a sharp left and continue hiking to the Paradise Falls amphitheater. The Paradise Walls are sub-divided into three distinct sections, which each have a slightly different approach. Head left at the top of the trail to access Paradise Lost and West Paradise. Head right at the top of the trail to access Paradise East.

Alternatively, if you are coming from the Wasteland, the Amphitheater, or Orange Blossom Walls, you can access the Paradise Walls simply by hiking west (left) along the cliff base trail. At the end of the Wasteland you will enter the right side of Paradise East, as depicted in the photo below.

The split in the main T-Wall trail marked by a cairn. Head left to access the Paradise Walls.

Alternate Access: Approaching East Paradise from the left side of the Wasteland.

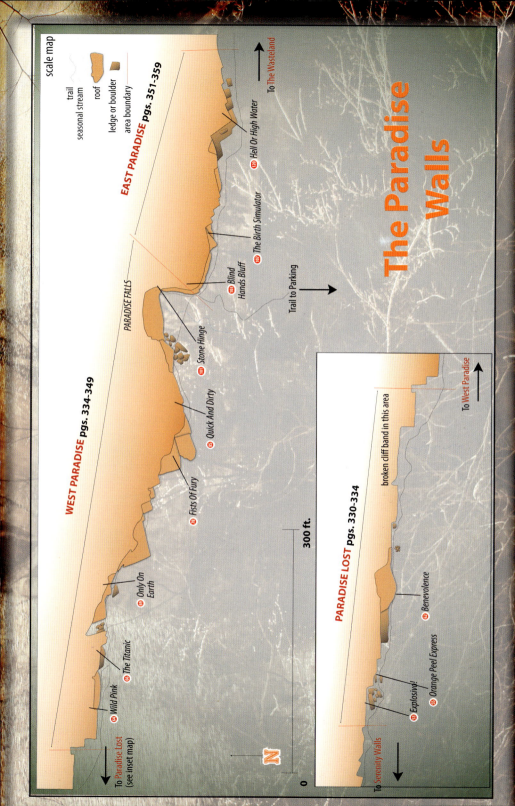

TENNESSEE WALL

PARADISE WALLS

PARADISE LOST

35 mins

Paradise Lost is the left-most section of the Paradise Walls. It is about 100 yards beyond West Paradise. Keep in mind that the climbs are listed from left to right, but as you are walking from West Paradise, you will encounter them right to left. The first route you will encounter is, *The Gleaning*.

50 Maxwell House 5.11- ★
Start: At the base of a steep incline in the trail and 80' right of Falling Out and at the left side of a tall buttress sporting lots of roofs.
Pitch 1: 5.11-. Climb a juggy overhanging wall to a 6' roof with crack and side wall. Belay over lip at stance. (40') Pitch 2: 5.9+. Continue up obvious line over small roof to the top. (60')
FA: Steve Goins, Judd Layman (10/98)

Insider's Tip: Might yield better gear if a flake-filled pocket under the roof was cleaned out.

51 Sedimental Attachment 5.10 ★
Start: 45' right of Maxwell House. Diagonal left through white rock to a band of orange rock; continue through body-length roof via flakes. Continue up and left to a stance. Pull a 3' roof at top of wall. 100'
FA: Steve Goins, Judd Layman, Rob Robinson, Darrow Kirkpatrick (1/98)

52 Pocket Pussy 5.12- ★★★
Start: 15' right of Sedimental Attachment. Climb a scalloped white wall; turn a small roof capping a right-facing corner. Work up and left (crux) to a large "hueco." Continue up and right a bit following flat holds, then straight up to a huge flat roof. Traverse left on thin face moves, now jug haul right out the roof to ring bolts at the lip. 100'
FA: Harrison Shull, Tyler Stracker (5/05)

TENNESSEE WALL

53 Explosivo! 5.12-
The severe angle of this pitch — which overhangs its base by 15' or so — is softened somewhat by a profusion of good holds. No single move is harder than 5.11, but there are several of these "animals" that must be tamed.
Start: 25' right of Pocket Pussy, atop a big stack of large, angular boulders. Crank through a band of tiered roofs past a bolt (crux). Turbo up the beautiful orange wall above past a second bolt and several more cruxes. When feasible, explode right and up a short, left-facing corner capped by a small roof; exit right and continue to a pair of bolt anchors. 60'
FA: Rob Robinson (top-rope 3/05) First Lead: Tyler Stracker, Rob Robinson (3/05)

54 Protect And Serve 5.12-
Start: Same as for Explosivo! Crank through a band of tiered roofs past a bolt. Diagonal right and follow a thin crack system splitting the bulging wall to a pair of bolt anchors. 60'
FA: Tyler Stracker, Kirk Brode (4/05)

55 Orange Peel Express 5.10+ ★★
A tasty piece of fruit plucked fresh from the T Wall sandstone orchard.
Start: At trailside, 15' right of Protect and Serve.
Follow a hand crack in an orange wall and right-facing flake to a ledge. Climb to an unlikely bulge; peel over this at a thin, vertical seam. Continue to the top following a right-facing corner to a large cedar tree. 90'
FA: Rob Robinson, Darrow Kirkpatrick (10/97)

56 Trimmed And Burning 5.10+ ★★
Full-on, full-tilt face climbing — with a burly bulge to boot.
Start: 8' right of Orange Peel Express. Climb a steep face to a ledge. "Boulder" past a small overhang and continue to an improbable bulge. Turn this (crux), follow a short thin seam above in black face. Continue straight to the top, staying right of the Orange Peel Express right-facing corner. 90'
FA: Tyler Stracker, Kirk Brode (3/05)

TENNESSEE WALL

PARADISE WALLS

57 Heat Vision 5.10 ★★
Here's one sure to set your soles on fire.
Start: 9' right of Trimmed and Burning.
Scamper up an easy face past a very short and shallow right-facing corner. Trend right, turn a small overhang above "cave." Climb to a smooth-looking bulge. Work right a few moves, then up water grooves (crux). Continue directly to a pair of bolt anchors. 90'
FA: Tyler Stracker, Rob Robinson (2/05)

59 Voodoo That You Do 5.10- ★★
T Wall sandstone magic well worth sampling. Zombie dust optional.
Start: 12' right of Step Into My Dream.
Climb a shallow, left-facing corner capped by a 1' roof. Make a couple of tricky face moves (crux) on the blank-looking face above. Meander directly up the wall via sustained climbing with great moves all the way to a pair of bolt anchors. 90'
FA: Tyler Stracker, Rob Robinson (2/05)

> Insider's Note: Comparable in quality and a smidgeon harder (but much less sustained) than Voodoo That You Do.

> Insider Tip: It might not be a bad idea to use double ropes to protect the first few gear clips.

58 Step Into My Dream 5.10+ ★★
Steep, sustained, and varied face climbing capped off by a classic boulder problem crux.
Start: 7' right of Heat Vision.
Boulder a few moves and turn a small roof past a single bolt (crux). Ease through a spot of choss and turn another small roof. Fire straight up the wall above through a notch and over a bulge (crux) past a single handjam-sized solution pocket. Finish on Voodoo That You Do to a pair of bolt anchors. 90'
FA: Rob Robinson, Kirk Brode (2/05)

60 Personal Victories 5.10- ★★
"A vertical crusade through a sea of gorgeous orange sandstone."
Start: 30' right of Voodoo That You Do.
Ascend the wall for 25' to a broad and spacious ledge. Climb through the small overhang above and continue up a short face to a second overhang split by cracks and sporting a large, block-like feature. Turn this, then diagonal right and up a featured dihedral to the top. 90'
FA: Judd Layman, Dustin Cole (2/97)

Ryan Johnson on Hands of Stone, 5.11b

Photo Credit: Micah Gentry

TENNESSEE WALL   PARADISE WALLS

🔴 Elevation Of The Soul 5.11 ★

Or is it ... Splattering of the Body? The crux roof flake on pitch two is reportedly a "deck master special." Start: 15' right of Personal Victories and just left of a tree growing smack against the wall.
Pitch 1: 5.9. Boulder past an overhang and climb face up and right to ledge. (25') Pitch 2: 5.11. Climb through "suspect" rock, then up a short, left-facing corner. Zigzag up the wall to a buzzard nest. Rail out a roof flake to the crux. Trend up and right and on to an obvious finish. (75')
FA: Steve Goins, Judd Layman (3/97)

Diagonal right and turn a flat roof using a handrail flake. Escape 10' right along a weakness in the cresting overhang above; gain vertical face and a poor stance. Crank left into overhangs and make a hard pull (contrived crux) onto a steep headwall and continue to the top. 90.

Alternate Finish ★ (recommended): 5.11-. Past the above mentioned "cresting overhang" make a few moves up to a small hole, trend left and continue to the top.

Insider's Tips: Carry the complete "trad war arsenal," up to and including a couple of big #4 cams, plus 20 full-length runners. Double ropes advised.

Insider's Note: Double ropes recommended, along with some big cams to help "protect" the crux.

🔴 Benevolence 5.11- ★★★

Recommended to the "sandstone lifer," this route has it all and will take all you've got! Originally graded 5.10c — NOT!
Start: 30' right of Elevation of the Soul, at a low, wide and deep roof at trailside. Boulder over an obstinate roof to gain a tenuous stance on a dead vertical face. Ease up to a ledge about 15' higher. "Boulder" over a crispy bulge (dubious fixed blade here ... possibly a knotted sling).

🔴 The Gleaning 5.11 ★

Start: 45' right of Benevolence.
Pitch 1: 5.10+. Scamper up an easy left-facing orange corner for 15' to a ledge. Muscle up and left through tiered 10' roof with big solution pockets; belay above the lip. (40') Pitch 2: 5.11. Continue straight up the wall to a thin stance; break right and up a ladder of small, sloping holds (crux); continue to the top. (60')
FA: Steve Goins, Tim Presley (3/97)

Insider's Note: Goins said he was praying on the last 20' during the first ascent.

334 www.rockerypress.com

TENNESSEE WALL

WEST PARADISE

This stretch of cliff line, about a quarter mile long, adjoins East Paradise on its right side. It begins at a broken up buttress (see Paradise Walls overview map, Pg 329) that forms the right side of the Paradise Falls amphitheater where the trail from below meets the cliff line. Heading left from Paradise Falls, keep in mind that you will encounter routes from right to left as you walk west. The first route you will encounter is *Dogfight*.

64 Wild Pink 5.9 ★
Start: Approximately 300' right of The Gleaning, at a small outcrop.
Follow a right-facing corner with a good crack to a large cave. Traverse left and through an overhang split by a jam crack with jugs. 60'

Alternate Start ★:
5.10-. Start 10' left of the original route. Climb straight up the face and join the regular route at the roof. 60'
FA: Rob Robinson and students (mid 80's)
FA Alternate Start: Steve Goins (rope solo, '98)

65 Hands Of Stone 5.11b (sport) ★
Start: 20' right of Wild Pink.
Climb a convoluted face and power through a 12' overhang. Finish up a short face. 45'
Variation: 5.11. Top-rope over the roof ... traverse right and up to the top. 45'
FA: Rob Robinson, Marvin Webb (top-rope, mid 80's)
First Lead: Penny Jordan and Louie Rumanes (early 90's)

Insider's Note: The bolts were added subsequent to the route being top-roped.

66 The Titanic 5.9+ ★
Start: 30' right of Hands of Stone.
Top-rope a shallow, left-facing corner to a ledge. Clamber atop a jutting block; continue to the top following the nose of a rounded arete. 60'
FA: Rob Robinson (mid 80's)

30 mins

TENNESSEE WALL

PARADISE WALLS

⑥⑦ Relative Humility 5.11 ★★★
Hungry for adventure? Serves up a big ole slice of delicious (humble?) sandstone pie ... this is one dessert few climbers will make a quick snack of.
Start: 100' right of The Titanic.
Pitch 1: 5.11. Boulder a few moves on the scalloped face. Follow a seamy weakness in the wall to an interesting-looking overhang with an obvious, body-sized scoop. Belay on the wall above. (50') Pitch 2: 5.11. Continue up the face; zigzag through crack weaknesses in the monolithic overhang above. (50')
FA: Steve Goins, Judd Layman (6/97)

⑥⑧ Heaven's Gate 5.11+ ★★★

Members of "the sandstone cult" will flip over the iron cross roof sequence ... one of the T Wall's finest. Higher up, a climactic bulge will likely make a true believer out of you.
Start: 35' right of Relative Humility. Climb a left-facing corner/ramp for 30'. Jug up a few moves to a big flat roof. Work right to gain a shallow, left-leaning crack (crux). Float over the bulge above (crux, with run-out) to a small recess. Ease left, then hard right a bit and over a much easier bulge. 90'
FA: Rob Robinson, Darrow Kirkpatrick (10/97)

Insider's Note: Double ropes recommended.

⑥⑨ Only On Earth 5.11+

There are few roof cracks like this in the solar system, one presumes. Features world-class hand jamming, with a harmonic convergence on the wall above.
Start: 30' right of Heaven's Gate.
Pitch 1: 5.11+. Follow a hand crack out a 20' roof to a small standing belay. (35') Pitch 2: 5.11. Climb a short ramp/corner, blast over a fingery bulge with a bit of a run-out. Finish up an easy dihedral. (60')
FA: Hugh Herr, Neil Cannon (1/85)

Like Mother, like son. Theresa & Cody Averbeck clmbing in West Paradise.

Photo Credit: Andrew Miller

TENNESSEE WALL

PARADISE WALLS

70 Nuclear Winter 5.12+ A0 ★★

Annihilating the final point of aid on this tendon-blaster will require ... some strategic arms control.
Start: 20' right of Only On Earth.
Pitch 1: 5.12+ A0. Explode through a cresting roof past a bolt and a few fixed pieces. Belay on the wall above. (40')
Pitch 2: 5.10-. Continue to a ledge with a tree, now on to the top. (60')

★★ **Direct Finish:** 5.11-. From the belay at the end of pitch 1 ... climb through an obvious weakness in tiered roofs; "smoke" face above and continue to the top. 100'
FA: Steve Goins, Judd Layman (4/97) FA Direct Finish: Steve Goins, Judd Layman (7/97)

71 A Turn Of The Page 5.10c (sport) ★★★

This classic sandstone novella should keep you glued to the wall from start to finish.
Start: 80' right of Nuclear Winter. Climb an easy wall for about 25'. Step right across ledges and climb a steep, exposed face to a pair of anchors. 90'
FA: Darrell Jordan, Chris Watford ('92)

72 Open Boat Whalers 5.10 ★★★

Ready to set sail on the sandstone sea? Navigating the run-outs on the headwall will be less nerve-racking if your belay crew includes a seasoned "rope rigger."
Start: Same as for A Turn of the Page. Climb a left-facing corner for 15'. Traverse right across a slightly overhanging wall via horizontal cracks for about 20'. Breech the vertical face above via short run-outs (crux) on small holds to a pair of bolts. 90'
FA: Rob Robinson, Peter Henley (2/85)

73 Dumpster Proof 5.12d (sport) ★★

Start: In a short, white corner 30' right of Open Boat Whalers.
Swing through steepness to a "no hands lay down rest." Jump for a jug ... break through to the moderate face up high. Chain anchors. 90'
FA: Cody Averbeck, Nathaniel Walker ('06)

74 Burn! 5.13a (sport)

Welcome to ... the fire! Loaded with lots of hot moves: heel hooks, a dyno here and there — and at least one killer iron cross sequence.
Start: 10' right of Open Boat Whalers. Clip the first bolt of The Message (see below). Diagonal left through bulges and over two flat roofs. Finish on Leftover Message (see below).
FA: Luis Rodriguez (7/00)

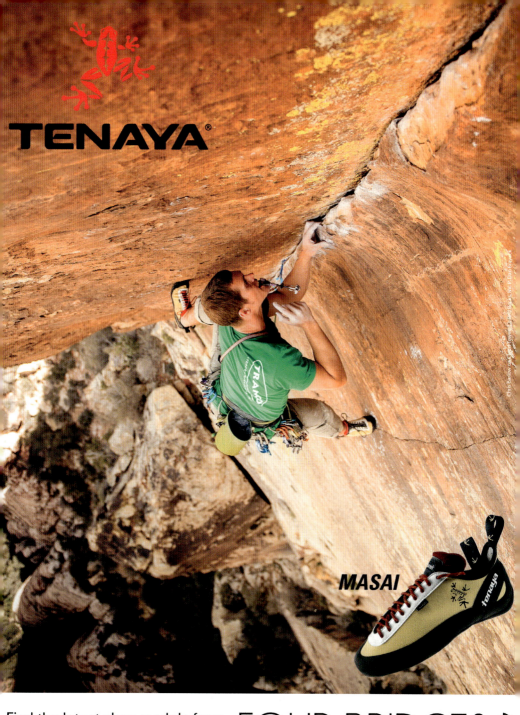

TENNESSEE WALL
PARADISE WALLS

75 Leftover Message 5.13a (sport) ★★★ ☐
Decipher this! Combines several of the Message's cryptic cruxes, with a fitting epilogue. Start: Same as for Burn!
Climb The Message (see below) for 40' (to its leftmost point). Continue clawing left into an obtuse corner with wild stemming; pull a final roof and continue up easy ground to bolt anchors. 75'
FA: Jerry Roberts (6/00)

76 The Message 5.13d (sport) ☐
Start: Same as for Burn!/Leftover Message.
Dive into a tsunami of cresting overhangs; turn the final roof (crux) past a flake and short crack. 60'
FA: Rob Robinson (5/91) FFA: Jerry Roberts (9/01)

> **Insider History:** This was one of my old projects. I freed it out to the lip, but decided it was so hard that I didn't want to spend a lot of time working it. (Hat tip to Jerry.) The route may be as difficult as 5.14a.

(77) Keelhauled 5.13a (sport) ★★★ ❒

Definition: to be punished by being dragged lengthwise from bow to stern beneath the keel of a ship. (You're going to love every minute of it too.)
Start: 10' right of The Message.
Climb a large, left-facing corner to a 12' roof with a flake. Turn roof at the shallow bowl above via a spectacular sequence; cross Fists Of Fury, finishing right to The Gangplank anchors (see below). 75'
FA: Travis Eiseman (6/00)

(78) Fists Of Fury 5.12 ❒

Ready to rumble? Break out the brass knuckles, load the big cams and put on your game face. One of the Sandstone Belt's meanest, "ass whupper" roof cracks.
Start: 10' right of Keelhauled.
Pitch 1: 5.12. Wiggle through a tricky roof slot. Climb a huge corner capped by "big daddy" — a 25' bombbay roof crack. Rig a hanging belay in a long, shallow, left-facing corner above the lip. (60') Pitch 2: 5.6. Continue up the corner to the top. (70')
FA: Rob Robinson, Steve Goins (6/85)

Insider's Note: Seem pretty hard? Occasionally graded 5.12+.

(79) The Gangplank 5.12a (sport) ★★★ ❒

Arrrgh ... time to walk the plank, laddy!
Start: 30' right of Fists of Fury.
Pitch 1: 5.12a. Swashbuckle through a low roof ... move left to a stance. (30') Pitch 2: 5.11a. Step left and climb the leftmost crack and arete to the base of a large roof. Continue working left to a bolt belay at stance. (75') Pitch 3: 5.8. Climb a blunt arete to the top. (40')
FA: Travis Eiseman (6/00)

Insider's Note: The second clip seems a bit sketchy; a stick clip might be in order.

John Bacahr on Open Boat Whalers, 5.10

Corey Kline disposing Dumpster Proof, 5.12+   Photo Credit: Luke Laeser

TENNESSEE WALL

⑧⓪ Slim Shady 5.12a ★★★
The companion climb to "the Punch"; a bit higher in quality.
Start: Same as for The Gangplank.
Climb the low roof. Diagonal left a few feet to a splitter finger and hand crack; follow it up through corners and over small roofs to the top. 85'
FA: Travis Eiseman (6/00)

> **Insider's Note:** Can be done in two pitches: turn the roof and belay.

⑧① Sucker Punch 5.12a ★★
On the prowl for a little street fight? Sandstone brawlers will enjoy knocking out the opening roof moves ... look forward to more civilized climbing above.
Start: Same as for Slim Shady.
Punch through a 10' roof past a couple of bolts. Climb the long headwall above following beautiful cracks to the top. 85'
FA: Travis Eiseman (6/00)

> **Insider's Note:** Can be done in two pitches: turn the roof and belay.

⑧② Silver Linings 5.11- ★
Start: 10' right of Sucker Punch.
Pitch 1: 5.11-. Pop over a small overhang onto a steep face. Now climb straight up past a fixed pin? to a ledge with a pine tree. (50') Pitch 2: 5.7. Traverse left 10' to a flake; climb a crack to the top. (40')
FA: Hillman Mann, Philip Hyman (alternate leads, 2/92)

⑧③ Ribbon Cracks 5.7 ★★
Start: 10' right of Silver Linings.
Blast up a vertical crack system packed with good finger and hand jams. 80'
FA: Rob Robinson, Peter Henley (4/85)

⑧④ Seam Stress 5.11+ ★
Start: 10' right of Ribbon Cracks.
Climb a steep wall with a nice, thin seam. 60'
FA: Rob Robinson, Forrest Gardner, top-rope (12/84) First Lead: Steve Goins (12/96)

> **Insider's Tip:** Reportedly protected using Lowe Ball nuts and marginal Metolious.

⑧⑤ Quick And Dirty 5.8 ★★★
Something of a misnomer; should be called ... long n' nice. The only climb of its grade in Paradise, but well worth a visit.
Start: 5' right of Seam Stress.
Climb a nice-looking, left-facing dihedral to the top. 60'
FA: Peter Henley, Rick Beckman (12/84)

TENNESSEE WALL / PARADISE WALLS

86 Stand And Deliver 5.11+ (sport) ★★★
Features a "squeamishly thin" crux, but the gear is good and the climbing is great, so the show must go on...
Start: 10' right of Quick and Dirty. Climb a delicate, steep face past a couple of red bolts (crux). Continue straight up the wall above to the top, passing a small roof. 100'
FA: Unknown.

87 Balls To The Wall 5.11 ★★★
Difficult to nut, with a "nutcracker" of a crux; not a pitch to pussy foot around on.
Start: 10' right of Stand and Deliver. Climb 25' to a tiny, right-facing (creaky) corner. Tweak over the bulge above (crux) to reach ... the chill zone. Cruise up jugs to a small overhang. Turn this and pump to the top. 100'
FA: Rob Robinson, Arno Ilgner (12/84)

> **Insider's Tip:** Lace as much pro as possible in the vertical seam right of the creaky corner at the crux. Double ropes recommended.

88 Southern Exposure 5.12+ ★★★
Sooo good!, but sooo reachy!
Start: 7' right of Balls to the Wall. Climb the face for 20' ... span straight up the wall past a short, thin vertical seam. Make a huge iron cross left, continue directly up the wall to the top. 100'
FA: Sam Adams (top-rope, 2/94)

> **Insider's Note:** Unfortunately, the moves past the crux seam are height dependent and practically impossible for anyone shorter than six feet tall.

89 Come And Get It! 5.11 ★★★
Hungry for some high quality face climbing? The sandstone dinner bell is ringing....
Start: 5' right of Southern Exposure.
Pitch 1: 5.11. Climb a right-facing corner. Diagonal right a few moves to a flexible flake beneath a large, flat ceiling with a dangerous-looking, detached flake. Skirt this on the left ... belay at stance above. (50') Pitch 2: 5.11-. Face climb directly up the steep, water-polished wall to the top. (50')
FA: Rob Robinson, Tim Cumbo (7/85)

> **Insider's Note:** Although this route doesn't garner a danger symbol, it is still a serious proposition. Of especial note is "the flake traverse" beneath the first pitch roof.

T-Wall

TENNESSEE WALL

🔴90 Tommy Knocker 5.11 ★
Start: 5' right of Come And Get It. Power over a small roof onto a steep wall with sloping holds. Work right to a seam ... now up to a small roof with a "sporty" loose flake. Gain the short diagonal finger crack above and continue to bolts on Respect For The Spider where you can lower off. 40'

FA: Rob Robinson, Randy Lane (7/89)

🔴91 Respect For The Spider 5.13c (sport) ★★★
Start: 10' right of Tommy Knocker. Follow bolts up a steep face. Spin out a 15' roof with a pinched-off crack and flake holds. Turn the lip (crux) and continue to anchors. 75'
FA: Jerry Roberts (8/00)

> **Insider's Note:** Could be as hard as 5.13d.

🔴92 Trail Of Tiers 5.11- ★★
This venerable old trad line migrates through a maze of overhangs. Worthy, but rarely done due to the difficult-to-protect crux arete on pitch two. Start: 15' right of Respect For The Spider. Pitch 1: 5.10. Climb a gently overhanging wall (with small roofs) for 15'. Traverse right to a stance by a flat, 3' roof. (45') Pitch 2: 5.11-. Continue traversing right ... follow a crack around an arete. Climb the arete (protection difficult) favoring the right wall (crux) to the left margin of the massive roof. Traverse left to standing belay. (40') Pitch 3: 5.8. Finish to the top following a crack in the face. (40')
FA: Rob Robinson, Peter Henley (4/85)

> **Insider's Note:** Pitch one and two can be done as one if you watch your rope drag.

www.rockerypress.com 345

TENNESSEE WALL PARADISE WALLS

93 Rockgasm 5.12d (sport)
Did someone say ... sex on the rocks? "Orgasmic" climbing on some of the T Wall's hottest stone.
Start: 5' right of Trail Of Tiers.
Handrail right following a horizontal crack just above the lip of a long flat roof; ease up the face above to a pair of short, side by side left-facing corners capped by roofs. Squirt right through these via an intricate and beautiful sequence. Surge over cresting wave of a roof above to anchors. 70'
FA: Jerry Roberts (6/00)

94 Grace 5.13b (sport)
Mother of Mary! A divine addition to the "sandstone cathedral's" ever-expanding collection of ethereal routes.
Start: 20' right of Rockgasm.
Rail left 15' through a big low roof, turn lip. Float into a beautiful stem sequence in the shallow box above; turn a thin, fingery bulge (crux). Finish through a cresting roof to a pair of anchors on the wall above. 70'
FA: Jerry Roberts (6/00)

> **Insider's Tip:** Stick clip bolt(s) above lip of roof. You might want to rig a back rope to protect the opening traverse.

TENNESSEE WALL

95 Stinger 5.12c ★★★ (sport)
A sandstone four leaf clover: "bee-utiful" rock, the sweetest moves — a honey of a pitch!
Start: 5' right of Grace.
Climb Dark Star (see below) for 15', traverse left below a roof. Trend left up stacked corners capped by small roofs. Buzz past a high and bulging overhang; continue straight up a spectacular exposed headwall and crack to a double bolt anchor. 100'
FA: Jerry Roberts (6/00)

> **Insider's Tips:** Stick clip the first bolt. Consider placing a long runner on the second bolt for a smooth-running belay.

96 Dark Star 5.13a (sport)
May the force be with you ... you're going to need it! Stellar holds galore, but the first 70 feet overhangs by half as much. A space odyssey worthy of Luke Skywalker.
Start: Same as for Stinger.
Blast straight up an overhanging wall with two small roofs (joined by a thin seam) to the base of an enormous roof. Launch out into roof (past an enormous, spooky block), crawl into the "dark star" cave! Bail here, or if you're psyched (and the wall above is dry) continue to the lip of the roof following a crack; finish up a psychotic headwall on thin holds. 100'
FA: Jerry Roberts (7/00) FA Variation: Jerry Roberts (7/00)

> **Insider's Tips:** This route clocks in at a great 5.12b if you end it from the anchor in the 'Dark Star.'

★★★ **Variation:** Skip the full body rest in the "dark star" cave for a phenomenal pump!

> **Insider's Tip:** Stick clip the first bolt. Rope drag may present a problem: I recommend the judicious use of double ropes and/or plenty of strategically placed full length runners. A good portion of this route remains dry in the rain.

97 The Bailiff 5.11- ★
Start: Same as for Dark Star.
Climb a right-facing corner to a gigantic roof. Traverse left 20' or so beneath this to a two bolt rappel station found on the wall above. 80'
FA: Steve Goins, Steve Atkin (5/89)

98 Behind The Waterfall 5.11 ★
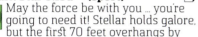
Start: 25' right of The Bailiff. Piece together a couple of power boulder problem moves ...you're rewarded with a bolt clip. Now ease through a short run-out to a small overhang. Follow a hand crack over this, and up to a fixed piece. 45'
FA: Peter Henley (aid solo, 1985) FFA: Steve Goins, Steve Atkin (5/89)

99 Aqua Lung 5.10 ★
Start: 15' right of Behind the Waterfall. Start off with a tricky boulder problem. Turn two roofs, (favoring the wall on the left.) Finish up a small dihedral with a finger crack to a single bolt. 50'
FA: Steve Atkin, Steve Goins, Rob Robinson (5/89)

Rockgasm, 5.12d

TENNESSEE WALL   PARADISE WALLS

T-Wall

100 Gates Of Testosterone 5.13a (sport)
From the Halls of Mentholyptus, head west for several leagues past the Pillars of Atlantis. Just left of Mount Olympus look for a huge sandstone tower sporting a pair of giant granite balls — you're almost there!
Start: 20' right of Aqua Lung.
Attack a gently overhung wall with a flat, crackless (and impossible-looking) 5' roof midway up. Conquer the roof using a Herculean iron cross sequence ... continue pumping upwards to the edge of a massive roof. Escape right to the anchors atop Stone Hinge. 80'
FA: Rob Robinson (9/91)

Insider's Tip: Stays mostly dry in the rain save the last few moves traversing to the anchors on Stone Hinge.

101 Stone Hinge 5.12d
Sandstone just doesn't get any better than this. In my 30+ years of climbing "the Hinge" stands out as one of my all time personal favorites; you'll love it too! Features beautiful "kung-fu style" corner stemming. Hi ... yah!
Start: 10' right of Gate of Testosterone. Climb a moderate wall with superb grit-textured holds; continue up an awesome, left-facing, hanging dihedral. At roofs, clock right. The race is on for the ledge above. 80'
FA: Rob Robinson, Marvin Orio (10/89)

Insider's Note: Originally graded 5.12a/b, some climbers think its 13a! What do you think?

348 www.rockerypress.com

TENNESSEE WALL

Stone Hinge, 5.12d

102 Dogfight 5.13a ★★
Feeling feral? "A small holds snarl fest."
Start: Same as for Stone Hinge.
Snarl up easy terrain past bolts on big holds to the base of the Stone Hinge dihedral. Attack a thin bulge out right, turn 1' roof above, finish on the final stretch of Stone Hinge. 80'
FA: Travis Eiseman (1/02)

Dogfight, 5.13a

BROADVIEW BUTTRESS

2 DAYS

Carl Buch on Property Man 5.12e   Photo Credit: James Arnold

❶ Handy Man 5.10+ ★★★★★ ☐
This beaut' looks even better after a little elbow grease. Start 118 miles north of Atlanta. Work out the huge cantilever before leveling out to face the prominent tapering crack that starts as thin fingers and erupts into an all-out off-width war zone--you may as well just call a real Handy Man to do it. **Chuck Berry 1958**

❷ Property Man 5.12e ★★★★★★★ ☐
Searching for your next dream line? Property Man begins just right of Handy Man. Start low and sell high on this investment opportunity. And with the proper guide, you won't need to bring your big nuts to the sale. Find your sequence through the opening moves to the quaint two finger pocket for the frantic lunge to the garage sized hueco where you can park that new caddy before the run out finish—are you a Property Man? I am...
Mark Livasy 1981

❸ Rock Climber Man (project) ☐
You warmed up on Handy Man, sent Property Man and still have time for more? May as well hop on the 'ole proj, right? Rock Climber Man is the 2,000 ft. extension of Real Estate Man. Personally, I'd ask Carl Buch and Broadview Property Solutions what they would do before buying a 1200 meter rope.
The advertisement is just below!

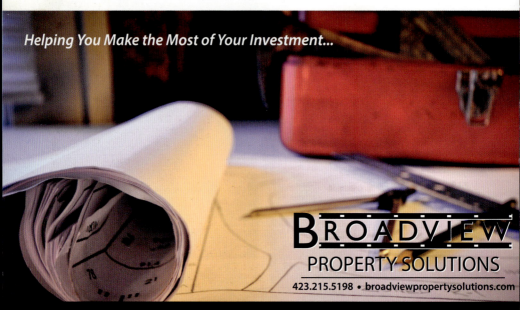

Helping You Make the Most of Your Investment...

BROADVIEW
PROPERTY SOLUTIONS
423.215.5198 • broadviewpropertysolutions.com

Broadview Property Solutions • Complete Contractor Services • Carl Buch Owner/Operator

TENNESSEE WALL

EAST PARADISE

This stretch of cliff line — about 150 yards long — adjoins West Paradise to its left. It begins at a broken up buttress that forms the right side of the Paradise Falls amphitheater, at the point where the trail from below meets the cliff line. From this point head right and you will be in East Paradise. The routes are listed from left to right, the same way you will encounter them, and the first route you encounter will be, Blind Hands Bluff, which is right above you.

103 Blind Hands Bluff 5.11 ★
Start: 30' right of Stone Hinge and at the point where the trail from below meets the cliff line.
Climb the left edge of the buttress at a thin vertical crack. Intercept a left-facing corner. Work up through this and "bluff" past the bulge above (crux) to gain a ledge. 75'
FA: Rob Robinson, Bruce Rogers (12/84)

Insider's Trivia: The second route done at the Tennessee Wall. Originally graded 5.11-.

104 El Chupacabra 5.11- ★
Start: 15' right of Blind Hands Bluff. Climb a left-facing corner with large roofs on its right wall. At the top of corner climb straight up through a bulging overhang (crux). Work right (crux) into a short, left-facing corner capped by roofs; angle left to the top. 80'
FA: Cody Averbeck, Sam Miles ('06)

105 Cryptid 5.9+
Start: Same as for El Chupacabra.
Pitch 1: 5.9+. Climb El Chupacabra to the top of the initial corner. Traverse right to a belay at the base of a short and heavily featured crack. (50') Pitch 2: 5.8. Climb the crack and join a splitter hand crack that leads to the top. (45')
FA: Sam Miles, Cody Averbeck ('06)

25 mins

Insider's Note: The upper crack will be classic once it has been cleaned out.

106 The Crisis Before The Norm 5.11 ★
Start: 15' right of El Chupacabra. Power out a low roof (crux) at a single hand jam slot; trend up and left via small holds to a stance. Continue up a right-facing corner above; wander up face to the top. 100'
FA: Steve Goins, Truly Bracken (date unknown)

www.rockerypress.com 351

TENNESSEE WALL

PARADISE WALLS

107 The Birth Simulator 5.12- ★★★
By all accounts this is one mean little baby. "Birthing the crux" will be a lot less painful, perhaps, if you use a bit of tape.
Start: 25' right of The Crisis Before The Norm. Amble up moderately difficult rock for about 40' to an enticing roof with a hand-sized crack. Strain? into the flared, hanging slot. Finish over a small and airy overhang. 90'
FA: Rob Robinson, Steve Goins (6/85)

Insider's Note: Originally graded 11+, but upgraded subsequent to climber feedback.

108 Parade Of Skeletons 5.10 ★
Start: 10' right of The Birth Simulator. Rattle up a wide, left-facing dihedral with a bulge. Exit right to a ledge. 75'
FA: Rob Robinson (12/88)

TENNESSEE WALL

110 Mouthful Of Cavities 5.11 ★
Start: 5' right of Whistlin' In The Boneyard. Pull through a small roof at the base of a short, right-facing corner. Continue straight up to a pillowed tan roof. Good holds above lead to a good stance. Trend up and right on face, then break left out in tiers (crux). End on a large ledge above with anchors. 70'
FA: Cody Averbeck, Chuck Crawford, Michael Wurzel ('07)

111 Out On A Whim 5.10+ ★★
Start: Same as for Mouthful Of Cavities. Pull through a small roof at the base of a short, right-facing corner. Traverse right around an arete and climb a straight-in finger and hand crack to a ledge. Rap from the rings on Mouthful Of Cavities (or The Moaning Weigh, see below). 70'
FA: Rob Robinson, Arno Ilgner (12/84)

> **Insider's Note:** Most climbers start the opening moves from atop a small pile of rocks; the first holds can be hell to reach.

109 Whistlin' In The Boneyard 5.11+ ★★
Nothing to be scared of here! Great gear and "killer" climbing.
Start: 20' right of Parade Of Skeletons. Boulder a few moves up the wall to a good "hueco." Diagonal left and climb a nice corner to a bulging roof with a single bolt. Conquer this (crux) and continue to the top. 90'
FA: Rob Robinson, Jim Herrington (12/93)

> **Insider's Notes:** Originally graded 5.11, it has been upgraded subsequent to climber feedback and could be as hard as 5.12-. This is also an excellent 5.10+ A0 if you simply aid past the crux bolt.

Out on a Whim, 5.10+

Queen Bitch 5.11- ★★

Check this one out if you're looking for something a little short n' sassy.
Start: Same as Loading The Reactor.
Climb seemingly suspect, but solid, rock to a ledge. Step left onto face and follow good holds to a stance below tiered roofs. Climb right through roofs, clip a bolt, gain a good hold at the lip. Power through slopers (crux) to gain a thin left-facing corner. Technical moves through the corner, then a step right provides an exit to the anchors on The Moaning Weigh. 70'
FA: Cody Averbeck, Theresa Averbeck ('05)

Climber: Andrew Miller Photo Credit: Micah Gentry

TENNESSEE WALL

112 Loading The Reactor 5.11- ★★
Start: Around the corner and 15' right of Out On A Whim.
Climb a few moves in a corner ... scrunch left beneath 5' roof to stance. Surge through a couple of small tiers (crux) onto steep face with good holds. Continue straight up into a smooth-looking, left-facing corner past a small roof. Rap from the rings on Mouthful Of Cavities or the Moaning Weigh. 70'
FA: Rob Robinson, Darrow Kirkpatrick (10/97)

Alternate Finish (Just Another Toothpick): 5.11- ★
Climb Loading The Reactor for approximately 30'. Diagonal left to a stance in a hidden, right-angling ramp. Break left up the face following a thin crack system to the ledge and anchors.
FA: Alternate Finish: Cody Averbeck, Theresa Averbeck ('05)

113 Queen Bitch 5.11- ★★
See description on page 354.

114 The Moaning Weigh 5.10
Start: Same as for Queen Bitch et al.
Pitch 1: 5.9. Climb seemingly suspect, but apparently solid, rock to a ledge. Traverse right to a large, left-facing corner system at the base of tiered roofs and belay. (35')
Pitch 2: 5.10. Climb the corner, diagonal right through roofs, link with hand crack and finish to ring anchors. (35')
FA: Cody Averbeck, Brion Voges, Ben Tsui ('05)

115 A Parting Of The Ways 5.12- ★★★
A complicated trad masterpiece.
Start: 30' right of Just Another Toothpick et al.
Pitch 1: 5.11+. Boulder over a small roof; continue to a ledge. Power out a 4' roof with seam to gain a horizontal slot. Climb the rounded, outside corner above with minimal, hard-to-place gear and a 5.10 move or two. Exit left above onto face and traverse to a standing belay beneath massive overhangs. (70')
Pitch 2: 5.12-. Insanely sloping holds (crux) lead over a 5' roof above split by a thin seam. Gun straight up the bulging wall (5.11-) above to the top. (40')

> **Insider's Tips:** Consider carrying a big #4 cam or equivalent for a hidden horizontal above the 4' roof on pitch 1. Use double ropes, bring a "master" trad rack. Part of pitch 1 was retro-bolted, but it may have been chopped.

Variation (Sport)(Diggity Dank):
5.12b. ★★ From the end of pitch 1 climb straight up through tiered overhangs following a line of bolts.
FA: Steve Goins, Rob Robinson (combined effort, 1/94) FA Variation: Anthony Meeks (date unknown)

TENNESSEE WALL   PARADISE WALLS

117 The Shadow 5.13a (Sport) ★

Bring a flashlight ... you might get lost up there. An awesome addition to the T Wall's collection of monster roofs.
Start: 35' right of Homeland Insecurity, atop a block.
Climb a face, turn a 20' roof to gain short wall. Continue out 10' roof (crux) to anchor above. 75'
FA: Travis Eiseman (2/02)

> Insider's Tip: Travis says a single rope runs well.

118 Belly Of The Beast 5.10 ★

Start: In the big corner, 20' right of The Shadow.
Step onto the face from atop a block. Climb right around a small roof capped by a short, left-facing corner. Continue to the top via an easier, but overhanging, offwidth crack/chimney. 80'
FA: Rob Robinson, Tom Campbell (5/85)

116 Homeland Insecurity 5.12

This beautiful, serpentine line winds up a fabulously featured wall packed with magnificent features. The quintessential T Wall trad line.
Start: 15' right of A Parting Of The Ways.
Scramble 10' to a ledge. Jam a hand-sized crack through a small roof. A line of jugs leads up and right. Turn a tricky bulge (5.11) split by an obvious crack; continue up the crack to a band of massive roofs. Penetrate these, work right (crux) and up to hidden ledge with anchors. 100'
FA: Kirk Brode, Rob Robinson (2/02)

> Insider's Tips n' Notes: Climbing to the base of the crux roof is an excellent pitch in and of itself; plus, it stays dry in the rain. Consider carrying a #4 Camalot or equivalent to place at the base of the 5.11 bulge. Double ropes might be nice to have; especially for clipping your last piece of gear in the crux overhang.

TENNESSEE WALL

⑲ Midget Cage 5.11 ★★
Start: Same as for Hell Or High Water. Climb Hell Or High Water until it is feasible to traverse right into a short, left-facing corner capped by a huge flat roof. Climb to the roof, work right, then up and back left in roof tiers. When possible, start gunning up the exposed arête, aiming for the top. 70'
FA: Harrison Shull, Tyler Stracker ('03)

⑳ Hell Or High Water 5.11-
See description on page 358.

㉑ Two Bums Are Better Than None 5.9 A0
Start: 15' right of Midget Cage, at the base of the huge detached slab leaning against the wall.
Climb the slab face, heading left to a flat roof. Do a few aid moves out the roof, gaining an easy corner. Climb the corner and a fun and exposed face, eventually step right; continue to the top. 80'
FA: Cody Averbeck, Sam Miles ('06)

㉒ Every Raisin Was A Grape 5.11 ★★
Start: Same as for Two Bums Are Better Than None.
Climb the slab. Turn a 2' overhang (crux); merge with the straight-in thin crack above. A final face sequence (crux) guards the summit. 80'
FA: Cody Averbeck, Sam Miles ('06)

TENNESSEE WALL — PARADISE WALLS

Hell Or High Water 5.11-
An intimidating block of overhanging rock (inexplicably!) ignored for the better part of two decades. Arguably the best "easy" 5.11 jug haul in the Chattanooga area; it is also one of my personal favorites.
Start: 30' right of Belly Of The Beast.
Boulder right across face on scrappy holds to gain the top of a huge flake leaning against cliff's base. Diagonal left across a bit of sketchy crackle; climb a short, right-facing corner to large band of overhangs with a jutting "ship's prow." Traverse left along prow into the center of the overhangs. Churn straight to the top past a single bolt (crux). 70'
FA: Rob Robinson, Kirk Brode (2/02)

Insider's Note: If you're careful how you rig your protection up and out the ship's prow, you can manage this on a single rope lead.

Laban Swafford on Hell or High Water, 5.11 Photo Credit: Micah Gentry

THE WASTELAND

Parking: Park at the main Tennessee Wall parking lot.

Approach: This stretch of cliff line is situated in between East Paradise and the Amphitheater. It encompasses several hundred yards of cliff line. Hike up the main Tennessee Wall trail for about a quarter mile to a fork. Bear right and continue to the large cove of rock known as "the Amphitheater." Hike left to the left margin of the Amphitheater, where you will encounter the first climb listed in that area, Circling Buzzards. At this point the trail will be right next to the cliff, and as you walk around an obvious prow, you will be entering the Wasteland.

Note: It is also possible to access this area if you approach from the Paradise Walls area. Hike up the main Tennessee Wall trail to a fork (look for a cairn) and make a sharp left. At the top of the trail, head right (east) and continue through East Paradise and to a seasonal stream at a long, low-angled and bushy section of the cliff. This constitutes the left boundary of the Wasteland. You may want to utilize this approach if you plan on climbing at the far left (west) side of the Wasteland.

Routes are numbered left to right, however you will encounter them walking right to left (east to west) if you approach from the Amphitheater.

25 mins

Around this buttress, you are leaving the Amphitheater and entering the Wasteland.

At this seasonal drainage, you are leaving East Paradise and entering the Wasteland.

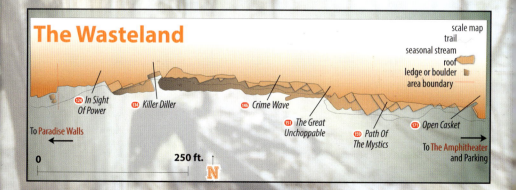

TENNESSEE WALL

THE WASTELAND

123 Ground Effects 5.10 ★★

An enjoyable and unexpectedly exciting romp up a wall that — at first glance — looks somewhat less than promising.
Start: Just right of a tree-filled gully and several large boulders.
Begin with an intricate face crux: step up ... step right ... step up again. Easy climbing leads to a very short, left-facing corner capped by a small roof. Turn this (crux) and continue straight up the wall to the top. 120'
FA: Steve Goins, Truly Bracken (11/92)

Insider's Tips: This is a "trad master special"; there's just enough pro, but you'll have work hard to ferret it out. Small Metolious or Aliens are helpful, as are a couple of the pink and red Tri-cams (past the second crux.) Also bring a small wire brush and nut tool. Double ropes recommended.

124 In Sight Of Power 5.8+ ★★

Start: 75' right of Ground Effects. Climb a long, left-facing corner to anchors. 80'
FA: Rob Robinson, Peter Henley (12/84)

Insider Trivia: This was the T Wall's first route and was named so because you can see a hydroelectric power station across the river from the summit.

TENNESSEE WALL

THE WASTELAND

This area's name, "The Wasteland" (taken from Four Quarters by T.S. Eliot), would seem to suggest a plethora of poor quality rock. That said, nothing could be further from the truth. Perhaps I should have called this area something like "The Thousand Roof Walls" since it is home to a chaotic mix of tall and exposed faces dominated by hundreds of small-to-medium sized roofs (with a couple that jut out a distance of 20' or more.)

25 mins

125 Super Wave 5.11+
This sandstone tsunami frequently swamps the sea-faring ambitions of the typical 5.11 trad leader. A big, open face of a romp — jam packed with scads of wild climbing. Start: 15' right of In Sight of Power. Follow a spectacular, mostly overhanging, line slicing left through a prominent roof with a bolt at its lip (crux). Trend left up the giant headwall into a shallow right-facing corner. Finish up face above. 100'
FA: Harrison Shull, Kirk Brode ('04)

Insider's Tip: Bring cams up to 5" (heavy on "the big stuff" for the roof). The very last moves may be wet if raining.

126 Steep Eye For The Slab Guy 5.12 ★★
Start: Same as for Super Wave. Follow a spectacular, mostly overhanging, line to a wide roof about midway up the wall. Diagonal right, turn the roof, clip bolt at crux then continue stylin' right. Finish on moderately difficult but sparsely protected face climbing to bolted anchors atop Stink Finger (see below). 100'
FA: Harrison Shull, Kirk Brode ('04)

Insider's Tip: Bring cams up to 5" (heavy on "the big stuff" for the roof).

127 Stink Finger 5.11+ ★
Start: 10' right of Steep Eye For The Slab Guy. Wander up a blunt arête to past a ledge. Continue up the left side past a big, right-facing system. Work right, then back left in roofs to gain face above. Diagonal right to a huge roof, rail left, and claw (crux) onto face above. Finish at anchors. 100'
FA: Kirk Brode, Tyler Stracker ('04)

128 Run With The Horseman 5.9+ ★
Start: 10' right of Stink Finger. Climb a wide, left-facing dihedral to a large roof band. Work right to a pair of bolt anchors on a ledge. 50'
FA: Rob Robinson, Peter Henley (12/84)

Andrew Miller cresting the roof on Superwave, 5.11

Photo Credit: Micah Gentry

T-Wall 'Big Air' Routes
Circus Circus, 5.8
Where Lizards Go to Die, 5.10-
Solar Circus, 5.10-
Crankenstein, 5.11-
Voodo Roof, 5.12+

TENNESSEE WALL
THE WASTELAND

129 Pump Failure 5.12- ★★★
The opening arête is longer and comparable in quality to pitch one of The Prow located on Lookout Mountain's Sunset Rock. Sustained and reachy power climbing on bullet hard sandstone. Start: 15' right of Run With The Horseman. Claw through a bulging overhang for 15'. Tweak right into face moves when possible, then back left onto the nose of a rounded arete. Churn for an out of sight ledge above. Finish up a long headwall, or set directionals and traverse left to bolt anchors at the end of pitch 1 of Run With The Horseman. 100'
FA: Harrison Shull, Stuart Chapin (3/02)
FFA: Brad Holroyd

130 Moon Of The Crow 5.11 ★★
Start: 25' right of Pump Failure, at the right edge of a low roof.
Climb up and left, just above the low roof on easy but unprotected ground to a small ledge. Continue up a shallow, left-facing corner; trend left past horizontals to a ledge. Follow seams through a roof, climb past horizontals and a thin face section protected by a bolt. Finish to bolted anchors. 95'
FA: Stuart Chapin (3/02)

In Sight of Power, 5.8+

Dave 'Willy' Wilson grinnin' through the fun upper bulge of Killer Diller. Photo Credit: Andrew Miller

TENNESSEE WALL — THE WASTELAND

131 Tribal Babysitter 5.8 ★★
Start: 5' right of Moon Of The Crow, in a low dihedral.
Pitch 1: 5.7. Move up and right via ledges and cracks, then back left to a ledge halfway up the wall. (45') Pitch 2: 5.8. Follow an orange dihedral to a roof, escape left to anchors. (45')
FA: Heidi Chapin, Stuart Chapin (3/02)

Insider's Tips: Consensus is that it is better to climb straight up from the ground (following William Perry, see next route) past the belay ledge and combine pitches 1 and 2 into one long lead.

132 William Perry 5.10 ★★
Start: Same as for Tribal Babysitter. Climb straight up to a ledge via a short crack and horizontals. Continue up a steep section, then finagle up and left onto an arete with a vertical crack. A bit higher, skirt right past a large roof and continue up a right-facing dihedral. Push straight over a final boulder problem bulge to earn the summit anchors. 100'
FA: Stuart Chapin, Harrison Shull (3/02)

TENNESSEE WALL

133 A Good Place To Come 5.9 ★★
And indeed it is! Sustained and enjoyable, mostly moderate, climbing capped by a tricky 5.9 crux.
Start: At trailside, 10' right of William Perry. Scramble 10' and climb a short, diagonal "slash of a hand crack" capped by an easy slab (with a tinsy little run-out.) Continue to a small flat roof above. Pass this on the left, step right and up to another small flat roof ... pull straight through this, then follow thin cracks and good holds up the steep face above to a good stance. Unlock boulder problem moves guarding access to the final headwall anchors (crux). 100' **FA: Unknown**

Insider's Tip: A green Camalot might work well in a shallow vertical pocket just before the anchors.

134 Killer Diller 5.10
A short, but killer piece of T Wall stone, and one of my favorite "short" 5.10 pitches at the T Wall.
Start: Atop a small ledge about 20' right of A Good Place To Come. Pull low roof and climb short overhanging finger crack (crux) splitting a tan band. Turn bulge split by crack (crux) ... face climb up and right. Finish to anchors via short "v" groove capped by a small overhang. 70'

FA: Rob Robinson (11/01)

Insider Note: The name comes from a Clyde Edgerton novel.

Laban Swafford charging to the goal line on William Perry, 5.10   Photo Credit: Micah Gentry

TENNESSEE WALL

135 Faunal Succession 5.11 ★
Start: 5' right of Killer Diller.
Climb horizontals to the base of a bulge.
Fight over the bulge via a seam and
face holds. Edge your way up to rings.
70' FA: Cody Averbeck, Tyler Stracker ('07)

136 Sole Searcher 5.6 ★
Start: 15' right of Faunal Succession.
Trend right up blocky rock, work
left, then straight up the center of a
steep face (crux) with intermittent small
holds. 60'
FA: Rob Robinson, Susan Robinson (12/91)

137 One Slip 5.5 ★★
A rare find for the grade, at least at the
T Wall.
Start: Same as for Sole Searcher.
Trend right up blocky rock on big holds
and bomber gear. Finish straight up the
wall (crux) staying on the right side of
an arete. 80'
FA: Rob Robinson, free solo (10/92)

> Insider's Note: From the Pink Floyd song "One Slip."

138 Path Of The Misfits 5.8 ★
Start: At trailside, 20' right of One Slip.
Face climb up to a corner system
capped by small roofs. Continue up the
wall just right of an arête (joining the
finish of One Slip) to the top. 80'
FA: David Vartanian, Ward Smith (1/90)

139 Wood Spirit 5.10 ★★
An often overlooked and neglected
"sleeper" classic worthy of your attention; it yields steep and nicely sustained
climbing on surprisingly good rock.
Start: 15' right of Path Of The Misfits, at 10'
cedar stump.
From atop the cedar stump: Climb a
short, shallow slot. Work more or less
directly up the wall above, passing
through the center of a prominent
orange band to anchors. 80'
FA: Jeff Achey, Kirk Brode ('98)

> Insider's Note: "Purists" can start from the ground to either side of the tree.

TENNESSEE WALL

THE WASTELAND

140 Hammer Time 5.10- ★★
"Leave hammer, bring heart."
Start: 35' right of Wood Spirit.
Boulder over a low roof. Climb a long, left-angling flake system to the top and anchors. 80'
FA: Ward Smith, David Vartanian (2/90)

141 Back From The Storm 5.12- ★
Start: 10' right of Hammer Time.
Tweak over a big roof past a (hard to spot) bolt. Work up and right over a smaller roof split by a thin crack; continue to the top. 80'
FA: David Vartanian, Ward Smith (1/90)

142 The Riff 5.10
Start: 15' right of Back From The Storm.
Climb a bit of sketchy rock. Traverse right and turn a 6' overhang; pull bulge above lip. Continue up a tiny corner and exposed face to the top. 100'
FA: Steve Goins, Truly Bracken (6/92)

143 The Oasis 5.10 ★
Start: 20' right of The Riff.
Work left a few moves out a low overhang with horizontal holds and handjams, then "ummph" over a bulge. Turn a small overhang above with a couple of elegant moves ... wander up an open face. Conquer a 3' summit roof split by an obvious thin crack, or finish just right on easier holds. 100'
FA: Steve Goins, Truly Bracken (9/92)

Hammer Time, 5.10-

TENNESSEE WALL

144 Class Action 5.11+ ★★
Takes an "appealing," although circuitous, route through a labrinyth of overhangs.
Start: 20' right of The Oasis.
Pitch 1: 5.11+. Boulder out a low roof onto an overhanging face (beneath a 15' crack.) Pass a bolt, rail left 15', turn a roof and head up a slab. Handrail out the roof to a belay. (50') Pitch 2: 5.10+. Turn the 4' roof above using a thick flake. Continue to the top following a shallow, left-facing corner. (50')
Variation - Conviction: 5.10. Start 20' right of the regular start, atop a block. Turn a bulge and climb to a hole below a massive roof. Traverse left 10', then up and left to join the regular route.
FA: Steve Goins, Truly Bracken (10/92)
FA Variation: Truly Bracken, Steve Goins (10/92)

145 Stay Of Execution 5.11 ★★
Start: 25' right of Class Action.
Pitch 1: 5.11. Fire straight up through a band of tiered overhangs to a standing belay. (40') Pitch 2: 5.9+. Work up and then right over jutting pedestal above. Traverse left a bit, then up a bulging wall to a standing belay. (40') Pitch 3: 5.10-. Escape over a 5' roof just right of a vegetated crack. (20')
FA: Steve Goins, Truly Bracken (9/92)

146 Crime Wave 5.12- ★★
Start: 30' right of Stay Of Execution. Face climb a little; continue up a short, shallow, overhanging crack capped by a short left-facing corner (hidden fixed pin) capped by a small roof. Escape right to a hidden ledge with fixed gear. 60'
FA: Forrest Gardner, Jack Noonan (4/86)

TENNESSEE WALL

THE WASTELAND

147 The Donkey Show 5.11 ★
Start: 30' right of Crime Wave.
Power into a band of small tiered overhangs, make a big move right to the base of a shallow vertical crack. Conquer this (crux), now ease up a crusty left-facing corner for 15'. Turn a small but tricky roof and make a few more corner moves. Exit right and continue up easier rock to the top. 100' FA: Tyler Stracker, Kirk Brode (3/05)

> **Insider's Tip:** There are placements for a couple of brass nuts in the first 15'. The key is having the guns to hang in there and place them.

148 Danglo Saxon 5.11-
Start: 20' right of The Donkey Show.
Climb a left-facing dihedral. Arch left up to and under an overhang. Step left, climb another left-facing dihedral; continue to the top following a weakness. 110'
FA: Steve Goins, Kent Ballew (12/90)

149 Tweedledee 5.11 ★
Start: 20' right of Danglo Saxon.
Crank through tiered roofs on good holds to a 3' overhang with a small alcove at its base. Turn this on the left; climb out close to the left side of a huge roof above past a bullet-shaped block. When feasible, rail left to roof's margin and escape up a headwall to the top. 100'
FA: Steve Goins, Kent Ballew (12/90)

Tweedledum 5.10- ★
Boulder past an overhang (crux). Face climb a stretch of blobby rock; fan left around a large, cresting overhang; jog right beneath a large triangular roof. Finish up a left-facing corner to the top. 100'
FA: Fritz Lovingood, Bear Thurman (12/90)

150 Tunnel Ratz 5.11+ ★
Start: 15' right of Tweedledum.
Climb 10', follow a crack through small overhang (crux) into unusual shallow vertical tube (a.k.a. the rat pipe.) At the top of tube, exit right, turn a tricky bulge, climb a totally run-out 5.8-ish face to gain a short vertical crack. Traverse right 15' to a small ledge on an arete and belay. Bail from fixed anchors (could be some knotted slings behind a large flake) or finish up the second pitch of Elephus Maximus (see subsequent route description.) 60'
FA: Rob Robinson, Chris Chesnutt (2/02)

> **Insider's Beta:** Carry a "full spectrum rack," including two each gold and blue Camalots for "the tube" and beyond.

TENNESSEE WALL

151 The Great Unchoppable 5.11+ ★★★
Pitch one is reportedly as good as — but a bit harder than — Fly With The Falcon (another classic T Wall crack.)
Start: 10' right of Tunnel Ratz.
Pitch 1: 5.11+. Traverse left along wide weakness, climb an overhanging crack (behind cedar tree) capped by a bulge. Traverse right to small ledge and belay. (50') Pitch 2: 5.10. Follow pitch 2 of Elephus Maximus. (See next route description.) (50')
FA: Chris Chesnutt, Travis Eiseman (2/02)

152 Elephus Maximus 5.11 ★★
Tilt-a-whirl trip through the vertical circus world.
Start: Same as for The Great Unchoppable.
Pitch 1: 5.11. Zig left along a wide weakness. Zag right to small cave (capped by a pointed horn and grapefruit-sized hole). Follow good holds right and up (crux). Belay on the first good small ledge you encounter. (50') Pitch 2: 5.10. Climb to the left margin of tiered roofs. Work through these; climb a short face and angle right to the top. (50')
FA: Steve Goins, Truly Bracken (5/92)

> **Insider's Note:** Doesn't look that great from the ground, but appearances can certainly be deceptive.

153 Pop Life 5.10+ ★
Start: 10' right around the corner from Elephus Maximus, on a small, exposed ledge.
Pitch 1: 5.10+. Climb a small, rounded, right-facing corner with a "small wires" crack. Turn a roof and climb another rounded (but not quite as steep) right-facing corner. Continue with a moderately difficult run-out up an apron arete to a belay. (60') Pitch 2: 5.4. Finish to the top following an easy, wide corner. (40')
FA: Rob Robinson, Robyn Erbesfield (11/85)

154 Talon 5.9- ★
Start: Same as for Air Raid.
Pitch 1: 5.8. Climb past a small overhang with horizontal bands. Scamper up a couple of ledges to a classic belay ledge at the base of a beautiful, left-facing orange corner. (40') Pitch 2: 5.9-. Climb the corner (crux) to a roof. Traverse left and up a few moves to another (smaller) ledge and belay. (60') Pitch 3: 5.4. Continue up the corner to the top. (40')
FA: Eric Peterson, Brett Fundak, Paul Stucky (11/89)

> **Insider's Notes:** At least one star for the stupendous belay ledge at the start of second pitch corner. (The corner is pretty good too!) Pitch one is a bit sketchy; I suggest starting a little further left: Follow a series of short corners linked by vegetated ledges to the belay ledge at the base of pitch two.

TENNESSEE WALL

THE WASTELAND

155 Air Raid 5.10 ★★★
Start: Scamper down a steep hillside beneath Pop Life et al and walk right about 20' along the trail.
Pitch 1: 5.8. Climb past a small overhang with horizontal bands. Scamper up a couple of ledges to a classic belay ledge at the base of a beautiful, left-facing orange corner. (40') Pitch 2: 5.10. Climb a beautiful splitter crack on the right wall of a super classic corner. Just below the largest roof, traverse right for about 25'. Escape to the top. 100'
FA: Chris Chesnutt, Travis Eiseman (2/02)

> **Insider's Note:** Nathaniel Walker has freed the final straight-out roof finish at 5.12 making for one spectacular airy pitch!

156 Wrectum Wrecker 5.12+
Be prepared to open up a can of old fashioned Southern whup ass on this one. Start: About 20' right of Talon. Scamper up some easy ledges, then make an exposed 5th Class traverse left about 15' to gain a small belay ledge.
Diagonal right up the wall ... work left to gain a small, white-frosted overhang with jams. Grunt into the shallow "toilet bowl" above; exit right via bulging seams to bolt anchors. 75'

★★★ Alternate Finish: Spinal Wrecker: 5.12. Follow "the Wrecker" into the bowl. Step left and follow a thin crack past a couple of bolts through a spectacular and airy, tiered overhang. Anchors await you on the wall above. 75'
FA: Rob Robinson, Forrest Gardner (11/85)
FA Alternate Finish: Travis Eiseman (2/02)

> **Insider's Note:** A twisted name for such an awesome climb, "butt" before you're finished with it (or vice versa) Forrest and I are confident you will figure out where the name came from!

157 Circus Circus 5.9 ★★★
Spectacular and exposed climbing through monolithic overhangs reminiscent of the best of the best that the Shawangunks in New York has to offer. Start: Same as for Wrectum Wrecker.
Pitch 1: 5.8+. Follow "the Wrecker" for about 20'. Ease right for about 30' on a slab face footing a huge flat roof (a.k.a. "the big top") to a small and exposed belay perch. (50')
Pitch 2: 5.9. Work left around a small roof above and climb a perfect left-facing corner to a good ledge (optional belay.) Jug through small overhang above (technical crux) and continue to the top. (75')
FA: Kirk Brode, Rob Robinson (alternate leads) (2/02)

> **Insider's Note:** All parties attempting this climb should be solid at the 5.9 grade ... a very intimidating and serious route.

TENNESSEE WALL

158 Two Clowns On A Rope 5.8+ ★★
A spectacular aerial feat of climbing that serves as a nice alternate finish to Circus Circus. You should consider doing both. Start: Same as for Circus Circus. Pitch 1: 5.8+. Climb Circus Circus to the first belay. (50') Pitch 2: 5.8. Diagonal right across the face following an obvious crack system in a very exposed face to a pair of bolt anchors beneath a large roof. (50') Pitch 3: 5.7. Climb right around the large roof and continue to the top. (35')
FA: Kirk Brode, Stuart Chapin (3/02)

Insider's Notes: It is possible to combine the first two pitches into one long lead. The last pitch is optional and indeed many parties simply bail from the bolt station at the end of pitch two. Like *Circus Circus*, this is a long, serious and intimidating climb recommended only to seasoned 5.9 climbers.

159 Path Of The Mystics 5.12-
Nothing mystical here save a superb jug haul on bomber holds leading out a huge roof to a mystifying crux. Start: On a spacious ledge above the trail, immediately right of the start of Two Clowns On A Rope et al. 15' of easy climbing leads to a 25' roof (periodically equipped with a few fixed pieces.) Muscle out and over the lip to fixed anchors. 50'
FA: Rob Robinson, Steve Goins, Jeff Gruenberg (1/87)

Insider's Tips: There are tons of places to do "leg drapes" over deep flakes, so I suggest wearing reversed knee pads strapped to your calves for some much appreciated padding. A good tape job for the hands will also make things a bit more pleasant.

TENNESSEE WALL

THE WASTELAND

160 Where Lizards Go To Die 5.10-
... and climbers go to live their dreams. An enticing, but intimidating, route that winds through a gauntlet of imposing roofs capped by a stunning and exposed dihedral.
Start: At trailside, about 20' right of Path Of The Mystics.
Wander up the wall and through weaknesses in small, stacked overhangs. Turn wide roof above (crux) to access a large, left-facing dihedral. At the large roof above step left to a pair of belay/rappel bolts. 80'
FA: Heidi Chapin and partner (5/02)

Insider's Tip: Turn the crux roof by traversing out left a few feet.

161 First Dance 5.10- ★
Start: 15' right of Where Lizards Go To Die.
Climb a long, left-facing dihedral peppered with small roofs. Finish to the top on the left wall. 120'
FA: Rob Robinson, Dan Canale (10/85)

162 Heavy Petting Zoo 5.11 ★★
Start: Same as for First Dance.
Climb First Dance for 10'. Work right along lip of small roof, then climb a steep face sporting a series of shallow, stacked right-facing corners barred by small roofs. At hidden thank God ledge above: turn rounded orange roof above near right margin staying left of bolt (which protects Bible Black Pre-Dawn, see below). Fire left into sea of cresting overhangs and follow line of least resistance (and available protection) to the top. 100'
FA: Kirk Brode, Rod Thomas ('05)

Bible Black Pre-Dawn 5.11-
Start: Same as for Heavy Petting Zoo.
Follow Heavy Petting Zoo to the bolt. Break hard right and climb an exposed and sparsely protected face. Near the arête, gun for the top. 100'
FA: Harrison Shull, David Draper ('05)

163 Dixie Wet Dream 5.12+ ★★★
Start: 15' right of Bible Black Pre-Dawn.
Wander up the wall, trend left, and climb a 15' roof peppered with big solution pockets and a bit of a crack. Continue up the wall above via fingercrack to fixed anchors. 90'
FA: Stuart Chapin, Cody Averbeck, ('05)
FFA: Cody Averbeck, Tyler Stracker ('07)

Insider's Note: Seasonally wet.

164 Combustion Cycle 5.11 ★★★
Welcome to the T Wall lab. Today's experiment: add one block carbonate of magnesium, two stout biceps and one part body English. Mix thoroughly, and see what sort of reaction you get....
Start: Same as for Dixie Wet Dream.
Amble up the face about 40' to a long roof band with several hanging corners perched just above the lip. Cycle into the very narrow, polished-looking corner; inch up to a hidden ledge with bolt anchors. 90'
FA: Rob Robinson, Forrest Gardner (11/85)

Carl Buch pulling the final roof of Where Lizards go to Die, 5.10-   Photo Credit: Corey Wentz

TENNESSEE WALL
THE WASTELAND

165 Violence Is Golden 5.11- ★
Start: 25' right of Combustion Cycle. Face climb scrappy rock for 30' or so. Diagonal right to small, tiered roofs. Jug up to a precarious position on the overhanging wall above. Jam a crack through a bulge (crux) to bolt anchors on a hidden ledge. 100'
★ **Alternate Start: 5.10**
Start 5' left of Magnum Bro/Crow (see below). Trend left across face via horizontals to join Violence is Golden at the overhangs.
FA: Forrest Gardner, Jack Noonan, Rob Robinson (10/85) FA Alternate Start: Harrison Shull, Kirk Brode ('05)

> Insider's Tip: Bring up to 5" cams for the alternate start.

166 Magnum Bro 5.11- ★★
Start: 40' right of Violence is Golden. Climb Magnum Crow (see description below) for 12'. Turn small roof at left side. Follow left-facing corner system to base of a giant roof. Bail from bolt anchors. 90'
Back Door Man: 5.10. Optional Finish. At the huge roof traverse left and then up a left-facing corner to the top. 40'
FA: Kirk Brode and partners ('04) FA Optional Finish: Kirk Brode and partner ('04)

167 Guerillas In The Mist 5.11 ★★
Start: Same as for Magnum Bro.
Pitch 1: 5.11-. Climb Magnum Bro to the bolt belay at the base of the huge roof. (90')
Pitch 2: 5.11+. Work right into roof then back left following obvious weaknesses, then up face above to the top. (50')
FA: Kirk Brode ('04)

168 Voodoo Roof 5.12+ ★★★
Start: Same as for Magnum Bro. Climb Magnum Bro to the base of the huge roof. Fire straight out the center and turn the lip (crux); continue to the top. 120'
FA: Kirk Brode, Chad Wykle ('04)

169 Magnum Crow 5.10+ ★★
See description on page 381.

170 Circling Buzzards 5.11 ★★
Pick this sandstone bone clean, and you'll have something to flap your gums about.
Start: 25' right of Magnum Crow.
Pitch 1: 5.11. Climb a thin crack through swatch of white rock. Arc left to a wide dihedral capped by a roof. Boulder up into this feature via delicate stemming. At the roof, traverse left, then up a hanging belay at a vertical crack. (80') Pitch 2: 5.10-. Ease over a small overhang onto the headwall. Angle left to the top. (40')
FA: Rob Robinson, Pat Perrin (alternate-leads, 3/86)

> Insider's Tip: Try a red Tricam (placed like a nut in a very shallow, vertical slot) for the opening sequence of the crux dihedral. Although the climb does offer protection: the name is suggestive of a potentially serious line.

Magnum Crow 5.10+ ★★

Magnum mind trip is more like it: the final roof is the most exposed "easy" 11 at the T Wall. Did I say 5.11?! LOL. Start: Same as for Magnum Bro.
Pitch 1: 5.9. Scratch over a loose bulge and conquer a small overhang. An easy dihedral leads to a spacious belay ledge. (40') Pitch 2: 5.10+. Continue up a second dihedral (pink-streaked rock). At the top of the corner: zaq right and hard left to a body-length roof split by a thin crack. Flap over this and finish to the top via a short, wide corner. (80')
FA: Rob Robinson, Bruce Rogers (4/85)

Insider Tips: Avoid the loose rock encountered on the opening moves of pitch one by climbing a tree just right of the start. Use double ropes for pitch 2.

Photo Credit: Nathalie Dupre

THE AMPHITHEATER

Small but intensively developed, this portion of the cliff line yields one of the most diverse concentrations of high-quality, hard free routes in the Sandstone Belt.

At the left side of the Amphitheater is a bulging wall bursting with a stack of intimidating roofs, along with a prow, which the guide designates as the cove's left boundary.

Pan right, and you'll see a huge, open face lined with long and inviting crack systems guarded by a wide swath of gnarly-looking roofs at the base of the wall.

The right side of the Amphitheater balloons out in a chaotic swirl of overhanging rock, rad roofs, and obtuse hanging corners. Pockets and bulges, in all shapes and sizes, are liberally sprinkled throughout. Taken together, these features constitute one big grab bag of "all things steep and crazy."

Andrew Miller courting Hands Across America, 5.12

Parking: Park at the main Tennessee Wall parking lot.
Approach: This stretch of cliff line is situated in between the Wasteland and the Orange Blossom Walls. It encompasses about a hundred yards of cliff line. Hike up the main Tennessee Wall trail for about a quarter mile to a fork with a cairn. Bear right and continue up the trail. Where it reaches the cliff is directly beneath the center of the Amphitheater at the base of the waterfall. The trail splits here and heads in each direction along the cliff. If you head left, you will quickly encounter the left margin of the Amphitheater, where you will encounter the first climb listed in this area: Open Casket. Routes are numbered from left to right.

TENNESSEE WALL

THE AMPHITHEATER

20 mins

The amphitheater is a one in a million section of Sandstone that has no rival in quality and density of classic, difficult lines. As the name implies, a bulk of these mega steep routes are located in the Sandstone 'bowl' at the terminus of the approach trail.

171 Open Casket 5.9 ★★
Start: 5' right of Circling Buzzards. Climb a coffin-like chimney barred by several roofs to anchors. 80'
FA: Rob Robinson, Peter Henley (2/85)

> **Insider's Note:** This route has become more popular in recent years.

172 Stormin' Norman 5.12d (sport) ★★
Start: 15' right of Open Casket. Follow a line of bolts up a spectacular orange-hued face and tackle a couple of massive overhangs along the way. 75'
FA: Steve Deweese (date unknown)

173 Face-off 5.12c (sport) ★★
Start: 10' right of Stormin Norman. A similar looking line to Stormin' that climbs up a sustained face to a cruxy roof.
FA: Edward Yates & John Dorough

174 Poweropolis 5.13 ★★
This "sprawling metropolis" of a pump offers up a double dose of finger-wrecking roof action.
Start: At the left side of the Amphitheater, and just right of a prominent outside corner.
Climb through a 20' band of junk rock to an 8' roof with a few bolts above the lip. Turn this (crux), then face climb following a seam to a 12' roof. Power out this on the right. Yard left to fixed anchors above the lip. 60'
FA: Rob Robinson (11/89)

> **Insider's Note:** A key hold broke off at the lip of the first overhang after the first ascent. It was subsequently repeated by Nathaniel Walker in 2008, sans hold, and thereafter was upgraded from 5.13- to 5.13.

T-Wall

Jeff Gruenberg on the F.F.A. of Tamper Proof, 5.13

384 www.rockerypress.com

Tamper Proof 5.13-
How could two incredible climbs like this exist side by side?! King of the 5.13 cracks.
Start: Same as for Psycho Path.
Scramble up a couple of ledges, then climb an unbelievably cool-looking crack line slicing through an overhanging orange wall capped by a 12' roof. 60'
FA: Rob Robinson (3/86) FFA: Jeff Gruenberg ('87)

Insider's Tip N' Notes: Wear rubber knee pads. Gruenberg snagged the free ascent after Robinson blew a crumbly fingerlock at the base of the roof (and re-started the pitch from a no hands rest instead of lowering to the ground.)

Climber: Pat Goodman   Photo Credit: Ben Ditto

TENNESSEE WALL — THE AMPHITHEATER

175 Psycho Path 5.13b (sport)
Arguably one of the finest, and most unique, pitches for the grade in the Deep South.
Start: 10' right of Poweropolis. Climb a severely overhanging arete embedded with a line of perfect (all natural!) finger pockets. Break right through a band of tweaky tiered roofs (crux) to chain anchors. 60'
FA: Rob Robinson (12/90)

> **Insider's Tip:** The crux is the very last move. Many climbers have made it to this point, only to fail. Wear rubber knee pads.

176 Tamper Proof 5.13-
See description on page 385.

177 Tough Guys Don't Dance 5.12- ★★
Actually, a lot of fancy footwork is necessary....
Start: Same as for Tamper Proof. Scramble up a few ledges. Turn a small overhang and step into a little corner. Work up to a wider, left-facing corner. Salsa right along a finger crack in a major roof; work up a few feet up to an overhang (crux). Tango into a short, left-facing dihedral over the lip and continue to a ledge. 60'
FA: Rob Robinson, Robyn Erbesfield (12/85)

178 Puntang 5.13b (sport) ★★
Sweet n' juicy power climbing.
Start: 25' right of Tough Guys Don't Dance. Climb through a short choss band, then turn a pocketed roof and continue up an orange arete. Turn the roof above on the left and continue to anchors on a ledge. (80') **FA: Anthony Meeks ('01)**

TENNESSEE WALL

179 Crankenstein 5.11- ★★

Starts out as a climbing lab experiment gone wrong, however, the bad quickly boils off and you're left with pure sandstone gold.
Start: 10' right of Puntang.
Pitch 1: 5.11-. Tiptoe up through friable rock, past a bolt in small roofs, to a short, left-facing corner capped by a small cresting roof. Work right around this (crux); ease up a narrow, left-facing corner above to an exposed and small standing belay. (75') Pitch 2: 5.9. Climb straight to the top on the spectacular, sheer face. (75')
FA: Rob Robinson, Peter Henley (3/85)

Insider Notes: Can be done in one long monster pitch if you take pains to float the first 50' of rope. This route originally began a bit to the left (where Puntang starts), however Stuart Chapin straightened it out with the directissima start (now considered the best way to do the line).

180 Blood Meridian 5.12- ★★

This would be one of the finest combo roof and crack lines at the T Wall if not for the first 15'. Bloody extraordinary climbing...
Start: 25' right of Crankenstein.
Pitch 1: 5.12-. Inch through a shale band for 15' (protection tricky, but feasible). Blast out a beautiful, 12' two-tiered roof (crux). Climb a perfect finger crack above for 20 or so feet to a hanging belay. (60')
Pitch 2: 5.9+. Climb a shallow, left-facing corner for a ways. Wander to the top. (85')
FA: Rob Robinson, Pat Perrin (alt. leads, 2/86)

Insider Notes: Watch out for rope pinch turning the first pitch roof. A bolt added to the start (22 years after the FA) was recently chopped. The bolt in the middle of the crux overhangs was added after an old fixed pin rotted out. May be undergraded.

T-Wall

TENNESSEE WALL

THE AMPHITHEATER

181 Tiers For Beers 5.11- ★★
A hefty piece of high quality trad work. Top it out, and you'll have more than earned your brewskies when you return to the T Wall parking lot at the end of the day.
Start: 10' right of Blood Meridian.
Pitch 1: 5.10+. Boulder over a (seasonally drippy) shale bulge in a small cave. Diagonal right through tiered roofs; shoot through the notch and rail left for 10' to a nice hidden belay ledge. (60') Pitch 2: 5.11-. Climb through "shoe box" in tiered roofs; gun right and follow a bulging, thin crack (with nice wall position). Fire for the top. (85')
FA: Rob Robinson, Eric Janoscrat (12/85)

Insider Beta: There may be a honeybee nest on pitch two (see pink-stained rock), which the route narrowly avoids; therefore, I recommend you attempt the climb on a warm winter day when the bees are hibernating.

182 Moms Are Marvelous 5.11+ ★★
Start: Same as for Tiers For Beers.
Pitch 1: 5.10+. Follow pitch one of Tiers For Beers to the gap. Continue right a bit further to a hanging belay at the base of a thin, bulging seam. (60') Pitch 2: 5.11+. Teeter over a delicate bulge (crux), turn a small roof, step right and fire for the top. (85')
FA: Hidetaka Suzuki, Rob Robinson (5/86)

Insider's Note: The next climb listed "bolt tracked" over the crux of pitch two — a not-so-marvelous fact that you'll have to try and ignore.

183 T Rex 5.13a ★★
"For the sandstone carnivore": a bloody good sandstone feast dripping with cruxes.
Start: 15' right of Tiers/Moms.
Follow a line of bolts through baby Godzilla roofs and up the steep wall above to anchors. 80'
FA: Anthony Meeks ('01)

184 Death By Boobalooba 5.11+ ★★
Start: Atop a ledge system 15' right of T Rex.
Pitch 1: 5.11+. Worm left out a 20' roof to a small ledge belay on wall above. (35')
Pitch 2: 5.10-. Climb a narrow, right-facing corner to a very small roof, work left onto a ramp. Continue face climbing directly to the top. (85')
FA: Forrest Gardner, Peter Henley (3/85)
FFA: Rob Robinson, Robyn Erbesfield (3/85)

Insider Note: Neglected classic deserving of more traffic.

185 Over The Rainbow 5.13a (sport)
"The true harvest of my life is intangible — a little star dust caught, a portion of the rainbow I have clutched." —Thoreau.
Start: 10' right of Death By Boobalooba.
Pitch 1: 5.12c. Claw out 20' or so of tiered roofs to a standing belay on the wall above. (40') Pitch 2: 5.13a. Continue up a blank-looking face above to anchors. (40')
FA: Jerry Roberts ('01)

Insider's Tip: Can be done as one pitch if you work the line using two ropes.

Sean Stone on the brilliant upper headwall of 'Over the Rainbow,' 5.13a

Photo Credit: Corey Wentz

DEATH BY BOOBALOOBA, 5.11+

CHATTRAD

Climber: Tim Derohen　　　　Photo Credit: Micah Gentry

TENNESSEE WALL

THE AMPHITHEATER

Hands Across America, 5.12

188 Ho' Baggin 5.12d ★ (sport)
Start: Same as Abortion Contortion. Climb abortion to the first roof and then break left out several overlaps, eventually ending back right at the anchors of Abortion.
FA: Ryan Johnson

> Insider Note: May gets its own independent start which will increase the grade and quality.

186 Space Sequential 5.11 ★
Start: 30' right of Over The Rainbow.
Pitch 1: 5.11. Boulder up (crux) into a wide corner. Face climb left linking "letterbox slots" above the lip of a massive roof. Belay at a shallow cave. (40') Pitch 2: 5.9. Continue up a right-facing corner in purplish rock; wander over small overhangs to the top. (85')
FA: Rob Robinson, Robyn Erbesfield (11/85)

189 Abortion Contortion 5.13a (sport)
Wide open, bizarro, no holes (or holds!) barred power climbing. Famous for a nasty finger—wrecking pocket at the crux.
Start: 15' right of Hands Across America. A line of bolts leading up through a wasteland of overhanging rock beckons. 75'
FA: Rob Robinson (3/90)

> Insider Note: Occasionally downgraded to 5.12+ by taller climbers. Great training route to top-rope laps on.

187 Hands Across America 5.12
One of the crown jewel crack lines of the Sandstone Belt.
Start: 15' right of Space Sequential. Climb an intimidating-looking crack line through a series of stacked roofs. 75'
FA: Rob Robinson (5/86)

> Insider Notes: Tape! Tape! Double ropes! First led using a swami belt and a pair of old "E.B.'s" to plus the challenge.

TENNESSEE WALL

190 Twistin' In The Wind 5.12c (sport)
Or is it twitchin' in the nylon web? Flash or fall — no matter — this is one sport mega classic you won't want to miss.
Start: 10' right of Abortion Contortion.
An overhanging wall packed with roofs awaits you. 60'
FA: Rob Robinson (9/91)

Insider Trivia Note: Named after a dead lizard that was found hanging in a spider's web near the upper crux.

191 The Meeker Rat 5.12d ★★ (sport)
Start: 10' right of Twistin' In The Wind. Boulder up into shallow corners, surge to a big pocket out right. Turn the bulge (crux), continue to a horizontal crack. Shoot through hueco roofs and up the face above. When possible, step right a bit into a scoop and finish at Paleface anchors. 65'
FA: Anthony Meeks (10/01)

192 Paleface 5.12b ★ (sport)
Start: 15' right of The Meeker Rat. Traverse left across the left wall of a wide, open book to an arete; follow bolts through the bulge to chain anchors. 65'
FA: Travis Eiseman (10/01)

Insider's Note: Reportedly needs an extra bolt somewhere below the crux to mitigate a potentially bad fall.

193 Turbo Zone 5.11+ ★★
Looking for a real power trip? This line's got your name on it. Jet fuel optional.
Start: Same as for Paleface.
Fan left across the wall of the wide dihedral. Turbo into a short, right-facing corner capped by a smooth, arching overhang. Tweak left over a bulge (crux) and continue to the top following a break. 100'
FA: Rob Robinson, Bruce Rogers, Bob Ordner (3/85)

www.rockerypress.com 393

Memory Fog

A perfect stack of three, monolithic roofs, split by a spectacular crack, juts forth from the maw of a massive overhanging wall — what more could you, the crack climbing "addict," hope for! It took me two days to get the protection for the route squared away and, along with that, a nasty rope drag problem sorted out. On the third day I put the whole package together; to "plus" the challenge I wore a swami belt with no leg loops, and traded my sticky soled Fire climbing shoes out for an ancient pair of worn out E.B.s. Today, 28 years later, Hands Across America still commands respect. No doubt it will continue to amaze and inspire future climbers for generations to come — as well it should!

Rob Robinson on the First Ascent of Hands Across America, 5.12

Photo Credit: Rob Robinson Collection

TENNESSEE WALL

194 Grand Contusion 5.13
The original "Muhammad Ali" of the T Wall roofs, and as fine a horizontal thrash as you'll find in the Sandstone Belt.
Start: Same as for Turbo Zone.
Climb a (tricky) white dihedral; traverse 10' right beneath a roof to a small stance. Cruise out a 15' roof crack/flake to an iron cross move; mantle onto sloping ledge above (crux) to gain stance. 60'
★ Alternate Start: 5.10. Start 15' right of the original start. Climb the face past a few bolts and join the regular route at the roof. FA: Rob Robinson (5/86) FA Alternate Start: Travis Eiseman (1/02)

> **Insider's Notes:** A) The "Eiseman roof variation": Climb about midway out the roof and claw onto the sloping ledge above. B) Originally a trad route; however, I had discussed with Eiseman the possibility of replacing two mank fixed pieces in the roof with bolts. Well ... they're in now! If they remain, they may need some repositioning.

195 Squatter's Rites 5.10+ ★★
A rare piece of ramp climbing, capped off by a classic sandstone roof.
Start: 15' right of Grand Contusion.
Climb a classic ramp leading left to a large, rectangular roof. Squat left, turn the lip and finish up a left-facing corner capped by a smaller roof. 80'
FA: Rob Robinson, Roy Briton, Robyn Erbesfield (6/85)

196 All Rites Reserved 5.11- ★
Start: 5' right of Squatter's Rites.
Wing through 20' of finger pockets on a bulging wall to a small "cave." Clear the lip on the left and climb shallow, stacked, right-facing corners barred by small roofs to the top. 80'
FA: Rob Robinson, Pat Perrin, Curt Merchant (1/86)

197 Art 5.8+ ★★★
Start: By a big boulder 20' right of All Rites Reserved.
Climb a classic, right-facing dihedral. 80'
FA: Rob Robinson, Bruce Rogers (1/85)

198 Ruby Fruit Jungle 5.12d (sport)
Carry the big guns for this vertical safari through the big orange sandstone jungle; feral free climbing at its finest.
Start: 10' right of Art, atop a large boulder. Span the gap and claw onto the wall proper; surge up a steep orange face to a short left-facing corner; conquer the small (but vicious!) overhang above. Sustained boulder problem moves lead up a short section of overhanging wall and through 10' of small tiers to anchors above the lip. 80'
FA: Rob Robinson (4/90)

> **Insider's Note:** Traversing right to a ledge to cop a rest before tackling the final crux section is considered off route.

199 Code Warrior 5.11 A0 ★★
Start: 10' right of Ruby Fruit Jungle. Power through gap in overhang to gain a steep, orange wall. As soon as possible, trend left following a nice crack system and then up past a tricky bulge. Turn the roof above at crack (crux) and continue through second roof above past a single bolt (A0). Finish in a right-facing corner. 80'
FA: Rob Robinson and partners (3/05)

> **Insider's Note:** This will make for a decent 5.13 route once someone gets around to eliminating the aid on a couple of finger-wrecking shallow pocket moves past the bolt.

T-Wall

www.rockerypress.com   395

T-WALL

By: John Bachar

I first got to climb at the T Wall with Rob Robinson in the fall of 2008. I have to say I wish I had gotten there earlier in my career because I was quite intimidated and impressed by the trad routes that had been established over twenty years ago.

This is truly a world class cliff and boasts some of the raddest trad stuff I have witnessed in my entire climbing career. The rock is of superb quality and the protection is all there, even if you can't see it from the base.

I think the first day I climbed there I didn't break the 5.10 barrier. It all looked un-protectable from the ground, but when I started climbing there was always some feature that provided a place for a cam or a wire. Once I got used to trusting that the rock would yield itself to protection, I got a little more confident and actually did a 5.11- called Hell or High Water. I was still spooked and intimidated however.

This type of climbing demands the best of any climber. One must have excellent rock reading skills for the T Wall classics. You've got to know how to protect as well as route find as well as maintain your cool while performing the moves.

The climbs at the T Wall serve as mini-monuments to what climbers can do when they believe in themselves and never give up on their dreams. We can all be proud of this fine area and the magnificent routes that have been done, and the route potential that still exists for future generations.

Bachar was born in 1957. He grew up in Los Angeles and started climbing at Stony Point and Joshua Tree at the age of 14. Obsessed with the sport, Bachar immersed himself in books on physical training and nutrition, and soon was able to outperform his fellow climbers.

Bachar made a name for himself in Yosemite with his unroped ascents of *New Dimensions* (5.11a) and *The Nabisco Wall*, a three-pitch affair [*Waverly Wafer* (5.10c), *Butterballs* (5.11c), *Butterfingers* (5.11a)]. Bachar's superb

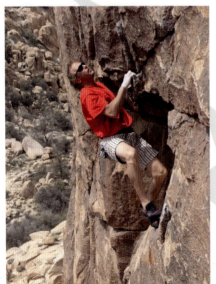

physical fitness gave him an edge; his campsite in Camp 4 was filled with exercise equipment, including the hanging ladders that became known as Bachar ladders. At his peak Bachar was able to perform a one arm pull up with 12.5 lbs of weight attached.

Confident of his free soloing ability, Bachar posted a note in 1981 promising a "$10,000 reward for anyone who can follow me for one full day." No one took the challenge. That same year he put up *Bachar-Yerian* (5.11c, X) with Dave Yerian. One of the boldest first ascents of the time, the 500-foot face climb is protected by 13 bolts. Bachar was a vocal critic of climbing tactics such as bolting on rappel which came into vogue during the 1980s.

Editor's Note: Sadly, John Bachar died on July 5th, 2009, from injuries sustained in a free-soloing fall in Mammoth Lakes, CA.

TENNESSEE WALL — THE AMPHITHEATER

200 Sugar In The Raw 5.11-
100% pure, unadulterated sandstone candy.
Start: Same as for Code Warrior. Power through gap in low overhang (crux) to gain a steep, orange wall. Continue straight up a short, shallow, left-facing corner capped by a tricky bulge (crux). A bit higher, crank over a 3' roof and shoot for a fixed anchor station just below the summit. 80'
FA: Rob Robinson, Shannon Stegg, Robyn Erbesfield (3/85)

201 History Of My Heart 5.12- ★
Start: 10' right of Sugar In The Raw, atop a small boulder.
Top-rope over a small overhang. Face climb following a right-facing flake on the wall above to a small ledge. 45'
FA: Rob Robinson (top-rope, 12/89)

202 Curb Sandwich 5.11d ★★★ (sport) One-course wonder meal.
Start: Same as for History Of My Heart. Boulder over a small roof, climb past a cresting overhang with pockets. Squeak left and climb a smooth-looking arete to double bolts. 45'
FA: Rob Robinson, top-rope (12/89) First Lead: Travis Eiseman, Justin Eiseman (bolted, '90)

203 Sly Willie Snores 5.11- ★★★
Guaranteed you won't fall asleep on this one! Good initial buzz provided by the face, but it's the final roof that serves as the real eye opener.
Start: 15' right of Curb Sandwich.
Zig-zag up a steep orange face with a few bolts. Jug and jam through (crux) 12' of tiered overhangs. 80'
FA: Kent Ballew, Bear Thurman (6/89)

TENNESSEE WALL

204 Changnurdle 5.11- ★
Start: 15' right of Sly Willie Snores.
Hop up into an "ice cream scoop" bowl. Exit left past a (fixed?) pin; follow an outside corner to the (right) margin of a large roof. Traverse right 10' and up a headwall to the top. 80'
FA: Kent Ballew and Bear Thurman (6/89)

205 Tweeter And The Monkey Man 5.10 ★★
Must be a movie or something; create your own show following the script below....
Start: 5' right of Changnurdle.
Climb a steep wall with small holds and shallow pockets. Work right to a small roof split by a crack. Turn this and continue to the top via big holds. 90'
FA: Jack Noonan, Tim Williams (1/91)

206 Nappy 5.7 ★
Start: 5' right of Tweeter And The Monkey Man. Climb a wide dihedral with a good jam crack. 90'
FA: Bear Thurman, Sharon Thurman (12/88)

207 New Beginnings 5.5 ★
Start: Same as for Nappy.
Climb a few moves up the dihedral. Diagonal right up a ramp system to an arete; work straight up this, then scamper up intermittent ledges to the top. 90'
FA: Rob Robinson, Susan Robinson (12/92)

208 Ain't So Eazy 5.9
Start: Atop a large, tilted boulder 10' right of New Beginnings.
Step off boulder onto an arete and follow it to the top. 90'
FA: Jack Noonan, Tim Williams, Curtis Sharp (1/91)

209 Plastic Toys 5.7 ★
Start: Same as for Ain't So Eazy.
Step across a gap and climb a wide corner to small roofs. Move left, thread through notch; weave to the top. 80'
FA: Bear Thurman, Fritz Lovingood (11/88)

> **Insider Note:** A very popular route that is, unfortunately, also the scene of the occasional splatterfest.

210 Wild Hair 5.9 +
FA: Bear Thurman, Fritz Lovingood (11/88)
Start: Same as for Plastic Toys.
Span gap and climb a wide corner. Move right; climb an arete to the top. 80'

ORANGE BLOSSOM WALLS

20 mins

The Orange Blossom Walls yield about a mile's worth of the finest stone the "Sandstone Belt of the South" has to offer — here you'll find scads of straight-forward and easy-to-protect trad lines, including lots of long corners, countless clean faces, classic straight-in cracks, and knife-like aretes. Roofs are sprinkled throughout, adding a little "spice to the T Wall sugar."

To facilitate locating routes, the Orange Blossom Walls have been divided into four "subdivisions." They are as follows: West Blossom (pg 402), Middle Blossom (pg 411), East Blossom (pg 434), and Lost Blossom (pg 451).

Parking: Park at the main Tennessee Wall parking lot.

Approach: This stretch of cliff line is situated to the right of the Amphitheater. It encompasses upwards of one mile of cliff line. Hike up the main Tennessee Wall trail for about a quarter mile to a fork. Bear right and continue to the large cove of rock known as the Amphitheater. Hike to the right side of the Amphitheater and pass beneath a low, flat roof next to a huge, tilted boulder. This marks the entrance to the Orange Blossom Walls.

Climbs are listed from left to right, the same way that you will encounter them.

Orange Blossom Walls as seen from Raccoon Mountain

Stone Wave, 5.11-

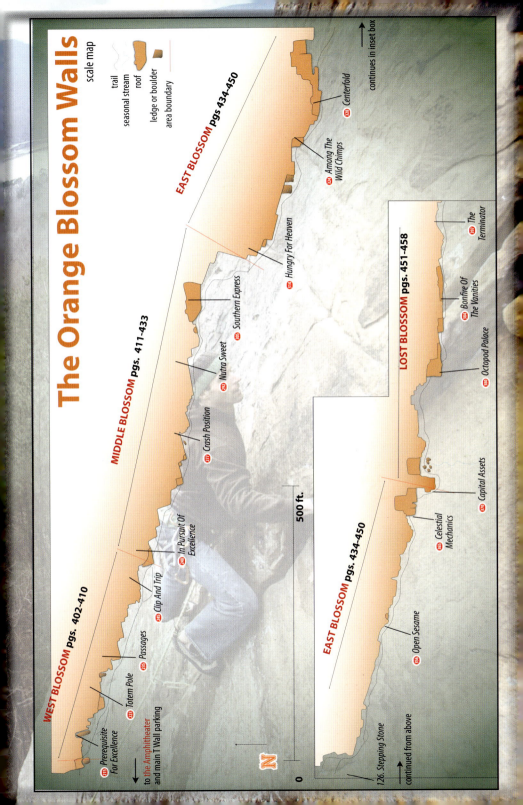

TENNESSEE WALL

ORANGE BLOSSOM WALLS

211 Rain Check 5.9 ★
10' right of Wild Hair.
Climb a short left-facing corner. Work left past under roof, continue up the wide corner above to small ledges. Traverse right and follow heavily featured arete to the top. **FA: Unknown**

212 March Hare 5.10- ★
Start: 20' right of Plastic Toys in the Amphitheater section) and a huge trailside boulder.
Climb a skinny dihedral with a finger crack for 15', turn a bulge with a thin crack. Wander to the top. 80'
FA: Marvin Webb, Steve Kerchner (4/85)

213 Mad Hatter 5.9 ★
Start: 10' right Rain Check.
Scramble atop a small ledge. Climb a short, right-facing corner with jam crack. Continue up the face above to a bulging headwall. Traverse right a few feet and climb a shallow, right-facing corner to the top. 80'
FA: unknown

214 Multiple Use Area 5.9 ★
Start: 10' right of Mad Hatter.
Climb a crosshatching of disconnected, vertical cracks. 80'
Variation: 5.9. Start 10' right of the regular start. Climb a left-facing corner past a small scoop to a 1' roof. Slip over this, or head left, and link up with Multiple Use Area.
FA: Marvin Webb and students (2/85)

402 www.rockerypress.com

TENNESSEE WALL

215 Prerequisite For Excellence 5.8 ★★
The "poorer cousin" of one of the T Wall's most famous 5.9's: In Pursuit Of Excellence.
Start: 10' right of Multiple Use Area.
Climb a short corner to a small ledge. Continue up a long, left-facing corner to the top. 80'
FA: Bob Ordner, Roy Briton, Rob Robinson (2/85)

216 Love Handle 5.10 ★★★
A tricky line that might put the squeeze on you at a few points.
Start: 10' right of Prerequisite For Excellence.
Climb a dihedral to a large scoop with a spot of crispy rock. Tweak onto face above (crux) and clip a "thank God" bolt. Turn the roof above at its right margin. Bolt anchors. 80'
FA: Stuart Chapin, Cody Averbeck (2/03)

217 Short Arm Inspection 5.11 ★★
A few rounds shy of a 21 gun salute, but still deserving of accolades.
Start: 20' right of Love Handle.
Pitch 1: 5.10. Power past a trailside overhang at the base of a short arete, then climb a vertical crack to a nice ledge. (20')
Pitch 2: 5.11. Climb the face/arete to a small overhang with a fixed pin. Turn this and continue to the top. (70')
★ Alternate Finish: 5.11. From the large ledge about 60' up on the route: Step right beneath an overhang, stretch around this and fire for the top.
FA: Steve Goins, Truly Bracken (12/92) FA: Alternate Finish: David Draper ('08)

218 No More Tiers 5.11- ★★★
Too bad! The only thing that could make this route any better is if it went on forever…
Start: 10' right of Short Arm Inspection.
Pitch 1: 5.10. Turn a low roof and follow forked cracks to a nice belay ledge. (20') Pitch 2: 5.11-. Tiptoe up a tweaky thin seam, slip through a flared slot and swing over a 3' roof. A casual corner continues to the top. (70') FA: Forrest Gardner, Rob Robinson (alt. leads, 3/85)

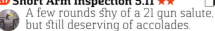
Insider's Tip: Frequently done as a single pitch.

219 Morning Sickness 5.11- ★★
Start: Same as for No More Tiers.
Pitch 1: 5.10. Climb the first pitch of No More Tiers. (20') Pitch 2: 5.11-. Climb the wall and follow a crack through a 10' roof. A bit higher, conquer a small overhang and weave to the top with tricky face climbing. (70')
FA: Curt Merchant and partners ('86)

220 Infinite Pursuit 5.10 ★★★
You've found your sandstone prey — let "the hunt" for the summit begin!
Start: 15' right of No More Tiers/Morning Sickness.
Climb a long, right-facing corner with a wide jam crack to a flat, 4' roof. Pursue holds above (crux); trend left to the top. 80'
FA: Rob Robinson, Robyn Erbesfield (1/86)

TENNESSEE WALL — ORANGE BLOSSOM WALLS

221 Standard Deviation 5.10- ★★
Strange bit of figuring, this one — a brain teaser of sorts.
Start: 10' right of Infinite Pursuit.
Cruise up a left-facing corner for 20' or so. Deviate left onto a smooth, orange slab split by shallow, vertical seams, then merge with a short, left-facing arch. Weave left through bulging overhangs to the top. 80'
FA: Pat Perrin, Curt Merchant (1/86)

222 Sunday Gardening 5.8 ★
Start: Same as for Standard Deviation.
Follow a left-facing corner to a band of roofs. Work right, turn bulge, finish up a short corner to the top. 80'
FA: Oliver Muff, Mark Thompson (3/86)

223 Totem Pole 5.9 ★
Start: 10' right of Sunday Gardening.
Follow a hand-sized crack up a long, right-facing corner; turn a 5' roof and continue up a corner through summit overhangs to the top. 80'
FA: Shannon Stegg, Robyn Erbesfield, Rob Robinson (3/85)

224 Contents Under Pressure 5.9 ★
Start: 10' right of Totem Pole.
Climb a wide crack (past a chockstone) which jogs left to an overhang. Step right and face climb the right wall of an arete to the top. 80'
FA: Rob Robinson, Tim Cumbo (4/85)

225 True Colors 5.8 ★
Start: 20' right of Contents Under Pressure.
Climb a left-facing corner to a good ledge. Subdue a small overhang and continue in the corner to the top. 80'
FA: Rob Robinson, Michael Austin, Gary Westcott, Carylon Austin (10/89)

> **Insiders Note:** Can easily be divided into two pitches.

226 Three Stars From God 5.11- ★
Start: 2' right of True Colors.
Climb a steep face with no pro using small holds (crux); cruise past two bolts. Fade right over blocky ledges to a prominent pine tree and the top. 100'
FA: Tim Williams, Jack Noonan (2/91)

TENNESSEE WALL

227 Kid's Fears 5.9+ ★
Start: 8' right of Three Stars From God. Climb a poorly-protected steep face with good holds; diagonal right to an arete. Climb the arete a bit; traverse left, and finish up Three Stars From God. 100'
FA: Jack Noonan, Tom Herring (1/91)

228 Creaky Tweaks 5.10 ★
Start: 5' right of Kid's Fears.
Boulder through a low overhang and climb a short, steep face with some flexible flakes to a large ledge with a stout pine tree. A long, lower-angled arete with good holds leads to the top. 100'
FA: Rob Robinson, Marvin Webb (4/85)

229 Wing And A Prayer 5.10+ ★
Start: 15' right of Creaky Tweaks.
Wing it past an overhang and follow a thin crack to a large ledge. 30'
FA: Rob Robinson, Tim Cumbo (4/85)

230 Let's Face It! 5.7 ★★
One of the T Wall's few moderate routes, so savor it.
Start: 5' right of Wing And A Prayer.
Pitch 1: 5.7. Climb a 4" to 6" crack, or a left-facing corner with a small tree to a belay on a large ledge. (30') Pitch 2: 5.7. Continue up a orange-colored corner to a stack of loose (?) blocks beneath a giant ceiling. Traverse left a few feet around these; finish to the top in a left-facing dihedral. (60')
FA: Ed Clark, Karen Clark (5/86)

231 Twitterville 5.10 ★
Start: 5' right of Let's Face It!
Scramble up a face and climb a short and narrow right-facing corner. Continue up the wall above and finish following the Steeplechase arete. 100'
FA: Rob Robinson ('08)

232 Steeplechase 5.11 ★★★
Hardly a route to horse around on: Delicate, and daring.
Start: Right around the corner and atop a small ledge 15' right of Twitterville. At the base of the Super Slide corner: Boulder left across a gnarly steep face past a short thin seam (crux) to access a long arete. Follow the arete to the right side of a big flat roof; prance right around this and on to the top. 100'
FA: Rob Robinson, Forrest Gardner (6/85)

Insider's Note: Above the crux is a nerve-racking run-out of 20' or so capped by a 5.10- sequence.

405

ROCK/STEADY

For over 26 years, Rock/Creek has been Chattanooga's local climbing shop. The gear may have changed, but the attitude remains the same. Patagonia and Rock/Creek grew up together, blazing new trails in the outdoor industry. But neither one of us rests on the past. The tradition continues with new climbing packs and clothing from Patagonia, and a new Rock/Creek store at The Block, next to High Point Climbing and Fitness.

rock/creek
patagonia®

ROCK/CREEK
patagonia®

Patagonia continues to innovate with new gear like the Ascensionist Pack pictured to the left. Designed in sizes from 25L to 45L, this will be your go-to climbing pack. Responding to ambassador feedback, Patagonia stripped out everything but the essentials and kept the weight to a minimum.

Come see us at Rock/Creek for the largest selection of Patagonia in the region.

rockcreek.com

Photos: Rock/Creek co-founders Dawson Wheeler (left) climbing in style at Sunset, and Marvin Webb (right) rocking the tube socks in Oregon.

TENNESSEE WALL

ORANGE BLOSSOM WALLS

233 Super Slide 5.10
  Excellent face climbing, pretty good gear ... but watch out for the infamous "sliding board" crux!
Start: Same as for Steeplechase.
Climb a shallow, left-facing corner capped by a 1' roof. Slide past the roof (crux) and follow thin cracks up a steep slab to the top. 100'
FA: Rob Robinson, Steve Goins (2/85)

234 The Sweep 5.10- ★★★
Start: 15' right of Super Slide.
Climb a shallow "V" shaped corner (crux). Sweep left across a moderately difficult slab, sans gear. Join a short jam crack and continue to the top. 100'
FA: Forrest Gardner, Peter Henley, Rob Robinson (2/85)

Insider's Tip: You'll need a good selection of gear, but skip the broom. A nice swath of face climbing with a well-protected crux; the run-out section is fairly reasonable.

235 Passages 5.8
The mother of all 5.8 corners.
Start: 5' right of The Sweep.
Climb a long, left-facing dihedral with lots of hand jams until you arrive at a 5' roof. Face climb left beneath this obstacle (crux), then directly to the top. 100'
FA: Bruce Rogers, Rob Robinson (1/85)

236 Don't Tell A Soul 5.10d ★★
Start: 5' right of Passages.
Climb a steep and exposed arete sprouting a couple of bolts. 100'
FA: John Vermont (early 90's)

237 Shiva's Last Dance 5.9 ★★
Start: 10' right of Don't Tell A Soul.
Climb a low-angle corner with big holds, then dance up through a bulging, left-facing corner. Continue right over another bulge and on to the top. 100'
FA: Rob Robinson, Tim Cumbo (4/85)

T-Wall

408 www.rockerypress.com

TENNESSEE WALL

🔴 **238** **Seam Like Nothing 5.12-**
Start: 10' right of Shiva's Last Dance. Sketch over an incredibly blank-looking bulge (crux) split by a short, vertical seam. Follow a shallow crack/corner above to a pine tree. 40'
FA: Rob Robinson, Curt Merchant, Pat Perrin (1/86)

🔴 **239** **False Alarm 5.9** ★
Start: 5' right of Seam Like Nothing. Climb a skinny, orange dihedral with a finger crack for 15'. Ring past a bulge and wander to the top. 100'
FA: Rob Robinson, Bruce Rogers (4/85)

🔴 **240** **Sanscrit 5.8** ★★★
Start: 10' right of False Alarm. Climb a left-facing corner with a jam crack to a shallow cave. Continue up the corner to the top. 100'
FA: Rob Robinson, free solo (12/85)

Insider's Note: Recently upgraded from two stars status; long, classic and sustained with good gear.

🔴 **241** **Day's Work 5.10-** ★★
A beautiful piece of climbing ... guaranteed to lighten your load.
Start: 5' right of Sanscrit.
Wriggle up a short, but classic, flared slot with a hand crack to a spot of bad rock. Traverse right and follow an arete to the top. 90'
★★ **Day's Work Direct (a.k.a. Night Shift): 5.10+**. At the top of the flared slot ... work straight up through a spot of poor quality rock and tackle a small overhang. Face climb past a thin, vertical crack to the top. (90') FA: Forrest Gardner, Rob Robinson (3/85) FA Direct Finish: Sean Hunt, Stuart Chapin (11/89)

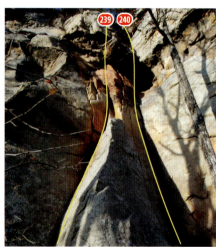

T-Wall

TENNESSEE WALL | ORANGE BLOSSOM WALLS

242 Proof Of Purchase 5.11+ ★★★
Break out your best rubber for this baby ... superb and sustained edging and smearing, with one or two hair-raising run-outs.
Start: 20' right of Day's Work.
Climb the face split by forked thin cracks. "Boulder" over a bulge above at a small, pointed flake (crux). High step into a smooth bowl (crux) with a thin, vertical seam. Follow this (crux) to a ledge above. 60'
FA: Rob Robinson, Mike Artz, Eric Janoscrat (12/85)

> Insider's Note: Some climbers have been following the bolts on Spirit Of The Game (see below), thinking they are on the upper face of Proof Of Purchase. Not even close...

243 Spirit Of The Game 5.11- ★★★
Down-in-the-dumps? Here's one that'll lift your spirits.
Start: 3' right of Proof Of Purchase.
Climb straight up the face to a short right-facing corner capped by a bulge. Make a few moves up and left to a bolt. "Boulder" up face to a second bolt, clip, and continue directly to the top. 60'
FA: Rob Robinson, Darrow Kirkpatrick (5/99)

244 Pinga Boys 5.9
Start: 5' right of Proof Of Purchase.
Climb a tree-filled crack to the top. 80'
FA: Peter Henley, Danny Abshire (5/85)

245 Clip And Trip 5.11- ★★
A great little sandstone vacation; all it'll cost you is a couple of biner clips.
Start: 30' right of Pinga Boys.
Trip up a small, flared corner with a crack. Face climb following a thin seam in an orange streak. Escape right, zig-zag to the top. 90'

★ Clip and Trip Direct Finish 5.11
Climb straight up the face above the orange streak and turn a bulge with very thin holds.
FA: Robyn Erbesfield, Shannon Stegg, Rob Robinson (3/85)
FA Direct Finish: Darrow Kirkpatrick, Rob Robinson (top rope) 1/12

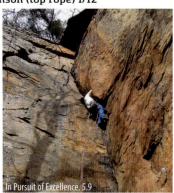

In Pursuit of Excellence, 5.9

TENNESSEE WALL

MIDDLE BLOSSOM

Just past the wide, left-facing corner full of grassy hummocks is a flat, low-to-the-ground roof. This feature marks the start of Middle Blossom. The trail leads beneath this roof. Coming out the middle of the roof is route #246, Finagle 5.9, which is the first route in Middle Blossom.

25 mins

246 Finagle 5.9 ★★★
You'll have to do a bit (of finagling), but by most accounts you should love every minute of it!
Start: 30' right of Clip And Trip.
Pitch 1: 5.9. Conquer the right margin of a large, flat roof (crux) with a long, horizontal crack (just over its lip). Diagonal left and tiptoe up a thin, bottoming crack in a steep, smooth slab (crux) ... scrape left to an arete to gain a scenic belay perch. (50') Pitch 2: 5.6. The arete leads to the top. (40')
FA: Robyn Erbesfield, Shannon Stegg, Rob Robinson (3/85)

247 Dirt Bag 5.8 ★★★
Start: 5' right of Finagle.
Climb a long, vertical crack system.
90' **FA: Peter Henley, Rick Beckman (5/85)**

248 In Pursuit Of Excellence 5.9+
 Your quest to find southern sandstone's 5.9 "holy grail" of corners is over ... one of the finest pitches for the grade in the region. Start: 10' right of Dirt Bag.
Layback, stem, and jam up a beautiful left-facing corner; at the summit roof traverse left to the top. 90' **FA: Bob Ordner, Roy Briton, Rob Robinson (2/85)**

T-Wall

www.rockerypress.com 411

Scamper Proof 5.12

A hard one to flash, but it has been done. Power trad climbing on perfect stone.
Start: 15' right of Guardian Of The Gate. Climb a left-facing corner for 15'. Scamper left and over a small roof ; continue up a narrow, right-facing corner capped by a bulge. Finish up a shallow, flared finger crack to the top. 90'

★ Direct Start: 5.12. Climb the face past two bolts. Join the regular route at the roof. **FA: Rob Robinson, Curt Merchant, Pat Perrin, Mark Cole (2/86) FA Direct Start: unknown**

Insider's Note: Throwing the feet out right to body stem off the corner is off route.

Climber: Tim Derohen   Photo Credit: Micah Gentry

TENNESSEE WALL

249 Litto 5.12a ★★ (sport)
Should have been named "The Infringer" since the first few bolts impinge on a previously established route. Nevertheless, great face climbing on gorgeous orange stone.
Start: 10' right of In Pursuit Of Excellence. Face climb a steep orange wall following a line of widely spaced bolts to the top. 90'
FA: Shannon Stegg (1990's)

250 Guardian Of The Gate 5.10+ ★★★
Start: Same as for Litto.
Face climb a steep orange wall; finagle right to, and then up, an arete capped by a short, shallow dihedral with a small roof. Step right and climb a bulge split by a short thin crack; continue to the top. 90'
FA: Rob Robinson, Tom Campbell (5/85)

> **Insider's Tip:** Clip the first few bolts of Litto, or if you're a purist, protect the lower face by slinging a tree alongside the route.

251 Scamper Proof 5.12 ★★★
See description on page 412.

252 Points O' Contact 5.10+
"220 volt quality" ... beautiful crack and face climbing capped by an electrifying crux.
Start: Same as for Scamper Proof. Climb a left-facing corner to the roof, ease right and jam a nice, hand-sized crack. Step left, then up, past a pair of shallow cracks (crux). Finish directly up the steep face. 90'
FA: Rob Robinson, Bob Ordner, Roy Briton (2/85)

253 Slay Ride 5.11- ★★
No walk in the park here ...
Start: 5' right of Points O' Contact. Boulder over a small overhang (jug) and climb a shallow crack to a stance. Solve a short, blank-looking (crux) steep face; finish via the high bulge of Finger Lockin' Good. 90'
FA: Rob Robinson, Robyn Erbesfield (3/85)

> **Insider's Note:** It is "legal" to sling the top of a nearby tree for protection.

T-Wall

Finger Lockin' Good, 5.10

www.rockerypress.com 413

TENNESSEE WALL — ORANGE BLOSSOM WALLS

254 Finger Lockin' Good 5.10 ★★★
Arguably the best piece of straight in 5.10 finger crackin' in the Chattanooga area.
Start: 5' right of Slay Ride.
Climb a sustained and bouldery 40' finger crack. Trend left, then over an obtuse bulge split by a thin crack; romp to the top. 90'
FA: Rob Robinson, Jay Dautcher (3/85)

255 Jay Walker 5.7 ★★★
Likely the T Wall's best 5.7; classic corner climbing loaded with excellent jams.
Start: 10' right of Finger Lockin' Good.
Climb a long, left-facing corner with two cracks. Bail at a cave on the left with anchors, or cruise right on to the top. 90'
FA: Jay Dautcher, free solo (3/85)

> **Insider's Note:** Watch out for the big "death spike" buried at the base of this pitch.

256 Restless Pedestrian 5.8 ★★
A toddler's version of the first pitch of the Yosemite Valley's Outer Limits.
Start: 5' right of Jay Walker.
Climb a long, "lightning bolt" crack which eventually merges with Jay Walker. 90'
FA: Rob Robinson, free solo (3/85)

257 Exposed Aggregate 5.7 ★
Start: 5' right of Restless Pedestrian.
Climb a vertical crack system to a ledge. 70'
FA: Bruce Rogers, Mike Wright (summer, '86)

258 Digital Display 5.9 ★
Start: 5' right of Exposed Aggregate.
Climb a 15' fingertip crack. Follow one of two cracks above to a ledge. 70'
FA: Rob Robinson, free solo (2/86)

259 Frenzy 5.11+ ★
Start: 20' right of Digital Display. Power out a low roof using finger pockets (tech crux) to gain a smaller roof above. Now climb a shallow, crescent-shaped crack capped by a bulge (thin holds); continue to the top. 90'
FA: Rob Robinson, Gene Smith (4/86)

Puppy Ride, 5.9

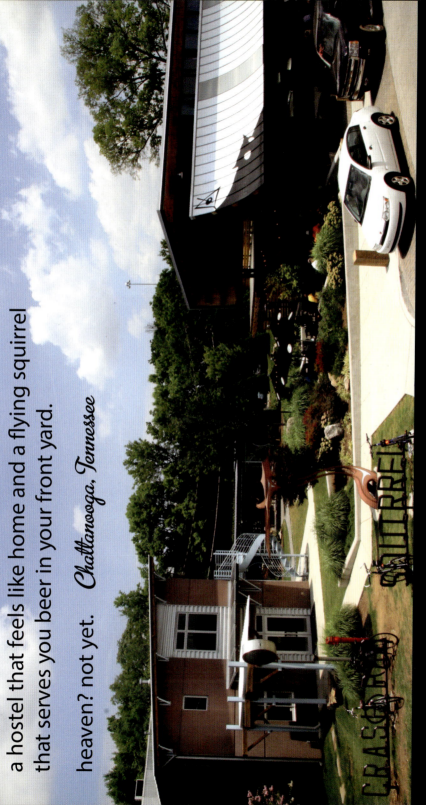

a hostel that feels like home and a flying squirrel that serves you beer in your front yard.

heaven? not yet. *Chattanooga, Tennessee*

423.648.8393
flyingsquirrelbar.com
crashpadchattanooga.com

TENNESSEE WALL

ORANGE BLOSSOM WALLS

260 Fear On Ice 5.12 ★★
Features a stack of sustained 5.11 moves capped by a hard crux, with hard-to-place gear.
Start: 15' right of Frenzy.
Power through double roofs and climb a marbleized bulge split by a thin vertical seam. 50'
FA: Rob Robinson (4/86)

> Insider's Note: Came close to decking on this one ... I'm living proof that backing up supposedly "bomber" gear never hurts.

261 Fly With The Falcon 5.11
A perfect Yosemite-style jam crack rips through a wall of incredible "faux marble" sandstone.
Start: 5' right of Fear On Ice.
Jug through small roofs, then jam a perfect hand and finger crack splitting a marbleized wall. Bolted anchors. 50'
FA: Marvin Webb, Steve Kerchner (3/85)

262 The Heaven Of Animals 5.11- ★★
Welcome to cloud nine ... more T Wall "climber heaven."
Start: 20' right of Fly With The Falcon. Yard over a low roof; climb a left-facing corner to a sloping ledge. Traverse left and climb a fun jam crack. Bobble over a small, bulging overhang (crux) and continue to the top. 100'
FA: Rob Robinson, Bruce Rogers (5/85)

> Insider's Tip: Look for a shallow sliver of a slot that'll take a small brass to protect the crux.

263 Puppy Ride 5.9
A bit of, shall we say, a teething toy for young sandstone Dobermans.
Start: Same as for The Heaven Of Animals. Yard over the low roof; climb the long, left-facing corner to the top. 100'
FA: Peter Henley, Rob Robinson (2/85)

> Insider's Tip: Aid the roof (one or two moves) and you'll have yourself a great pitch of 5.8!

T-Wall

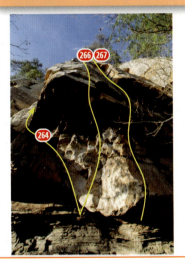

416 www.rockerypress.com

TENNESSEE WALL

264 Steel Puppies 5.11- ★★

Some artful name twisting by Gardner gave this route its unusual moniker. Deciphered, it means you'll need steel fingers for a couple of the crux moves.
Start: 15' right of Puppy Ride.
Hump up into a bomb-bay roof. Steel left ... climb a rounded, right-facing corner. Diagonal left to Puppy Ride, or finish up a long stretch of moderate face climbing. 100'
FA: Forrest Gardner, Rob Robinson (3/85)

265 Chocolate Puppies 5.11- ★★

Third and final contribution to the "puppy trilogy."
Start: As for Steel Puppies.
Follow Steel Puppies to a small overhang in a rounded, right-facing corner. Traverse right 15' to an arete; climb this for about 20'. Step right around the arete and follow a pebble-studded "tips" crack till it ends. A bit higher, climb right to gain a nice handcrack. Continue up this and on to easier rock and the top. 110'
FA: Harrison Shull, Andy Kluge (1/01)

Insider's Tips: A bit tricky to protect. Bring a couple of long runners.

T-Wall

www.rockerypress.com 417

TENNESSEE WALL

ORANGE BLOSSOM WALLS

266 Gift Of Power 5.12a ★★★ (sport)
Features full throttle, "four wheel drive" power climbing through a short span of tiered hangs. Jumper cables, afterburner optional.
Start: Just right of Steel Puppies/Chocolate Puppies.
Monkey through 12' of tiered overhangs. Face climb following a thin crack to a mass of fixed slings at a flake, or continue up and left (carry a rack) to the top. 100'
FA: Rob Robinson, Justin Eiseman (1/90)

Insider's Trivia: A bolt gun was used to "saw" a small pine tree down which was blocking the start of the route — hence the name.

267 Calves Of Steel 5.11 ★★

Corralling this mad cow of a pitch will require steady nerves and a fistful of brass nuts.
Start: 5' right of Gift Of Power.
Clear two small roofs and climb a shallow, right-facing corner. Cowpoke right (crux) to the left edge of a large, rectangular roof. A casual trail ride up a long, left-facing corner leads to the top. 100'
FA: Rob Robinson, Jay Dautcher (3/85)

268 Riddle On The Roof 5.13- ★★★
A dastardly and ridiculously difficult spot of climbing that, by most accounts, can be as frustrating as trying to solve a Rubick's cube.
Start: 20' right of Calves Of Steel.
Scamper up a short, left-facing corner barred by a low roof. Break left and turn a small roof to gain a thin crack leading up and over a body length roof (crux). Continue following the crack to the top. 100'
FA: Chris Chesnutt, Travis Eiseman (90's)
FFA: Nathaniel Walker (2/08)

269 Reptile Analysis 5.10 ★★
Get in touch with your inner lizard....
Start: Same as for Riddle On The Roof.
Scamper up a left-facing corner barred by a low roof; gecko right and around a 6' roof (crux). A long, left-facing corner leads to the top. 100'
FA: Forrest Gardner, Bob Ordner, Rob Robinson (3/85)

Nathaniel Walker on the First Ascent of Riddle on the Roof, 5.13

Photo Credit: Luke Laeser

Stone Wave 5.11

Sandstone surfing just doesn't get any better than this. Start: 15' right of Hold Your Horses! Boulder (good spotter) over a low overhang (tech crux). Follow a magnificent crack system up to and over a small but spectacular cresting overhang (11-) to the top. 100'
Insider's Tip: If the start stymies you... consider climbing Molly And Rocket for about 10' and then traversing left on big face holds.
FA: Rob Robinson, Gene Smith (2/85) FFA: Gene Smith, Laura Smith (4/85)

Insider's Note: The free ascent was snagged after a small tree stump was hacked out of the crack above the "stone wave."

Climber: Tim Derohen Photo Credit: Micah Gentry

TENNESSEE WALL

270 Hold Your Horses! 5.10 ★★★
A challenging T Wall chariot ride for aspiring Ben Hur's of the vertical world.
Start: 10' right of Reptile Analysis/Paralysis. Climb a wide, left-facing corner; work right around a big roof, climb a narrow, left-facing dihedral for 10' or so, join the regular route (see below), and continue to the top. Traverse left to bolted anchors atop Reptile Paralysis. 100'

★ Alternate Start: 5.11. Start 15' right of the regular start. Boulder over a low roof (tech crux). Diagonal left and climb a rounded arete (5.8 or 5.9) with no pro. Step through bowl above and continue to the top.
FA: Forrest Gardner, Robyn Erbesfield (7/85) FA Alternate Start: Rob Robinson, Arno Ilgner (3/85)

> **Insider's Note:** The alternate start was actually the original route. The hope is that by making the Gardner/Erbesfield version the standard start this route will begin to see some much deserved traffic.

271 Hold Your Reptile 5.10+ ★★
Start: Same as for Hold Your Horses. Climb a wide, left-facing corner; work left at the junction of a big roof; merge with the long, left-facing corner that comprises the upper half of Reptile Analysis and continue to the top. 110'
FA: Tyler Stracker, David Draper (3/05)

> **Insider's Tip:** Bring a big #4 cam for the roof traverse.

A Tension Span, 5.9

272 Stone Wave 5.11
See description on page 420.

273 Molly And Rocket 5.8 ★
Start: 10' right of Stone Wave, at a large rock spike.
Step to the wall from the spike and climb a long, vertical crack system. 100'
FA: Kyle Patrick, Buddy Baldwin (3/86)

274 Who Needs A Thnead? 5.10- ★
Start: 10' right of Molly And Rocket. Climb a shallow, vertical crack to a sloping ledge. Continue past a bolt to the top. 90'
FA: Tim Williams, Marvin Webb (1/91)

275 A Tension Span 5.9 ★★★
Start: 20' right of Who Needs A Thnead? Climb a narrow, right-facing corner. Trend left and up a wide, right-facing corner. 80'
FA: Arno Ilgner, Rob Robinson (3/85)

276 Surf's Up 5.11c (sport)
Hang ten? Rope up and you'll find out why this perfect wave of sandstone is a favorite ride of the local sandstone beach bums.
Start: 15' right of A Tension Span. Climb the face following a line of bolts. Surf right at the last bolt (crux) and up to anchors. 80'
FA: Eddie Whittemore ('92)

> **Insider's Note:** The grade is height dependent. Shorter climbers should be prepared for far harder moves.

277 Crash Position 5.9
Clear the sandstone runway and prepare to enjoy a scenic air voyage. Plenty of "gear depots" along the way, so don't be intimidated by the route's name.
Start: 10' right of Surf's Up.
Climb through a bulge split by a crack. Ramble up and right onto a long arete which leads to the top. (Crux is the last 15'.) 80'
FA: Sean Hunt, Stuart Chapin (10/89)

TENNESSEE WALL — ORANGE BLOSSOM WALLS

278 Defcon Five 5.11- ★★★
Defcon Five: a military term referencing a general state of readiness ... well, get ready!
Start: 25' right of Crash Position.
Climb a steep wall for 25' with thin, parallel cracks ... battle left to the arete (crux) via bouldery moves. Near the top of the arête, march right up a small, right-facing corner. 90'
★★ Direct Start: 5.11+. Start a few feet left of the regular start. Climb dead straight up the bulging nose (challenging gear placements) of the arete past a single bolt (crux) and continue to the top.
FA: Rob Robinson, Tim Cumbo (4/85) FA Direct Start: Rob Robinson (5/99)

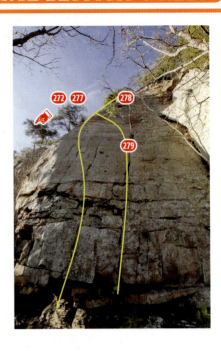

279 Mean Cuisine 5.10 ★★
A zesty sandstone entree with a side dish combo which includes several spicy run-outs. Serious take-out food for the well seasoned trad climber.
Start: 5' right of Defcon Five.
Climb a vertical crack (the appetizer) which mutates into a sustained stretch of freaky face climbing. Traverse left (even freakier) via snap n' crackle holds past a small scoop. Finish via the Defcon arete. 90'
★★ Direct Finish: 5.12-. Climb Cuisine's appetizer crack and freaky face; continue straight to the top past two bolts using fingernail-width holds and slopers.
FA: Rob Robinson, Peter Henley (2/85) FA Direct Finish: Tim Williams ('94)

280 Over The Hills And Far Away 5.9 ★
Start: 15' right of Mean Cuisine.
Boulder up a rounded, crackless arete, sans gear. Coast straight up a smooth sweep in the wall, finishing in an orange streak to the top. 90'
FA: Forrest Gardner, Peter Henley (2/85)

281 Blind Date 5.7 ★
Start: 5' right of Over The Hills And Far Away.
A left-facing dihedral, formed by a huge semi-detached flake, leads to a nice cedar tree. 50'
FA: Sherburne Sentell, John Gore (3/85)

282 Digital Macabre 5.10 ★★★
See description on page 423.

Digital Macabre 5.10 ★★★
Classic, thin fingers rainbow crack arcing across a sandstone sky.
Start: 5' right of Blind Date.
Scamper up a short corner capped by a scoop. Turn the lip and savor a perfect thin crack arcing left to a ledge. 50'
FA: Marvin Webb, Steve Kerchner (3/85)

Photo Credit: Micah Gentry

TENNESSEE WALL — ORANGE BLOSSOM WALLS

283 Fill In The Blanks 5.10 ★★★
For the face climbing sketch artist — the perfect sandstone canvas.
Start: 15' right of Digital Macabre.
Pull a low hang, then climb a pebble-studded face capped by a thin crack arching right. From the top of the crack continue on for a few more moves ... climb a 2nd thin crack splitting a bulge; continue to the top. 100'
★★**Variation: 5.9** Cruise up the wall to the base of the thin, arching crack. Sketch left to an arete (short run-out) and cruise to the top.
FA: Rob Robinson, Tim Cumbo (4/86) FA Variation (original route): Rob Robinson, Peter Henley (3/85)

284 Razor Worm 5.9
Start: 10' right of Fill In The Blanks. Cruise up the right side of a large, semi-detached flake; follow the crack line above over a bulge (crux) and continue to the top. 100'
FA: Peter Henley, Rob Robinson (2/85)

285 Cake Walk 5.10-
A "Valley style" crack line, and one of the T' Wall's tastiest sandstone pastries.
Start: 10' right of Razor Worm.
Putter up a perfect, left-facing dihedral to a 2' roof. Work right round this to gain a delightful crack system above which continues to the top. 100' FA: Rob Robinson, Peter Henley (2/85)

TENNESSEE WALL

286 Fingernails On A Chalk Board 5.12- ★★
Very thin, as the name implies. Rewarding and sustained face climbing with a couple of honest-to-God "fingernail width" holds. Start: 5' right of Cake Walk.
Face climb to the top of a shallow, vertical crack. Tiptoe straight up the face (staying well left of the bolts on Competitive Edge, see next route) to a small ledge. "Boulder" up a blank-looking headwall for 12' to a polished bulge. Step right; exit on the final moves of Competitive Edge. 100'
FA: Rob Robinson, top-rope (10/92)

Insider's Note: Use of the left outside corner for a move on the final headwall is "o.k."

287 Competitive Edge 5.11 ★★★
Gold medal quality face climbing. Start: 10' right of Fingernails On A Chalk Board. Climb a bottoming, vertical crack. Edge past four bolts; finish via a thin seam. 100' FA: Robyn Erbesfield, Roy Briton (3/89)

Insider's Note: Protecting the final seam is tricky, but it's all there.

288 Golden Locks 5.9
Hand jam heaven! One of the best "24 carat" cracks for the grade in the Sandstone Belt.
Start: 10' right of Competitive Edge. Scamper over a small (crux) overhang; jam and face climb following a solid gold, straight-in, finger and hand crack to the top. 100'
FA: Rob Robinson, Marvin Webb (2/85)

Memory Fog

The Tennessee Wall is home to vast inventory of jam-i-licous jam cracks. Among this landscape laden with vertical (and overhanging!) cracks, Golden Locks stands out as the best straight-in 5.8 hand job. Did I say 5.8? The start is more like 5.9. Anyway, looking up from the base, you can almost imagine you've been magically transported to crack heaven: Yosemite Valley. Since it was first climbed, Golden Locks has likely received a few thousand ascents. No doubt it will see many, many more. It's alway been a favorite of mine, and for years I included it in my T-Wall free solo circuit.

Rob Robinson free solo on Golden Locks, 5.9   Photo Credit: Rob Robinson Collection

TENNESSEE WALL

289 Gravity Creeps 5.10 ★★

This fine piece of face climbing deserves a wider climbing audience — even if on top-rope.
Start: 15' right of Golden Locks.
Climb a sustained face following a disconnected crack system to a 2' overhang. Creep left and finish up Golden Locks. 100'
★★ **Direct Finish:** 5.11+. From the 2' overhang: Climb straight up a freaky thin face past two bolts to the top.
FA: Rob Robinson, Forrest Gardner (7/85)
FA Direct Finish: Michael Emelianoff ('90)

290 Greenwich Garden Party 5.9+

Start: 10' right of Gravity Creeps.
Skitter up a slick n' shallow left-facing corner. A "veggie crack" leads to the top. 100'
FA: John Harlin, Rob Robinson (11/85)

291 Some Girls 5.12b ★★

....can put up wickedly thin climbs like this one! "Good luck, gentlemen."
Start: 10' right of Greenwich Garden Party. Climb into shallow box formed by opposing corners. Meander up the water-polished face above (multiple cruxes) past a few bolts and a fixed pin? to the top. 90'
FA: Jennifer Cole, Mark Cole (mid 80's)

292 Nutrasweet 5.7 ★★★

Nutritious, delicious, and good for you, too.
Start: 10' right of Some Girls.
Climb a giant, left-facing corner with a hand crack. 90'
FA: Robyn Erbesfield, Rob Robinson (3/85)

293 Sun King 5.12a ★★ (sport)

Start: 10' right of Nutrasweet.
Climb a beautiful orange wall peppered with bolts to a double bolt anchor. 80'
FA: Eddie Whittemore (12/89)

Insider's Tip: Good late afternoon winter route ... gets the last rays of the sun.

294 Margin Of Profit 5.10-

A truly spectacular and airy arete. You can take this one to the bank.
Start: 5' right of Sun King.
Follow a thin finger crack diagonaling left. Ease up and right (a bit run-out, but moderately difficult) to a superb arete. Cruise to the top finishing on the right side. 110'
★ **Direct Start:** 5.10+. Start 10' right of the regular route. Jam a nice crack through small roofs; join the regular route.
FA: Rob Robinson, Robyn Erbesfield (3/85) FA Direct Start: Rob Robinson (mid 80's)

Insider's Tip: Good late afternoon winter route ... gets the last rays of the sun.

TENNESSEE WALL

ORANGE BLOSSOM WALLS

295 Hidden Assets 5.10-
Greenbacks are nice, but if you want to be a sandstone millionaire, then add this — one of the finest 5.10 corners in the Sandstone Belt — to your vertical portfolio.
Start: 15' right of Margin Of Profit. Climb a short, left-facing corner; step right to a small ledge. Now look up! A beautiful hand crack leads up a perfect left-facing corner. Finish via elegant stemming through a bulge capping the corner (crux); easier rock above leads to the top. 100'
FA: Rob Robinson, Peter Henley (2/85)

296 Point Of Departure 5.10+ ★★
Occasionally the scene of a real air show; bring a good "air traffic controller" for your belay.
Start: 10' right of Hidden Assets. Crank over a low roof; bearhug, body wrap, and heel hook the blunt arete above ... easier rock above leads to the top. 100'
FA: Rob Robinson, Curt Merchant, Pat Perrin (2/86)

> **Insider's Tip:** Good late afternoon winter route ... gets the last rays of the sun.

T-Wall

Razor Worm, 5.9

Some Girls, 5.12

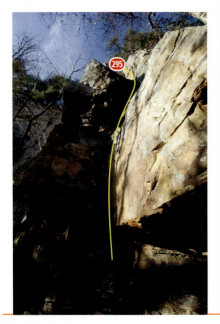

428 www.rockerypress.com

TENNESSEE WALL

297 Steepopolis 5.12-
This legendary T Wall test piece has earned a fearsome reputation throughout the years. Most of the climbing, however, is fairly reasonable, although at times difficult to protect.
Start: 10' right of Point Of Departure. Blast up the wall past a pair of thin, vertical seams. Work through a faint notch above, then follow more thin seams up a very sustained face to the top. 100'
FA: Rob Robinson, Curt Merchant (4/86)

> **Insider's Tips & Trivia:** Double ropes recommended, along with a couple of biners worth of brass and steel nuts. Originally graded 5.11+.

298 Mrs. Socrates 5.12-
Southern sandstone cracks like this are as rare as the Hope diamond. Whether you're ready for it now, or working your way up through the grades: This magnificent crack belongs at the top of your "must do" list.
Start: 10' right of Steepopolis. Breeze up to a small recess. Conquer a short but obtuse right-facing corner (crux). Jam a long finger and hand crack to a sloping ledge. Step right and continue straight to the top, or diagonal right to a pine tree just below the summit. 110'
FA: Rob Robinson, Bruce Rogers, Marvin Webb (2/85)

> **Insider's Notes:** If you like this route, then don't miss Suck Creek's Rainbow Delta or Confetti Fingers. Originally graded 5.11+.

299 Defender Of The Crown 5.13a
(sport) King of the T Wall face climbs. Royal stone, royally difficult, rarely repeated.
Start: Same as for Mrs. Socrates. Charge through low hangs to a shallow recess. Power over a mean little roof, continue to top of seam above. Cognitively complex face climbing past multiple cruxes leads past a final bulge to easier rock above. 85'
FA: Rob Robinson (12/89)

> **Insider's Notes:** A bit "slabby" perhaps, however the plethora of beautiful, complex, and intricate sequences make this route one of my all-time T Wall favorites. Stepping left to snag a rest jam in the Socrates crack is verboten.

Carl Buch finding a keen gear placement in the crux of Mrs. Socrates, 5.12- Photo Credit: Nathalie Dupre

TENNESSEE WALL

300 Electric Rats 5.10 ★★★
Welcome ... to Mr. Gardner's lab. Features a scrappy "rat pipe" of a roof followed by a bit of a grovel up a somewhat tamer crack. Start: 10' right of Defender Of The Crown. Grovel? through a maze of tiered roofs (crux) split by a crack which continues up the wall above to the top. 110'
FA: Forrest Gardner, Peter Henley (2/85)

> **Insider's Tip:** Judicious use of runners down low will save you a world of rope drag hell on the wall above.

301 Bugs From Hell 5.11+ ★★
Cocky leaders beware: This is a finger stinger of a pitch that could also turn out to be a real ego exterminator.
Start: 15' right of Electric Rats.
Boulder over a small overhang. Clamber through pebbled bulges to a stance atop a small horn. Sketchy face moves (crux) past a fixed pin give way to a fingertip seam that leads to the top. 110'
FA: Forrest Gardner, Rob Robinson (6/85)

> **Insider's Tips n' Trivia:** The first ascent protected the crux using several hand placed long knife blades. There is a fixed pin in place now. Named after a scorpion found in the crack above the crux encountered during the first ascent that tried to sting me on the second.

302 Motor Boody 5.9 ★★
Start: 10' right of Bugs From Hell.
Climb a right-facing corner. Steer left onto the steep wall below a big flat roof. Conquer a bulge and continue to the top. 110'
FA: Steve Goins, Rob Robinson (6/85)

303 Life In High Definition 5.11- ★
Start: 10' right of Motor Boody, in a crack on the right side of a box alcove.
Begin with a strenuous move into a leftward arching undercling crack. Follow this into a large right-facing corner. At a conglomerated hole, traverse left to gain a small, right-facing corner system. Follow this up ledges to the base of a large right-facing corner/roof. Traverse under the roof to the anchor on Motor Boody. 100'
FA: Cody Averbeck, Luke Laeser, Nathaniel Walker ('08)

www.rockerypress.com 431

TENNESSEE WALL
ORANGE BLOSSOM WALLS

304 Grandma's Couch 5.11- ★
Start: 15' right of Life In High Definition.
Pitch 1: 5.11-. Boulder over a low roof, continue to a small alcove. Diagonal left up a ramp, now right over a "wave," followed by a wild traverse left (at the margin of the big roof.) Belay on a small ledge above (known as "the couch.") (75')
Pitch 2: 5.6. Finish with a short stretch of moderate face climbing. (25')
FA: Pat Perrin, Mark Henley, Curt Merchant (3/86)

305 Southern Express 5.12+ ★★★ (sport) One of the last great T Wall "super roofs." Recently set free. Start: Same as for Grandma's Couch.
Wander up the wall and out an imposing 25' roof split by a bolt-protected thin crack. 100'
FA: Nathaniel Walker, Luke Laeser ('08)
FFA: Laban Swafford, Nathaniel Walker

306 Time Takes A Cigarette 5.9
Start: 15' right of Grandma's Couch/Southern Express.
Follow a big, right-facing corner to a big flat roof. Traverse right beneath the roof following its 4" inch crack ... roll right around lip and finish with a short spate of easy face climbing. 75'
FA: Forrest Gardner, Jack Noonan (10/85)

307 Saint Valentines Day Massacre 5.12- ★
Start: Same as for Time Takes A Cigarette.
Climb T.T.A.C. for 10'; work right and over a flat, 4' roof past a bolt. Continue up the face above to the top. 60'
FA: Steve Goins, Truly Bracken (5/83)

308 Exodus 5.10 ★★
Start: 20' right of Saint Valentine's Day Massacre.
Climb a jam crack on the right side of a rounded arete. 60'
FA: Pat Perrin, Rob Robinson (3/86)

309 Genesis 5.10 ★
Start: 15' right of Exodus.
Climb a steep wall with a hard-to-spot, reachy bolt clip about 30' off the deck. 60'
FA: Pat Perrin, Mark Henley (3/86)

> **Insider's Note:** Even using double rope technique ... clipping the bolt can be a real head trip.

To reach the following two climbs: Just right of Genesis ascend a moderately difficult 5th Class corner. The climbs will be more or less right overhead.

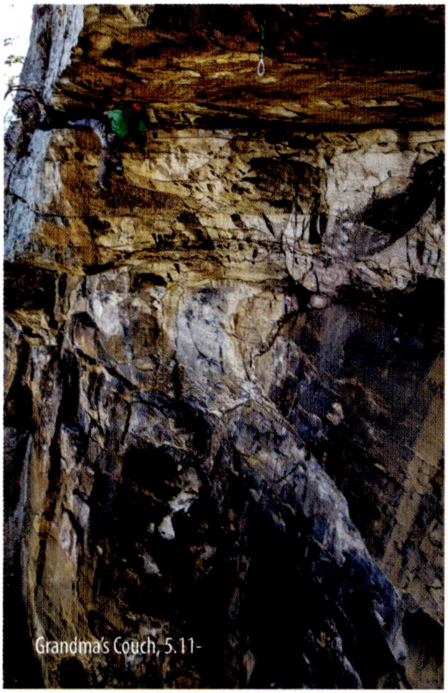

Grandma's Couch, 5.11-

(310) Zenmania 5.11+ ★★ ❒
You'll probably find this one rather inspiring if you're working up through the 5.11 grades.
Start: On the wall directly above Genesis.
Climb a huge roof split by a crack. 60′
FA: Ron Davis, Kevin Thomas (4/85)

(311) Riverbend Festival 5.10+ ★ ❒
Start: 30′ right of Zenmania.
Wander up the wall; a thin, crescent-shaped crack breaches an exposed 5′ roof. Conquer this and continue to the top. 100′
FA: Rob Robinson, Robyn Erbesfield (6/85)

(312) Slug Trail 5.8 ★ ❒
Start: 25′ right of Genesis.
Climb a right-slanting crack into a brown band; wander up the wall above to the top. 50′
FA: Jamie Silliman and partner (3/86)

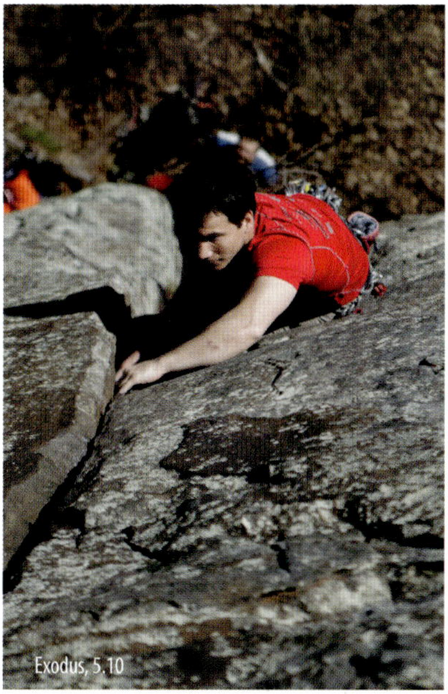

Exodus, 5.10

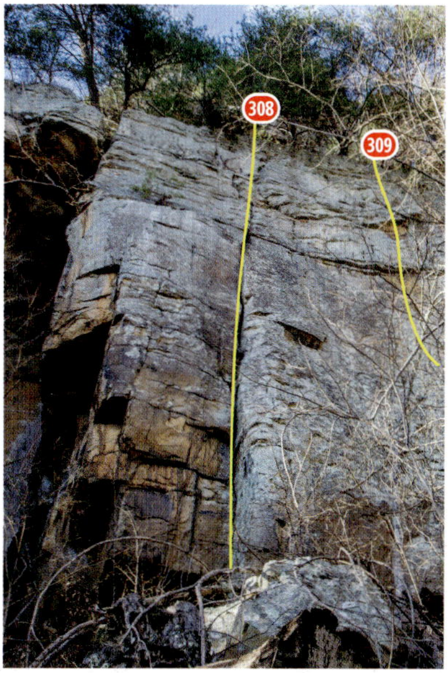

TENNESSEE WALL
ORANGE BLOSSOM WALLS

30 mins

EAST BLOSSOM

Approach: East Blossom begins just past the alcove to the right of the 25' roof of Southern Express. The trail breaks away from the cliff as it passes this recess, then continues directly beneath the cliff as it enters East Blossom.

313 Full Belly In Hell 5.10- ★
Start: 20' right of Slug Trail.
Climb a steep face and outside corner. 70'
FA: Forrest Gardner, Peter Henley (11/85)

314 Hungry For Heaven 5.10
For the sandstone priest or priestess — a gift from rock gods.
Start: 10' right of Full Belly In Hell. Boulder over a small roof split by a shallow crack. Work up (crux) and inch left a few moves to gain a steep, left-facing corner. Sinker fingerlocks and classic laybacks lead up this and the wall above to the top. 70'

★★★ Hungry For Heaven: Variation 5.10
Start: Same as for the regular route. Climb Hungry For Heaven past the low roof to jug holds in the short bowl above. Work right to the arete and follow thin cracks up the face. Merge with the headwall crack on the regular route and continue to the ledge with ring anchors.
FA: Rob Robinson, Robyn Erbesfield (3/85) Variation FA: Rob Robinson (2013)

315 Full Coleman 5.11+ ★★
Named for an exploding fuel canister; come prepared for long moves on bomber orange streaked rock.
Start: 10' right of Hungry For Heaven. Toprope from right to left using several unique iron pockets to a thin face up high.
FA: Dave Wilson, Chad Fowler, Cody Averbeck ('12)

Insider's Note: Needs one lead bolt placed for a reasonably safe lead. In the meantime, it makes for a nice top rope from the anchors of Hungry for Heaven.

316 Board Walk 5.10 ★★
A bit of a vertical chessboard. Checkmating the summit might take some doing ...
Start: 50' right of Hungry For Heaven. "Walk" over a bulge to a stance on a steep wall. A thin, squiggly crack leads to the top. 70'
FA: Rob Robinson, James Dobbs (12/85)

317 The Garden 5.7 ★
Start: 10' right of Board Walk.
Follows a long vertical crack system to the top. 70'
FA: Eric Peterson, Brett Fundak, Paul Stuckey (11/89)

318 Corner Pockets 5.10- ★
Start: 20' right of The Garden.
Pocket a short left-facing corner. 40'
FA: Sandy Stewart, Steve Kerchner (4/85)

TENNESSEE WALL

319 Cathedral Crack 5.8 ★★
Great jamming and face climbing. Highly recommended.
Start: Up the hill side just a bit and approximately 20' right of Corner Pockets. Climb a slabby face and crack line to a ledge with ring anchors. 50'
FA: Rob Robinson, Michael O'Donnell, Chad Burdyshaw (3/13)

320 Jewel In The Sun 5.9 ★★
Start: 5' right of Cathedral Crack. Face climb a shallow bowl with no protection for 20' to a stance. Continue up face and climb a short, right-facing corner with hand crack. Diagonal up the steep wall above through a shallow notch to the top. 50' FA: (top rope) Chad Burdyshaw (3/13)
First Lead: Rob Robinson (3/13)

Insider's Tip: If you don't want to risk the lead you can always do Cathedral Crack to top rope it.

321 Molecular Bypass 5.10+ ★★
Start: 10' right of Jewel In The Sun. Climb a short corner and continue up a steep face with discontinuous cracks line past two bolts to ledge with ring anchors. 40' FA: (top rope) Rob Robinson (3/13)

Insider's Tip: A bolt has been placed at the crux however this would be a death route without the addition of a second protection bolt a bit higher in a crackless section of the wall.

322 Soil Mechanics 5.8 ★
Start: 10' right of Molecular Bypass. Climb a short, left-facing crack and corner capped by a small roof to ledge. 40'
FA: Ryan Little, (3/13)

Cathedral Crack, 5.8

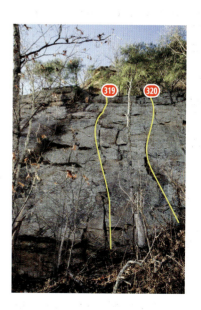

TENNESSEE WALL — ORANGE BLOSSOM WALLS

323 Trungle 5.8 ★
Start: At trailside, approximately 25' right of Soil Mechanic (or 50' right of Corner Pockets)
Climb a left-facing corner beneath a band of massive, tiered roofs. 60'
FA: Roy Briton, Bob Ordner (2/85)

324 Among The Wild Chimps 5.11 ★★
You might be able to monkey around on pitch one, but the wild roof on pitch two is a habitat best left to the sandstone gorilla.
Start: Same as for Trungle.
Pitch 1: 5.10. Step right out of a hole (minimal protection) in the wall and climb to the top of a small, left-facing corner on the orange wall. Traverse right along pockets and step into a hidden dihedral. Belay by a pine tree a bit higher. (60')
Pitch 2: 5.11. Swing left through tiered roofs. Finish up a short corner with spectacular position. (40')

★★ **Variation Pitch 1: Brazen Serpent: 5.11+ (sport)**. Face climb the steep orange face past a faint arch following a few bolts.
FA: Forrest Gardner, Robyn Erbesfield, Rob Robinson (6/85) FA Variation Pitch 1: Van Eitel, Allan Fuhr, Dan Russell (11/90)

Insider's Note: Some of the bolts of Brazen Serpent cross and impinge upon the original line of Among The Wild Chimps.

325 Mirage 5.11a ★★ (sport)
Start: 5' right of Among The Wild Chimps. Follow a line of bolts up the face to a pine tree. 60' FA: Bernard and Kiki Vanwestingham ('92)

326 The Velvet Jesus 5.11 ★★
Velvety smooth, divine climbing in spite of a somewhat disappointing start.
Start: Same as for Mirage.
Pitch 1: 5.9. Clip the first two bolts on Mirage, work right around the corner to a decent stance in an alcove with a single belay bolt. (25') Pitch 2: 5.11. Climb the corner around a roof to gain a steep finger crack. Climb with great gear and locks up black and orange rock to the base of a smooth slab. Clip a bolt and finish out a roof with a fixed anchor at the lip. (80')
FA: Cody Averbeck, Nathaniel Walker, Joseph Staub ('07)

327 Crematorium 5.11+ ★
Start: 20' right of Mirage.
Pitch 1: 5.11+. Traverse left below a rounded bulge split by a seam. Claw into "potato chip" roofs. Work right a bit ... climb through more roofs via an overhanging finger crack to a hanging belay. (40') Pitch 2: 5.7. An easy pitch leads to the top. (70')
FA: Rob Robinson, Forrest Gardner (7/85)

Insider's Tip: Try double ropes to eliminate the hanging belay.

328 Centerfold 5.10+ ★★
Start: 25' right of Crematorium.
Climb a large, right-facing corner. Finagle through a weakness in the roof above. Continue up an easy face the top. 80'
FA: Rob Robinson, Jay Dautcher, Phil Reilly (3/85)

Massive Attack 5.9+ ★
Start: same as Centerfold.
Follow a large right-facing flake to a massive roof. Escape right to anchors on House (see below). 50'
FA: Stuart and Heidi Chapin 3/03

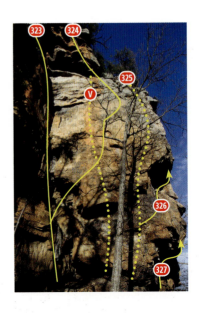

TENNESSEE WALL

329 House Of The Rising Sun 5.10d ★★
(sport) Start: 8' right of Massive Attack. Boulder through a low roof to balance on a thin face. Follow five bolts past multiple cruxes to anchors. 50'

★★ Direct Finish (Farmer Roof) 5.13a. (sport) Above the anchors, Continue through imposing roofs following a line of bolts.
FA: Stuart Chapin, Kirk Brode (4/03) FA Direct Finish: Steven Farmer

330 Up In Arms 5.11+ ★★★
"Full metal jacket" roof problem. Start: 7' right of House Of The Rising Sun. Follow a thin crack up the wall ... arm? through a tiered roof (crux) split by a crack. 100'
FA: Rob Robinson, Mark Cartwright (4/85)

> **Insider's Tip:** Not this time! You'll appreciate the subtleties of this obtuse pitch much more without guidebook beta.

331 Olympic Alchemy 5.13a ★★★
(sport) Conquering this bad ass roof will require a gold medal effort. Practice those one finger pull-ups ...
Start: 5' right of Up In Arms.
Conquer a tiny, right-facing corner, motor up the face to a tiered roof — conquer it. 75' FA: Rob Robinson (5/92)

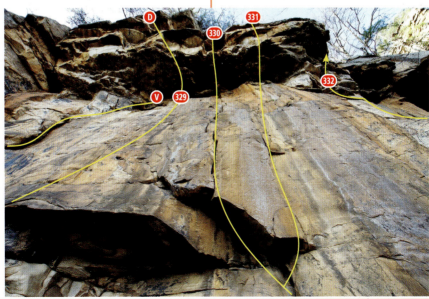

TENNESSEE WALL

ORANGE BLOSSOM WALLS

332 Atom Smasher 5.10+ ★★
An experiment, of sorts, for the sandstone physicist. Watch out for the "nuclear flake" on the crux overhang.
Start: 15' right of Olympic Alchemy.
Climb a right-facing corner; smash through tiered, white overhangs (crux); finish up an easy, right-facing corner. 100'
FA: Rob Robinson, Pat Perrin (3/86)

333 Airborne 5.9+ ★★
Bring a rack of big cams and an Army Ranger's attitude to the landing zone. Parachute optional.
Start: 15' right of Atom Smasher.
Climb a long, left-facing flake that slices through the left margin of a big roof. 100' FA: Arno Ilgner, Rob Robinson (3/85)

334 Board Of Corrections 5.11+ ★★★

Offers more than enough grounds for a peel, with an unappealing ground fall. That said, this is an excellent, well-protected (and neglected) route provided the alternate start is used.
Start: 30' right of Airborne.
Climb a small, left-facing corner on the right side of an arete ... sketch right and up face (very thin pro, one move of 11-) to gain a thin crack splitting a bulging (crux) wall. 60'
★ Alternate Start: 5.9. Start 15' left of the regular start. Climb a large, left-facing corner and follow the thin crack through the bulge.
FA: Rob Robinson, James Dobbs (12/85)
FA Alternate Start: Rob Robinson, Robyn Erbesfield (12/85)

> **Insider's Note:** Carry lots of small wires. Double ropes advised.

335 Smooth Operator 5.11
Bring your 5.11 calling card, and be prepared for a spot or two of "911" climbing.
Start: 20' right of Board Of Corrections.
Climb a perfect, right-facing corner with a thin crack ... at a horizontal band, step left, then onto the steep face (at a thin seam just right of an arete.) Weave up the center of wall; exit through tiered roofs. 70'
FA: Rob Robinson, Pat Perrin (3/86)

> **Insider's Notes and Tips:** Carry plenty of small wires, brass and TCU's. Double ropes recommended. While it is possible to reach right and clip the first bolts on Lord Of The Dance, it would result in a bad pendulum if you fall. If you do this route on a warm winter day you might see the hundreds of lizards that hang out in the dihedral crack. Please be kind to them ... you are a guest in their home.

336 Lord Of The Dance 5.12a ★★★
Welcome to the Tennessee Wall ballroom ...
Start: 5' right of Smooth Operator.
Climb a long, intricate, and intermittently pumpy face past a left-facing arch capped by a bulge and small roof. 70'
FA: Rob Robinson, Darrow Kirkpatrick (5/98)

> **Insider's Tip:** Some of the bolts may have been mysteriously removed.

337 Precious Orr 5.10-
Panning for gold in the T Wall river of sandstone? Check this 24 carat crack line out ...
Start: 5' right of Lord Of The Dance. A straight-in, "solid gold" hand crack slices through the wall ... climb it! 60'
FA: Marvin Webb, Rob Robinson (2/85)

> **Insider's Tip:** There are lots of hidden holds inside the crack.

TENNESSEE WALL

Golden Gloves, 5.10

Precious Orr, 5.10-

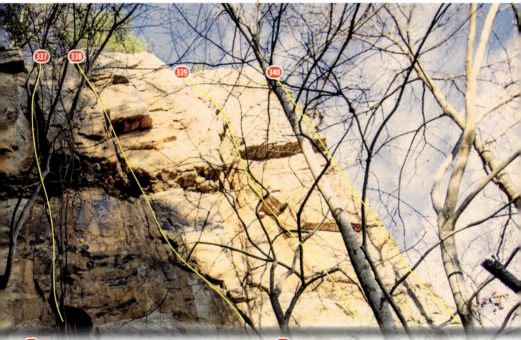

338 Golden Gloves 5.10 ★★★
Start: 10' right of Precious Orr.
Climb a long crack through a box-like overhang. 60'
FA: Rob Robinson, Arno Ilgner (3/85)

339 Can O' Worms 5.8
Start: 10' right of Golden Gloves.
Climb a chimney. 60'
FA: Robyn Erbesfield, Rob Robinson (3/85)

340 Stepping Stone 5.10-

Step right up ... this is one arete you'd better not miss! Start: On the right wall of an arete, 20' right of Can O' Worms.
Face climb the right wall of the arete to a good stance; a serpentine path winds up the edge to the top. 60'
FA: Rob Robinson, Pat Perrin (3/86)

Insider's Tip: Carry a good selection of brass to help protect the initial 15' or so.

T-Wall Scenic Routes
Passages, 5.8 ☐
Open Sesame, 5.8-+ ☐
A Good Place to Come, 5.9 ☐
Crash Position, 5.9 ☐
Stepping Stone, 5.10- ☐

Brooke Hadden on the upper arete of Stepping Stone, 5.10

Photo Credit: Andrew Miller

TENNESSEE WALL

341 Above And Beyond 5.10- ★★★
If you do Stepping Stone you can easily set up a top rope to do this mega classic line.
Start: Same as for I'm Late.
Diagonal left and climb face with a 5.8 move or two, then turn a small roof. At base of short, left-facing corner above, step left and follow the Stepping Stone arete for a few body lengths. At a small ledge above, step right a few feet, then climb a superb fingercrack with ratchet locks supplemented by face moves to anchors. 60'
FA: Rob Robinson (top rope) 2011

342 I'm Late 5.7 ★
Start: Same as previous.
Climb a little, left-facing corner with a jam crack. Wander up the wall to the top. 60'
FA: Kevin Thomas, Ron Davis (12/85)

343 Micro Genie 5.11- ★
Start: 5' right of I'm Late.
"Boulder" straight up an orange wall for 15' to 20'. Step right and up a short corner capped by a small overlap; follow a flake system above to a second overlap. Finagle right to a blunt arete. Layback water worn crack above ... high step (crux) to big horizontal. Step right to a tree. 40'
FA: John Barr, Ann Barr ('99)

344 Family Planning 5.7
Start: 15' right of Micro Genie.
Climb a long, left-facing corner to the top.
FA: Unknown

345 Chesnutt Arete 5.12- ★
Start: 10' right of Family Planning.
Top-rope a steep arete. Step right and pull through a 10' pocketed roof. Continue up the short face above to the top. 70' FA: Chris Chesnutt ('89)

> **Insider's Note:** A key arete hold has reportedly broken off; it may be easier (or harder) now.

346 Blood On The Rocks 5.10
Hungry for a bit of bloody good rock? Sink your fangs and fingers into this pitch.
Start: 10' right of Chesnutt Arete.
Climb the face with a thin crack to boulder problem moves over a small bulge (crux); continue up a left-facing corner. Jam n' jug over 5' summit roof (crux) with a hand crack. 70'
FA: Rob Robinson, Mark Cartwright (4/85)

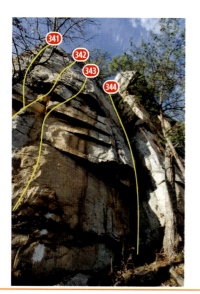

TENNESSEE WALL — ORANGE BLOSSOM WALLS

347 Auger Drive 5.10+ ★★
Start: 5' right of Blood On The Rocks. Climb a short, left-facing dihedral to a shallow scoop. Sketch past a smooth, right-facing corner, jugs lead through an easy overhang ... continue to the top. 70'
FA: Rob Robinson, Forrest Gardner (4/86)

Insider's Note: "Protected" by a slew of #0 and #1 brass. I always felt the route offered decent protection, a notion which, it seems, has been widely rejected. Definitely worth sampling on top-rope if you choose not to lead it.

348 Auger Lite 5.10 ★
Start: 10' right of Auger Drive.
Boulder onto the wall above a low overhang. Climb straight up the face (crux) following a thin crack, staying right of a shallow scoop. Skirt left around overhang above, then right and up the face to the top. 70'
FA: Tyler Stracker, Rod Thomas (2/06)

349 Unexpected Ease 5.9 ★
Start: Same as for Auger Lite.
Boulder onto wall above a low overhang. Diagonal right and climb a broken, left-facing system past a small roof. Continue on face above to the top. 70'
Alternate Start: 5.9. Start 10' right of the regular start. Boulder onto the wall above the low overhang.
FA: James Dobbs, Oliver Muff (12/85)

350 Benign Humor 5.11+ ★★
Start: 20' right of Unexpected Ease.
Climb along the right side of a scary-looking, semi-detached pillar; continue up the face, staying left of a prominent dark hole. Turn a bulge to gain a vertical seam; continue straight up to a small roof and on to the top. 100'
FA: Steve Goins, Truly Bracken (12/93)

Insider's Tip: If this innocuously named route is anything like Benevolence (another Goins route in Paradise Lost) its a got a real "punch line" or two to deal with.

351 People's Express 5.10- ★★★
Recommended without reservation to the climbing masses ... massively popular, and understandably so.
Start: 20' right of Benign Humor.
Turn a tricky 2' roof (crux). Follow stellar cracks up long, steep, and sustained left-facing corners to the top. 100'
FA: Arno Ilgner, John Harlin (11/85)

Insider's Tip: You can plug a big #4 cam above the lip of the roof.

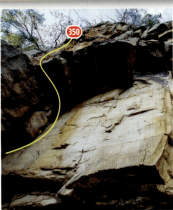

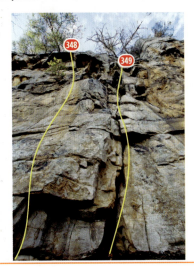

TENNESSEE WALL

352 Espirit Nuvo 5.10
For the free climbing spirit: a spirited and spiritually refreshing climb.
Start: 15' right of People's Express. Spirit up the face ... merge with a shallow finger crack splitting a black slab. When feasible, transmigrate right a few moves and climb a series of small, right-facing corners. Finish through a slot at the top of the wall. 100'
FA: Rob Robinson, Bruce Rogers (2/85) FA Super Direct: Forrest Gardner, Rob Robinson (4/86)

353 Viva La Balance! 5.11+
Start: From the top of the Nuvo finger crack.
Tiptoe more or less straight up the wall on balancy face moves with one notable run-out. Finish over a strenuous and techy bulge (crux). 100'
FA: Forrest Gardner, Rob Robinson (4/86)

> **Insider's Tip:** If the run-out in the middle of the route gives you the "heebee jeebee's" you can skirt it by weaving right and then back left to get around it.

354 Crackattack 5.10-
It's a heart attack you might have the first time you look up at this splitter line; a sandstone "crack addict's" dream come true.
Start: 15' right of Nuvo/Balance!, at the left side of a cave just above the trail. Attack a long, straight-in jam crack breaching a small roof about 70' up. Finish via a short, exposed chimney slot. 100'
FA: Rob Robinson, Bruce Rogers (2/85)

355 Ravin' Maniac! 5.11+ ★★★
Welcome ... to the T Wall mental ward. Deranged face climbing on a beautiful "Arapilean" orange face.
Start: Same as for Crackattack. Climb a bulging, orange wall (above the cave) laced with vertical seams (sustained and thin). Power over 8' summit roof using a jam crack. 100'
FA: Rob Robinson, Robyn Erbesfield (1/86)

> **Insider Tip:** Use double ropes and carry lots of brass nuts.

www.rockerypress.com 443

TENNESSEE WALL

ORANGE BLOSSOM WALLS

356 Open Sesame 5.9
Comparable in quality to Stan's Crack at Sunset Park on Lookout Mountain. Although it may look like 5.10 from the ground, trust me, it opens up "like magic."
Start: 15' right of Ravin' Maniac!, at the right side of the cave.
Climb a long, steep, left-facing dihedral with good jams and excellent holds. Finish right around a roof. 100'
FA: Steve Goins, Rob Robinson (2/85)

Insider's Tip: The crux is right above the cave. A big #4 cam might come in handy.

357 Forbidden Fruit 5.11- ★★
More juicy sandstone from the T Wall gift basket.
Start: 10' right of Open Sesame.
Climb past a bolt (stick clip) through a spot of loose rock to a ledge. Follow pockets right, turn a roof. Continue up left-facing corners, turn another roof. Angle up slab to anchor with fixed? webbing. 100'
FA: Steve Jones, Jonathan Clardy ('98)

358 Yo Bro ... Got Any Crank? 5.10 ★★
Sorry ... an invigorating sandstone tonic is all you'll find here.
Start: Immediately right of Forbidden Fruit. Climb past three bolts (stick clip the first one) to a left-facing corner. Turn a roof and continue to a second roof. Cut left through the weakness and up a slab to fixed? webbing anchors on Forbidden Fruit. 100'
FA: Jonathan Clardy, Perry Key ('98)

359 Cold Day In Hell 5.11 ★★
Start: On a ledge just above the trail, 20' right of Yo Bro.
Pitch 1: 5.11. Work up and left through bulging overhangs to a long, right-facing corner. Rig a standing belay at small stance. (40') Pitch 2: 5.9. The corner leads to the top. (75')
FA: Rob Robinson, Steve Goins (1/87)

360 Devil's Guard 5.7 ★
Start: 10' right of Cold Day In Hell. Scamper up into a shallow, cave-like recess. Climb right, then up a jam crack to the top. 100'
FA: Rob Robinson, Bruce Rogers (7/85)

361 The He-Man Woman Hater's Club 5.11 ★★
An absolutely bitchin' piece of climbing — in spite of its misogynistic appellation.
Start: 5' right of Devil's Guard.
Pussy foot through a bit of choss to a stance. "Boulder" into a bowl (crux) above a small roof and bolt. Step right to second bolt. Skirt another small roof ... merge with a superb steep crack and shallow left-facing corner. As the system ends, step right to a stance at the base of a summit slab. Fire straight up (5.10, run-out for a few moves), or zig right, zag left, then on to the top. 100'
FA: Jonathan Clardy, Scott Carter ('98)

TENNESSEE WALL

362 Seal Test 5.8 ★
Start: 15' right of The He-Man Woman Hater's Club.
Follow a hand/fist crack up corners (with roofs) to the top. 100'
FA: Bruce Rogers, Rob Robinson (7/85)

363 Stand Your Ground 5.11 ★
Start: 5' right of Seal Test.
Crank through hard-to-protect small roofs; mantle (crux) onto face above. Climb straight up the wall above through a small overhang and continue to the top. 100'
FA: David Draper, Spring Kurtz (2/06)

364 Solar Circus 5.10 ★★
A golden ray o' sandstone; guaranteed to light up your day.
Start: 10' right of Stand Your Ground.
Pitch 1: 5.10. Clamber through a bit of spotty rock and into a tan band split by a short flake/crack. Diagonal right around a small roof above and belay. (50') Pitch 2: 5.10. A spectacular thin finger crack in the headwall leads to the top. (50')
★ Pitch 1 Variation: 5.10. Clamber through the spotty rock band, turn a rounded overhang (split by a thin crack) capped by a short left-facing corner. Join the regular route.
★★★ Alternate Finish: 5.10+. Follow a pair of squiggly cracks in purplish rock that parallel the fingercrack on the regular route; finish via the right one.
FA: Rob Robinson, Curt Merchant, Pat Perrin (1/86) FA Pitch 1 Variation: unknown.
FA Alternate Finish: Steve Goins and partner (3/95)

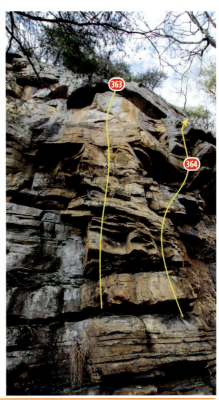

TENNESSEE WALL

ORANGE BLOSSOM WALLS

365 Celestial Mechanics 5.12
Classic spacewalk out a giant roof following an otherworldly crack.
Start: 40' right of Solar Circus, atop a boulder.
Climb a thin crack through a mossy bulge to a 30' roof crack. Belay/rappel above lip. 60'
★ Alternate Start: 5.11-. Start 15' left of the regular start. Climb a clean thin crack through a stripe of tan rock, merge with the roof crack.
FA: Rob Robinson, Steve Goins (7/85) FA: Alternate Start: Rob Robinson, Steve Goins (7/85) FFA: Rob Robinson (7/85)

Insider's Tips: The base of the roof seeps, but it is usually dry during the summer. (The day of the free ascent the high was 105.) The best way to start the route is via the alternate start.

366 Super Nova 5.13- ★★★
An unusually bright spot of roof climbing that lit up the southern sandstone skyscape in the mid 1980's. Universally appealing, but rarely repeated.
Start: 25' right of Celestial Mechanics. Warm up with an easy corner. Explode over a small but very technical roof. Face climb following a tricky thin (5.11) crack above to fixed? anchors at the margin of giant roof. 60'
FA: Rob Robinson (2/86)

Insider's Note: The South's first 5.13. Featured on the cover of Climbing in June, 1986.

367 Space Dancer 5.10 ★★
Start: 20' right of Super Nova.
Ease up a (loose?) left-facing corner, turn a small roof. A striking, thin crack system splitting the steep face above leads to a spacious ledge. 70'
FA: Rob Robinson, Peter Henley (7/85)

Insider's Tip: Make sure to "float" your rope through the lower roofs to reduce rope drag.

TENNESSEE WALL

368 Bad Omega 5.10 ★
Start: Same as for Space Dancer. Follow Space Dancer through the roof. Traverse right on the face above a wide roof. Climb a finger crack system and face to the top. 100'
FA: Harrison Shull, Tyler Stracker (4/04)

Insider's Tip: Make sure to "float" your rope through the lower roof to reduce rope drag.

369 Take No Mess 5.11
Start: A few feet right of Space Dancer/Bad Omega.
Climb a junky corner, diagonal left and crank through a roof with a fist-sized crack; continue up the crack and face to the top. 100'
FA: Tyler Stracker, Harrison Shull (4/04)

Insider's Tip: Bring at least one larger camming device in the range of a #3.5 to a #4.

The First Ascent of Celestial Mechanics

-By Rob Robinson

I waited until the middle of summer to do Mechanics, because it was the first time I had seen this 30' roof crack dry since we had first discovered the wall. It was in the middle of July and over 100 degrees, with hideous humidity, when I hiked in to do the climb with Steve Goins, my long time partner and friend.

Although there was an obvious and easier start to the climb off to the left, I decided to tackle the monster head on ... climbing straight up a steep face below the roof following a thin crack. I remember there was a big, very shallow recess in the wall right at the start, and thinking how it reminded me of a planet.

The view looking out the roof from the base was awesome; it was going to require doing a partial inversion and then actually climbing down the roof crack — and then out horizontally. The climbing through this section was very awkward, since the crack was actually bottled up in a flare that scraped my shoulders. Once the roof leveled out the climbing became a bit more civilized— at least for a few feet. The hand jams became kinder, and the flaring, down-tilted aspect of the roof gave way to a flat plane. But the hand crack disappeared midway out the roof. So I hung there in the crack for awhile, trying to figure out how to get around this blank section to pick the crack back up where it began again in a long, shallow slot. The lactic acid clock was ticking and, finally, I dropped onto the rope and hung there. After taking a few minutes to collect myself, I pulled back up on the rope, asked for tension, and peered past the blank section into the slot ahead. I spied a hold, but it looked difficult to reach, much less use. Yet it appeared that was going to be it. I went back into lead mode, powered past the blank section, and managed to snag the hold. A bizarre sequence followed, and suddenly I was past the blank section and in the slot! A few more twisty-turnsy crack moves and it was over. I hauled up a tube chock from the ground, fixed it in a hole and lowered off. I pulled the rope and sic'd Steve on it, who also managed to power through with just one hang (at the same spot that had stymied me.) Final success seemed imminent, but exhausted from the extreme heat and humidity we opted to clean the pitch and come back the following day for what we hoped and believed would be the successful free ascent.

When I got home that evening I was completely filthy. My lycra was practically glued to my legs. My T-shirt was rancid and soaked through with sweat. I was covered in a thick patina of sweaty grime from head to toe. But the idea of cleaning up and returning to the climb the next day seemed like it might disrupt this— bond — I felt with the climb. Anyway, as far as I was concerned, night time was just going to be a quickie intermission. So I skipped showering, kept my tape job on, and hit the bed still wearing my dirty climbing clothes!

***

I woke up the next morning feeling great. I met Steve at the T Wall parking lot, and was also joined by my girlfriend Robyn Erbesfield. We hiked back up to the wall, strolled along the base to the climb, and immediately picked back up where we'd left off from the day before. It was very hot already, and was soon to be over 100 degrees again, with the same sweltering humidity.

From the day before I recalled how hard it had been to retrieve gear from my waist and place it in the crack, so this time I opted to "loose clip" several cam units directly to the front of my T shirt. My strategy was to carry them balanced on my chest like it was a dinner plate.

I climbed to the roof to a heel stance rest, stilled my mind, then launched out the roof, snatching the cams off my T shirt and placing them ... no problem! I was psyched. I got to the crux, and although I felt strong, it was clear I was not going to be able to hang around forever. I still had both feet and hands jammed in the crack, but wanted some sort of rest before I tackled the crux. I decided to cut my feet loose and see how it felt. It felt great! This seemed to require a lot less energy, and allowed me the luxury to leisurely survey the whole roof. It was huge!

I could feel the burn coming on in my forearms, and there was no way to engineer a better rest. The next best thing, I decided, was to see how switching from one hand jam to the other felt. I disengaged one hand from the crack, and hung there on a single jam. I heard rising but unintelligible voices from below. I felt like I was ... disappearing ... into some bizarre void; my energy and the climb's seemed to fuse, and then in a flash I felt like I had merged with the Center of the Sandstone Universe in a spectacular and incomprehensible way. This was ... a harmonic convergence!

I hung there, switching jams until I felt recovered enough to continue, then swung my feet back up into the crack, and readied for the crux. I made the reach past the blank section, and wormed into the shallow slot. The hardest part was over. I was soon over the lip and on my way back to earth.

***

As I arrived back on earth Steve and Robyn were congratulatory — and very impressed by the one hand jam hang! (They dubbed it "the Rambo hang.") I was just psyched it had worked. Although I had used this technique before on other climbs, I hadn't planned on doing it, or even thought about it as an option — but I had listened to the climb, did what it asked me to do, and it worked.

I was so pumped I couldn't untie the knot in my rope. My forearms were massively dilated. Every vein, muscle and tendon popped out in graphic relief. I remember smiling and thinking to myself: now that's a set of forearms even John Long would be proud of. Robyn undid the knot for me, then grabbed me by both forearms, and laughing in her little pixie way, said " don't tell me you haven't been doing steroids big boy ... I've got the proof right here." She shook my forearms, looked me in the eyes and just laughed. Although I repeatedly and emphatically denied her assertion (which was the truth) I could not dissuade her otherwise. I still think to this day she believes that!

Memory Fog

After stripping a couple of small brass placed on the face above the roof during a fall, a nervous visitor (watching from the trail below) started hollering for me to place a knifeblade piton at the lip for pro. The request struck me as amusing; after all, this was (as least as far as I was concerned) just standard fare southern sandstone hardcore trad climbing. To humor him, however, I hauled up a pin he had stashed in his backpack, and then banged it in with a rock. The crux above the pin featured a boulder problem move with a small and greasy, sloped heel hook. Once standing up, a series of beautiful and technical layaways led up tiny corners to a stance beneath a big roof where I placed a couple of bail pieces and lowered off. Super Nova was born...

Photo Credit: Rob Robinson Collection

TENNESSEE WALL

LOST BLOSSOM

Approach: Just past the route Take No Mess, which is located on the right margin of a crack-laced buttress, is the beginning of the Lost Blossom section. The trail rounds this point before encountering the routes below.

370 Capital Assets 5.8 ★★

Though many years have passed since the T Wall's "initial public offering," the crag continues to issue investment grade, "triple A" classics like this one.
Start: On the center face of a buttress, 15' right of Take No Mess.
Diagonal right over a small overhang, climb incut, horizontal banding to a stance some 30' up. Work past 1' roof (crux) and continue up the slabby wall following a thin crack system; trend right and finish up the center of a summit headwall. 100'
★★Variation: 5.8. At the above mentioned crux: step right and climb a right-facing flake with rounded knobby holds; merge with the final summit headwall.
FA: Rob Robinson, Jared Chastain (9/01)

371 Live And Direct! 5.10+ ★★

Some real star power here ... deserves a wider climbing audience.
Start: Around the point, 25' right of Capital Assets and beneath a huge square roof.
Pitch 1: 5.10. Scurry up an overhanging, right-facing corner with good jams; traverse left to a ledge and belay. (25') Pitch 2: 5.10+. A long, thin crack/corner diagonalling right leads to the top. (60')
Alternate Start: 5.10+. Start 5' left of the regular start. Climb the face, turn a small overhang. Belay at stance on ledge. Join pitch two.
FA: Rob Robinson, Pat Perrin (alt. leads) (3/86) FA Alternate Start: Steve Goins, Truly Bracken (3/92)

TENNESSEE WALL

ORANGE BLOSSOM WALLS

372 Quality Control 5.9 ★★
Start: 35' right of Live And Direct.
Tiptoe up alongside a long, vertical crack system bisecting a steep slab. Turn a tiny roof; continue to the top. 80'
FA: Pat Perrin, Rob Robinson (3/86)

373 Self Control 5.11 ★★
Start: 10' right of Quality Control. Dance up the face past a manky fixed? blade into a shallow arch (crux); ease up the wall to the top. 80'
FA: Mike Artz, Eric Janoscrat, Rob Robinson (12/85)

374 Johnny Get Your Roundup 5.9+ ★
Start: 5' right of Self Control.
Work through a tricky start and follow a crack system to the top. 80'
FA: Stan Pritchard, Amy Wood (date unknown)

375 Tunnel Vision 5.7 ★
Start: 15' right of Johnny Get Your Roundup.
Wriggle, jam and backstep a long chimney crack slicing through the cliff line. 80'
FA: Eric Janoscrat, Mike Artz, Rob Robinson (12/85)

376 Wit's End 5.11+ ★★
Welcome to the Big House? A heady arete — complete with a nutter of a roof — and packed with a plethora of puzzling pockets. "Tin foil hat optional."
Start: 15' right of Tunnel Vision.
Face climb following a short thin crack to a small flat roof. Break left and turn a jug-filled overhang. Surge left across the orange wall above, following finger pockets to access a striking arete. Climb past the flat, 3' roof above (crux); continue up arete to the top. 70'
FA: Rob Robinson, Pat Perrin (3/86)

377 Rape Ammo 5.9 ★
Start: 5' right of Wit's End.
Face climb following a short thin crack to a small flat roof. Break left, then up and right past a hole in the wall. Climb a short, left-facing corner stacked between two roofs. A jam crack above leads to fixed anchors beneath an overhang formed by a huge, hanging boulder. 75'
FA: Arno Ilgner, Rob Robinson (3/85)

TENNESSEE WALL

378 Rape Conducive 5.8 ★★★
One of the T Wall's most classic 5.8 corners for the grade — as good as the Passages corner in West Blossom.
Start: 15' right of Rape Ammo.
Cruise up a long, left-facing corner to fixed anchors beneath an overhang formed by a huge, hanging boulder. 75'
FA: Rob Robinson, Arno Ilgner (3/85)

379 Fox On The Run 5.11+ ★★★

You'll have to climb like one since "ole' man gravity" will be hounding you at the crux.
Start: 10' right of Rape Conducive.
Jam a crack over a small roof; stem up a right-facing corner. Step right, turn a small overhang ... tiptoe up small corner/ramp capped by a bulge (crux). Polish off moves up a final tricky headwall. 75'
FA: Rob Robinson, Mike Artz, Eric Janoscrat (12/85)

> **Insider's Tip:** You might find Lowe Ball nuts, small Tri cams ... and a biner full of #1 and #2 small stoppers will come in handy (the latter for the final headwall).

380 Octopod Palace 5.10+ ★★
A great cave line suitable for spinning a "nylon web."
Start: 20' right of Fox On The Run.
Boogie up a 4" crack; spin through the long roof of a large cave (with a nice crack) to a belay/rappel spot on the wall above. 60'
FA: Rob Robinson, Steve Goins (6/85)

T-Wall

TENNESSEE WALL

ORANGE BLOSSOM WALLS

381 Mojo 5.11 ★
Start: Around the point and 20' right of Octopod Palace.
Climb a finger crack at the wall's left margin to a small tiered roof replete with creaky blocks. Attack the roof, working roundabout out right then up and over and back left (contrived.) Wander up and left via thin cracks to a pair of ring anchors. 100'
FA: Stuart Chapin, Cody Averbeck (11/03)

382 The Song Of The Bullet 5.11- ★
Start: 10' right of Mojo at an obvious splitter finger crack.
Climb the beautiful splitter until the rock begins to deteriorate. From here, engineer an easy traverse right and up to a stance below a roof. Pull the roof on the left via a hand and finger crack. Follow a faint right-facing corner system — eventually trend up and left to a bolted anchor. 100'
FA: Cody Averbeck, Theresa Averbeck, Jennifer Baxter ('08)

383 Of Vice And Men 5.10- ★★★
Start: 15' right of Mojo.
Follow a handcrack up a left-facing corner and through a roof slot. Finish up an offwidth crack to a ledge with trees. 80'
Alternate Start: 5.9. Start 10' left of the regular start. Climb the face following a thin finger crack. Diagonal right to the roof and join the regular route.
Variation: 5.10. Climb the left-facing corner to the roof. Work left and turn the roof via thin cracks. Rejoin the regular route, or join the alternate finish.
Alternate Finish: Unknown grade. Above the roof, follow a shallow, right-facing corner to a blank bulge; step left and climb a moderately difficult face, sans protection, to the top.
FA: Steve Goins, Truly Bracken (1/95) FA Alternate Start: Unknown. FA Variation: Steve Goins, Truly Bracken (1/95) FA Alternate Finish: Kirk Brode and partner ('03)

> **Insider's Tip:** Bring a couple of really big cam units for the offwidth on the regular route.

384 Bonfire Of The Vanities 5.11 ★★
Start: 20' right of Of Vice And Men.
Burn through a concave overhang split by a crack. Shallow, left-facing corners lead to an eye-catching roof ... step left. Finish up a prominent headwall following a thin seam. 80'
FA: Rob Robinson, Robyn Erbesfield (12/85)

TENNESSEE WALL

385 Fuel Injected Suicide Machine 5.12
★★★

"I'm a fuel injected suicide machine — I'm the rocka and the rolla — I'm the out of controlla." Classic pocket pulling on a steep blunt arete.
Start: Same as for Bonfire Of The Vanities. Climb Bonfire past the low roof. Shift to a leftward arching system. Step right and climb a series of difficult, shallow corners that lead to the base of a large roof. Clip fixed gear and hit the gas. Do a series of powerful moves via jug pockets — culminating in a tenuous snatch that garners entry to the spectacular blunt arete. Follow amazing edges on perfect stone to the anchor on Bonfire. 100'
FA: Cody Averbeck, David Draper, Nathaniel Walker ('08)

386 Unknown Soldier 5.12 ★★★

Killer climbing through a vertical sandstone battlefield. Few victory flags are carried through to the summit.
Start: 10' right of Bonfire Of The Vanities/Fuel Injected Suicide Machine. Grunt through low roof into a short left-facing dihedral capped by a small roof. Turn this and continue straight up the face past a single bolt to a 8' roof split by a finger crack. Conquer this and continue for another 50' to bolted anchors. 100'
FA: Stuart Chapin, Kirk Brode, Cody Averbeck (2/04)

387 Catch Me In The Wry 5.9

Start: 20' right of Unknown Soldier. Follow a wide, left-facing dihedral capped by a roof. Step right round this and continue up a dirty corner to a vegetated ledge. A steep handcrack leads to the top. 100'
FA: Cody Averbeck, Stuart Chapin ('04)

Insider's Note: This route could be upgraded to one or two stars with a bit of cleaning.

Bosom of the Rat, 5.9

Cody Averbeck on the splitter upper crack of Intruders in the Dust, 5.10

TENNESSEE WALL

388 A Brief History Of Time 5.9
Start: Same as for Catch Me In The Wry. Traverse right across the face to an arete and follow it to a ledge with trees and brush. Continue to the top following a right-angling crack. 100'
FA: Rod Thomas, David Draper (1/06)

389 The Poop Chute 5.10
Start: 35' right of A Brief History Of Time. Pitch 1: 5.9. Turn a minor overhang and climb a slabby wall past small roofs to a spacious belay ledge. (40') Pitch 2: 5.10. Climb a striking crack and corner system to the top. (60') FA: Unknown

> **Insider's Note:** Pitch two looks great from the ground. Unfortunately, the cracks are perpetually filled with dirt that funnels down from above.

390 In Search Of The Source 5.11+

You just found it. One of the finest pitches of hard "trad style" 5.11 face climbing in the Chattanooga area: Magical moves and incredible sequences on bullet-hard sandstone.
Start: Same as for The Poop Chute.
Pitch 1: 5.9. Turn a minor overhang and climb a slabby wall past small roofs to a spacious belay ledge. (40') Pitch 2: 5.11+. Zip up a thin 15' finger crack. Diagonal right across face, then left over a spectacular and airy bulge past two bolts to bolt anchors above. (50')
FA (top-rope): Rob Robinson (1/06) First Lead: Tyler Stracker, Amy Wood (2/06)

> **Insider's Tip:** Small to medium wires, small TCU's or Aliens, and a couple of Camalots up to size #1.

391 Bath Party Politics 5.9 ★
Start: 15' right of In Search Of The Source. Pitch 1: 5.9. Climb a short slot capped by a huge, square chock stone; belay on spacious ledge above. (40') Pitch 2: 5.9. Follow a wide, left-facing corner with a crack (and tree) to the top. (70')
FA: Stan Pritchard, Stuart Chapin (11/03)

392 The Omen 5.11+

The T Wall's most spectacular-looking arete. The climbing's not too bad either...
Start: 15' right of Bath Party Politics. Pitch 1: 5.10-. Follow thin cracks to a 10' roof. Traverse left and up to a spacious ledge. (40') Pitch 2: 5.11+. Traverse right across the face and climb a spectacular arete past three bolts. (70')
FA: Stuart Chapin, Cody Averbeck ('03)

> **Insider's Tip:** TCU's for the arete.

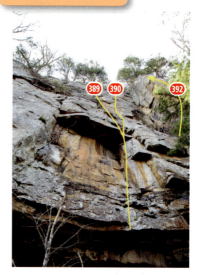

Hell Bent for Leather, 5.11+

TENNESSEE WALL

ORANGE BLOSSOM WALLS

393 Hell Bent For Leather 5.11+ ★★★
Standard issue, full tilt, no-holds-barred, go-for-broke southern sandstone fare.
Start: 10' right of The Omen.
Pitch 1: 5.11+. Inch up the face alongside a thin crack, ease through a bulge; turn a body-length roof split by a hand crack. Belay at the "grass paddocks" on the wall above. (50') Pitch 2: 5.9. A crack system slices through a small roof; cruise to the top. (70')
FA: Rob Robinson, Forrest Gardner (alt. leads, 6/85)

394 Intruders In The Dust 5.10 ★★
A long neglected classic which languished for years until the dirt-filled upper crack was dug out with a Yo hammer. Well worth sampling.
Start: 25' right of Hell Bent For Leather. Climb a short finger crack. From the ledge above; climb straight through a blank-looking section past a single bolt (crux). Continue over a small overhang. A long and occasionally tricky jam crack leads to the top. 100'
FA: Rob Robinson, Bruce Rogers (7/85)

Insider's Note: A special thanks to David Draper and crew for straightening this route out and cleaning it up.

395 Game Of Thrones 5.10+ ★★
Start: Same as for Intruders in the Dust. Climb through crux past the bolt on Intruders. Traverse left a few feet and climb a brown, water-polished face via hard sand up moves using narrow, sloping ledges to the top. 100'
FA: Rob Robinson, top rope (2012)

396 Bosom Of The Rat 5.9 ★
Start: 10' right of Intruders In The Dust. Climb left-facing dihedrals to a small roof. Follow the crack through this; continue up the corner to the top. 120'
FA: Steve Goins, Rob Robinson (6/85)

397 The Terminator 5.11
See description on page 459.
★ **Alternate Start (The Govinator):** 5.10. Start 20' left of the regular start. Climb through a slot in small, square overhangs. Trend right over a small roof (crux); follow the line of least resistance up the moderate face above, gradually merging with the second pitch of The Terminator.
Insider Note: The alternate start avoids the hard-to-protect first pitch (which shuts many climbers down.) But if you don't do that first pitch … you haven't done The Terminator!
FA Alternate Start (top-rope): Rob Robinson, Tyler Stracker (1/06) First Lead Alternate Start: David Draper (1/06)

Insider's Note: The second pitch was originally graded 5.11+ before a couple of loose plates were removed from the corner.

398 Anarchy 5.11a
Start: A hop, skip and a jump (or two) right of The Terminator.
Climb a short face with several bolts. 40'
FA: Eddie Whittemore ('89)

399 Dictator 5.11d ★
Start: On the obvious arete, a few feet right of Anarchy.
Climb the arete. 40'
FA: Eddie Whittemore ('89)

400 Martial Law 5.11c ★
Start: Some 20' right of Dictator.
Climb an arete. 40'
FA: Eddie Whittemore ('89)

401 Rising Force 5.13b
Start: About 35' right of Martial Law.
Climb a bulging arete. 30'
FA: Eddie Whittemore ('89)

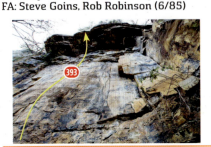

The Terminator 5.11

Hasta la vista, baby? The last great show at this end of the T Wall — and it's a blockbuster.
Start: 30' right of Bosom Of The Rat.
Pitch 1: 5.11-. Climb a bulging, left-facing corner (thin gear) capped by a flat roof. Traverse left round the lip to a small ledge belay. (50') Pitch 2: 5.11. Step out left and climb a steep, shallow, and sustained corner with tricky jamming to a small roof. Turn this (tech crux) and continue to the top. (60')
FA: Rob Robinson, Peter Henley (5/85)

Climber: Cody Averbeck   Photo Credit: Micah Gentry

Most visitors to Chattanooga will have heard of the 24,686 acre Prentice Cooper State Forrest being associated with world-renowned areas like the Tennessee Wall (T-Wall) and Suck Creek Canyon. But, few will have heard of the several high quality satellite areas also found in this large tract of land that are tucked deep within the park and hidden or obscured by lengthy approaches, seasonal closures, and general layers of inconvenience and adventure.

PROMISED LAND

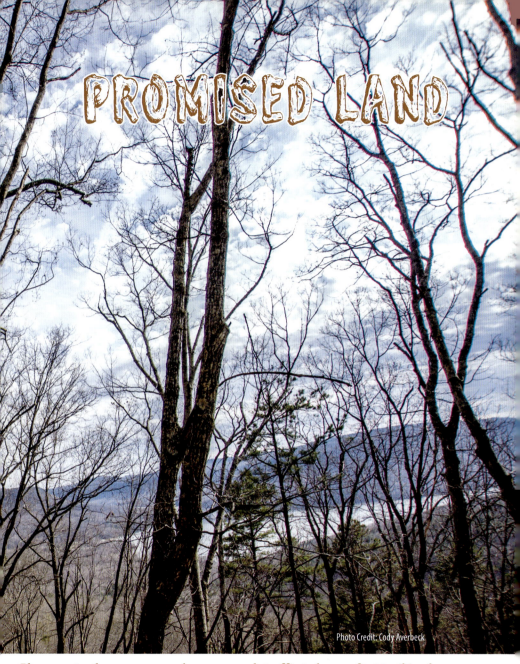

Photo Credit: Cody Averbeck

Please note, these areas rarely see enough traffic to keep a foot-trail in place. Therefore, do not expect a convenient or even straightforward approach. Consult materials in this guide and supplement them with satellite imagery surfing and orientation at home. In other words, come prepared with a general sense of the lay of the land.

PRENTICE COOPER

Area History

This unique wilderness cliff was discovered by Amber Johnstone in 2000 while out on one of her marathon hiking jogs. Later, she returned with Travis Eiseman and the process of doing new routes began.

The walls of the Promised Land are in some way reminiscent of the Tennessee Wall; perhaps this is due to the area's noticeable amount of eye-catching, orange rock. (The area's most dramatic display is a beautiful, deep orange face situated near center of the cliff; its so pretty I'd almost recommend visiting the area just to see it.) However the area doesn't quite rise to th T Wall standard of quality.

Of course, how many cliffs could ever hope to measure up to the Tennessee Wall?! Suffice to say: I think you'll find enough good stuff here that you won't be disappointed. At minimum, I expect you'll get at least one fabulous day of climbing out of the area. If the area strikes your fancy ... no doubt you come back for more.

The little time I have spent at Promised Land makes me think back to a few trips I made, back in the late 70's and early 80's, to another remote and obscure cliff—Buzzard Point. I would have never dreamed that area would become so popular. So you never know.

The cliff line: is approximately one half mile long, and has a mostly flat trail running its length at the base. The walls average 80', or half a rope length, in height. The rock is generally very solid. Climbs are often steep face or steep face following cracks, with enough overhangs thrown in to keep things interesting.

The area is (at best) only partially developed; undoubtedly some great new pitches are yet to be added. All said and done, I'd guess the Promised Land might one day be home to as many as 100 routes.

Rules & Regs

1.) The park is closed from Sunset to Sunrise.

2.) Have you checked to make sure that it's not a Prentice Cooper scheduled hunt date? In this case, climbing will be temporarily prohibited within the park until the end of the hunt.

You can check scheduled hunt dates by following this link:

http://www.tn.gov/agriculture/forestry/stateforest07.shtml

3.) Firearms are prohibited in park if not under a Wild Hunt permit.

4.) Possession of drugs or alcohol is prohibited.

5.) Camping is permitted in only designated areas (none of which are near to the crags).

6.) Do not take motorized vehicles on roads designated as Closed (some gates are seasonally locked. Do not go around them!)

Climbing Specific Regulations

1.) All new routes requiring fixed hardware must be approved through Prentice Cooper Management. Consult the SCC website for more information.

PRENTICE COOPER

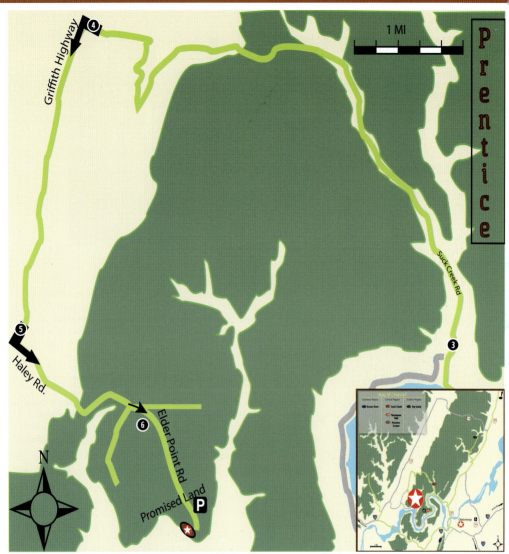

The Promised Land

❶ From Chattanooga, Take I-27 North and get off at the Signal Mountain Road exit. ❷ Continue 1.5 miles on US 127 North until you reach the base of Signal Mountain. ❸ At the base of the mountain, take a left onto Suck Creek Road (TN Highway 27 West). Follow Suck Creek Road for approximately 12.0 miles passing a bridge that crosses suck creek (turn for T-Wall) and climbs up, over, and down Suck Creek Canyon. ❹ Once over the mountain (now in Sequatchie Valley) locate the stoplight at Powell's Crossroads (the 12.0 mileage referenced above) and take a left onto Griffith Highway. Drive this road for 4.2 miles until reaching Haley Road on your left (unmarked gravel road) ❺ Take a left onto Haley Road (set your odometer here!), crossing into Prentice Cooper (will pass through State Forest Gate), and drive 3.7 miles to Elder Point Road. ❻ Take a right turn and drive 1.8 miles on Elder Point Road to parking.

45 mins

PRENTICE COOPER

Driving Landmarks

Promised Land Approach

❶ From the pull-out ... continue downhill (the road becomes noticeably steeper, with more mud ruts than a Carolina hog farm) on foot, mountain bike or mule for about 1/8th of a mile. (Do not attempt to negotiate this section of road, even if you have a four wheel drive vehicle; you've probably got a 50/50 chance of making it.) Towards the foot of the hill look for a white-blazed pine tree on the left; this marks the "old" entrance into The Promised Land.

❷ If routes you want to do are located near this end of the cliff it makes sense to take the old approach. Follow a trail down through the woods, paralleling a tiny creek, to a break in a small cliff outcrop. From here, the "trail" drops down a rapidly steepening hillside just right of the creek. About 100 yards down the slope, you'll come to another break in a big cliff line. This is the main wall. Contour right, thread through a couple of boulders— and you've arrived. Orientation: the first line that jumps out at you should be a long, straight-in crack line called Jack of all Trades pg 486.

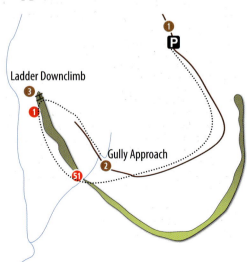

PRENTICE COOPER

Area Logistics

Emergency

Attempt to Dial 911 (Cell Service is Limited)

The option of rescue in this remote area of the park is very unlikely and will further require parties to have the knowledge and capabilities to self-rescue or control accidents until regional SAR teams arrive.

Season

Fall-Spring

Camping

The only camping available in Prentice Cooper are the Davis Pond and Hunter's Check Station Camping areas, none of which are immediately accessible on this side of the park.

Your best bet is to retreat back to Chattanooga or find your way to the T-Wall campground (see page: 299).

Food

The small town of Powell's Crossroads has a few poorly stocked Gas Stations that you can buy beer and snacks at. For the best selection of eats, back-track to Chattanooga. In particular, check out Shuford's BBQ at the base of Signal Mountain.

❸ A second point of ingress (Insider's Tip: this is the way to go) is as follows: continue past the first access point for about 1/4th mile to another white-blazed tree on the left. Contour left through the woods and follow white blazes down a gently steeping hillside for a few hundred yards to the top of the cliff. Blazes will further guide you to a hand-line bolted to the wall of a gently sloping ledge; at its base resting against the wall is a nice 2" x 4" pressure treated 12' ladder. Descend to the cliff's base. Insider's Note: Even if the handline happens to be missing you will still be able to "3rd class" down at this point.

At the base of the ladder you'll be greeted by a lovely, zen-like "wilderness bubble" (which Chris Chesnutt named Beautiful Cove.) Giant, old growth hemlocks lord over a shaded glen resplendent with moss-covered boulders and a trickling creek.

Orient yourself to the cliff line by locating an obvious huge band of overhangs adjacent to the base of the down climb.

www.rockerypress.com 465

PRENTICE COOPER

PROMISED LAND

BEAUTIFUL COVE

25 mins

On the far left end of the Promised Land cliff is a short and very steep overhanging buttress located in a lush evergreen cove with an access ladder on the left side of the wall. There are two routes located here and one more unfinished sport line right and around the corner from this wall. The rest of the established routes are located a few minute's walk climber's right of this small cluster of sport routes.

❶ Bought By Blood 5.12 (sport) ★★
Start: In a big alcove of overhangs, just right of the base of the ladder down climb. Climb the steep left-most bolted line to a double bolt anchor. 50'
FA: Jerry Roberts (5/00)

❷ Unsent 5.12 (sport) ★★★
Start: Same as Bought By Blood. Climb the steep right route out through overhangs to a two bolt anchor.
FA: Jerry Roberts (5/00)

❸ Unfinished Deweese
Start: 50' right of Unsent. This line will climb the beautiful and blank looking knife blade arete.
Bolted by Steve Deweese

PRENTICE COOPER

CHESTNUTT'S WALL

This is the tallest and most striking section of cliff at the Promised Land. It is also where a Southern legend, Chris Chestnutt, had a terrible accident, falling to the ground from 80'.

❹ Chestnutt's Crack 5.10+
Start: Same as Charmed. Climb a flaring straight in finger crack to some ledges and a steepening wall passing a thin seam system with face holds. Finish at a new 2 bolt anchor. 75' **FA:** Travis Eiseman, Robert McSween (5/00)

❺ Charmed 5.10 ★★★
Start: same as Chestnutt's Crack. Boulder around roof and climb a long left-facing corner to a small roof. Step right and continue to the top, ending at a new two bolt anchor. 75' **FA:** Travis Eiseman, Robert McSween (5/00)

❻ Tunnel of Love 5.9
Start: around the corner from previous in a big right facing corner; climb it.

❼ Ride the Snake 5.11 ★
Start: 30' right of Charmed. Climb a long left-facing corner (with a spot of suspect rock) to a prominent roof. Trend right and finish on Ironic (see below). 80'
FA: Travis Eiseman, Robert McSween (5/00)

❽ Ironic 5.11
Start: 10' right of Ride The Snake. Climb a long right-facing corner with good hand jams. Finish directly through overhangs capping a steep headwall. 80' **FA:** Travis Eiseman, Chris Chesnutt (5/00)

PM

25 mins

> **Insider's Lament:** As Chris rigged a rappel, he tripped and "took the big one." He was severely injured but alive. He climbs today.

Promised Land

www.rockerypress.com 467

Philip Wilcheck on the technical seam of Chestnutt's Crack, 5.10   Photo Credit: Cody Averbeck

PRENTICE COOPER

9 House Of Cards 5.11- ★★
Start: 30' right of Ironic. Climb a short left-facing corner capped by roofs. Step right and climb a rounded arete (tricky pro) for a few moves (crux) until passing roofs, now rejoin the corner. Continue up obvious crack system (crux) to a small cave ... turn lip and continue up juggy wall to the top. 80'
FA: Travis Eiseman, Rob Robinson (5/00)

10 Unclean Spirit 5.11+
Start: 18' right of House Of Cards. Climb a long straight-in crack system in a black streak to a 5' roof festooned with big flakes. Turn this and continue to the top. 80' FA: Travis Eiseman, Chris Chesnutt (5/00)

11 Project
Start: A few feet to the right of Unclean Spirit. Take on a thin start that leads to a tiny seam and corner system that finishes out roofs.

12 Chesnutt's Corner 5.10+ ★★
Start: 15' right of Unclean Spirit. Climb a left facing corner capped by a 10' roof with footwall. Turn this and mosey up the wall following a crack past a small ledge to the top. 80'
FA: Chris Chesnutt, Travis Eiseman (5/00)

Chestnutt's Crack, 5.10

Promised Land

www.rockerypress.com 469

PRENTICE COOPER

PROMISED LAND

⑬ Uninvited 5.11-, A1 ★★
Start: 20' right of Chestnutt's Corner. Aid a few moves to turn a roof. Follow a long, right-diagonaling crack to a ledge; continue up and right to a pine tree. 80' FA: Travis Eiseman, Robert McSween (5/00)

⑭ Persona Non Grata 5.11 ★★
Start: 10' right of Uninvited. Stand on a stack of stones and jump left to a jug. Trend left to meet up with the face on Uninvited 80' FA: Travis Eiseman, Robert McSween (5/00)

⑮ Shenanigans 5.11- ★★
Start: 10' right of previous. Identify this route by a high first bolt with perma-draw above lip of roof. Stick clip the bolt and make a crux roof pull to two more bolts above. Meander of the steep wall to the top. FA: Scott Perkins, Matt Harris (04)

⑯ Sinner 5.12b ★★ (Sport)
Start: 15' right of Shenanigans. This tantalizing little arete challenge will be easy to spot due to its unique geometric figure involving a few well-endowed changing corner and roof maneuvers. FA: Steve DeWeese (04)

⑰ Slim's Route 5.8 ★★
Start: Just right of Sinner. Climb a right-facing corner for 20', face climb right beneath a big ship's prow roof for 15' to a nasty-looking gully. Follow a small right-facing corner for 25' to a small roof … jog left and up juggy rock to the top. 80' FA: Robert McSween, Travis Eiseman (5/00)

Emily Hon on the splitter, Jerry & Lynn's Crack, 5.9

Photo Credit: Cody Averbeck

PRENTICE COOPER

PROMISED LAND

18 Orb Weaver 5.10 ★★
Start: In a classic box-like formation, 65' right of Slim's Route. Climb the back wall of the box to a roof. Stem n' step out left to a stance; continue up a final headwall past a small ledge and tricky bulge to the top. 80' FA: Travis Eiseman, Amber Johnstone (7/00)

19 Jerry And Lynn's Crack 5.9 ★★
Start: Same as for Orb Weaver. Follow an excellent, straight-in hand crack on the right wall of the "box" to a ledge. Lower from a pair bolts. 75'
FA: Jerry Roberts, Lynn Baroussa (5/00)

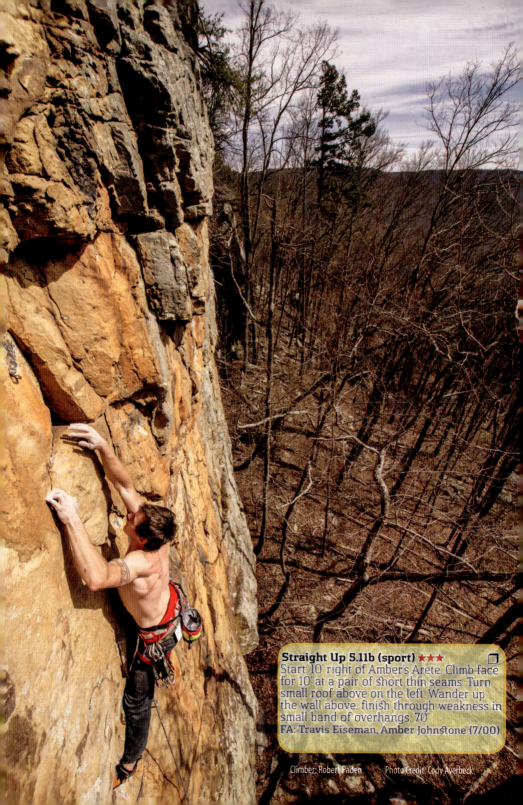

Straight Up 5.11b (sport) ★★★

Start: 10' right of Amber's Arete. Climb face for 10' at a pair of short thin seams. Turn small roof above on the left. Wander up the wall above; finish through weakness in small band of overhangs. 70'

FA: Travis Eiseman, Amber Johnstone (7/00)

Climber: Robert Paden Photo Credit: Cody Averbeck

PRENTICE COOPER

PROMISED LAND

⓴ Amber's Arete 5.10c (sport) ★★
Start: 10' right of Jerry And Lynn's Crack. Climb a classic arete with great movement to a ledge and bolted anchors.
FA: Amber Johnstone, Travis Eiseman (7/00)

㉑ Straight Up 5.11b (sport) ★★★
See description on page 473.

㉒ Lockdown 5.11c (sport) ★★★
Start: 10' right of Straight Up. Climb a nice face to the ledge. 60'
FA: Travis Eiseman, Amber Johnstone (7/00)

㉓ Chopping Block 5.10 ★
Start: 10' right of Lockdown. Climb a short left-facing corner to stance. Step up face at short thin crack. Jog right and following a long right-facing corner to the top. 85' FA: Travis Eiseman, Amber Johnstone (7/00)

㉔ Emotional Rescue 5.9 ★★
Start: Just right of previous. Climb the 'steep slab' past two bolts. 70'
FA: Fernando Paulete (03)

㉕ Fun in the Bun 5.9 ★
Start: 10' right of Emotional Rescue. Low angle climbing leads to a steep step left to a rounded flake/arete. 70'
FA: Sean McGahee (03)

㉖ Hostess with the Mostest 5.8
Climb the long right facing corner. 70'
FA: Scott Perkins (03)

PRENTICE COOPER

㉗ Tethered Goat 5.11 ★★★
Superb appetizer (or main meal) for sandstone lions. Start: 50' right of Chopping Block? Climb an excellent face past bolt. Turn small overlap with second bolt. Power over small overhang (crux) past third bolt. Fix anchors at ledge, or continue up a short headwall to the top. 70'
FA: Rob Robinson, Darrow Kirkpatrick (10/00)

㉘ The X Files 5.9 ★
Start: On the right side of an arete, 40' right of Tethered Goat. Boulder up right side of arete, merge with a short and shallow left-facing corner. From ledge, finish up a short headwall crack. 70'
FA: Rob Robinson, Darrow Kirkpatrick (10/00)

㉙ Slim's Corner 5.8 ★★★
Start: 10' right of The X Files. Climb a classic right-facing corner capped by a roof. Wind left around this and continue up a crack to a ledge, then on to the top. 70' FA: Robert McSween and Travis Eiseman (00)

㉚ Hard Eight 5.10
Start: 20' right of Slim's Corner. On the opposite side of this 'box' formation, climb another right facing corner chocked with vines, mud, and other unpleasentires. 70' FA: Scott Perkins and Fernando Paulette (03)

Promised Land

Emily Hon on Amber's Arete, 5.10c with the scenic TN River snaking through the background.

Photo Credit: Cody Averbeck

PRENTICE COOPER

PROMISED LAND

Promised Land

Shadows and Tall Trees
This is the orangest wall at the promised land and includes a pair of high quality sport routes on immaculate sun-burnt Sandstone.

31 Project
Start: 10' right of Hard Eight. Climb a steep face passing a roof at 3/4 height with a steep, technical face up high. 80'

PM
25 mins

PRENTICE COOPER

Promised Land

32 Cure for Pain 5.11c (sport) ★★
Quite the dose of orange Sandstone potent enough to satisfy the most hardy of Sandstone habits! Start: 10' right of Previous. Stick clip the high first bolt and climb the dark orange face to a difficult crux before trending right into a right facing corner system and anchors above. 70'
FA: Sean McGahee (03)

33 Shadows and Tall Trees(Sport) 5.12b ★★★
Foretold was the Promised Land of Orange Sandstone-- Behold! Start: 10' right of Cure for Pain. Climb the tiger-striped orange face to a crux roof pull up high. 70'
FA: Rich Plummer (03)

Insider's Tips: Unfortunately, the last moves are contained within a black streak that is often seasonally wet.

PRENTICE COOPER

PROMISED LAND

㉞ Velvet Elvis 5.10+ ★★
Start: 100' right of Shadows and Tall Trees. Climb a long right facing corner to a mid-way roof, that leads to a finishing corner up high. 60'
FA: Scott Perkins (03)

㉟ Grandma's Muscle 5.6
Start: 100' or so feet right of Velvet Elvis, past a maze of giant fallen-down blocks and boulders. Climb a low angle, wide flake and crack system to the top. 60'
FA: Sean McGahee, Cristina Gonzalez (03

㊱ Arete 5.11+ ★★
Start: just right of previous. Toprope the beautiful, blunt arete.

㊲ Aftershock 5.10-
Start: 15' right of the arete. Climb the gradually steepening face past minimal gear.
FA: Scott Perkins (03)

㊳ Golden Corral 5.10- ★
Start: 10' right of Aftershock. Climb the tight left facing corner, to a midway ledge and to a nice right-facing corner crack in an orange face above.
FA: Scott Perkins and Matt Harris (03)

㊴ Dick Trickle 5.9
Start: 10' right of Golden Corral in a black, water streaked face. Climb up into a left facing flake that transitions into a left facing corner up high.

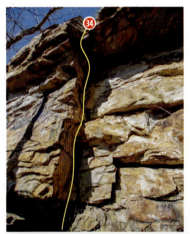

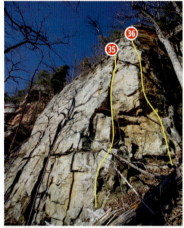

Robert Paden on the classic, Bag of Tricks 5.10+   Photo Credit: Cody Averbeck

PRENTICE COOPER

PROMISED LAND

PM
25 mins

THE CROWN JEWEL

If you're just passing through the area for an afternoon, do yourself a favor and settle in on this wall. If ever there was a 'downtown' Promised Land -- this would be it. Here, you'll find several well protected classics on bullet orange rock. Make sure and don't miss classics like Bag of Tricks, the Crown Jewel, and Jack of all Trades...

④⓪ Corner 5.10-
Start: 20' right of Dick Trickle, on the right side of a dark colored face. Climb a wide crack in a right facing corner.

④① Project
Start: 10' right of the corner. Toprope the beautiful orange and tan face passing several difficult bulges.

④② Bag Of Tricks 5.10+ ★★
Start: Just right of previous - at the base of a nice left facing corner and crack system. Climb up the corner and pull a crux or two our of your... hat... and take on a bulge with a nice, short headwall to the top. 75' **FA:** Travis Eiseman, Rob Robinson, Robert McSween

④③ Slim's Slab 5.12 ★★★
Start: 5' right of Bag Of Tricks. Toprope a difficult and bouldery face, passing multiple cruxes to a bulge. Climb over this then straight up easier ground to the top. **FA (toprope):** Robert McSween (5/00)

④④ Crown Jewel 5.10
Start: 5' right of Slim's Slab. King Me! --- an area classic! Boulder problem moves (crux) guard access to the corner. Conquer these and continue up an obvious, beautiful stemming corner. 80' **FA:** Travis Eiseman, Robert McSween (5/00)

Promised Land

482 www.rockerypress.com

PRENTICE COOPER

PRENTICE COOPER

PROMISED LAND

45 Sugar and Spice 5.12-
Start: 20' right and around the corner from Crown Jewel. A Travis "T-Bone" Eiseman classic! Boulder into a small, right facing corner and climb a splitter, straight-in crack in an orange wall to a cruxy step left.
FA: Travis Eiseman, (03)

46 Liquid Plummer 5.12- ★
Start: 15' right of Sugar & Spice. Climb a finger crack to a striking hairline seam that snakes up and left in gold rock.
FA: Richard Plummer (03)

Insider's Tips: Bring an arsenal of tiny cams and wires.

47 Get it Boy! 5.10c ★
Start: 15' right of previous. Begin on a left-leaning ram and follow a striking finger and hand crack in a black and brown streaked wall. FA: Sean McGahee & Scott Perkins (03)

48 Easy Corner 5.7
Start: On the right side of the wall. Climb the obvious short left-facing corner.
FA: Scott Perkins & Jonna Beiletti (04)

49 Dust Up 5.10- ★
Start: Just right of previous. Climb the striking short arete past a single bolt.
FA: Scott Perkins (04)

Philip Wilcheck on the mega classic, Jack of All Trades, 5.10+

Photo Credit: Cody Avenbeck

PRENTICE COOPER — PROMISED LAND

50 Satellite Flyer 5.9 ★
Start: Just right of Dust Up. Climb a face to a crack and flake system. 80'
FA: Scott Perkins, Sean McGahee (03)

51 Jack of All Trades 5.10+
Start: 50' right and around the corner from Satellite Flyer. Roof, crack, face...this climb has it all and will require a Sandstone Mr. Fix type with a versatile set of tools and skill at his disposal! Boulder out a low roof crack with excellent hand jams. Up this, then right into a slot. Continue over a small roof following the crack system to the top. 80' FA: Travis Eiseman, Chris Chesnutt, Jerry Roberts (5/00)

52 Close Call 5.10+ ★★★
Start: just right of Jack of all Trades. Pull up onto the wall via a difficult roof maneuver. Merge with a left-facing flake system with a roof up high that is passed by an awkward traverse right to a grassy ledge and top-out. 80'
FA: Chuck Crawford, Wolfgang Geist (03)

Climber's right of this downclimb, the cliff continues for another 1/2 mile ranging between 45-60' in height, and there are many more climbs established in this area known as the 'Sugar Plumb Walls.'

FOR YOUTH DEVELOPMENT®
FOR HEALTHY LIVING
FOR SOCIAL RESPONSIBILITY

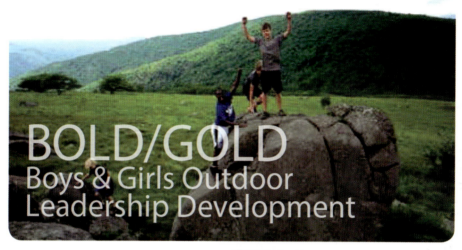

BOLD/GOLD
Boys & Girls Outdoor Leadership Development

What is BOLD/GOLD?
BOLD & GOLD is an youth development program using experiential learning in the wilderness environment to foster personal growth and leadership skills. Extensive summer courses and year round programming available.

Who Is This For?
BOLD & GOLD is for anyone 12-18

What We Do?
Outdoor Skills Sessions & Personal Growth, Multi-Day Excursions, Day Adventures, Mountain Biking, Paddle Boarding, Backpacking, Canoeing, Climbing & more!

Visit Facebook.com/chattboldgold or contact dkadwell@ymcachattanooga.org or bpercy@ymcachattanooga.org for more information!

J.A. HENRY COMMUNITY   YMCA
301 West 6th Street Chattanooga, TN 37402
ymcachattanooga.org/bold/gold-wilderness-school.

Josh Livasy on his super project, Triple Kaioken, 5.13c

The cliffs at Big Soddy are owned and managed by the Cumberland Trail State Park. Big Soddy is named for its namesake watershed that drops through the Cumberland Plateau raging through the class 4 & 5 whitewater river gorge that is located within a 15 minute hike from its neighbor, Deep Creek. The cliff, however, stands in stark contrast to its nearby counterpart. While the crags of Deep Creek are nestled away in a steep & shady drainage, the cliffs at Big Soddy soar above the tree line and are bathed in sun.

Photo Credit: Aaron Matheson

To this end, Big Soddy compliments the summer cragging at Deep Creek, offering south facing winter cragging yielding wildly tall & exposed routes on vertical to severely overhanging terrain. Of special interest are the many splitter cracks and mixed lines in the area that together with the remote approach and big air give Big Soddy an adventurous style.

BIG SODDY GORGE

Rules & Regs

Approach: Warning! The Deep Creek & Big Soddy parking lot is nestled in a rural residential area whose residents appreciate their privacy and peace & quiet. While driving, parking, and hiking, please keep this in mind and drive slowly, yield to residents, and please keep a low-profile while in the parking lot & hiking to the crags.

The parking lot and trailhead is owned and managed by the Southeastern Climbers Coalition, and you must obtain a **GATE CODE** to access the lot by following this link and agreeing to the terms of use.

seclimbers.org/deep-creek

SCC General Rules & Regulations

Drive slowly through the community and please respect that families and their children live and play here.

The parking lot is closed from Sunset to Sunrise. You will be ticketed and/or towed for unattended vehicles left in the lot past dark.

Please close and lock the gate behind you.

Please keep dogs leashed while in the lot and first 300' until down into the gorge.

No Car Camping is permitted in the lot.

No Overnight Parking is permitted in the lot.

Stick to established trails. Do Not trespass within adjacent private properties.

There are 26 marked spaces for parking. Illegally parked vehicles will be **TOWED**.

Climbing Specific Regulations

Do not Leave Fixed Gear (Quickdraws) ever. .

No bolting or new route development without a permit. For more information, please contact John Dorough at jwdorough@comcast.net or Chad Wykle at chad@rock-creek.com

BIG SODDY GORGE

Approach: Warning! The Deep Creek & Big Soddy parking lot is nestled in a rural residential area whose residents appreciate their privacy and peace & quiet. Drive Slowly! **Directions:** STOP! The Deep Creek & Big Soddy access is locked and requires a gate code that is accessed on-line through www.seclimbers.org.

❶From Chattanooga, Take I-27 North for approximately 19 miles to a right turn for the Hixson Pike Exit. ❷Take a left on Tsati - go 0.3mi. ❸Right on Dayton Pike- go 0.7mi. ❹Left on Durham- go 0.5mi. ❺Right on Black Valley Road - go 0.1 mi. ❻Left on Hotwater Road- go 2.1mi (up the mtn). ❼Sharp right on Old Hotwater- go 0.5mi. ❽Sharp left on gravel private drive (Follow Signage). ❾Go 0.1mi and fork left onto gravel road following SCC Signs- go 50ft. STAY LEFT AT THE SPLIT. ❿Right into gravel parking area.

30 mins

BIG SODDY GORGE

Driving Landmarks

Area Logistics

Emergency
Dial 911

Season
Fall-Winter

Camping

There is no overnight parking or camping permitted in the SCC lot and no camping available in the Deep Creek and Big Soddy Gorges.

Violators of theses policies will be ticketed and/or towed. The lot is patrolled daily.

The closest camping accommodations are found at Chester Frost Campground located at 2318 North Gold Point Circle, Hixon, TN 37343. (P) 423-842-0177

The local Chattanooga hang out, The Crashpad, is also a great option for those willing to commute from Chattanooga. You can find them on the web at: crashpadchattanooga.com or give them a call at: (423) 648-8393.

Food

The towns of Soddy & Daisy (now Soddy daisy) have a good selection of fine establishments. Just cruise the main drag (head south on Dayton Pike back towards Daisy), and you will encounter some nice options.

BIG SODDY GORGE

Big Soddy Approach

WARNING!! The parking lot is closed from Sunset to Sunrise. You will be ticketed and/or towed for unattended vehicles left in the lot past dark. Big Soddy requires a long hike, so give yourself ample enough time to make it out before nightfall!!

Approach for Big Soddy (Visor Right & Left):
❶ From the parking lot, locate the trail head next to the kiosk. Follow the trail across the plateau until it veers slightly right and down a series of stone stairs. ❷ At the base of these stairs, cross a logging road and head down to a sign directing you to a lower logging road that leads downhill and right to the intersection with the Cumberland Trail (signage here). ❸ From this point, head left downhill on the CT to a point where the trail crosses another logging road and eventually Deep Creek via a bridge. ❹ Cross Deep Creek and take a few switchbacks where the Main Wall of Deep Creek will become visible. ❺ Head right along the CT for approximately 15 minutes where the trail will wind around the Point of Deep Creek and start to descend into the Big Soddy Gorge. ❻ The trail then crosses Big Soddy Creek via a beautiful suspension bridge. Cross this bridge and head up uphill along the CT via several switchbacks to a point where the cliff at Big Soddy becomes visible. ❼ Identify the visor (see pg 496) and walk either climber's left or right of this formation for routes. See following 'Visor Right,' or 'Visor Left' sections for routes.

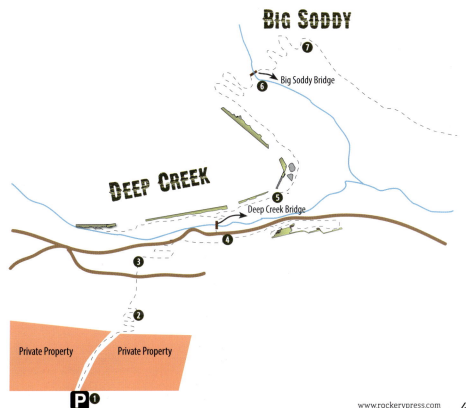

BIG SODDY GORGE

Area History

For a long, long time, the towering cliffs of Big Soddy were left undeveloped by rock climbers. If anyone did venture into the Soddy Creek Section of the Cumberland Trail to climb, their vertical adventures went unrecorded, and their chalk has long since washed away.

It wasn't until 2007 when John Dorough, Chad Wykle, and Chad Fowler walked the cliff and established several ground-up climbs that are still considered area classics. If you make the trip yourself, make sure to check out Departure 29 and Liberator to name a couple of these early classic lines. Large sections of the 'Visor Right' cliff remained more or less untouched until Micah Gentry scouted the cliff and put up a few more lines in early 2011.

Meanwhile, during 2011-2012, John Dorough, who was also apart of the development of the Deep Creek climbing area, was tirelessly spearheading the movement to get the State to give the 'all clear' for fixed anchor installation to begin at Big Soddy. Dorough took many hikes throughout the area accompanied by Park Rangers and Biologists to ensure that no endangered plants (such as Scutellaria Montana or Large-flowered Skullcap, which is federally protected by the Endangered Species Act of 1973) were threatened due to climber impact. He also organized a proper climbing management plan to implement a development standard that can provide a working climbing model for other cliffs that run along the Cumberland Trail to be opened for future development.

Dorough and other local ambassadors also built many bridges--literally and figuratively--during the process in order to secure safe passage across Deep and Big Soddy Creeks and build positive relations with State officials. Ultimately, Dorough and company managed to once again work their magic in early 2013 when they opened the majestic cliffs of Big Soddy up for not only

Construction of the Deep Creek bridge.

John Dorough and Anthony Jones (CT Ranger) celebrate the completion of the Deep Creek bridge.

BIG SODDY GORGE

more amazing traditional climbs, but also for a few bolted gems here and there scattered amongst the miles of bullet cliff line.

Bolting more or less began at one of the more remote cliffs in the gorge in early 2013 when Joshua Livasy explored Big Soddy along with Paul Whicker on a tip from Dorough. The first route to be bolted was Air Nimbus at Dragon Wall. Gentry also joined Livasy subsequently to finish bolting the Dragon Wall feature. Access to this remote cliff became difficult as the temporary Soddy bridge continued to wash out in high waters leaving Soddy Creek much too high to cross safely in the middle of winter. Enter the Biggie Board - a 10 foot 2 x 6 adorned with skateboard grip tape depicting the late Notorious B.I.G. was used to cross the creek's exposed boulders during times when the bridge was out. Although completely unsafe, the Biggie Board never failed and development didn't have to wait on another temporary bridge to be built in lieu of the planned suspension bridge project that is currently still under construction.

By late 2013, Conspiracy Buttress was the next cliff to be developed. Gentry and Livasy put up Chemtrail Surfer and Monatomic Gold, respectively, and by the next weekend under the drills of Dorough, Cody Averbeck, Dave Wilson, Laban Swafford, Zachary Lesch-Huie, Gentry and Livasy, the rest of the wall was just about developed in a single day.

By the next few months, FA's of Trad lines and sport climbs alike were being put up at an astonishing pace and even though the cliff still has much more potential for amazing rock climbs, there are plenty of classic climbs in the 5.10 to 5.13 range that make Big Soddy well worth the trek for the adventurous spirit.

Endangered Species, Scutellaria Montana or Large-flowered Skullcap

BIG SODDY GORGE

VISOR RIGHT

40 mins

THE VISOR, RIGHT

The visor marks the middle point of Big Soddy route development. Areas to the right are lumped into the 'Visor Right' section, while areas to the left are lumped into the 'Visor left' section. Routes located in the Visor area feature tall, bullet stone with maximum exposure situated on a prominent point.

❶ **Whiskey Slings 5.10-** ★★★

A striking natural line that begs to be climbed.
Start: just right of the visor in an acute right facing corner. Trend left to a series of ledges leading to a beautiful marbelized right facing flake/corner. Follow the system to a ledge and out a steep hand and fist crack in a white bulge (takes a few big cams here). Follow a series of horizontals to the top and a bolted anchor with a great view. 80' FA: Cody Averbeck & Alex Whiteman. '13

> Insider's note: A leaky flask soaked the slings used on the first ascent - hence the name.

❷ **Maui Gold 5.12a (sport)**

Mahalla, Bro! Ride this Sandstone giant for as long as you can.
Start: 30' right of the visor. Climb a boulder problem to a perfect 3 finger pocket, work right to a high side pull to gain access under the roof. From here, pull out a flaring crack corner, and you will gain access to a bullet proof face. Conquer this to one last rest before you blast up jug hauling fun! 14 bolts, 80'
FA: John Dorough. '13

❸ **Oddjob 5.10+**

Start: 25' right of Whiskey Slings. Climb out a low roof into a striking right facing corner to a deteriorating finish and anchor on ledge. 60'
FA: Andrew Miller, Carl Buch '13

2nd ascent of Oddjob, 5.10+

BIG SODDY GORGE

Alex Whiteman on the 2nd ascent of Whiskey Slings, 5.10- Photo Credit: Micah Gentry

BIG SODDY GORGE

Double Buttress

The Double Buttress is a small, condensed section of cliff that holds a collection of short, steep sport climbs and few nice cracks.

40 mins

❹ Camp Crack 5.6
Located behind a large leaning boulder, scramble up to wide splitter and transitioning right to seam. Start: in fist size splitter that peters out into seams leading to some face climbing. Gear up to 4". 50'
FA: Micah Gentry, Richard Parks. '13

❺ Vajazzled (sport) 5.10+ ★★
Located around the corner from Camp Crack. Climb up face for 1 bolt and transition left onto slopey shelves leading to namesake holds. 7 bolts, 60'.
FA: Micah Gentry. '14

❻ Mrs. Big Stuff 5.8 ★★★
Start: In a right facing corner left of huecoed wall. Climb wide crack off ground and through several wide sections. Usually only dry in the summer. 60'
FA: Verena Draper, Micah Gentry. '14

Insider's note: Take some larger cams (5-6")

❼ Big Black Furry Creature 5.10d (sport) ★★
Start: Left of tree. Steep moves out first roof yields vertical climbing on solid rock. A popular spot for Raccoons...as you will see. 7 bolts 60'
FA: Micah Gentry. '14

❽ Strange Design 5.11c (sport) ★★
Start: right of the tree. Boulder up to steep moves out roof to sustained jug pulling. Bouldery start leads to pumpy series of jugs finishing on face climbing. 8 bolts 60'
FA: Micah Gentry. '14

BIG SODDY GORGE

VISOR RIGHT

❾ Bittersweet 5.11- (sport) ★
Start: 15 ft right of Strange Design. Climb into awkward stance for long moves leading to positive holds up to and out a roof. 6 bolts. 60'
FA: Micah Gentry. '14

> Insider's note: Seeps most of the year

❿ Miller/ Gentry 5.10 ★
start: 5' right of bittersweet. Make a few moves up face to a splitter crack going up to a roof.
FA: Andrew Miller, Micah Gentry. '13

> Insider's note: Seeps most of the year

⓫ Ivy Trail 5.7
Start: in a corner right of Miller/Gentry. Climb seams along a wide crack on low angle terrain through lots of greenery. Finished straight up the wall. 80'
FA: Verena Draper, Micah Gentry. '14

⓬ Blight 5.10b (sport) ★★★
This is the far left route on this wall just around corner from Ivy Trail. A constantly dirty start leads to great climbing to and out the upper roof to a gorgeous upper section. 8 bolts 60'
FA: Micah Gentry. '14

⓭ Picking up the Pieces 5.10- ★★★
Start 15 ft right of Blight. Climb the seam in the middle of the wall to roof flake and finish on Ain't Life Grand by traversing right at the top. Shares anchors with the adjacent sport route. 75'
FA: Micah Gentry. '14

⓮ Ain't life Grand (project) (sport)5.12+
Start in a depression and climb slopey slots to the upper slab with knobs. 5.11ish climbing leads to 3 bolts of serious slabbing on gobstopper knobs. 10 bolts 75'
F.A. Micah Gentry. '14

CAVE-CLIFF TECHNICAL

RESCUE

WORLD CLASS ROCK CLIMBING MEETS WORLD CLASS RESCUE TEAM

Unfortunately, each year the unthinkable happens and self rescue is not an option. At times like this, it is good to know that the professionals of the Chattanooga Hamilton County Cave/Cliff/Technical Rescue team have your back.

Our mutual aid services are based in the Chattanooga area and extend through Tennessee, Alabama, Georgia, and beyond. They include cutting edge equipment, the area's most advanced medical-ready team, and world class climbers, cavers, technical riggers, and support staff on the ready. Though you may not need us this year, many will. Our services are free of charge and are primarily supported by donations.

While you are here in Chattanooga, enjoy the adventure! If you can, consider making a donation. Call it an insurance policy for you or your climbing buddies, or just pay it forward. Help us provide the services that climbers in trouble need.

chcrs.org | info@chcrs.org | (423) 899-5910

BIG SODDY GORGE

VISOR RIGHT

SODDY MALL

The Soddy Mall is a long, continuous section of cliff line that is conveniently located just off of the CT and may one day be considered the 'main wall' at the cliff, but currently route development is spotty due to sections of less than perfect rock between patches of bullet stone.

⑮ NC calling 5.9 ★
Up the hill and right of ALG about 150'. Climb the splitter corner through some thought provoking moves. 50'
FA: Verena Draper, Micah Gentry

⑯ Dark side of the flake 5.11a (sport)
★★★
Start 100 yards to the right of NC Calling. Climb steep shelves through a roof crux leading to a unique bit of fin climbing up to an airy arete. 9 bolts 90'
F.A. Micah Gentry. '14

⑰ Great corner in the sky 5.10- ★★
Starts left of tree on left crack option. Climb a finger crack left of tree to ramp moving left past huge flake to a beautiful right-facing corner. 80'
FA: Micah Gentry, Verena Draper. '14

Insider's Tip: Anchors under roof but with deadfall removed from top, there will be left and right extensions to the top.

Modern Problems, project

Elden Earhart on Over My Head, 5.11a Photo Credit: Micah Gentry

BIG SODDY GORGE

VISOR RIGHT

⑱ The Roost 5.10 ★★
50 ft right of Great Corner in the Sky. Climb left facing corner to ledge and continue left through wide right facing corner to gain slab and go left into dihedral until pulling onto face at top. 75'
FA: Micah Gentry, Verena Draper. '14

⑲ White n' Sight 5.9 ★★
It's hard to miss this striking, straight in wide crack splitting the white and gold wall. Bring some larger cams. 75'
FA: John Dorough, Zachary Les-Chuie. '14

⑳ Beefcake 5.10d (sport) ★★
Start on ledge and climb thin moves up seam to barely there holds and a delightful crux. Sustained climbing. 4 bolts. 40'
FA: Elden Earhart. '14

㉑ Holed Up 5.10c (sport) ★★
Begin on ledge above start for white corner. Climb positive holds to the large hole on the wall and make continuous long moves up the face. 5 bolts. 50'
FA: Micah Gentry. '14

BIG SODDY GORGE

㉒ Over My Head 5.11a (sport) ★★
Start: just right of an arete. Take on a strong roof start to a thin finish where at the last bolt you can climb straight up for 12a or escape right for an 11a grade. 5 bolts 50'
FA: Elden Earhart. '14

㉓ Buzz Muscle 5.11a (sport) ★★
2nd line right of arete. Hefty roof pull start to thinner face and a mantle finish
5 bolts. 50'
FA: Elden Earhart. '14

㉔ Getting Medieval 5.10- ★★★
The first route past upper ledges. Climb face through questionable rock to steep roof moves on big holds and on to top. 75'
FA: Verena Draper, Micah Gentry. '14

㉕ Modern Problems 5.13(sport) ★★
The imposing 15' roof just right of the corner of Getting Medieval. 12 bolts 70' Bolted by: Zachary Pyke. '14

Verena Draper on Holed Up, 5.10c

Photo Credit: Micah Gentry

BIG SODDY GORGE

㉖ Germans Express 5.10 ★★
Burly starting move protected by a bolt yielding great climbing through slabby face moves and two dihedrals. 85'
FA: Micah Gentry, Verena Draper. '14

㉗ Half Percentile 11a (sport) ★★★
20 right of Germans Express. Climb a striking black and green slab following sculpted features on bomber rock. Bolts 75' FA: Zachary Pyke. '14

㉘ Park's Flake 5.9 ★★
Start: 300 ft to the right of Half Percentile. Follow the striking left facing flake passing a wide section and a step left to a ledge that finishes climbing a higher corner to bolted anchor. 60'
FA: Richard Parks, Micah Gentry. '11

㉙ Gold Finger 5.12- ★★
24 karat finger lockin' in bullet orange and yellow stone.
Start: 5 feet right of Parks Flake. Climb the splitter finger crack in the golden wall next to Parks Flake. 60'
FA: Andrew Miller, Alex Whiteman. '13

Insider's Tip: Bring extra TCUs

BIG SODDY GORGE

VISOR RIGHT

SODDY MOTEL

It's hard not to utter an 'Oh Man' or 'Whoa' as the Soddy Motel comes into view as the Cumberland Trail snakes just below its base. The defining feature of this sector is the 25' cap roof that sports one of the hardest roof cracks in the Sandstone Belt - Sea of Moses...

AM
45 mins

Park's Flake, 5.9

Soddy

30 Room Service 5.8
Start: 50' right of previous. Follow easy crack negotiating around trees/shrubs. 60' FA: Chad Fowler, Chad Wykle, John Dorough. '11

31 Wake up call 5.11+ ★★★
Start: 5' right of Room Service. Climb a WAKE UP boulder problem for 10' following bomber protection along a seam that leads to and out a 3' roof. 60'
FA: Chad Fowler, Chad Wykle, John Dorough. '11

508   www.rockerypress.com

BIG SODDY GORGE

32 No Tell Motel 5.11+ ★★★
Climb out of the bum shelter to a splitter roof crack and right facing corner that leads to easier climbing and bolted anchors. 65'
FA: Cody Averbeck. '13

Insider's tip: look for small face holds on the left side of the corner when turning the low lip ---- attentive belay.

33 Sea of Moses (project) 5.13+
Then Moses stretched out his hand over the sea, and the LORD drove the cliffs back and the roof was divided.
The obvious massive roof crack that splits the 25' roof.
FA: Laban Swafford, John Dorough. '13

Insider's tip: Grade is approximate.

Laban Swafford works out the crux of Sea of Moses, 5.13+

BIG SODDY GORGE

㉞ To Live is to Fly ★★★ (project) (sport) 13b
"To live is to fly, all low and high." A 'high gravity' line that will keep all but the most hardy grounded.
Start: 25' right of Sea of Moses. Climb up an easy face to the base of a 6' roof seam. No feet Houdini out the roof to a large left facing corner. Finish out a classic multi-tiered roof system to anchors above.
FA: Cody Averbeck. '14

Insider's tip: Grade is approximate.

㉟ Room for Two 5. 12b ★★ (sport)
Start: 10' right of To Live is to Fly. Climb a well featured start to the base of a double stack of tiers to a desperately thin and slopey crux that thrutches up and right. At this horizontal break, climb hard left to a system and corners and arete perches that lead to an anchor below the final cap roof.
FA: John Dorough. '14

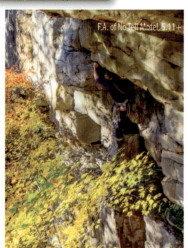

F.A. of No Tell Motel. 5.11+

Laban Swafford & John Dorough on the F.A. of Sea of Moses

BIG SODDY GORGE

VISOR RIGHT

45 mins

GOOD SAMARITAN BUTTRESS

This is the next buttress immediately to the right of the Soddy Motel. These killer climbs will feel like a blessing. The Good Samaritan Buttress is a narrow, vertical buttress with attractive orange rock and a short, but striking hand crack in its middle.

㊱ Trailside Parable 5.10 ★★
Start on an arete 50' right of the Soddy Motel. Gain ledge. At crack, move left. Pull through awesome orange rock and finish through a small roof up high.
FA: John Dorough, Zachary LesChuie. '13

㊲ Good Samaritan 5.11-
"Gooder Samaritan." Do yourself a solid and do it. This route is sustained with wonderful rock. Start: 10' right of previous at a flake. Climb a nice face to ledge (small cams). At the top of the crack, reef once right, then pull techy mantle up (crux). Continue up face to top. 80'
FA: Zachary LesChuie, John Dorough. '13

㊳ Gospel of Luke 5.11+
Start at undercut arete 5' right of Good Samaritan. Boulder-mantle over the 'nose' directly onto the slab. Pad up to gear. Clip a bolt, climb past the seam (crux). Continue straight up face. Gain sub-ledge, angle left to top anchor. Fantastic. Amazing rock and moves. Treat yourself and do this route. 80'
FA: John Dorough, Zachary Leshuie. '13

㊴ Romper Room 5.7
Start 5' right of Gospel of Luke. Start in an acute left facing corner crack that leads to a tree covered ledge. From here, identify a large 6" splitter crack splitting a low-vertical wall that leads to another ledge and on to the top of the cliff.
FA: Cody Averbeck, John Dorough. '14

BIG SODDY GORGE

THE SIRENS

This wall is located immediately before the wall takes a hard 90 degree turn downstream.

The two seams' siren call will lure you into this quality zone. The right wall offers a corner and two splitter seams. To the left are some tasty, technical mixed climbs.

AM

45 mins

④⓪ August West 5.12
You'll be singing his name! A unique, technical climb with great rock.
Start: Several hundred feet past the Good Samaritan Buttress. This is the face with pockets above the flat, blank roof. Climb ledges right of large blank overhang. Mantel up then dance left using a horizontal. Tech up past a bolt and pocket crux to ledge relief. Romp it to the top. 70'
FA: John Dorough. '14

④① Sprankles 5.11+ ★★
Start: same as August West. Climb ledges right of large blank roof. Get some small cams then initiate face techniques past crimps and two bolts. Gain the ledge, swing right, then up to anchors. Quality technical face. 70'
FA: Zachary LesChuie. '14

④② Laban's Route 5.10- ★
Start in corner on the right side of this wall. Stem and jam to roll around right onto face. Tech up face to anchors. Don't overlook this nice corner crack with some quality face climbing higher up. 60'
FA: Laban Swafford, Ben Johnson

(arete variation start) 5.10+
Bust some technical arete moves past two bolts to finish up the climb above. Bullet white stone. 60'
FA: Laban Swafford, Ben Johnson

④③ Siren Left 5.10-
What a sweet siren song this lovely climb sings. A pleasure from bottom to top. Start: the obvious left seam starting off ledge located 10' right of previous. Scramble onto ledge. Climb seam using Southern crack-face technique. Roll out a small alcove onto face above. Head straight to anchors just right of tree. 60'
FA: Zachary LesChuie, John Dorough

④④ Siren Right 5.10- ★★
Straight-ahead fun climb with some tech in the seam for added interest. Great position and view of gorge at the top.
Start: 10' right of Siren left. This is the obvious right seam starting off a black slab. Pad up to seam. Climb through seam. Pull small roof higher up to gain anchor ledge. 70'
FA: Zachary LesChuie, John Dorough

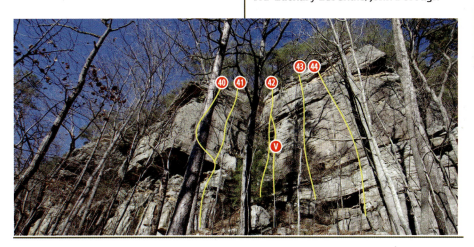

www.rockerypress.com 513

Andrew Miller on the First Ascent of Gold Finger, 5.12-
Photo Credit: Micah Gentry

BIG SODDY GORGE

SUNRISE WALL

This attractive buttress holds a handful of routes that start up on a ledge. Access the ledge climber's left of the buttress proper. These routes feature extremely steep starts one bullet white rock to a nice headwall elevated high above the gorge canopy.

45 Man Songs ★★★ 5.10-
Start: far left on the ledge and follow a striking splitter seam that snakes up the wall to a two bolt anchor. 70'
FA: Zachary Leschuie. '14

46 Crack of Dawn ★★★ 5.12-
Start: 10' right of Man Songs. Start off the ledge and clip 2 bolts through initial tiered roof intro to a cruxy lip turn. Continue up the face via a splitter crack and face to an anchor station on top of the cliff. 70'
FA: John Dorough. '14

47 Break of Day 5.12d/13a ★★ (sport)
Start just right of Crack of Dawn. Follow a line of bolts that traverses rightward along a handrail, passing a hard boulder problem that gains the swooping white swath just below the point of the buttress. 60'
FA: John Dorough. '14

AM
45 mins

48 Soddy Bottom Boys ★ 5.11+
Start: on the right side of the ledge. Climb out a very steep crack / corner to a broken face above to a two bolt anchor.
FA: Zachary Leschuie. '14

Soddy

www.rockerypress.com 515

AM

45 mins

Departure Buttress

This wall features one of the highest density of classic traditional and mixed climbs in the Big Soddy Gorge. This wall is packed with a large variety of excellent climbs on high quality Sandstone. To boot, these routes offer fantastic scenic views of the gorge below.

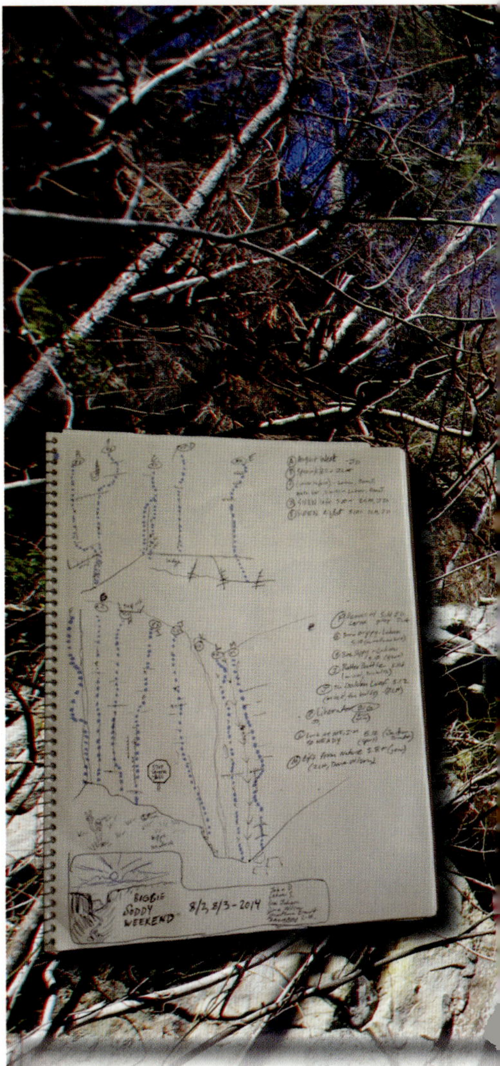

㊾ Dances with Lorax 5.4 ❐
Start: dirt corner at left end of wall. Negotiate ledge-corner moves. Grab tree. Traverse left then right and maybe back again. Kick mud steps then grab bushes to top it out. 50'
FA: John Dorough, Zachary LesChuie. '14

Insider's Note: Unique, but requisite. Litmus test for the uninitiated Southerneer.

㊿ Born Grippy 5.10+ ★ ❐
Start just right of previous route. Climb left facing flake-crack to horizontals. Bust through crimps to a bolt. Stay on point for the tic tac to the anchor.50'
FA: Laban Swafford, John Dorough '14

Insider's Note: Not as classic as climbs to the right, but this is still a sweet sweep of stone.

(51) Born Slippy 5.10 ❐
Crack to orange face above. Cap rock hangs over top. Jam through funky crack to cool jugs. Awesome face climbing tic tacs through horizontals in the orange face. Fantastic climbing from bottom to top; killer face climbing. 50'
FA: Laban Swafford '14

(52) Butter Battle 5.11+ ❐
Start up right facing flakes. Hit two juggy breaks then bust a crimpy crux on radical rock and sweet holds. Hang tight at the end. What a sweet slice of face climbing. Beautiful crux sequence on exquisite stone. Mixed, two bolts. 60'
FA: John Dorough '14

(53) Jector the Golden Loaf 5.12- ❐
Start in a small gulley 10' right of Butter Battle. Climb the finger crack, move left where crack ends then back right. Pad through bullet white rock. After small overhang, crank a powerful and puzzling crux sequence (bolt). Grab a TCU to the left at a rest, clip last bolt and finish with a final tricky move. Gorgeous rock, varied climbing and a crux you won't soon forget. 70'
FA: Zachary Leschuie '14

Soddy

BIG SODDY GORGE

54 Liberator 5.10+ ★★★
Let my people go Rock Climbing! A classic wide crack that leads to the tip top of the Departure Buttress. Start: 10' right of Jector. Climb the top to bottom splitter wide crack and chimney. 80'
FA: John Dorough, Mike Womax '11

Insider's Tip: bring some wide cams.

55 Look At Me, I'm So Heady 5.12a (sport) ★★★
Start: immediately right of Liberator OW. Crimp through tough sequential moves to gain the ledge 35' up. Rest up then launch into funky corner. Depart right for heady moves on beautiful white stone. Roll onto arete ledge for a rest, then pull back left for final moves to anchor. So heady. Feels like a journey. Quality rock, great moves and a rewarding position at the top. 80'
FA: Johnathan Brandt '14

BIG SODDY GORGE

VISOR RIGHT

56 Gift From Nature 5.8+ ★★★
Start: Just around right from I'm So Heady. Rides right side of long arete. Jam through two small roofs off the bat. After short white corner skirt overhang around right. Romp up face just right of arete on sweet sandstone features. Anchor on right side of arete at the top. A fantastic moderate with varied climbing, quality stone and great position over Soddy gorge. Do it. 90'
FA: Dave Wilson & Zachary LesChuie '14

57 Alert 5 5.9 ★
Start: 10' right of Gift from Nature. Climb a mossy crack that splits the face above. Scared of hairy monsters? Face your fears!
FA: John Dorough '11

58 Departure 29 5.11+
The classic of the area. Start: 5' right of Alert 5. Pull a low roof and follow crack to a ledge system, traverse hard right and follow striking flake system to top. Top it out! A beautiful rock climb with unparalleled position. 80'
FA: John Dorough '11

Did Someone Say Roofs?

By: Rich Romano

As a Shawangunks climber in the seventies, it was easy to believe that "the Gunks" was the undisputed king of overhangs. The known climbing areas of the era did little to refute this claim. The closest rivals were perhaps Colorado's Eldorado Canyon and Seneca in West Virginia. But their overhangs were actually a very small proportion of the total climbing as a whole.

In the late seventies and early eighties, a few adventurous Gunkies began to explore a region in the southeastern United States known as "the Sandstone Belt." They came back with stories of giant roofs of different shapes and sizes ... some with splitter cracks, some with overhanging walls linking up roof systems. Of course, a proud Gunkie such as myself dismissed these rumors as overblown. I had to see it to believe it.

Well, seeing was believing! In the spring of 1985, I swung south on my way back from Big Bend, Texas to visit my old friends Shannon Stegg, Rob Robinson and Gene Smith. The first climb to diffuse the mysticism surrounding the earlier rumors was Steggasaurus Slab, at Yellow Creek, which featured five feet-dangling overhangs in 200 feet. Next in line was the beautiful and continuous Fire Wall, which featured a striking crack line through the steepest section of the canyon. I would soon learn that these routes epitomized southern sandstone. The rest of the week was spent sampling classics from Sandrock, Steele, and a few other areas.

Returning to the Gunks, I viewed our overhangs in a different light: they didn't seem as big anymore. I was also awed by the amount of quality rock the Sandstone Belt possessed. The following year I visited the South again. After a few days crag hopping, I found myself back in Yellow Creek with Gene. The routes we did that day were overshadowed by the ultra classic Grand Dragon. This uniquely overhanging hand and finger crack will forever be etched in my memory. Regrettably, I have since learned that Yellow Creek is closed— which demonstrates the potentially fragile relationship between climbers and landowners.

The following day was spent at the Tennessee Wall. With its classic cracks, steep faces and massive overhangs, I would venture to say that a trip to the South is not complete without a visit to this amazing cliff.

The last day of my trip was unforgettable. Rob was eager (or rather psychotic) to try a new route on a cliff he recently discovered. Gene and I followed him through the woods until we were below the largest roof I had ever seen. Rob proceeded to attack this thing with maniacal intensity. Realizing his passion, I decided to just hang out and take pictures. After he finished it, Gene and I took turns climbing. What a thrill it was to climb such a giant roof!

How do I feel now that the Gunks have been dethroned? Fine, I am better crack climber anyway ... but then again, the South has plenty of that too! See Bio on pg 539

BIG SODDY GORGE

VISOR LEFT

PM
45 mins

The Visor, Left

The visor marks the middle point of Big Soddy route development. Areas to the left are lumped into the 'Visor Left' section. Routes located in the Visor area feature tall, bullet stone with maximum exposure situated on a prominent point.

59 Climbers Cough 5.10a (sport) ★★★
A troubling condition after exposure to years of prolonged route development... This is the first route left of visor. This route can be done in 2 pitches but a 70m will get you to the ground. 1st pitch is a mossy pitch of face and slab climbing while the 2nd pitch starts with a bolt off the anchor followed by a perma draw and a hanging arete. Climb positive holds to the top pedestal which has one of the best views in the canyon. 110'
FA: Micah Gentry '13

60 Emily the Hon 5.7 ★
Start: 15 ft left of Climber's Cough. Begin on a low bulge in front of a tree and climb into corners to ledge down and right of the tree. Climb 2nd pitch by traversing out right into an airy position before pulling steep section. Finish through final ledges 110'
FA: Emily Hon, Micah Gentry '13

Insider's Tip: Watch for loose rock

61 Patient Zero 5.11a (sport)
Start: Under a shallow right facing corner 25' left of Emily the Hon. Symptoms may include sweaty palms, pumped forearms, delusions of grandeur, and desire to do it all again. Boulder through lower corner to great holds and a crux which yields to fun climbing up an exposed upper section. Stick Clip. 14 bolts. 110'
FA: Micah Gentry '13

BIG SODDY GORGE
VISOR LEFT

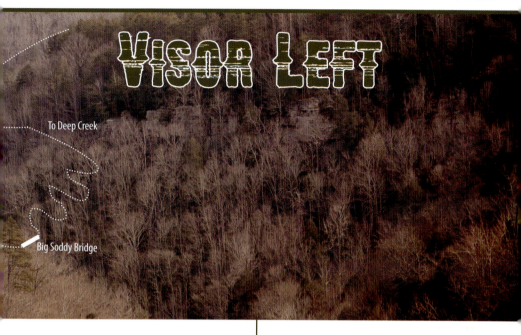

To Deep Creek

Big Soddy Bridge

www.rockerypress.com 521

James Pullum on Climbers Cough 5.9

Photo Credit: Micah Gentry

PM

45 mins

LEDGE BUTTRESS

The ledge buttress, like the routes previously encountered in this area, starts off with lackluster starts up muted gray stone, but at the halfway point, these routes change character and provide increasing quality rock and moves with a fantastic all-around wall position above Big Soddy.

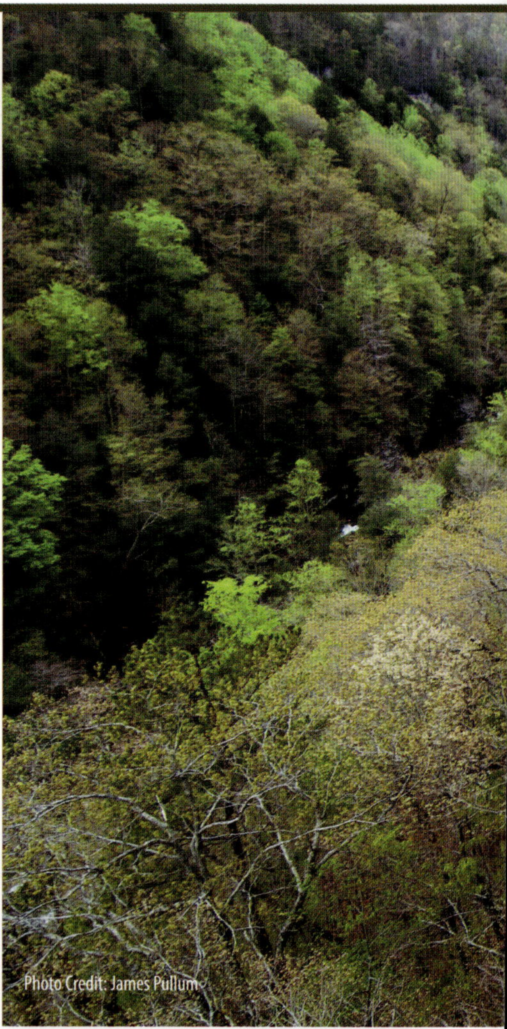

Photo Credit: James Pullum

(62) General Ledger 5.10b (sport) ★★ ❒
Start: 200' left of Gentrification.
Climb a few bolts of dirty rock to a few steep moves to gain a tall vertical face joining up near the top of a hanging arete. 13 bolts. 90'
FA: Micah Gentry '13

(63) Purple crack 5.8 ★ ❒
Start: same as General Ledger.
Climb the first few bolts of General Ledger and at the ledge, climb up purple crack to a roof and then traverse out right before getting to a scary flake where you will then meet up with General Ledger again. 90'
FA: Micah Gentry, Verena Draper, '13

Insider's Tip: Bring lots of runners. Climbing to the traverse is 5.5 ,but the traverse is scary 5.8.

(64) Unfinished Business 5.9 ❒
Start: A few feet left of General Ledger.
This is a short line of bolts to the ledge that will probably extend to the top, eventually... 5 bolts 40'
FA: Micah Gentry

(65) Ledgendary 5.9 ★★★ ❒
Start: 20 ft left Unfinished Business.
Start on dark conglomerate rock and climb up through corners all the way to the top. 90'
FA: Verena Draper, Micah Gentry '13

(66) Living on the ledge 5.7 ★ ❒
Start: 20' left of previous. Climb up past low ledge to splitter left facing corner. 40'
FA: Verena Draper, Micah Gentry

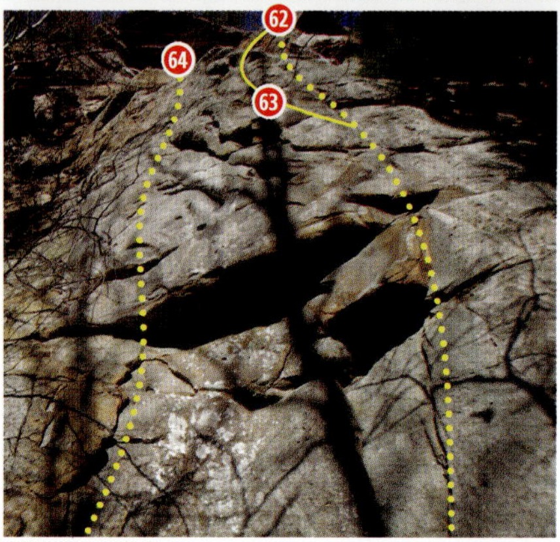

Soddy

BIG SODDY GORGE

Micah Gentry on Patient Zero 5.11a (and yes, that is Dragon Wall in the distance)

BIG SODDY GORGE

VISOR LEFT

PM

50 mins

Disheveled & Old Walls

The Disheveled & Old Walls has some of the least developed cliff line at Big Soddy. There are still many more lines to be done. Currently, route development is limited to a cluster of three routes on a bullet but short piece of gray stone.

67 Superannuated 5.12a ★★
Start: several hundred feet left of living on the ledge. Climb out the roof via technical stemming to a jug rest. Difficult climbing leads to a perfect thank god jug out to the right 40'
FA: John Dorough '13

> **Insider's Tip:** save some 0&00 cams to pull the 'changing corner' crux

68 Bleary Eyed and Bonking (Sport) 5.13 ★★
Start just left of previous. Pull left then up a small right facing corner feature which ends at two pockets. Apply bouldering magic to gain finishing jug. 40'
Bolted by: Dave Wilson, '13

69 It Never Fails 5.12d (sport) ★★
Start: same as Bleary Eyed and Bonking. Pull further left. Conjure a feasible sequence out bulge on perfect stone. 4 bolts. 40'
Bolted by: Dave Wilson, '13

www.rockerypress.com

John Dorough, Laban Swafford, Zach Lesch-huie, Josh Livasy, and Cody Averbeck on the single-day development of the Conspiracy Buttress.

BIG SODDY GORGE

VISOR LEFT

PM — 35 mins

CONSPIRACY BUTTRESS

Ok, well Trad guide or not, this is a fantastic wall made up of all sport climbs. The climbs are wildly varied, tall, exposed, and feature some of the best rock around that you'd swear was straight out of the New River Gorge. If you fancy a hard sport climb once in awhile, then pay this wall a visit... but keep a close eye, your Trad Big Brother is watching you...

70 War for Oil 5.10-
Start: on the far right side of the conspiracy buttress. Climb the "Astroman" crack/corner to ledge. Clip bolt then climb face to overhang. Pull it on the left. Climb face above, and bring a blue TCU for the top. 70'
FA: John Dorough, Cody Averbeck '13

71 Chemtrail Surfer (aka Genstral Stain) (Sport) 5.11b
Bloody good climbing on insane pink rock in an impeccable setting. One of the best 5.11s in the area. Start: 5' left of War for Oil. Climb up the technical slab into the pink and white chemtrail (aka Genstral Stain), then head out a small roof to fun face climbing and chains. 70'
FA: Micah Gentry '13

Insider's tip: stick clip the first 2 bolts

72 Illuminati Alumni 5.10d(Sport) ★★★
Start: 5' left of Chemtrail Surfer. Stick clip and conquer a technical slab passing unique underclings and knobs to a fun middle section and juggy roof up high. 70'
FA: Micah Gentry '13

73 33° 5.12a (Sport) ★★★
Start: just left of Illuminati Alumni. Follow bolts up a fun face to a boulder problem after the small roof. 80'
FA: Josh Livasy '13

Insider's Tip: did you find the Thumbdercling?

74 Man on the Moon 5.11d (Sport) ★★★
The bizarre crux on this one will convince you of the unlikelihood of ever landing a man on this moon. Begin a few feet left of 33°. Start off belay bench under slab. Climb slab right of small, granite-like corner. After ledge, negotiate a puzzling crux. Enjoy exposure and more sustained movement to the top. 12 bolts 90'
FA: John Dorough '13

528 www.rockerypress.com

BIG SUDDY GORGE

Dave Wilson on Chemtrail Surfer, 5.11b

Photo Credit: Micah Gentry

SuperDARN 5.13a (Sport) ☐
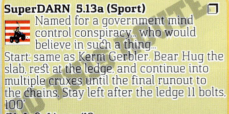 Named for a government mind control conspiracy, who would believe in such a thing...
Start: same as Kerm Gerbler. Bear Hug the slab, rest at the ledge, and continue into multiple cruxes until the final runout to the chains. Stay left after the ledge 11 bolts. 100'
FA: Josh Livasy '13

Josh Livasy & Zachary Lesch-Huie climbing into the mist. Photo Credit: Micah Gentry

BIG SODDY GORGE — VISOR LEFT

75 Butter Dish (project) (Sport) ★★★
Mmmm, butter Sandstone...
Start off same belay bench under slab. Start same as Man on the Moon. Follow a tricky black slab to the ledge. Power out the overhang, then hang on through the buttery panel to a big rest. A tough final sequence may spread you thin. 90'
FA: Zachary Leschuie '13

76 Man on the Grassy Knoll 5.11d (Sport) ★★★
Look over there! You'll have to distract others parading their way to this climb so you can get your own shot at it... Start: same belay bench under slab. From slot, climb slab up and slightly left. After ledge, pull a crux then chase shaply jugs to another ledge. Negotiate moves up then right to finish. 12 bolts 80'
FA: Zachary Leschuie '13

BIG SODDY GORGE

77 Kerm Gerbler Abduction 5.12+ (Sport) ★★
Start: same as SuperDARN. Climb SuperDARN to the ledge, plus a few more bolts, then move right to an independent line of bolts. Bust a crux then monkey bar to a banana ledge. Get abducted as you travel through the final roof boulder problem. 100' FA: Laban Swafford '13

78 SuperDARN 5.13a (Sport)
See description on page 530.

79 Monatomic Gold 5.13a (Sport)
One of the best 13a's in the region. Start: 20 ft. Left of SuperDarn. Climb the slab onto and through multiple golden tiered roofs to finish on the point of the Big Soddy wilderness. 14 bolts 100'+ FA: Josh Livasy '13

80 Elvis Lives! 5.12d (Sport)
Start: 25' left of Monatomic Gold. Begin on an orange and gold streaked face that leads to the base of a blank right facing corner. A techy corner crux leads to another difficult sequence out steepness to a rest below the final roof. Climb the splitter finger crack to an anchor at the lip. There are fixed chain draws on the second steep half. 14 bolts 100'
FA: Cody Averbeck '13

81 The Magic Bullet 5.12 (Sport) ★★
This is currently the last route on the Conspiracy Buttress. Climb the face through a nice middle panel of white rock to several roofs above.
FA: Cody Averbeck '13

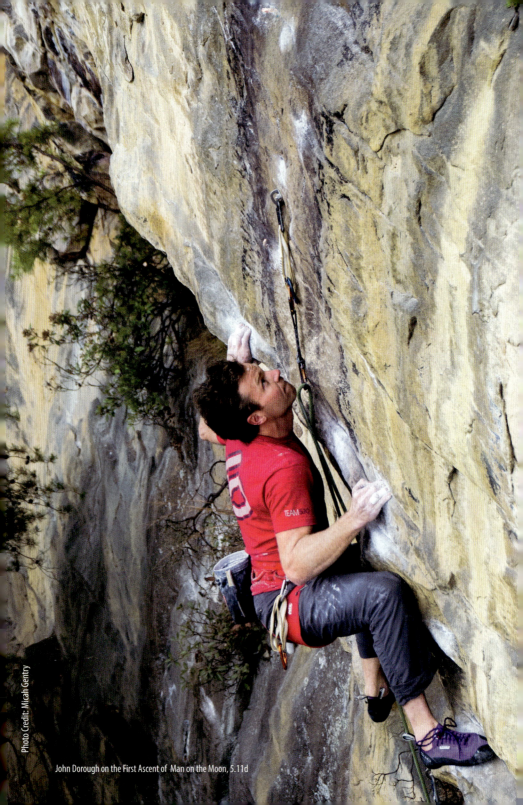

Photo Credit: Micah Gentry

John Dorough on the First Ascent of Man on the Moon, 5.11d

BIG SODDY GORGE

Dragon Wall

The Dragon Wallz are some of the deepest, most remote, and obscure collection of out-of-this world long, steep, and hard sport routes on a tilted world of 120' of atmospheric Southern Sandstone. To access this wall, continue left past the Conspiracy Buttress for at least 30 more minutes depending on the quality of the climber's trail at the moment.

87 Red Ribbon Army 5.13c (sport) Project ★★
Start: 15' left of Piccolo. This is the left most route on the ledge that climbs up the backside of the main buttress. Do this in 2 pitches. Anchors on left side of ledge. bolts 120'+
Bolted By: Josh Livasy '12

AM
1hr 15 mins

82 It's Over 9000 5.10- (sport) ★
This is the rightmost route on the wall. Follow a line of bolts. 60'
FA: Micah Gentry '13

83 Kame House 5.11- (sport) ★★★
Start: left of IO9000. This route shares a start with Piccolo but cuts right at the base of a corner and traverses up and right to anchors. 110'
FA: Micah Gentry '13

84 Piccolo 5.12b (sport) ★★★
An undeniable classic that would tower over routes at other areas if not for its neighbors to the left...
Start: same as Kame House. At the above mentioned corner, continue straight up to a roof and upper face. 110'
FA: Micah Gentry '13

85 Air Nimbus 5.13a/b (sport)
Hope you can DUNK! This is an amazing line that journeys straight up into the upper atmosphere of Southern Sandstone. Start: 10' left of Piccolo. Climb a face to a ledge and stay right at a split in the bolt line. 14 bolts. 120'+
FA: Josh Livasy '12

Insider's Tip: Watch the end of your 70 meter rope!

86 Triple Kaioken 5.13c (sport) project
Like a hot knife slicing towards heaven, have you ever seen such a thing? 15 bolts, 120'+
Bolted By: Josh Livasy '12

Insider's Tip: Need 80m cord

Piccolo, 5.12b

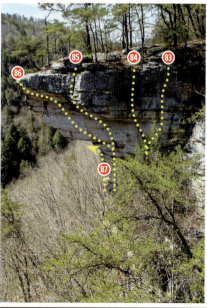

Soddy

Josh Livasy on Triple Kaioken, 5.13+   Photo Credit: Aaron Matheson

ABOUT THE PHOTOGRAPHERS

Micah Gentry took a lot of photos for Chattrad.

Cody Averbeck just pushes buttons.

Andrew Miller: nobody knows anything about him.

Nathalie Dupre
My dad always reminds me that my love for climbing started when he threw me on the boulders in our back yard, even before I could walk. Since then, i have grown as a climber from top roping my first route at sunset to leading my first route at fosters. I started taking pictures as a teenager of landscapes, photo shoots, music and other worldly passions . It wasn't until the fall of 2011 that i started bringing my camera to the crag and shooting crux moves and the classic movements that make climbers so passionate about this sport. I fell in love with the challenge of capturing the intensity of climbing while hanging hundreds feet in the air. Most of my work has been an attempt to showcase climbing as meditation through movement, between balance and strength.

Justin Hall
JustinHallphoto.com

Corey Wentz enjoys catching climbers in the moment, and has no shame in using photography as an excuse for not carrying the rope or belaying.

Mike Cork Hack climber and occasional photographer splitting time between Atlanta and Chattanooga.

ABOUT THE AUTHOR & PUBLISHERS

Rob Robinson is the author of four previous rock climbing guidebooks to crags located in the "Sandstone Belt of the South." His freelance articles have been carried through the years by Climbing, Rock & Ice and Mountain magazines.

In 1986, he appeared on the cover of Climbing magazine subsequent to the first ascent of a groundbreaking route called "Super Nova" located at the Tennessee Wall. That same year he was invited by the American Alpine Club to serve as a guest panelist for an event billed as "The Great Debate: The Future of Rock Climbing in the United States."

Robinson, who is referred to by some as "the father of southern sandstone," first began climbing in the Chattanooga, Tennessee area in 1975. Since that time he has completed more than 1,000 first, or first free, ascents throughout the region and beyond. His reputation for bold routes is legendary.

Robinson graduated with a degree in Communications from the University of Tennessee at Chattanooga. He is the managing broker and co-owner of Metro Real Estate, LLC, a Chattanooga-based full service real estate brokerage.

He lives with his wife, Susan, on Signal Mountain — about 20 minutes from the Tennessee Wall and other surrounding crags.

Micah Gentry likes climbing. He is a Co-founder at Rockery Press.

Cody Averbeck considers himself fortunate to have grown up in Chattanooga where he has been climbing on Southern Sandstone since 2000. He is a Co-founder at Rockery Press.

ABOUT THE ESSAYISTS

Matt Sims is a consummate athlete. He's a cyclist. A trail runner. An IronMan. However, his athleticism reaches back to Chattanooga's burgeoning climbing scene, where his efforts on and off the rock helped shape the direction of Southeast's climbing scene. Today, you'll still find Matt out there, trad climbing, bouldering, and putting up great lines for others to enjoy -- and send.

John Gill first began climbing on sandstone in the South in the late 1950's. He was, in all likelihood, the first climber in the history of climbing to make bouldering his primary focus. He is considered by many as the "father of modern bouldering."

In 1978, Master of Rock: The Biography of John Gill by Pat Ament was published. It was through this book that the climbing community at large came to know the extraordinary story of one of the world's most extraordinary climbers. Through his efforts, Gill inspired and influenced a generation of American climbers, myself included. I am honored to include a short essay piece in this guide by John (see pg. 85.)

In 2008, John Gill received the American Alpine Club's Robert & Miriam Underhill Award for outstanding climbing achievement.

John also maintains an Internet site that can be found at www.johngill.net

Jeff Achey has been making regular pilgrimages to Southern sandstone since the mid '90s. Once an aspiring climbing writer and avid trad climber, he now trains in martial arts, gardening, and bolting chossy limestone. He lives in New Castle, Colorado, but keeps a small cabin in the South.

Jeff is also the author of Climb!: The History of Rock Climbing in Colorado. He has to his credit an incredible list of ascents, including the visionary first ascents of the Free Nose (a.k.a. Black Magic) and The Serpent, both located in Colorado's legendary Black Canyon of the Gunnison.

Cody Averbeck see adjacent page.

John Bachar see pg 396.

Rob Robinson see adjacent page.

Rich Romano With a résumé of bold ground-up ascents stretching over thirty five years from the Sierras to the Cascades, Wind Rivers, Gunks, Adirondacks, and the Southwest, just to name a few, Rich Romano is one of the most prolific Eastern climbers ever, especially in the realm of 5.10 and above.

Richie recently turned 50, which puts him at the youngest end of the "newly old" spectrum of Gunks originals. He will tell you that injuries and other responsibilities and interests are slowing him down (he is a fine classical guitarist, and has a "guitar season" during which he maintains his fingernails and cuts back on climbing), but when you see him flying up 5.10's and 5.11's in his gym shorts, swami belt, and skimpy rack, you can only tremble at the prospect of him in full form.

INDEX

4
The Cobb ★		88
Towers Chimney ★		123
Dances with Lorax		516
Beginner's route		108
Inside moves		108

5
One Slip ★★		371
New Beginnings ★		399

6
Starting Point ★★		325
Sundance ★★		325
One-Ten ★★		89
Anteater ★★		151
Sole Searcher ★		371
Airbrush ★		183
Raptor Rapture		313
Transient Chronology		310
Grandma's Muscle		480
Camp Crack		499
Beginners Gauntlet		71
The Womb		87

7
Blonde Ambition JD		181
Jay-walker ★★★		414
Nutrasweet ★★★		427
Let's Face it ★★		405
Ribbon Cracks ★★		343
Little Steps ★★		325
Copperhead ★		94
Slip Stream ★		126
Afternoon Delight ★★		164
Jugular Vein ★		181
Nappy ★		399
Plastic Toys ★		399
Exposed Aggregate ★		414
Blind Date ★		422
The Garden ★		434
I'm late ★		441
Devil's Guard ★		444
Step Right Up ★		325
Mass Transit ★		323
Rainy Day ★		231
Emily the Hon ★		520
Living on the ledge ★		524
Righthand Crack ★		68
Yellowbrick Road ★		71
In the Corner ★		88
Whiz Bang ★		94
Test Tube ★		103
Little Pearl ★		140
Freedom Chimney ★		160
Jug Mania ★		163
Evening Flight out ★		183
Family Planning		441
Tunnel Vision		452
Easy Corner		484
Ivy Trail		500
Romper Room		512
The Diamond		68

8
Passages JD		408
Walk in the Park JD		164
Amplitude HB		240
Art ★★★		395
Sanskrit ★★★		409
Dirtbag ★★★		411
Rape Conducive ★★★		452
Slim's Corner ★★★		475
Mrs. Big Stuff ★★★		499
Thin Pockets ★★★		106
Bill's route ★★★		118
Broemel's route ★★★		118
Prerequisite for Excellence ★★		403
Restless Pedestrian ★★		414
Cathedral Crack ★★		435
Trungle ★★		436
Capital Assets ★★		451
Tribal Babysitter ★★		368
Slim's Route ★★		470
Corner Bar ★★		217
Shelob ★★		252
The Ramp ★★		264
Ghost Dancers ★★		106
Terrier in Trouble ★★		108
Sunday Gardening ★		404
True Colors ★		404
Molly and Rocket ★		421
Slug Trail ★		433
Soil Mechanics ★		435
Seal Test ★		445
Path of the Misfits ★		371
Big Orange Country ★		325
Golden Child ★		319
Cruise Control ★		277
Fist Pocket ★		294
Purple crack ★		524
Jungle Gym ★		91
Apes Only ★		91
Spring Break ★		106
Sudden Journey ★		154
Dreamway ★		155
Mercenary Territory ★		177
Squeeze Box ★		183
Room Service ★		508
Talisman		319
Fiddlehead		313
Disturbing Immortality		312
Hostess with the Mostest		474
Jawbone		272
End of the Road		290
Fat Crack		108
Heavy Hands		108
Disintegration		172
B-52		174
Space Flaps		177

8+
Razor Worm JD		424
Quick and Dirty ★★★		343
Dos Padres ★★★		237
Gift From Nature ★★★		518
S'more ★★★		73
Bombs Away ★★		260
Crazy Eights ★★		94
Crack-a-Smile ★★		153
In sight of power w		362
Mountaineer's Route w		216
Peace and Tranquility w		122
Overbearing Elders w		154
Sunset Sonata w		156
The Obvious Crack		210
Pilgrims Progress		227
Remain in Light		143
Terminal Impatience		183

9
Puppy Ride JD		416
Open Sesame JD		444
Stan's Crack JD		123
Liberty Bell JD		160
Golden Locks 4W		425
Crash Position HB		421
Windwalker HB		160
Finagle ★★★		411
Tension Span ★★★		421
Open Casket ★★★		384
Ballew Balls ★★★		220
Ledgendary ★★★		524
Rattlesnake route ★★★		71
The Grand Cave ★★★		90
Bubble Bath ★★★		126
Dodge City ★★★		142
Northwest Conversion ★★★		172
Talon ★★		375
Shivas last dance ★★		408
Fill in the blanks variation ★★		424
Motor Booty ★★		431
Jewel in the Sun ★★		435
Quality Control ★★		452
Two clowns on a rope ★★		377
Circus Circus ★★		376
Jerry and Lynn's Crack ★★		472
Emotional Rescue ★★		474
Star Search ★★		257
Nifty Nine ★★		272
G.P.S. Crack ★★		284
White n' Sight ★★		504
Parks Flake ★★		507
Lefthand Crack ★★		69
Friday the Thirteenth ★★		88
Fault Line ★★		92
Broken arrow alt. start ★★		104
Devil Dog ★★		130
Alan's Gold ★★		130
The Cobbler ★★		143
Battle above the Clouds		146
Divinity Crack ★★		152
Pancake Flake ★★		165
Rain Check ★		402
Mad Hatter ★		402
Totem Pole ★		404
Contents under Pressure ★		404
False Alarm ★		409
Digital Display ★		414
Over the hills and far away ★		422
Board of Connections alt st. ★		438
Unexpected Ease ★		442
Rape Ammo ★		452
Bath Party Politics ★		457
Bosom of the Rat ★		458
A nice place to come ★		369
Wild Pink ★		335
Soylent Green ★		323
Gravity's Wake ★		321
Fun in the Bun ★		474
The X files ★		475
Satellite Flyer ★		486

INDEX

Temporary Like Immortality ★	198	
Dying on the Vine ★	203	
Weird Load ★	240	
Kandahar Falls ★	242	
Tora Bora ★	242	
Sandstone Cemetary ★	250	
Big Leg ★	257	
Bad Apple ★	280	
NC calling ★	502	
Alert 5 ★	518	
More fun with Dick and Jane ★	68	
Congo Bongo ★	91	
Hell in a Bucket ★	138	
Generation Gap ★	138	
Decoy Buckets ★	177	
Aerial Aviation ★	182	
Aint so eazy ★	399	
Pinga Boys ★	410	
Time takes a cigarette ★	432	
Catch me in the Wry ★	455	
A brief history of time ★	457	
Trample-Proof	319	
Tunnel of Love	467	
Dick Trickle	480	
Shock Collar	260	
Unfinished business	524	
Malfunction Junction	114	
Jungle Boobies	130	
Lizards in Action	134	
Trivial Pursuits	182	

9+

A Sense of Adventure **JD**	103	
Second Sun **JD**	181	
In Pursuit of Excellence **4W**	411	
R.J. Gold **HB**	115	
Little Tree ★★★	235	
Steggosaur ★★★	235	
Airborne ★★	438	
Electric Ambiance ★★	312	
Coach Banana ★★	237	
Amplitude Alt. Start ★★	242	
Finders Keepers ★★	260	
Stan's Direct 1 ★★	123	
Stan's Direct 2 ★★	123	
The View From Above ★★	183	
Kid Fears ★	405	
Massive Attack ★	436	
Johnny get your roundup ★	452	
Run with the Horseman ★	363	
Titanic ★	335	
Schrodinger Equation ★	323	
Squeezing Out Sparks ★	232	
The Last Detail ★	240	
Special Delivery ★	108	
Infidel Zombies ★	122	
Deceive Me ★	123	
Flarewell to Arms ★	134	
Diagonal ★	150	
Grim Reaper ★	154	
Wild Hare	399	
Greenwich Garden Party	427	
Cryptid	351	
The Suck	288	
The Day After	174	
House of Cards	177	

10-

Cake Walk **JD**	424	
Hidden Assets **JD**	428	
Where Lizards go to die **JD**	378	
Siren Left **JD**	513	
Broken Arrow **JD**	104	
Jefferson Airplane **JD**	115	
Silent Runner **JD**	174	
Precious Orr **4W**	438	
Crack Attack **4W**	443	
Rockwork Orange **4W**	252	
Margin of Profit **HB**	427	
Stepping Stone **HB**	439	
Climbers Cough ★★★	520	
The Sweep ★★★	408	
Above and Beyond ★★★	441	
People's Express ★★★	442	
Of Vice and Men ★★★	454	
Commandant's Choice ★★★	220	
Mr. Big Stuff ★★★	224	
Asleep at the Wheel ★★★	240	
The Rose ★★★	286	
Whiskey Slings ★★★	496	
Picking up the Pieces ★★★	500	
Getting medieval ★★★	505	
Man Songs ★★★	515	
Sinsophrenia ★★★	142	
Standard Deviation ★★	404	
Day's work ★★	409	
Hammer Time ★★	372	
Personal Victories ★★	332	
Voodoo that you do ★★	332	
Harvest Time ★★	327	
Virginia Reels ★★	321	
Panzer Leader ★★	198	
Lusk Point Horror ★★	203	
Wash Board Blues ★★	242	
Battle Wagon ★★	244	
Siren Right ★★	513	
Flute Loops ★★	73	
Lichen to Lose it ★★	94	
Off to See the Lizard ★★	134	
Beyond the Obvious ★★	142	
Windmill ★★	160	
Lichen or Not ★★	172	
March Hare ★	402	
Who needs a Thnead? ★	421	
Full Belly in Hell ★	434	
Corner Pockets ★	434	
First Dance ★	378	
Tweedle Dum ★	374	
Falling out ★	327	
Chalkdust Memories ★	321	
Safer by design ★	313	
Golden Corral ★	480	
Dust Up ★	484	
Angst ★	203	
The Faucet ★	206	
The Entrance Crack ★	206	
Roadkill Bill ★	240	
Fling Fortress ★	260	
Laban's route ★	513	
It's Over 9000 ★	535	
Another Fallen Angel ★	76	
Zenobia ★	87	
Green Hills of Africa ★	91	
Bare Elegance ★	104	
Hueco Twelve ★	143	
Slip Slot ★	149	

Safari with Friends w	150	
Ode to the South w	151	
Grip Stone w	162	
Draft Dodger w	177	
Aftershock	480	
Corner	482	
Lusk Variation	203	
Lusk Original route	203	
Elective Dentistry	229	
Psycho Fingers	277	
Up in Smoke	104	
Pete's Back	138	
Catatonia	143	
Train Time	164	
Ghostly Grabber	182	

10b

Blight ★★★	500	
General Ledger ★★	524	

10

Blood on the Rocks **JD**	441	
Killer Diller **JD**	369	
Crown Jewel **JD**	482	
Born Slippy **JD**	516	
Screamwall **JD**	77	
Pigs in Space **JD**	170	
Hungry for Heaven **4W**	434	
Black Magic **HB**	147	
Love Handle ★★★	403	
Infinite Pursuit ★★★	403	
Superslide ★★★	408	
Finger Locking Good ★★★	414	
Hold your Horses ★★★	421	
Digital Macabre ★★★	422	
Fill in the blanks ★★★	424	
Electric Rats ★★★	431	
Hungry for Heaven alternate finish ★★★	434	
Golden Gloves ★★★	439	
Air Raid ★★★	376	
Open Boat Whalers ★★★	338	
Cast Iron Image ★★★	318	
Charmed ★★★	467	
Mein Commandant ★★★	220	
Mein Kampf ★★★	220	
Golden Delicious ★★★	243	
The Headwall ★★★	71	
Alpha Omega ★★★	73	
Screamwall Direct Finish ★★★	77	
Nuclear Blue ★★★	130	
Optical Delusion ★★★	153	
Airy Arete ★★★	167	
Pigs in Space direct ★★★	170	
Tweeter and the Monkey Man ★★	399	
Reptile Analysis ★★	418	
Mean Cuisine ★★	422	
Gravity Creeps ★★	427	
Exodus ★★	432	
Boardwalk ★★	434	
Yo Bro. got any Crank? ★★	444	
Solar Circus ★★	445	
Space Dancer ★★	446	
Intruders in the Dust ★★	458	
The Wood Spirit ★★	371	
William Perry ★★	368	

www.rockerypress.com 541

INDEX

Entry	Rating	Page
Ground Effects	★★	362
Heat Vision	★★	332
Sinji	★★	322
Ghost Dance of the Rednecks	★★	312
Then Everything Begins	★★	310
Orb Weaver	★★	472
Club Fighter	★★	232
Art-A-Majig	★★	248
Sandtrap		290
Vajazzled	★★	499
Great corner in the sky	★★	502
The Roost	★★	504
Germans express	★★	507
Trailside Parable	★★	512
The shaft		104
Dennis the Menace	★★	114
Ambidextrous	★★	114
Illusions		138
Wigged Lycra Warrior	★★	147
Temple of Doom	★★	163
Facts of Strife	★★	163
Flash Dance	★★	177
Whistler's Mother	★★	181
Creaky Tweaks	★★	405
Twitterville	★	405
Genesis	★	432
Auger Lite	★	442
Bad Omega	★	368
The Oasis	★	372
Belly of the Beast	★	356
Parade of Skeletons	★	352
Sedimentary Attachment	★	330
Chopping Block	★	474
Violent Twisting	★	229
Karate Chop	★	237
Total Recall		237
Without Worms	★	243
Hate Crime	★	244
Clay Fighter	★	246
The Way with Girls	★	288
Miller/ Gentry		500
The Birth Canal	★	92
Roach Crack	★	103
Diamond in the Rough	★	103
Puppy Rodeo	★	103
Spud Boys	★	108
Trickle Down Effect	★	121
Jams and Shams	★	129
Saint Pauli Girl	★	138
Chaos out of Control	★	147
Greenpeace	★	152
Lesbians in Politics	★	154
King's Roof	★	162
Good Fortune	★	172
Aqualung	★	347
Steel Puppies	★	417
Poop Chute		457
The Riff		372
The Moaning Weigh		355
Wild Pink Direct		335
Hard Eight		475
Aryan Way		214
Crowbar		237
A Good Root		272
Flash or Crash		80
Replicons		136
Marty's Misconceptions		149
Prior Consent		172

10c

Entry	Rating	Page
A turn of the page	★★★	338
Amber's Arete	★★	474
Holed up	★★	504
Get it Boy!	★	484

10+

Entry	Rating	Page
Esprit Nuvo	4W	443
Jack of All Trades	4W	486
Layaway Plan	4W	228
Five Roofs in Reverse	4W	264
Chestnutt's Crack	HB	467
Guardian of the gate	★★★	413
Points of Contact	★★★	413
Arsonists for Christ	★★★	318
Close Call	★★★	486
Honeycomb Hideout	★★★	217
Tombstone	★★★	250
Liberator	★★★	517
Dire Straights	★★★	89
Sunset Boulevard	★★★	104
A Stitch in Time	★★★	100
Agrippa	★★★	155
Squatters Rites	★★	395
Night Shift	★★	409
Hold your Reptile	★★	421
Point of Departure	★★	428
Riverbend Festival	★★	433
Molecular Bypass	★★	435
Centerfold	★★	436
Atom Smasher	★★	438
Auger Drive	★★	442
Live and Direct!	★★	451
Octopod Palace	★★	453
Game of Thrones	★★	458
Magnum Crow	★★	380
Out on a Whim	★★	353
Step into my dream	★★	332
Trimmed and Burning	★★	331
Orange Peel Express	★★	331
All the Colors of Love	★★	315
Hookers and Blow	★	312
Chestnutt's Corner	★	469
Velvet Elvis	★★	480
Bag of Tricks	★★	482
Sudden Death Playoff	★★	198
Free, White and Twenty One	★★	210
A Matter of Degrees	★★	214
Crankus Maximus	★	237
Needle in the Haystack	★★	268
Pete and Rob's	★★	280
Ethiopia	★★	287
The Erroneous Zone	★★	92
Ghost Dancer alt. start	★★	106
Horribilus Maximus	★★	118
Confederate Arete	★★	142
Experimental Animals	★★	172
Bought the Farm	★★	182
Wing and a Prayer	★	405
Pop Life		375
Send Lawyers, Guns, and Money	★	311
Steggish Boy	★	212
Equal Rights	★	268

10c (cont.)

Entry	Rating	Page
Tight Cat	★	288
Born Grippy	★	516
Geek Motel	★	71
Screaming Turtles from Hellw		71
Trailside Trials	★	146
Shy Line	★	154
Barnyard Zen	★	167
La Pishnibulle	★	181
Agony to Ecstasy		257
Sand Jive		260
Jerry's Kids		277
Oddjob		496
Rusty's Crack		80

10d

Entry	Rating	Page
Illuminati Alumni	★★★	528
Don't tell a soul	★★	408
House of the Rising Sun	★★	437
Big Black Furry Creature	★★	499
Beefcake	★★	504

11a

Entry	Rating	Page
Patient Zero	JD	520
Mirage	★★★	436
Dark side of the flake	★★★	502
Half Percentile	★★★	507
Over My Head	★★★	505
Buzz Muscle	★★	505
All Rights Reserved	★	395
Anarchy		458

11-

Entry	Rating	Page
Hell or High Water	HB	358
Flagstone	HB	73
The Cornerstone	HB	119
Sugar in the Raw	★★★	398
Sly Willie Snores	★★★	398
No more tiers	★★★	403
Spirit of the game	★★★	410
Defcon five	★★★	422
Benevolence	★★★	334
Looking for Gold	★★★	319
Kentucky Fried Fingers	★★★	318
Where the Sidewalk Ends	★★★	310
Fascist Leader	★★★	211
The Auschwitz Crack	★★★	244
Sundown Syndrome	★★★	257
Strictly Ballroom	★★★	269
Bitch in Heat	★★★	288
Good Samaritan	★★★	512
Kame House	★★★	535
Prisoner of Zenda	★★★	69
The Arena	★★★	89
Golden Ledges	★★★	110
Stitch in time alt. finish	★★★	100
Dobermanns	★★★	129
Golden Years	★★★	143
Deck Party	★★★	156
Back Street Revelations	★★★	163
Morning Sickness	★★	403

www.rockerypress.com

INDEX

Route	Grade	Page
Clip and Trip ★★		410
Slay Ride ★★		413
The Heaven of Animals ★★		416
Chocolate Puppies ★★		417
Forbidden Fruit ★★		444
Tiers for Beers ★★		388
Queen Bitch ★★		355
Loading the Reactor ★★		355
Trail of Tiers ★★		345
House of Cards ★★		469
Shenanigans ★★		110
Soapstone ★★		211
This Ewe's For Bud ★★		217
Green Dreams ★★		235
Snag the Ear! ★★		235
Last Feast of the Crokadiles ★★		269
Pink Flamingos ★★		286
The Drainpipe ★★		98
Lost Arrow Chimney ★★		98
Bolt Pinnacle ★★		115
Mineral Fright ★★		115
Unleashed ★★		130
Afternoon Walk ★★		164
Changnurdle ★		399
Three Stars from God ★		404
Life in High Definition ★		431
Grandma's Couch ★		432
Micro Genie ★		441
Celestial Mechanics alt. start ★		446
Song of the Bullet ★		455
Crankenstein ★		387
Violence is Golden ★		380
Just Another Toothpick ★		355
El Chupacabra ★		351
Bailiff ★		347
Silver Linings ★		343
Maxwell House ★		330
Times Witness ★		321
Star Tide variation ★		248
Panty Raid ★		254
Happy Birthday ★		288
Complex Dexterities ★		71
Hallucinating Insects ★		87
Hit the Slopers ★		104
Rushin Roulette ★		108
New Age ★		134
Rude Awakening ★		134
Blade Runner ★		136
Yin ★		139
Yang ★		139
No Pro Glow ★		153
Magnum Bro		380
Bible Black		378
Danglo Saxon		374
Rumble Fish		313
Tweak Analysis		294

11b

Route	Grade	Page
Chemtrail Surfer (aka Genstral Stain) JD		528
Straight up ★★★		474
Hands of Stone ★		335

11

Route	Grade	Page
Fly with the Falcon 4W		416
Stone Wave 4W		421
The Terminator 4W		458
Pleasure Burn 4W		212
Rainbow Delta 4W		254
Special Olympics 4W		272
The Obsessed 4W		284
The Toothpick 4W		122
Euphoria 4W		77
Ironic HB		467
Train Time direct HB		165
Steeplechase		405
Competitive Edge ★★★		425
Come and Get it ★★★		344
Balls to the Wall ★★★		344
Relative Humidity ★★★		336
Tethered Goat ★★★		475
Rapture of the Steep ★★★		211
March into the Sea ★★★		221
The Thread That Runs So True ★★★		268
The Pearl ★★★		83
Final Frontier ★★★		110
Doberman's Direct ★★★		129
Baby Cats ★★★		167
Short Arm Inspection ★★		403
Calves of Steel ★★		418
Among the wild Chimps ★★		436
The Velvet Jesus ★★		436
Smooth Operator ★★		438
Cold day in Hell ★★		444
The He-Man women haters club ★★		444
Bonfire of the Vanities ★★		454
Circling Buzzard ★★		380
Guerillas in the Mist ★★		380
Combustion Cycle ★★		378
Heavy Petting Zoo ★★		378
Elephus Maximus ★★		375
Moon of the Crow ★★		366
Every Raisen was a Grape ★★		357
TommyKnocker ★★		345
No Name Number One ★★		319
Taming the Flaming ★★		311
Persona Non Grata ★★		470
Forearm Magazine ★★		210
Out to Launch ★★		294
Strategic Arms Control ★★		294
Dysphoria ★★		80
Scare Voyager ★★		87
Osmosis ★★		87
Boulder of Fortune ★★		90
Murfreesboro Blues ★★		136
Adaptive Radiation ★★		149
Grounds for a Peel ★★		152
Defender ★★		156
Midget cage ★★		357
Stand your ground ★		445
Turbo Zone ★		393
Mojo ★		454
Space Sequential ★		392
Tweedle Dee ★		374
Stay of Execution ★		373
Faunal Succession ★		371
Mouthful of Cavities ★		353
The Crisis before the norm ★		351
Blind Hands bluff ★		351
Behind the Waterfall ★		347
The Gleaning ★		334
Elevation of the Soul ★		334
Resident Alien ★		312
The Gambler ★		310
Ride the Snake ★		467
Another Roadside Attraction ★		294
Bittersweet ★		500
The Fang ★		71
The Widow Maker ★		134
The Donkey Show ★		374
Hold your Horses alternate start		421
Take no mess		369
Cranial Reconstruction		71

11c

Route	Grade	Page
Surf's up HB		421
Lockdown ★★★		474
Cure for Pain ★★		479
Strange Design ★★		499
Martial Law		458

11+

Route	Grade	Page
Superwave JD		363
Fox on the Run 4W		453
Only on Earth 4W		336
Unclean Spirit 4W		469
Butter Battle 4W		516
Viva La Balance HB		443
In Search for the Source HB		457
The Omen HB		457
Heaven's Gate HB		336
Confetti Fingers HB		256
Departure 29 HB		518
The Great White Fright HB		98
Proof of Purchase ★★★		410
Up in Arms ★★★		437
Board of Connections ★★★		438
Ravin' Maniac ★★★		443
Hell Bent for Leather ★★★		458
The Great Unchoppable ★★★		375
Stand and Deliver ★★★		344
Sewanee Gun Club ★★★		314
Extreme Prejudice ★★★		221
Diesel and Dust ★★★		228
The Cauldron ★★★		252
Native Tongue ★★★		254
The Puzzle Palace ★★★		264
Wake up call ★★★		508
No Tell Motel ★★★		509
Gospel of Luke ★★★		512
Dementia ★★★		110
Clip and Trip Direct ★★		410
Direct Finish ★★		427
Bugs from Hell ★★		431
Zenmania ★★		433
Full Coleman ★★		434
Brazen Serpent ★★		436
Benign Humor ★★		442
Wits End ★★		452
Death by Boobalooba ★★		388
Moms are marvelous ★★		388
Class Action ★★		373

www.rockerypress.com 543

INDEX

Route	Stars	Page
Whistln in the Boneyard	★★	353
Hot off the griddle	★★	323
Dreaming of Beauty	★★	311
Preparing to Dye		311
Born under a Bad Sign	★★	310
Grandma Muscle's arete	★★	480
The Jesus Chainsaw Massacre	★★	198
Free James Brown	★★	210
The Burn Ward	★★	214
Stracker/Eiseman		235
Reach for the Sky	★★	257
Welcome to the Machine	★★	277
The Entity	★★	287
Sprankles	★★	513
Typically French	★★	71
Total Eclipse	★★	73
Frenzy	★	414
Crematorium	★	436
Stink Finger	★	363
Seam Stress	★	343
Bomb Proof Roof	★	319
Shoot to Thrill	★	227
Soddy Bottom Boys	★	515
Kaleidoscope Eyes	★	98
Dynamic Salvage	★	103
Tequila Sunrise	★	143
Tunnel Ratz		374
Chestnutt's Roof		237
American Sportsman		280

11d

Route	Stars	Page
Man on the Moon **HB**		528
Man on the Grassy Knoll	★★★	532
Curb Sandwich	★★★	398

12a

Route	Stars	Page
Uncle Pervy's Playhouse **HB**		272
Maui Gold **HB**		496
Gift of Power	★★★	418
Lord of the Dance	★★★	438
Slim Shady		343
The Gangplank	★★★	341
Look At Me, I'm So Heady	★★★	517
The Litto	★★	413
Sun King	★★	427
Sucker Punch	★★	343
Superannuated	★★	526
33°	★★	528

12-

Route	Stars	Page
Homeland Insecurity **4W**		356
Mrs. Socrates **4W**		429
Protect and Serve **4W**		331
Explosivo **4W**		331
Going Off the Deep End **4W**		200
Suck Crack **4W**		203
Mountain Madness **4W**		224
Jector the Golden Loaf **4W**		516
The Prow **4W**		81
Jennifer's World **4W**		98

Route	Stars	Page
Raiders of the Lost Arch **4W**		136
The Beauty **4W**		152
Steepolis **HB**		429
Breaking the Waves **HB**		322
Any Way You Slice it **HB**		224
Space Ranger **HB**		111
Pump Failure	★★★	366
A parting to the ways	★★★	355
Pocket Pussy	★★★	330
Sugar and Spice	★★★	484
Deep End Direct Start	★★★	100
Star Tide Rising	★★★	248
Sea of Slopers	★★★	256
Crack of Dawn	★★★	515
Carte Blanche	★★★	73
Fingernails on a chalkboard	★★	425
Path of the Mistics	★★	377
Crime Wave	★★	373
Inches Despair	★★	210
Happy Holidays	★★	280
Gold Finger	★★	507
Tarantula	★★	69
Pagan Rites	★★	81
Invisible Touch	★★	88
Lost Digits	★★	92
Jennifer's world direct finish	★★	98
Water in Motion	★★	106
Twilight of the Idols	★★	119
No Hand's Land	★★	121
Rip Cord	★★	150
Escape from Ventura!	★★	155
St. Valentines Day Massacre	★	432
Chestnutt Arete	★	441
Blood Meridian	★	387
Tough guys don't dance	★	386
Back from the storm		372
Liquid Plummer	★	484
Fuhrer's Fury	★	228
Reach for the Sun	★	237
Muscle Shoals	★	87
Crux Busters	★	89
Stretcharete		90
Point of No Return	★	91
The Whitewall	★	103
Gut Strings	★	140
Apogee		182
Seam like nothing		409
Crispy Creme		103
Dyno Land		140

12b

Route	Stars	Page
The Odyssey **HB**		266
Piccolo	★★★	535
Some Girls	★★	427
Diggity Dank	★★	355
Sinner	★★	470
Room for Two	★★	511
Pale face		393

12

Route	Stars	Page
Celestial Mechanics **4W**		446
Fist of Fury **4W**		341
Tantrum **4W**		101
August West **HB**		513
The Beast **HB**		152

Route	Stars	Page
Fuel Injected Suicide Machine	★★★	455
Unknown Soldier	★★★	455
Slim's Slab	★★★	482
Burstin' At the Seams	★★★	224
The Knockout Artist	★★★	225
Primitive Man	★★★	290
Perfect Sinner	★★★	99
Hands Across America	★★	392
Scamperproof	★★	412
Fear on Ice	★★	416
Steep eye for the slab guy	★★	363
The Birth Simulater	★★	352
Fire in the Belly	★★	214
Battle of the Bulge	★★	272
The Magic Bullet	★★	533
A Carnival of sorts	★★	69
Scandals in the Twilight	★★	88
Strechum' Armstrong	★★	134
Idiot Savant	★★	174
Mean Cuisine direct finish	★	422
The Blue Wall of Silence	★	315
Goin's Route	★	237
Roper's Aid route	★	81
Bought by Blood		466
Unsent		466
Submission		121

12c

Route	Stars	Page
Homeside Sin **HB**		323
Twisting in the Wind	★★★	393
Stinger	★★★	347
Face Off	★★	384

12+

Route	Stars	Page
Milky Way **4W**		284
The Edge of Might **4W**		83
Southern Express	★★★	432
Voodoo roof	★★★	380
Southern Exposure	★★★	344
Two Sides to Wisdom	★★★	318
Wrectum Wrecker	★★	376
Kerm Gerbler Abduction (Laban's route)	★★	533
Hyena	★	83
Dixie Wet Dream		378
Ain't life Grand		500

12d

Route	Stars	Page
Stone Hinge **HB**		348
Rockgasm **HB**		346
Stormin Normin www		384
Elvis Lives! www		533
Ruby Fruit Jungle	★★	395
Dumpster Proof	★★	338
Nuclear Winter	★★	338
It Never Fails (Dave Wilson route)	★★	526
Ho Baggin	★	392
Meeker Rat		393

www.rockerypress.com

INDEX

13a
Gates of Testosterone **JD**		348
Dark Star	**JD**	347
Burn	**4W**	338
Defender of the Crown		
	HB	429
Over the Rainbow **HB**		388
Olympic Alchemy ★★★		437
Keel Hauled ★★★		341
SuperDARN ★★★		533
Monatomic Gold ★★★		533
HOTRS extension ★★		437
Supernova ★★		446
T-Rex ★★		388
Dog Fight ★★		348
Break of Day ★★		515
Dementol Bridge ★★		179
The Shadow ★		356
Crankin' Juicy		212

13a/b
Air Nimbus	**4W**	535

13-
Tamperproof **4W**		386
Direct Afraid **4W**		179
Riddle on the Roof ★★★		418
The Banshee ★		103

13b
Psycho Path **HB**		386
Grace	**HB**	346
To Live is to Fly ★★★		511
Grand Contusion ★★		395
Poontang ★★		386
Rising Force		458

13
Dance of the Demon		
★★★		121
Poweropolis ★★		384
Modern Problems ★★		505
Bleary Eyed and Bonking (Dave Wilson route) ★★		526
Abortion Contortion ★		392

13c
Triple Kaioken **HB**		535
Respect for the Spider		
★★★		345
Red Ribbon Army ★★		535
Sea of Moses **4W**		509

13d
The Message **4W**		340

14
Deaf, Dumb, and Blind ★		99
Power Ranger Project **4W**		
		111

Aid
Heavy Hor's D'oeures		10, A3
★★★		231
Buff Rubes	8, A2+	
★★★		206
Nazi Party Animal		9, A3
★★★		212
Mace and Chain		9, A3+
★★★		209
Fantastic Voyage		10, A2
★★		232
Kaboom!	10+, A2	
★★		232
Code Warrior		11 A0
★★		395
Uninvited	11-, A1	
★★		470
Redneck Direct		8, A3
★★		206
On Any Sunday		A2
★★		257
Caught Red-Handed		10-, A2
★		98
Cornhole	10, A4	
★		284
Moccasin Bend		10+, A2
★		126
Steve McQueen Memorial		7, A4
★		216
Whack and Dangle		8, A2+
★		246
Poultry Boy	9, A2+	
★		280
Colors like a Tropical Fish		9, A3
★		134
Twilight Zone		A2
★		121
Thin Slivers	A2	
★		126
Turkey and Coke		A3
★		101
The Ho Chi-Min Trail		11+, A1
		199
It's Bad	13, A4	288
Rolling Rock	5, A3-	244
Zyklon B	7, A4	216
Blue Collar	8, A2	206
Plate Lunch	8+, A2+	209
Two Bums are better than none		
	9, A0	357
Blood Assurance		9, C1
		244
Truancy	A2+	211
Caesar's Palace	A4	212

www.rockerypress.com

CHATTRAD

Rob Robinson

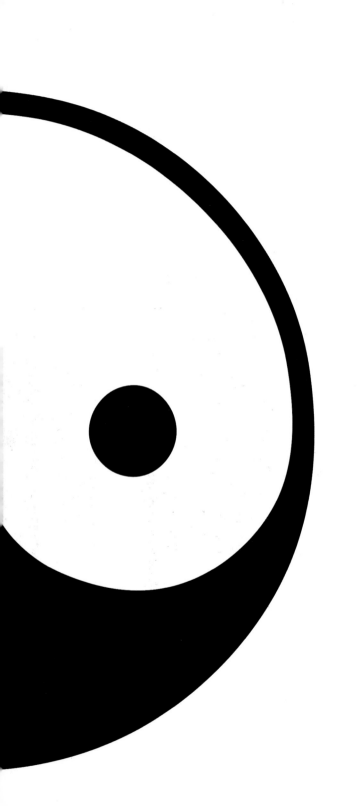

CHATT STEEL

AVERBECK & GENTRY

ROCKERY PRESS

Rockery Press is the realization of a local Chattanooga effort that has been building for over half a decade.

It's generally well known that Chattanooga has had a reputation for being tight lipped with regards to publicizing our regional climbing resources. Whether this conservative stance results from our seemingly never-ending battle with area access, or from a tradition of 'do it yourself' guidance, or maybe simply from a trend of general guidebook skepticism — the Chattanooga climbing community has long been divided on what to do about the "guidebook question."

With this conflict as our backdrop, it's important as publishers and community members to see both sides of what a guidebook offers. Oftentimes, the immediate local response to publication is to focus on the impact that guidebooks bring. Studies show that guidebooks result in a 30% rise in user visitation. Outside of the disgruntled 'not what it used to be' local perspective, this increase in traffic, if not mitigated through appropriate planning, can result in forms of negative impact.

On the other hand, a community without a guidebook runs the risk of having its future gym and web reared generations lose, forget, or never learn the histories and tall tales that distinguish a community's legacy.

Rockery Press recognizes both sides of what a guidebook does. For this reason, it's our mission to produce the most unique, local-born content and multimedia designs that preserve the authentic Chattanooga rock climbing record for past, present, and future generations. And in addition, as proactive local publishers committed to area access and stewardship, we pledge a portion of profits to local grass roots organizations and efforts committed to developing, sustaining, and protecting our local climbing resources.

We hope that this balance between publication and protection will help carry Southeast rock climbing into a healthy and vibrant future as it continues to grow throughout the TAG region.

★★★

We hope you have enjoyed Chattrad, our second title of many more works to come. Rockery Press is continually looking to refine our craft, and we greatly appreciate input from our audience. Please contact us with comments and ideas, and we look forward to seeing you next time!

See You Next Time!